S0-BQY-704

Death and Identity

Death
and Identity

Robert Lester Fulton

California State College at Los Angeles

John Wiley & Sons, Inc., New York/London/Sydney

SECOND PRINTING, APRIL, 1966

Library of Congress Catalog Card Number: 65-15762
Printed in the United States of America

CONTRIBUTORS

ARTHUR M. ADLERSTEIN, PH.D.
Psychologist, The Neurological Research Center, The Children's
Hospital of Philadelphia, Philadelphia, Pennsylvania

IRVING E. ALEXANDER, PH.D.
Professor of Psychology, Duke University, Durham, North Carolina

HERBERT BARRY, JR., M.D., PH.D.
Instructor in Psychiatry, Harvard Medical School, Cambridge, Massa-
chusetts; Associate Psychiatrist, Massachusetts General Hospital,
Boston, Massachusetts

FRANZ BORKENAU*
Political Commentator and Historian; Formerly Professor of History,
University of Marburg, Marburg, Germany

HENRY H. BREWSTER, M.D.
Instructor in Mental Health, Harvard School of Public Health, Cam-
bridge, Massachusetts; Research Associate, Department of Social
Relations, Harvard University, Cambridge, Massachusetts

* Deceased.

ADOLPH E. CHRIST, M.D.
Director, Psychiatric Inpatient Services for Children, School of Medicine, University of Washington, Seattle, Washington

RANDOLPH S. COLLEY, B.A.
Sometime Research Assistant, Department of Psychology, Princeton University, Princeton, New Jersey

ANDREW S. DIBNER, PH.D.
Chief Clinical Psychologist, Veteran's Administration Mental Hygiene Clinic, Boston, Massachusetts

JAMES C. DIGGORY, PH.D.
Associate Professor of Psychology, University of Pennsylvania, Philadelphia, Pennsylvania

CARL EISDORFER, PH.D.
Associate Professor, Division of Medical Psychology, Duke University, Durham, North Carolina

HERMAN FEIFEL, PH.D.
Chief Clinical Psychologist, Veterans Administration Mental Hygiene Service, Los Angeles, California; Associate Clinical Professor of Psychiatry (psychology), University of Southern California School of Medicine, Los Angeles, California

FERN FISK, M.A.
Research Associate, Laboratory of Human Development, Stanford University, Stanford, California

ROBERT FULTON, PH.D.
Associate Professor of Sociology, California State College at Los Angeles, Los Angeles, California

GILBERT GEIS, PH.D.
Professor of Sociology, California State College at Los Angeles, Los Angeles, California

THOMAS P. HACKETT, M.D.
Instructor in Psychiatry, Harvard Medical School, Cambridge, Massachusetts; Assistant Psychiatrist, Massachusetts General Hospital, Boston, Massachusetts

JOSEPHINE R. HILGARD, M.D.
Clinical Professor of Psychiatry, Laboratory of Human Development, Stanford University, Stanford, California

FRANCES C. JEFFERS, M.A.
Research Associate, Center for the Study of Aging, Duke University Medical Center, Durham, North Carolina

RICHARD KALISH, PH.D.
Associate Professor of Psychology, California State College at Los Angeles, Los Angeles, California

ALFRED G. KNUDSON, M.D., PH.D.
Chairman, Department of Pediatrics, City of Hope Medical Center, Duarte, California

ERICH LINDEMANN, M.D.
Professor of Psychiatry, Harvard Medical School, Cambridge, Massachusetts; Psychiatrist-in-Chief, Massachusetts General Hospital, Boston, Massachusetts

ROBERT J. LIFTON, M.D.
Associate Professor of Psychiatry, School of Medicine, Yale University, New Haven, Connecticut

DAVID G. MANDELBAUM, PH.D.
Professor of Anthropology, University of California, Berkeley, California

STANLEY T. MICHAEL, M.D.
Psychiatrist; Research Associate, Cornell University Medical School, Ithaca, New York.

JOSEPH M. NATTERSON, M.D.
Department of Pediatrics, City of Hope Medical Center, Duarte, California

MARTHA F. NEWMAN, M.A.
Research Associate, Laboratory of Human Development, Stanford University, Stanford, California

CLAUDE R. NICHOLS, M.D.
Assistant Professor of Psychiatry, Regional Center for the Study of Aging, Duke University, Durham, North Carolina

OCTAVIO PAZ
Author and Diplomat; Mexican Ambassador to India, Mexican Embassy, New Delhi, India

MIGUEL PRADOS, M.D.
Psychiatrist, Royal Victoria Hospital, Montreal, Quebec, Canada

PAUL J. RHUDICK, PH.D.
Research Associate, The Age Center of New England Inc., Boston, Massachusetts

DOREEN Z. ROTHMAN, PH.D.
Clinical Psychologist, Philadelphia Child Guidance Clinic, Philadelphia, Pennsylvania

MERVYN SHOOR, M.D.
Psychiatrist-in-Charge, Guidance Clinic, Santa Clara Juvenile Probation Department, San Jose, California; Clinical Instructor in Psychiatry, Stanford University School of Medicine, Stanford, California

SAMUEL D. SHRUT, PH.D.
Lecturer in Psychology, New York University, New York, New York; Research Associate, Home for Aged and Infirm Hebrews, New York, New York

MARY H. SPEED, M.A.
Coordinator and Psychologist, Juvenile Probation Department, Santa Clara County, San Jose, California

KARL STERN, M.D.
Professor of Psychiatry and Chairman of Department, University of Ottawa, Psychiatrist in Chief, St. Mary's Hospital, Montreal, Quebec, Canada

WENDELL M. SWENSON, PH.D.
Professor of Clinical Psychology, Mayo Clinic, Rochester, Minnesota

JOSEPH D. TEICHER, M.D.
Professor of Psychiatry (Child), University of Southern California, Los Angeles, California; Director of Children's and Adolescent Psychiatric Services, Los Angeles County General Hospital, Los Angeles, California

EDMUND H. VOLKART, PH.D.
Dean, Humanities and Social Science, Oregon State University, Corvallis, Oregon

CHARLES W. WAHL, M.D.
Associate Professor and Chief, Division of Psychosomatic Medicine, University of California at Los Angeles Medical Center, Los Angeles, California

W. LLOYD WARNER
University Professor, Michigan State University, East Lansing, Michigan

AVERY D. WEISMAN, M.D.
Associate Psychiatrist and Director, Psychiatric Consultation Service, Massachusetts General Hospital, Boston, Massachusetts

GWENDOLYN M. WILLIAMS, M.A.
Sometime Research Assistant, Department of Psychiatry, St. Mary's Hospital, Montreal, Quebec, Canada

Preface

In the last decade, and particularly since the publication in 1959 of Herman Feifel's book, *The Meaning of Death*, research into the problems caused by death has burgeoned in the United States. Although Feifel could, in truth, state six years ago that we possessed little systematic knowledge about attitudes or reactions toward death, and that not enough attention had been paid to the implications of the meaning of death in this country, the situation has now changed perceptibly. Research into grief and bereavement, studies of attitudes toward death, and recorded responses to death and dying have begun to appear in increasing plentitude in the social and medical science literature.

This book is an attempt to take notice of these developments, and, in turn, to provide impetus to their continuing progress.

By a systematic ordering of the most recent and pertinent research that has been conducted by psychiatrists, psychologists, sociologists, and medical personnel on various facets of death, it is hoped that a basis can be established for better comprehension of its dynamics and dimensions. The concern is not only for the almost two million persons who must directly confront death each year in the United States, but also for their immediate survivors and the larger society beyond. By bringing together these different clinical and experimental materials, results can be compared, analyzed, and assessed. Areas of agreement and disagreement, generalizations, and conclusions can all be held up to the light of modern research techniques and, in this way, theoretical or experimental error may be avoided, new insights stimulated, hypotheses formulated, and disparate information integrated.

The collection of readings for inclusion in this book has been selected on the basis of several criteria. Among the experimental or clinical studies, primary consideration was given to those recent studies which reflected, tested, or extended the work of the pioneers in this field whose writings, although important theoretically and historically, have but limited value for modern contemporary research. Pioneer works include such classic papers as: Sigmund Freud's, "Mourning and Melancholia" and his "Thoughts on War and Death"; G. Stanley Hall's, "Thanatophobia and Immortality"; Howard Becker's, "The Sorrow of Bereavement"; Mary Chadwick's "Notes Upon the Fear of Death"; and Smith E. Jelliffe's, "The Death Instinct in Somatic and Psychotherapy." The importance of these illustrative articles is seen in the interest they have provoked and the research they have inspired among contemporary scholars. In a very real sense the ground-breaking thoughts and ideas from these early studies will be found on a majority of the pages of this book.

Selection of the theoretical or expository essays and the articles on ritual and ceremony was based upon a desire to place the experimental reports within a framework which would not only provide perspective for the research reported, but which would also expose speculative statements to the hard glare of empirical evidence.

This book of readings is inevitably incomplete. It would require a volume several times the size of this to include all the material currently available. I believe, however, that the items included are representative of the major work that has been and is being done in the area of death.

The materials of this book are arranged into the following four parts: (1) Theoretical Discussion on Death, (2) Attitudes and Responses Toward Death, (3) Grief and Mourning: The Reaction Toward Death, and (4) Ceremony, The Self, and Society.

Introductions written by me serve to put into perspective each section as well as to explicate their several parts. In editing some of the selections, I deleted words and sentences and rearranged passages. This was done in order to keep the book within manageable form as well as to eliminate nonessential or repetitive materials.

The papers in this book—the theoretical statements, the empirical reports, as well as the discussions on ritual and ceremony—have as their common object the illumination of the problems that death presents to each of us. I will have realized my object in preparing this book if, through bringing these different efforts together, a stronger light is cast upon the face of death, and we are aided in preserving rather than losing our personal identity before its countenance.

I wish to thank the contributors to this volume and their publishers for permission to republish their essays. I also wish to acknowledge my appreciation to Dr. H. C. Meserve, Editor, *Journal of Religion and Health*, for permission to reprint in the several introductions to this book portions of my article, "Death and the Self," which originally appeared in the July 1964 issue of the journal. Special thanks are owed to the Board of Governors of the National Funeral Directors Association for materially supporting the editorial work on this book. In particular, I especially wish to thank Howard C. Raether, Executive Secretary for the Association, whose courage and foresight made this book possible.

I wish to thank Professor Robert Habenstein for the idea of the book and for contributing to initial stages of its preparation. He is not responsible, however, for whatever errors of judgment or fact the book may contain.

I am deeply indebted to my colleague Professor Gilbert Geis for his encouragement and assistance throughout the course of this project.

Finally, I wish to thank Julie Ann Rockman Fulton for her important contribution to the preparation of this book, and Joan Harris, Jennifer Young, and Pat Fulton for their valuable clerical and editorial assistance.

ROBERT FULTON

January 1965

Contents

PART 3.   GRIEF AND MOURNING: THE REACTION TO DEATH

PART 4. CEREMONY, THE SELF, AND SOCIETY

Part 1.

Theoretical Discussions on Death

INTRODUCTION

Death asks us for our identity. Confronted by death, man is compelled to provide in some form a response to the question: Who am I? The manner in which this question has been asked and the replies that it has received have varied from era to era and have reflected the personal aspirations and the social consensus of the time and place. It is only the implacable and challenging presence of death itself which has remained constant.

In Western culture the question of identity posed by death has traditionally been answered within the framework of sacred doctrine. Man was God's creature, fashioned after His image from the dust of the earth. Man's death, no less than the life that had been breathed into him, was an act of Divine Will.

Within such a theological structure man could stand secure in the knowledge that death was a personal matter between God and himself. The very purposefulness of his death placed him at the center of existence and elevated him above all other creatures as the principal subject of creation. As part of a Divine plan, death was the brother to life and as such could be confronted openly, spoken of freely, and treated as a natural phenomenon. For Western society the recognition of death was a prime requisite for life as well as an integral dimension of personal identity.

Traditional rites for the dead symbolized and gave expression to theological beliefs. They served to reinforce the social bonds of the group and, in so doing, compelled recognition of its elemental constituent—the individual. Ceremony for the dead thus served to link God, man, and society.

In America today we have come to a point in our history when we are beginning to react to death as we would to a communicable disease. Death no longer is viewed as the price of moral trespass or as the result of theological wrath; rather, in our modern secular world, death is coming to be seen as the consequence of personal neglect or untoward accident. Death is now a temporal matter. Like cancer or syphilis, it is a private disaster that we discuss only reluctantly with our physician. Moreover, as in the manner of many contagious diseases, those who are caught in the throes of death are isolated from their fellow human beings, while those who have succumbed to it are hidden quickly from view. The aged, those most susceptible to death, seek in ever-increasing numbers to remove themselves to segregated retirement communities, there to await fate in the same manner as the leper once did. Death, like a noxious disease, has become a taboo subject, and as such it is both the object of much disguise and denial as well as of raucous and macabre humor.

How have we come by these newer attitudes and practices and what are their consequences for society and for the individual?

The four articles in this section address themselves in different forms to this basic question and each in turn sheds additional light on various facets of the issue. Together they provide us with empirical documentation of individual and social responses to death as well as theoretical explanations of such responses, all set into the broader perspective of established intellectual disciplines.

A brilliant documentation of the psychological and sociological effects of the horrifying experience the residents of Hiroshima underwent following that city's devastation by the atomic bomb in 1945 is provided by Lifton in the initial contribution to this section. Lifton not only tells us a great deal about the behavior and the feelings of people in the face of disaster, but he also provides us with a vantage point from which to observe the interplay between death and its perception in different cultures.

In describing the reactions of the *hibakusha*, the 90,000 survivors of Hiroshima, Lifton reports that the most striking psychological feature observed was the sense of a sudden and absolute shift from the normal existence to an overwhelming encounter with death. The emotional theme of their encounter with the atomic bomb has, in fact, remained with the victims to this day, providing them with a special and rather exclusive self-definition, that of survivors of civilization's most frightful man-made tragedy.

Lifton describes the early impact of mass death upon the survivors; the weird, unreal, dream-like quality of the scene, and the essentially ineffectual, aimless, and rote nature of their behavior, and he reports as well a second reaction to the shock and horror of the bombing, that of psychological closure. People unable to remain receptive to the emotional experience of the intensity that took place at Hiroshima simply ceased to feel, moving in and out among the injured, the dying, and the dead without emotional response. Lifton reports, however, that after a time this closure merged into feelings of depression and despair. It is his hypothesis that the sense of shame and guilt that the survivors evinced so strongly in their interviews with him is a reaction to a basic psychic defense mechanism of closure. He reasons that the psychic defense mechanism could not afford full protection against the knowledge of being alive and strong, or against the sense of "helplessness" toward the victims. Lifton's account of how guilt was expressed toward specific family members whom the survivors were unable to aid or for whom they felt responsible, their focusing of their memory upon one sight or one particular ultimate horror, and their preoccupation with bodily concerns and physical disorders of apparent psychosomatic origin and, finally, their ultimate identification with the dead, all follow the classic pattern of grief reaction first described by Lindemann and subsequently confirmed by psychiatric researchers such as Stern and Berry.

The continuous encounter with death and, equally important, the significant inner encounters so graphically described by Lifton are, of course, not limited to Hiroshima or to Japan, but in varying degrees can be said to be the personal experience of all of us. Lifton's report is of particular value to us, therefore, because it provides us with a measure by which to gauge and assess our public and private responses to that inevitable encounter.

On the public level, Lifton's essay serves to bring the three subsequent articles into focus and we are able to see that their points of departure heighten rather than detract from their basic accord. His report encourages the thought that the effect of what transpired in Hiroshima in a matter of moments has been aborning in Western society since the Age of Reason. The telescoping effect upon time caused by the bomb and the mortal blow it dealt the structure of human existence in Hiroshima propelled the survivors of that city into the existential life of twentieth-century America.

The remaining three articles, then, shed theoretical light upon the phenomenon described so vividly by Lifton. Franz Borkenau, our second contributor, offers the provocative theory in his article, "The Concept of Death," that the shift in attitudes toward death is traceable to the conflicting feelings about death experienced by our unconscious. His thesis is that man is confronted with a self-contradictory experience of death which is rooted deep in his inner being. Man's unconscious is convinced of its own immortality, yet at the same time finds one of its motive forces to be the pursuit of death itself. The coexistence of these two incompatible elements within the unconscious of man provides an inherent contradiction in human existence. Although man struggles to resolve the conflict within, the embracing of one motive force perforce causes its primal opposite to reassert itself. Man is thus caught in a never-ending debate, which, Borkenau proposes, is a basic element in shaping the course of human history.

The conflicting attitudes toward death posited for the individual are also understood to be at work within the culture so that ultimately there emerge periods of time when the culture can be characterized as death-defying, death-accepting, or death-denying in outlook. A shift in the popular attitude toward death from one of these orientations to another is seen to mark an epoch in our historical evolution. Our age, Borkenau believes, is experiencing such a shift away from the death-defying stance it has traditionally taken toward one that is basically death-denying.

Wahl, in his article, "The Fear of Death," attempts to explain modern attitudes and reactions toward death in a somewhat different manner. He would reject Borkenau's psychoanalytically inspired reductionism which places man, ultimately, at the mercy of an unconscious forever in the throes of a life and death struggle within itself. Moreover, he disagrees with those neo-Freudians who propose that the fear of death is basically a displacement of castration anxiety following an unsuccessful resolution of the oedipus complex. For Wahl, as a psychiatrist, the fear of death is intimately associated with the development of symbol formation in the child and the concomitant formation of guilt reactions. Its source, he believes, is to be found in the general life shocks and intrafamilial stresses to which we are all exposed. That some of us can survive our childhood with no apparent fear of death and others cannot, Wahl attributes to the sense of adequacy and security engendered by the family experience that is differentially developed. Although both writers agree that our age is characterized by a denial and repression of death, they do so from grossly different "readings" of modern culture. Borkenau, for example, attributes what he would call our "present-day nihilistic secularism," to the disintegration of Christian faith in Western society and its belief in immortality. Wahl does not address himself to this question of historical change, believing that in the area of death our modern reactions are hardly different from those of our primitive ancestors. Borkenau, more historically minded, proposes that the synthesis of the death acceptance of Hebrew and Hellenistic religions with Christianity has meant for many the abandonment of the belief in an actual afterlife. But Christian thought teaches that life without immortality is meaningless. Moreover, the Western notion of personality is ultimately dependent upon the Christian belief of the immortal soul. To deny the latter is to question the relevance if not the reality of the former. For Borkenau, modern secularism, despairing of its own arid philosophy, is thus bent upon a nihilistic course in which the nullification of self is its ultimate goal, the achievement of which will signal man's mastery over his own mortality.

For Wahl, on the other hand, such religious and philosophical systems as Borkenau deals with are merely epiphenomenal. Indulging in a little reductionism and circularity of his own, Wahl finds the source of our elaborate social techniques and religious and philosophical systems which serve to disguise the fact of death in the interpersonal and intrapsychic paradoxes which individuals are heir to. For Wahl, the same factors of love and security which make an individual feel personally invulnerable to death and give him magical feelings of omnipotence force him to take the responsibility for his death wishes toward his significant persons. Wahl argues that since children reason magically, that is, to think a thing is to do a thing, and reason by the law of Talion, that is, to do a thing is to insure a similar punishment to the self, the hostile death wishes a child entertains toward others during his childhood come back to haunt him indirectly or symbolically during his adult life. Thus, with Wahl as with Borkenau, man is destined forever to be hoist with his own psychic petard.

In the final contribution to this section, Fulton and Geis in their article, "Death and Social Values," take up some ground left vacant by Borkenau and Wahl. They concur with Borkenau that attitudes toward death are changing in Western society and for them, more particularly, in the United States, but they differ with him and with Wahl concerning the source of this change. Fulton and Geis propose that the reversal noted in death attitudes is the result of shifts and changes within the culture itself and not a consequence of either unconscious strivings or intrapsychic paradoxes. Medical science discoveries, technological inventions, the Higher criticism, and other social and cultural factors have served, they suggest, to break the crust of religious belief and to bring us to our present condition.

Robert Jay Lifton

Psychological Effects of the Atomic Bomb in Hiroshima: The Theme of Death

Hiroshima commands our attention now, eighteen years after its exposure to the atomic bomb, perhaps even more insistently than when the event actually occurred. We are compelled by the universal threat of nuclear weapons to study the impact of such weapons upon their first human victims, ever mindful of the relevance of this question to our own future and to all of human survival.

Much research has already been done concerning the physical consequences of the Hiroshima and Nagasaki disasters, particularly in relation to their unique feature of delayed radiation effects.[1] But little attention has been paid to psychological and social elements, though these might well be said to be at present the most vivid legacies of the first atomic bomb.[2]

My own interest in these problems developed during two years

Reprinted from *Daedalus*, 92 (1963) pp. 462–497, by permission of the author and the publisher (Copyright, 1963, by the American Academy of Arts and Sciences).

of research, conducted in Tokyo and Kyoto from 1960–1962, on the relationship of individual character and historical change in Japanese youth.[3] I was struck by the significance which the encounter with nuclear weapons had for the Japanese as a whole, even for young Japanese who could hardly remember the event. Also involved in my undertaking a study in Hiroshima was concern with the psychological aspects of war and peace, as well as previous interest in the behavior of individuals and groups under extreme conditions.[4]

I began the work in April of 1962, first through two brief visits to Hiroshima, followed by four and one-half months of residence there. My approach was primarily that of individual interviews with two groups of atomic bomb survivors: thirty-three chosen at random from the more than 90,000 survivors (*hibakusha*),[5] listed at the Hiroshima University Research Institute for Nuclear Medicine and Biology; and an additional group of forty-two survivors specially selected because of their prominence in dealing with A-bomb problems or their capacity to articulate their experiences. Included among the latter were physicians, university professors, city officials, politicians, writers and poets, and leaders of survivor organizations and peace movements. I also sought out all those in Hiroshima (mostly Japanese, but also Americans and Europeans) who could tell me anything about the complex array of group emotions and social problems which had arisen in the city over the seventeen years that had elapsed since the disaster.

I was aware of the delicacy of my situation as an American psychiatrist conducting this study, and I relied heavily upon the continuous support and assistance of Japanese groups within the Hiroshima community, so that all meetings and interviews were arranged through their introductions. In the case of the randomly selected group, my first contact with each survivor was made through a personal visit to the home, in the company of a Japanese social worker from Hiroshima University. My previous experience in Japan—including the ability to speak a certain amount of Japanese—was helpful in eliciting the many forms of cooperation so crucial for the work. Perhaps of greatest importance was my conveying to both colleagues and research subjects a sense of my personal motivation in undertaking the work, the hope that a systematic study of this kind might clarify important problems often spoken about loosely, and thereby in a small way contribute to the mastery of nuclear weapons and the avoidance of their use.

Interviews were generally about two hours long; I tried to see each research subject twice, though I saw some three or four times, and others just once.   I tape-recorded all sessions with subjects of the randomly selected group, and did so with many of those in the special group as well, always with the subject's consent. Interviews were conducted in Japanese, and a research assistant was always present to interpret.   After making an initial appraisal of the problems involved, I decided to focus my questions upon three general dimensions of the problem: first, the recollection of the experience itself and its inner meaning seventeen years later:[6] second, residual concerns and fears, especially those relating to delayed radiation effects; and third, the survivor's sense of self and society, or of special group identity.   Subjects were encouraged to associate freely to these topics and to any feelings or ideas stimulated by them.   And in gathering these data I sought always to evaluate to what degree exposure to the atomic bomb in Hiroshima resembles psychological and social patterns common to all disasters, as described in the general literature on disaster, and in what ways it might be a unique experience.   What follows is a preliminary statement on work in progress; a composite description of some of the basic trends I have observed.

The Experience Recalled

The degree to which one anticipates a disaster has important bearing upon the way in which one responds, and the predominant tone in the descriptions I heard was that of extreme surprise and unpreparedness.   Since it was wartime, people did of course expect conventional bombing; there had been regularly occurring air raid warnings because of planes passing over Hiroshima, though only an occasional stray bomb had actually been dropped on the city. American planes did drop leaflets warning Hiroshima inhabitants that their city was going to be demolished and urging them to evacuate from it.   But very few people appear to have seen these leaflets, and those who did tended to ignore them as enemy propaganda.   Many wondered at Hiroshima's relatively untouched state, despite its obviously strategic significance as a major staging area for Japan's military operations in China and Southeast Asia.   There was general apprehension, the feeling that there was something dangerous about Hiroshima's strangely intact state and that the

Americans must be preparing something extraordinarily big for the city (though this latter thought could have been partly a retrospective construction). At 8:15 A.M. on August 6, 1945, the moment the bomb fell, most people were in a particularly relaxed state, since, following a brief air-raid warning, the all-clear had just been sounded. People thus had a false sense of immediate security, as well as a total incapacity to imagine the nature of the weapon that was about to strike them.

It was only those at some distance from the bomb's hypocenter who could clearly distinguish the sequence of the great flash of light in the sky accompanied by the lacerating heat of the fireball, then the sound and force of the blast, and the impressive multicolored "mushroom cloud" rising above the city. Two thousand meters is generally considered to be a critical radius for high mortality (from heat, blast, and radiation), for susceptibility to delayed radiation effects, and for near-total destruction of buildings and other structures. But many were killed outside of this radius, and indeed the number of deaths from the bomb—variously estimated from 63,000 to 240,000 or more—is still unknown. Falling in the center of a flat city made up largely of wooden residential and commercial structures, the bomb is reported to have destroyed or so badly damaged, through blast and fire, more than two-thirds of all buildings within 5000 meters—an area roughly encompassing the city limits—that all of Hiroshima became immediately involved in the atomic disaster.[7] Those within the 2000-meter radius could not clearly recall their initial perceptions: many simply remember what they thought to be a flash—or else a sudden sensation of heat—followed by an indeterminate period of unconsciousness; others recall only being thrown across a room or knocked down, then finding themselves pinned under debris of buildings.

The most striking psychological feature of this immediate experience was the sense of a sudden and absolute shift from normal existence to an overwhelming encounter with death. This is described by a young shopkeeper's assistant, who was thirteen years old at the time the bomb fell, and 1400 meters from the hypocenter:

I was a little ill . . . so I stayed at home that day. . . . There had been an air-raid warning and then an all-clear. I felt relieved and lay down on the bed with my younger brother. . . . Then it happened. It came very suddenly. . . . It felt something like an electric short—a bluish sparkling light. . . . There was a noise, and I felt great heat—

even inside of the house. When I came to, I was underneath the destroyed house. . . . I didn't know anything about the atomic bomb so I thought that some bomb had fallen directly upon me . . . and then when I felt that our house had been directly hit I became furious. . . . There were roof tiles and walls—everything black—entirely covering me. So I screamed for help. . . . And from all around I heard moans and screaming, and then I felt a kind of danger to myself. . . . I thought that I too was going to die in that way. I felt this way at that moment because I was absolutely unable to do anything at all by my own power. . . . I didn't know where I was or what I was under. . . . I couldn't hear voices of my family. I didn't know how I could be rescued. I felt I was going to suffocate and then die, without knowing exactly what had happened to me. This was the kind of expectation I had . . . .

I stress this sudden encounter with death because I believe that it initiates, from this first moment of contact with the atomic bomb, an emotional theme within the victim which remains with him indefinitely: the sense of a more or less permanent encounter with death.

This early impact enveloped the city in an aura of weirdness and unreality, as recalled by an elderly electrician, who at the time of the bomb was in his mid-forties, working at a railroad junction 5000 meters from the hypocenter.

I was setting up a pole . . . near a switch in the railroad tracks . . . I heard a tremendous noise. There was a flash . . . a kind of flash I had never seen before which I can't describe. . . . My face felt hot and I put my hands over my eyes and rushed under a locomotive that was nearby. I crawled in between the wheels, and then there was an enormous boom and the locomotive shook. I was frightened, so I crawled out. . . . I couldn't tell what happened. . . . For about five minutes I saw nobody, and then I saw someone coming out from an air-raid shelter who told me that the youngest one of our workers had been injured by falling piles . . . so I put the injured man on the back of my bicycle and tried to take him to the dispensary. Then I saw that almost all of the people in that area were crowded into the dispensary, and since there was also a hospital nearby, I went there. But that too was already full. . . . So the only thing to do was to go into (the center of) Hiroshima. But I couldn't move my bicycle because of all the people coming out from Hiroshima and blocking the way. . . . I saw that they were all naked and I wondered what was the matter with them. . . . When we spoke to people they said that they had been hit by something they didn't understand. . . . We were desperately looking for a doctor or a hospital but we couldn't seem to have any success. . . . We walked toward Hiroshima, still carrying our tools. . . . Then in Hiroshima there was no place either—it had become an empty field—so I carried him to a place near our company office where injured people were lying inside, asking for water. But there was no water and there was no way to help them and I myself didn't know what kind of treatment I should give to this man or to the others. I had to let them die right before my eyes. . . . By then we were cut off from escape, because the fire was beginning to spread out and we couldn't move—we were together with the dead people in the building—only we were not really inside of the building because the building itself had been destroyed, so that we were really outdoors, and we spent the night there . . . .

This rote and essentially ineffectual behavior was characteristic of many during the first few hours, in those situations where any attempt at all could be made to maintain a group co-operative effort; people were generally more effective in helping members of their immediate families, or in saving themselves. This same electrician, an unusually conscientious man, kept at his post at the railroad over a period of several weeks, leaving only for brief periods to take care of his family. Again his description of the scene of death and near-death takes on a dreamlike quality:

There were dead bodies everywhere. . . . There was practically no room for me to put my feet on the floor. . . . At that time I couldn't figure out the reason why all these people were suffering, or what illness it was that had struck them down. . . . I was the only person taking care of the place as all the rest of the people had gone. . . . Other people came in looking for food or to use the toilet. . . . There was no one to sell tickets in the station, nothing . . . and since trains weren't running I didn't have much work to do. . . . There was no light at all and we were just like sleepwalkers. . . .

And a middle-aged teacher, who was also on the outskirts of the city about 5000 meters from the hypocenter, describes his awe at the destruction he witnessed:

I climbed Hijiyama Mountain and looked down. I saw that Hiroshima had disappeared. . . . I was shocked by the sight. . . . What I felt then and still feel now I just can't explain with words. Of course I saw many dreadful scenes after that—but that experience, looking down and finding nothing left of Hiroshima—was so shocking that I simply can't express what I felt. I could see Koi (a suburb at the opposite end of the city) and a few buildings standing. . . . But Hiroshima didn't exist—that was mainly what I saw—Hiroshima just didn't exist.

And a young university professor 2500 meters from the hypocenter at the time sums up these feelings of weird, awesome unreality in a frequently-expressed image of hell:

Everything I saw made a deep impression—a park nearby covered with dead bodies waiting to be cremated . . . very badly injured people evacuated in my direction. . . . The most impressive thing I saw was some girls, very young girls, not only with their clothes torn off but with their skin peeled off as well. . . . My immediate thought was that this was like the hell I had always read about. . . . I had never seen anything which resembled it before, but I thought that should there be a hell, this was it—the Buddhist hell, where we were taught that people who could not attain salvation always went. . . . And I imagined that all of these people I was seeing were in the hell I had read about.

But human beings are unable to remain open to emotional experience of this intensity for any length of time, and very quickly—sometimes within minutes—there began to occur what we may term *psychological closure;* that is, people simply ceased to feel.

For instance, a male social worker, then in his twenties and in military service in Hiroshima, was temporarily on leave at his home just outside of the city; he rushed back into the city soon after the bomb fell, in accordance with his military duty, only to find that his unit had been entirely wiped out. A certain amount of military order was quickly re-established, and a policy of immediate mass cremation of dead bodies was instituted in order to prevent widespread disease, and in accordance with Japanese custom. As a non-commissioned officer and one of the few able-bodied men left, he was put in charge of this work of disposing of corpses, which he found he could accomplish with little difficulty:

After awhile they became just like objects or goods that we handled in a very businesslike way. . . . Of course I didn't regard them simply as pieces of wood—they were dead bodies—but if we had been sentimental we couldn't have done the work. . . . We had no emotions. . . .

Because of the succession of experiences I had been through I was temporarily without feeling. . . . At times I went about the work with great energy, realizing that no one but myself could do it.

He contrasted his own feelings with the terror experienced by an outsider just entering the disaster area:

Everything at that time was part of an extraordinary situation. . . . For instance, I remember that on the ninth or tenth of August, it was an extremely dark night. . . . I saw blue phosphorescent flames rising from the dead bodies—and there were plenty of them. These were quite different from the orange flames coming from the burning buildings. . . . These blue phosphorescent flames are what we Japanese look upon as spirits rising from dead bodies—in former days we called them fireballs.[8] —And yet, at that time I had no sense of fear, not a bit, but merely thought, "those dead bodies are still burning." . . . But to people who had just come from the outside, those flames looked very strange. . . . One of those nights I met a soldier who had just returned to the city, and I walked along with him. . . . He noticed these unusual fireballs and asked me what they were. I told him that they were the flames coming from dead bodies. The soldier suddenly became extremely frightened, fell down on the ground, and was unable to move. . . . Yet I at that time had a state of mind in which I feared nothing. Though if I were to see those flames now I might be quite frightened. . . .

Relatively few people were involved in the disposal of dead bodies, but virtually all of those I interviewed nonetheless experienced a similar form of psychological closure in response to what they saw and felt, and particularly in response to their overall exposure to death. Thus many told how horrified they were when they first encountered corpses in strange array, or extremely disfigured faces, but how, after a period of time as they saw more and more of these, they felt nothing. Psychological closure would last sometimes for a few hours, and sometimes for days or even months and merge into longer-term feelings of depression and despair.

But even the profound and unconscious psychic defensive maneuvers involved in psychological closure were ultimately unable to afford full protection to the survivor from the painful sights and stimuli impinging upon him. It was, moreover, a defense not devoid of its own psychological cost. Thus the same social worker, in a later interview, questioned his own use of the word "businesslike" to describe his attitude toward dead bodies, and emphasized the pity and sympathy he felt while handling the remains of men from his unit and the pains he took to console family members who came for these remains; he even recalled feeling frightened at night when passing the spot where he worked at cremation by day. He was in effect telling me not only that his psychological closure was imperfect, but that he was horrified—felt ashamed and guilty—at having behaved in a way which he now thought callous. For he had indulged in activities which were ordinarily, for him, strongly taboo, and had done so with an energy, perhaps even an enthusiasm, which must have mobilized within him primitive emotions of a frightening nature.

The middle-aged teacher who had expressed such awe at the disappearance of Hiroshima reveals that way in which feelings of shame and guilt, and especially shame and guilt toward the dead, break through the defense of psychological closure and painfully assert themselves:

I went to look for my family. Somehow I became a pitiless person, because if I had pity I would not have been able to walk through the city, to walk over those dead bodies. The most impressive thing was the expression in people's eyes—bodies badly injured which had turned black—their eyes looking for someone to come and help them. They looked at me and knew that I was stronger than they. . . . I was looking for my family member—but the eyes—the emptiness—the helpless expression—were something I will never forget. . . . I often had to go to the same place more than once. I would wish that the same family would not still be there. . . . I saw disappointment in their eyes. They looked at me with great expectation, staring right through me. It was very hard to be stared at by those eyes. . . .

He felt, in other words, accused by the eyes of the anonymous dead and dying, of wrong-doing and transgression (a sense of guilt) for not helping them, for letting them die, for "selfishly" remaining alive and strong; and "exposed" and "seen through" by the same eyes for these identical failings (a sense of shame).[9]

There were also many episodes of more focused guilt toward specific family members whom one was unable to help, and for whose death one felt responsible. For instance, the shopkeeper's assistant mentioned earlier was finally rescued from the debris of his destroyed house by his mother, but she was too weakened by her own injuries to be able to walk very far with him. Soon they were surrounded by fire, and he (a boy of thirteen) did not feel he had the strength to sustain her weight, and became convinced that they would both die unless he took some other action. So he put her down and ran for help, but the neighbor he summoned could not get through to the woman because of the flames, and the boy learned shortly afterward that his mother died in precisely the place he had left her. His lasting sense of guilt was reflected in his frequent experience, from that time onward, of hearing his mother's voice ringing in his ears calling for help.

A middle-aged businessman related a similarly guilt-stimulating sequence. His work had taken him briefly to the south of Japan and he had returned to Hiroshima during the early morning hours of August 6. Having been up all night, he was not too responsive when his twelve-year-old son came into his room to ask his father to remove a nail from his shoe so that he could put it on and go off to school. The father, wishing to get the job quickly over, placed a piece of leather above the tip of the nail and promised he would take the whole nail out when the boy returned in the afternoon. As in the case of many youngsters who were sent to factories to do "voluntary labor" as a substitute for their school work, the boy's body was never found—and the father, after a desperately fruitless search for his son throughout the city, was left with the lingering self-accusation that the nail he had failed to remove might have impeded the boy's escape from the fire.

Most survivors focus upon one incident, one sight, or one particular *ultimate horror* with which they strongly identify themselves, and which left them with a profound sense of pity, guilt, and shame. Thus the social worker describes an event which he feels affected him even more than his crematory activities:

> On the evening of August 6, the city was so hot from the fire that I could not easily enter it, but I finally managed to do so by taking a path along the river. As I walked along the bank near the present Yoko-gawa Bridge, I saw the bodies of a mother and her child. . . . That is, I thought I saw dead bodies, but the child was still alive—still breathing, though with difficulty. . . . I filled the cover of my lunch box with water and gave it to the child but it was so weak it could not drink. I knew that people were frequently passing that spot . . . and I hoped that one of these people would take the child, as I had to go back to my own unit. Of course I helped many people all through that day . . . but the image of this child stayed on my mind and remains as a strong impression even now. . . . Later when I was again in that same area I hoped that I might be able to find the child . . . and I looked for it

among all the dead children collected at a place nearby. . . . Even
before the war I had planned to go into social work, but this experience
led me to go into my present work with children—as the memory of
that mother and child by Yokogawa Bridge has never left me, especially since the child was still alive when I saw it.

These expressions of ultimate horror can be related to direct
personal experience of loss (for instance, the businessman who had
failed to remove the nail from his son's shoe remained preoccupied
with pathetic children staring imploringly at him), as well as to
enduring individual emotional themes. Most of them involved
women and children, universal symbols of purity and vulnerability,
particularly in Japanese culture. And, inevitably, the ultimate
horror was directly related to death or dying.

Contamination and Disease

Survivors told me of three rumors which circulated widely in Hiroshima just after the bomb. The first was that for a period of
seventy-five years Hiroshima would be uninhabitable—no one would
be able to live there. This rumor was a direct expression of the
*fear of deadly and protracted contamination from a mysterious
poison believed to have been emitted by the frightening new
weapon.* (As one survivor put it, "The ordinary people spoke of
poison; the intellectuals spoke of radiation.")
   Even more frequently expressed, and I believe with greater emotion, was a second rumor: trees and grass would never again grow
in Hiroshima; from that day on the city would be unable to sustain
vegetation of any kind. This seemed to suggest *an ultimate form
of desolation even beyond that of human death:* nature was drying
up altogether, the ultimate source of life was being extinguished—a
form of symbolism particularly powerful in Japanese culture with
its focus upon natural aesthetics and its view of nature as both
enveloping and energizing all of human life.
   The third rumor, less frequently mentioned to me but one which
also had wide currency in various versions, was that all those who
had been exposed to the bomb in Hiroshima would be dead within
three years. This more naked death symbolism was directly related to the appearance of frightening symptoms of toxic radiation
effects. For almost immediately after the bomb and during the
following days and weeks, people began to experience, and notice

in others, symptoms of a strange form of illness, nausea, vomiting, and loss of appetite; diarrhea with large amounts of blood in the stools; fever and weakness; purple spots on various parts of the body from bleeding into the skin (purpura); inflammation and ulceration of the mouth, throat, and gums (oropharyngeal lesions and gingivitis); bleeding from the mouth, gums, nose, throat, rectum, and urinary tract (hemorrhagic manifestations); loss of hair from the scalp and other parts of the body (epilation); extremely low white blood cell counts when these were taken (leucopenia); and in many cases a progressive course until death.[10] These symptoms and fatalities aroused in the minds of the people of Hiroshima a special terror, *an image of a weapon which not only kills and destroys on a colossal scale but also leaves behind the bodies of those exposed to it deadly influences which may emerge at any time and strike down their victims.* This image was made particularly vivid by the delayed appearance of these radiation effects, two to four weeks after the bomb fell, sometimes in people who had previously seemed to be in perfect health.

The shopkeeper's assistant, both of whose parents were killed by the bomb, describes his reactions to the death of two additional close family members from these toxic radiation effects:

My grandmother was taking care of my younger brother on the 14th of August when I left, and when I returned on the 15th she had many spots all over her body. Two or three days later she died. . . . My younger brother, who . . . was just a (five-month-old) baby, was without breast milk—so we fed him thin rice gruel. . . . But on the 10th of October he suddenly began to look very ill, though I had not then noticed any spots on his body. . . . Then on the next day he began to look a little better, and I thought he was going to survive. I was very pleased, as he was the only family member I had left, and I took him to a doctor—but on the way to the doctor he died. And at that time we found that there were two large spots on his bottom. . . . I heard it said that all these people would die within three years . . . so I thought, "sooner or later I too will die." . . . I felt very weak and very lonely—with no hope at all . . . and since I had seen so many people's eyebrows falling out, their hair falling out, bleeding from their teeth— I found myself always nervously touching my hair like this (he demonstrated by rubbing his head). . . . I never knew when some sign of the disease would show itself. . . . And living in the countryside then with my relatives, people who came to visit would tell us these things, and then the villagers also talked about them—telling stories of this man or that man who visited us a few days ago, returned to

Hiroshima, and died within a week. . . . I couldn't tell whether these stories were true or not, but I believed them then. And I also heard that when the *hibakusha* came to evacuate to the village where I was, they died there one by one. . . . This loneliness, and the fear. . . . The physical fear . . . has been with me always. . . . It is not something temporary, as I still have it now. . . .

Here we find a link between this early sense of ubiquitous death from radiation effects, and later anxieties about death and illness.

In a similar tone, a middle-aged writer describes his daughter's sudden illness and death:

My daughter was working with her classmates at a place 1000 meters from the hypocenter. . . . I was able to meet her next day at a friend's house. She had no burns and only minor external wounds, so I took her with me to my country house. She was quite all right for awhile but on the 4th of September she suddenly became sick. . . . The symptoms of her disease were different from those of a normal disease. . . . She had spots all over her body. . . . Her hair began to fall out. She vomited small clumps of blood many times. Finally she began to bleed all over her mouth. And at times her fever was very high. I felt this was a very strange and horrible disease. . . . We didn't know what it was. I thought it was a kind of epidemic—something like cholera. So I told the rest of my family not to touch her and to disinfect all utensils and everything she used. . . . We were all afraid of it and even the doctor didn't know what it was. . . . After ten days of agony and torture she died on September 14. . . . I thought it was very cruel that my daughter, who had nothing to do with the war, had to be killed in this way. . . .

Survivors were thus affected not only by the fact of people dying around them but by the way in which they died: a gruesome form of rapid bodily deterioration which seemed unrelated to more usual and "decent" forms of death.

We have seen how these initial physical fears could readily turn into lifetime bodily concerns. . . . Moreover, Hiroshima survivors are aware of the general concern and controversy about genetic effects of the atomic bomb, and most express fear about possible harmful effects upon subsequent generation—a very serious emotional concern anywhere, but particularly so in an East Asian culture which stresses family lineage and the continuity of generations as man's central purpose in life and (at least symbolically) his means of achieving immortality.[11] The Hiroshima people know that radiation *can* produce congenital abnormalities (as had been widely demonstrated in laboratory animals); and abnormalities have frequently been reported among the offspring of survivors—sometimes in very lurid journalistic terms, sometimes in more restrained medical reports. Actually, systematic studies of the problem have so far revealed no higher incidence of abnormalities in survivors' offspring than in those of control populations, so that scientific findings regarding genetic effects have been essentially negative. However, there has been one uncomfortably positive genetic finding, that of disturbances in sex ratio of offspring: men exposed to a significant degree of radiation tend to have relatively fewer daughters, while exposed women tend to have fewer sons, because, it is believed, of sex-linked lethal mutations involving the X chromosome—a finding whose significance is difficult to evaluate. Moreover, there are Japanese physicians who believe that there has been an increase in various forms of internal (and therefore invisible) congenital abnormalities in children of survivors, despite the absence so far of convincing scientific evidence.[12]

Another factor here is the definite damage from radiation experienced by children exposed *in utero*, including many stillbirths and abortions as well as a high incidence of microcephaly with and without mental retardation (occurring almost exclusively in pregnancies which had not advanced beyond four months). This is, of course, a direct effect of radiation upon sensitive, rapidly growing fetal tissues, and, scientifically speaking, has nothing to do with genetic problems. But ordinary people often fail to make this distinction; to them the birth of children with abnormally small heads and retarded minds was often looked upon as still another example of the bomb's awesome capacity to inflict a physical curse upon its victims and their offspring.

Fears about general health and genetic effects have inevitably affected marriage arrangements (which are usually made in Japan by families with the help of a go-between), in which survivors are frequently thought to encounter discrimination, particularly when involved in arrangements with families outside of Hiroshima.

A company employee in his thirties, who was 2000 meters from the bomb's hypocenter when it fell, described to me virtually all of these bodily and genetic concerns in a voice that betrayed considerable anxiety:

Even when I have an illness which is not at all serious—as for instance when I had very mild liver trouble—I have fears about its cause. Of course if it is just an ordinary condition there is nothing to worry about, but if it has a direct connection to radioactivity, then I might not be able to expect to recover. At such times I feel myself very delicate. . . . This happened two or three years ago. I was working very hard and drinking a great deal of *sake* at night in connection with business appointments and I also had to make many strenuous trips. So my condition might have been partly related to my using up so much energy in all of these things. . . . The whole thing is not fully clear to me. . . . But the results of statistical study show that those who were exposed to the bomb are more likely to have illnesses—not only of the liver, but various kinds of new growths, such as cancer or blood diseases. My blood was examined several times but no special changes were discovered. . . . When my marriage arrangements were made we discussed all these things in a direct fashion. Everyone knows that there are some effects, but in my case it was the eleventh year after the bomb, and I discussed my physical condition during all of that time. From that, and also from the fact that I was exposed to the bomb while inside of a building and taken immediately to the suburbs, and then remained quite a while outside of the city—judging from all of these facts, it was concluded that there was very little to fear concerning my condition. . . . But in general, there is a great concern that people who were exposed to the bomb might become ill five or ten years later or at any time in the future. . . . Also when my children were born, I found myself worrying about things the ordinary people don't worry about, such as the possibility that they might inherit some terrible disease from me. . . . I heard that the likelihood of our giving birth to deformed children is greater than in the case of ordinary people. . . . and at that time my white blood cell count was rather low. . . . I felt fatigue in the summertime and had a blood count done three or four times. . . . I was afraid it could be related to the bomb, and was greatly worried. . . . Then after the child was born, even though he wasn't a deformed child, I still worried that something might happen to him afterwards. . . . With the second child too I was not entirely free of such worries. . . . I am still not sure what might happen and I worry that the effects of radioactivity might be lingering in some way. . . .

Here we see a young man carrying on effectively in his life, essentially healthy, with normal children, and yet continually plagued by underlying anxieties—about his general health, then about marriage arrangements, and then in relationship to the birth of each of his children. Each hurdle is passed, but there is little relief; like many survivors, he experiences an inner sense of being doomed for posterity.

And a young clerk, also exposed about 2000 meters from the

hypocenter, but having the additional disadvantage of retaining a keloid scar resulting from facial burns, expresses similar emotions in still stronger fashion:

> Frankly speaking, even now I have fear. . . . Even today people die in the hospitals from A-bomb disease, and when I hear about this I worry that I too might sooner or later have the same thing happen to me. . . . I have a special feeling that I am different from ordinary people . . . that I have the mark of wounds—as if I were a cripple. . . . I imagine a person who has an arm or a leg missing might feel the same way. . . . It is not a matter of lacking something externally, but rather something like a handicap—something mental which does not show—the feeling that I am mentally different from ordinary people . . . so when I hear about people who die from A-bomb disease or who have operations because of this illness, then I feel that I am the same kind of person as they. . . .

The survivor's identification with the dead and the maimed initiates a vicious circle on the psychosomatic plane of existence: he is likely to associate the mildest everyday injury or sickness with possible radiation effects; and anything he relates to radiation effects becomes associated with death. The process is accentuated by the strong Japanese cultural focus upon bodily symptoms as expressions of anxiety and conflict. Thus the all-encompassing term "A-bomb sickness" or "A-bomb disease" (*genbakusho*) has evolved, referring on the one hand to such fatal conditions as the early acute radiation effects and later cases of leukemia; and on the other hand to the vague borderline area of fatigue, general weakness, sensitivity to hot weather, suspected anemia, susceptibility to colds or stomach trouble, and general nervousness—all of which are frequent complaints of survivors, and which many associate with radiation effects.[13] Not only does the expression "A-bomb disease" have wide popular currency, but it has frequently been used by local physicians as a convenient category for a condition otherwise hard to classify, and at the same time as a means of making it possible for the patient to derive certain medical and economic benefits.

These benefits also loom large in the picture. Doctors and survivors—as well as politicians and city officials—are caught in a conflict between humanitarian provision for medical need, and the dangers (expressed to me particularly by Japanese physicians) of encouraging the development in survivors of hypochondriasis, general weakness and dependency—or what is sometimes called

"A-bomb neurosis." During the years immediately after the war, when medical care was most needed, very little adequate treatment was available, as the national medical law providing for survivors was not enacted until 1957. But since that time a series of laws and amendments have been passed with increasingly comprehensive medical coverage, particularly for those in the "special survivors" group (those nearest the hypocenter at the time of the bomb and those who have shown evidence of medical conditions considered to be related to A-bomb effects). In the last few years the category of "special survivors" has been steadily enlarged: distance from the hypocenter, as a criterion for eligibility, has been extended from 2000 to 3000 meters; and qualifying illnesses—originally limited to such conditions as leukemia, ophthalmic diseases, and various blood and liver disorders, all of which were considered to be related to radiation effects—have been extended to include illnesses not considered to be necessarily directly caused by radiation but possibly aggravated by the overall atomic bomb experience, such as cancer, heart disease, endocrine and kidney disorders, arteriosclerosis, hypertension, and others.

Maximum medical and economic benefit, however, can be obtained only by those "certified" (through a special medical procedure) to have illnesses specifically related to the atomic bomb; but some physicians believe that this "certification"—which can be sometimes given for such minor conditions as ordinary anemia (as well as for more serious illnesses)—tends to stamp one psychologically as a lifetime A-bomb patient. The rationale of these laws is to provide maximum help for survivors and to give them the benefit of the doubt about matters which are not entirely scientifically resolved. But there remains a great deal of controversy over them. In addition to those who feel that the laws foster an exaggerated preoccupation with atomic bomb effects (not only among doctors but also among city officials, ordinary people, and even survivors themselves), there are other survivors who criticize them as being still insufficiently comprehensive, as having overly complicated categories and subcategories which in the end deny full care for certain conditions.

My own impression in studying this problem is that, since "A-bomb disease" is at this historical juncture as much a spiritual as a physical condition (as our young clerk made so clear)—and one which touches at every point upon the problem of death—it is difficult for any law or medical program to provide a cure.

The general psychological atmosphere in Hiroshima—and particularly that generated by the effects of the mass media—also has great bearing upon these psychosomatic problems. As one would expect, the whole subject of the atomic bomb and its delayed radiation effects has been continuous front-page news—from 1945-1952 within the limits of the restrictions upon publicizing these matters imposed by the American Occupation,[14] and without such restrictions thereafter. Confronted with a subject so emotionally charged for the people of Hiroshima—its intensity constantly reinforced by world events and particularly by nuclear weapons testing—newspapers in Hiroshima and elsewhere in Japan have dealt with it dramatically, particularly in circulating the concept of "A-bomb disease." Mass media are caught in a moral dilemma in some ways: there is on the one hand the urge to give full publicity to the horrors of nuclear weapons through vivid description of effects and suspected effects of atomic bomb radiation—thereby serving warning to the world and also expressing a form of sympathy to survivors through recognition of their plight—and on the other hand the growing awareness that lurid reports of illness and death have a profoundly disturbing effect upon survivors. Responsible media have struggled to reconcile these conflicting moral pressures and achieve balanced treatment of an unprecedentedly difficult problem; others have been guided mainly by commercial considerations. In any case, the people of Hiroshima have been constantly confronted with frightening descriptions of patients dying in the "A-bomb Hospital" (a medical center built specifically for the treatment of conditions related to the bomb) of "A-bomb disease." In the majority of cases the relationship of the fatal condition to delayed radiation effects is equivocal, but this is usually not made clear, nor does it in any way lessen the enormous impact of these reports upon individual survivors.[15] Also furthering this impact have been the activities of peace movements and various ideological and political groups—ranging from those whose universalistic dedication to peace and opposition to nuclear weapons testing lead them to circulate the effects of the bomb on the humanistic basis, to others who seek narrower political goals from the unique Hiroshima atmosphere.

What I wish to stress is the manner in which these diverse passions—compounded of moral concern, sympathetic identification, various forms of fear, hostility, political conviction, personal ambition, and journalistic sensationalism—interact with the psychosomatic preoccupations of survivors. But I would also emphasize that these passions are by no means simply manufactured ones; they are the inevitable expression of the impact of a disaster of this magnitude upon basic human conflicts and anxieties. And whatever the medical exaggerations, they are built upon an underlying lethal reality of acute and delayed radiation effects, and upon the genuine possibility of still-undiscovered forms of bodily harm.

Yet, in bodily terms or otherwise, human beings vary greatly in their capacity to absorb an experience of this kind. And one's feelings of health or invalidism—as well as one's symbolic attitude toward the bomb—have much to do with individual emotions and life-patterns. This is made clear by a middle-aged female artist who experienced the bomb just 1500 meters from the hypocenter, and during subsequent years suffered continuously from a variety of bodily symptoms of indefinite origin, as well as from general unhappiness in marital and family relationships:

> It looks as though marriage and the normal life one leads with marriage is good for the health. . . . Among A-bomb victims, those that are married and well established with their families have fewer complaints. Of course, even those who are settled in their families remember the incident. But on the whole they are much better off and feel better . . . their attitude is, "shoganai" (it can't be helped). "It is useless to look back on old memories," they keep saying. They are simply interested in their immediate problems of marriage and everyday life. They look forward rather than backward. . . . Those without families on the other hand keep remembering everything. Clinging to their memories, they keep repeating the experience. . . . They curse the whole world—including what happened in the past and what is happening now. Some of them even say, "I hope that atomic bombs will be dropped again and then the whole world will suffer the same way I am suffering now."

This kind of hostility is likely to occur together with psychosomatic complaints, and particularly in those people who feel that their life has been blighted by the atomic bomb—those who lost close family members or who in one way or another feel themselves unable to recover from the experience. The cosmic nature of the emotion—its curse upon (and in some cases wish for total annihilation of) the whole world resembles in some ways the retaliatory emotions of hurt children. But it contains additional elements of personal recollection: the experience of "world-destruction" at the time of the bomb. And it is a projection into the future: the even greater world-destruction one can envisage as a consequence of a repetition of the use of nuclear weapons.

Unwanted Identity

It is clear by now that exposure to the atomic bomb changed the survivor's status as a human being, in his own eyes as well as in others'. Both through his immediate experience and its consequences over the years, he became a member of a new group; he assumed the identity of the *hibakusha*, of one who has undergone the atomic bomb. When I asked survivors to associate freely to the word *hibakusha*, and to explain their feelings about it, they invariably conveyed to me the sense of having been compelled to take on the special category of existence, by which they felt permanently bound, however they might wish to free themselves from it. The shopkeeper's assistant expresses this in simple terms characteristic for many:

Well . . . because I am a *hibakusha* . . . how shall I say it—I wish others would not look at me with special eyes . . . perhaps *hibakusha* are mentally—or both physically and mentally—different from others . . . but I myself do not want to be treated in any special way because I am a *hibakusha*. . . .

To be a *hibakusha* thus separates one from the rest of humankind. It means, as expressed by a young female clerical worker left with a keloid from her atomic bomb exposure at 1600 meters, a sense of having been forsaken.

I don't like people to use that word (*hibakusha*). . . . Of course there are some who, through being considered *hibakusha* want to receive special coddling (*amaeru*). . . . But I like to stand up as an individual. When I was younger they used to call us "atomic bomb maidens." . . . More recently they call us *hibakusha*. . . . I don't like this special view of us. . . . Usually when people refer to young girls, they will say girls or daughters, or some person's daughter . . . but to refer to us as atomic bomb maidens is a way of discrimination. . . . It is a way of abandoning us. . . .

What she is saying, and what many said to me in different ways, is that the experience, with all of its consequences, is so profound that it can virtually become the person; others then see one *only* as a *hibakusha* bearing the taint of death, and therefore, in the deepest sense, turn away. And even the special attentions—the various forms of emotional succor—which the survivor may be tempted to seek, cannot be satisfying because such succor is ultimately perceived as unauthentic.

A European priest, one of the relatively few non-Japanese *hibakusha*, expresses these sentiments gently but sardonically:

> I always say—if everyone looks at me because I received the Nobel Prize, that's O.K., but if my only virtue is that I was 1000 meters from the atomic bomb center and I'm still alive—I don't want to be famous for that.

Hibakusha look upon themselves as underprivileged in other ways too. Not only are they literally a minority group (one-fifth of the city's population), but they are generally considered to be at the lower socioeconomic levels of society, and have even at times been compared to the *burakumin*, or outcast group. For once it was realized that Hiroshima was not permanently contaminated after all, not only did the survivors attempt to rebuild their homes, but hordes of outsiders—some from overseas areas, some from the industrial Osaka region, some of them black marketeers and members of gangs who saw special opportunity beckoning: all of them both physically and culturally more vigorous than the atomic-bombed, traditionalistic Hiroshima population—poured into the city, and became perhaps the main beneficiaries of the economic boom which later developed. Survivors have encountered discrimination not only in marriage but also in employment, as it was felt that they could not work as hard as ordinary people and tended to need more time off because of illness and fatigue. Of course, survivors nonetheless regularly work and marry; but they often do so with a sense of having, as *hibakusha*, impaired capacity for both. They strongly resent the popular image of the *hibakusha* which accentuates their limitations, but at the same time accept much of it as their own self-image. Thus, concerning occupational competition, older survivors often feel that they have lacked the overall energy to assimilate their economic, spiritual, and possibly physical blows sufficiently to be the equal of ordinary people; and young survivors, even if they feel themselves to possess normal energy, often fear that being identified by others as a *hibakusha* might similarly interfere with their occupational standing. Concerning marriage, the sense of impairment can include the need to have one's A-bomb experience more or less "cleared" by a go-between (as we have seen); fears about having abnormal children, or sometimes about the ability to have children at all;[16] and occasionally, in males, diminished sexual potency (thought of as organic but probably psychogenic in origin).

However well or poorly a survivor is functioning in his life, the word *hibakusha* avokes an image of the dead and the dying. The young clerk, for instance, when he hears the word, thinks either of the experience itself (". . . Although I wasn't myself too badly injured I saw many people who were . . . and I think . . . of the look on their faces. . . camps full of these people, their breasts burned and red . . .") or, as we have already heard him describe, of the aftereffects: "when I hear about people who die from A-bomb disease or who have operations because of this illness, then I feel that I am the same kind of person as they. . . ."

We are again confronted with the survivor's intimate identification with the dead; we find, in fact, that it tends to pervade the entire *hibakusha* identity. *For survivors seem not only to have experienced the atomic disaster, but to have imbibed it and incorporated it into their beings, including all of its elements of horror, evil, and particularly of death.* They feel compelled virtually to merge with those who died, not only with close family members but with a more anonymous group of "the dead." And they judge, and indeed judge harshly, their own behavior and that of other survivors on the basis of the degree of respect it demonstrates toward the dead. They condemn, for instance, the widespread tendency (which, as Japanese, they are at the same time attracted to) of making the anniversary of the bomb an occasion for a gay festival—because they see this as an insult to the dead. Similarly they are extraordinarily suspicious of all individual and group attempts to take any form of action in relationship to the atomic bomb experience, even when done for the apparent purpose of helping survivors or furthering international peace. And they are, if anything, more critical of a survivor prominent in such programs than they are of "outsiders," constantly accusing such a person of "selling his name," "selling the bomb," or "selling Hiroshima." The causes for their suspiciousness are many, including a pervasive Japanese cultural tendency to be critical of the man who shows unconventional initiative (as expressed in the popular saying, "A nail which sticks out will be hammered down"), as well as an awareness of how readily the Hiroshima situation can be "used" by ambitious leaders. But there is an ultimate inner feeling that any such activities and programs are "impure," that they violate the sanctity of the dead. For in relationship to the atomic bomb disaster, it is only the dead who, in the eyes of survivors, remain pure; and any self- or group-assertion can readily be seen as an insult to the dead.

The *hibakusha* identity, then, in a significant symbolic sense, becomes an identity of the dead. Created partly by the particularly intense Japanese capacity for identification, and partly by the special quality of guilt over surviving, it takes shape through the following inner sequence: I almost died; I should have died; I did die, or at least am not really alive; or if I am alive it is impure of me to be so; and anything I do which affirms life is also impure and an insult to the dead, who alone are pure.[17]

Finally, this imposed identity of the atomic bomb survivor is greatly affected by his historical perceptions (whether clear or fragmentary) of the original experience, including its bearing upon the present world situation. The dominant emotion here is the sense of having been made into "guinea pigs," not only because of being studied by research groups (particularly American research groups) interested in determining the effects of delayed radiation, but more fundamentally because of having been victimized by the first "experiment" (a word many of them use in referring to the event) with nuclear weapons. They are affected by a realization, articulated in various ways, that they have experienced something ultimate in man-made disasters; and at the same time by the feeling that the world's continuing development and testing of the offending weapons deprives their experience of meaning. Thus, while frequently suspicious of organized campaigns against nuclear testing, they almost invariably experience anxiety and rage when such testing is conducted, recall the horrors they have been through, and express bitter frustration at the world's unwillingness to heed their warnings. And we have seen how this anger can at times be converted into thoughts of cosmic retaliation. There remains, of course, a residuum of hostility toward America and Americans for having dropped the bomb, but such hostility has been tempered over the years and softened by Japanese cultural restraints—except, as we have also seen, in individuals who experienced personal losses and blows to self-esteem from which they have been unable to recover. More than in relation to the dropping of the bomb itself (which many said they could understand as a product, however horrible, of war), survivors tend to express hostility in response to what they feel to be callousness toward their plight, or toward those who died, and also toward nuclear weapons testing. Thus, in singling out President Truman as an object of hatred, as some do, it is not only for his having ordered that the bomb be used but also for being assertively unapologetic about having done so.[18]

Survivors tend to be strongly ambivalent about serving as symbols for the rest of the world, and this ambivalence is expressed in Hiroshima's excruciating conflict about whether or not to tear down the so-called "A-bomb dome" (or "peace dome")—the prominent ruins of a dome-shaped exhibition hall located almost directly at the hypocenter. The dome has so far been permitted to stand as a reminder of the experience, and its picture has been featured in countless books and pamphlets dealing, from every point of view, with the A-bomb problem. Three different sets of attitudes on the question were expressed to me. The first: Let it remain permanently so that people (especially outsiders) will remember what we have been through and take steps to prevent repetitions of such disasters. The second: Tear it down for any of the following reasons: it does no good, as no one pays any attention to it; we should adopt the Buddhist attitude of resignation toward the experience, the dome is unauthentic, does not adequately convey what we really experienced, and is not in fact directly at the hypocenter; it is too painful a reminder for *us* (*hibakusha*) to have to look at every day (perhaps the most strongly felt objection); and, we should look ahead to the future rather than back to the unpleasant past. And the third: Let it neither be permitted to stand indefinitely nor torn down, but instead left as it is until it begins to crumble of its own, and then simply removed—a rather ingenious (and perhaps characteristically Japanese) compromise solution to the dilemma, which the city administration has proposed. Most survivors simultaneously feel various conflicting elements of the first and second sets of attitudes, and sometimes of all three. The inner conflict is something like this: For the sake of the dead and of our own sense of worth, we must give our experience significance by enabling it to serve wider moral purposes; but to do so—to

be living symbols of massive death—is not only unbearably painful
but also tends ultimately to be insincere and to insult, rather than
comfort, the dead.

Beyond Hiroshima

We return to the question we raised at the beginning: Does Hiroshima follow the standard patterns delineated for other disasters,
or is it—in an experiential sense—a new order of event? We must
say first that the usual emotional patterns of disaster[19] are very
much present in what I have already described. One can break
down the experience into the usual sequence of anticipation, impact,
and aftermath; one can recognize such standard individual psychological features as various forms of denial, the "illusion of centrality" (or feeling of each that he was at the very center of the
disaster's path),[20] the apathy of the "disaster syndrome" resulting
from the sudden loss of the sense of safety and even omnipotence
with which we usually conduct our lives, and the conflict between
self-preservation and wider human responsibility which culminates
in feelings of guilt and shame; even some of the later social and
psychological conflicts in the affected population are familiar.[21] Yet
we have also seen convincing evidence that the Hiroshima experience,[22] no less in the psychological than in the physical sphere,
transcends in many important ways that of the ordinary disaster.
I shall try to suggest what I think are some of the important
ways in which this is true. And when these special psychological
qualities of the experience of the atomic bomb have been more
fully elaborated—beyond the preliminary outlines of this paper—I
believe that they will, in turn, shed light on general disaster patterns,
and, of greater importance, on human nature and its vicissitudes
at our present historical juncture. We may then come to see Hiroshima for what it was and is: both a direct continuation of the
long and checkered history of human struggle, and at the same
time a plunge into a new and tragic dimension.
    The first of these psychological elements is one we have already
referred to, the continuous encounter with death. When we consider the sequence of this encounter—its turbulent onset at the
moment the bomb fell, its shocking reappearance in association
with delayed radiation effects, and its prolonged expression in the
group identity of the doomed and near-dead—we are struck by

the fact that it is an interminable encounter. There is, psychologically speaking, no end point, no resolution. This continuous
and unresolvable encounter with death, then, is a unique feature
of the atomic bomb disaster. Its significance for the individual
survivor varies greatly, according to such factors as previous character traits, distance from the hypocenter at the time the bomb
fell, fatalities in his immediate family, and many other features
of his bomb experience and subsequent life pattern. There is little
doubt that most survivors lead reasonably effective personal, family,
and occupational lives. But each retains, in greater or lesser degree,
emotional elements of this special relationship to death.

In the light of the Hiroshima experience we should also consider
the possibility that in other disasters or extreme situations there
may also be more significant inner encounters with death, immediate or longer-term, than we have heretofore supposed. Psychiatrists
and social scientists investigating these matters are hampered by
the same factors which interfere with everyone else's approach to
the subject: first, by our inability to imagine death, which deprives
us, as psychiatrists, of our usual reliance upon empathy and leaves
us always at several psychological removes from experiential understanding; and second, by the elaborate circle of denial—the profound
inner need of human beings to make believe that they will never
die—in which we too are enclosed. But these universal psychological barriers to thought about death become much greater in
relation to a nuclear disaster, where the enormity of the scale of
killing and the impersonal nature of the technology are still further
impediments to comprehension. No wonder then that the world
resists full knowledge of the Hiroshima and Nagasaki experiences,
and expends relatively little energy in comprehending their full
significance. And beyond Hiroshima, these same impediments
tragically block and distort our perceptions of the general consequences of nuclear weapons. They also raise an important question
relevant for the continuous debate about the desirability of pre-
paredness for possible nuclear attacks: If the human imagination
is so limited in its capacity to deal with death, and particularly
death on a vast scale, can individuals ever be significantly "prepared" for a nuclear disaster?

The Hiroshima experience thus compels us, particularly as psychiatrists, to give more thought to psychic perceptions of death and
dying. Here I would particularly stress the psychological importance of identification with the dead—not merely the identification

with a particular loved one, as in the case of an ordinary mourning experience, but rather, as we have observed in atomic bomb survivors, a lasting sense of affiliation with death itself. This affiliation creates in turn an enduring element, both within, and standing in judgment of, the self—a process closely related to the experience of shame.[23] Also of great importance is the *style of dying*, real or symbolic, the way in which one anticipates death and the significance with which one can relate oneself to this anticipation. Among those I interviewed in Hiroshima, many found solace in the characteristically Japanese (partially Buddhist) attitude of resignation, but virtually none were able to build a framework of meaning around their overwhelming immersion in death. However philosophically they might accept the horrors of war, they had an underlying sense of having been victimized and experimented upon by a horrible device, all to no avail in a world which has derived no profit from their sufferings.

And this sense of purposeless death suggests the second special feature of the atomic disaster: *a vast breakdown of faith in the larger human matrix supporting each individual life, and therefore a loss of faith (or trust) in the structure of existence.* This is partly due to the original exposure to death and destruction on such an extraordinary scale, an "end-of-the-world" experience resembling the actualization of the wildest psychotic delusion; partly due to the shame and guilt patterns which, initiated during the experience itself, turned into longer-lasting preoccupations with human selfishness (preoccupations expressed to me by a large number of survivors); and partly due to the persisting sense of having encountered an ultimate form of *man-made* destruction. Phrased in another way, the atomic bomb destroyed the complex equilibrium which ordinarily mediates and integrates the great variety of cultural patterns and individual emotions which maintain any society, large or small. One must, of course, take into account here the disruption accompanying the extensive social change which has occurred all over Japan immediately following World War II; and one must also recognize the impressive re-emergence of Hiroshima as an actively functioning city. Nonetheless, this profound loss of confidence in human social ties remains within survivors as a derivative of the atomic bomb experience.

A third psychological feature of particular importance in the Hiroshima disaster is that which I have called *psychological closure*. Resembling the psychological defense of denial, and the behavioral state of apathy, psychological closure is nonetheless a distinctive pattern of response to overwhelmingly threatening stimuli. Within a matter of moments, as we have seen in the examples cited, a person may not only cease to react to these threatening stimuli but in so doing, equally suddenly, violate the most profound values and taboos of his culture and his personal life. Though a highly adaptive response—and indeed very often a means of emotional self-preservation—it can vary in its proportions to the extent at times of almost resembling a psychotic mechanism. Since psychological closure, at least in the form it took in Hiroshima, is specifically related to the problem of death, it raises the question of the degree to which various forms of psychosis might also be responses to the symbolic fear of death or bodily annihilation.

The psychological closure created by the Hiroshima disaster is not limited to the victims themselves, but extends to those who, like myself, attempt to study the event. Thus, although I had had previous research experience with people who had been exposed to extreme situations, I found that at the beginning of my work in Hiroshima the completion of each interview would leave me profoundly shocked and emotionally spent. But as the work progressed and I heard more and more of these accounts, their effects upon me greatly lessened. My awareness of my scientific function—my listening carefully for specific kinds of information and constantly formulating categories of response—enhanced the psychological closure necessary to me for the task of conducting the research (necessary also for a wide variety of human efforts which deal with problems in which death is a factor). It is the vast ramification of psychological closure, rather than the phenomenon itself, that is unique to nuclear disaster, so much so that all who become in any way involved in the problem find themselves facing a near-automatic tendency to close themselves off from what is most disturbing in the evidence at hand.

Finally, there is the question of *psychological mastery of the nuclear disaster experience.* Central to this problem is the task of dealing with feelings of shame and guilt of the most profound nature: the sense that one has, however unwittingly, participated in this total human breakdown in which, in Martin Buber's words "the human order of being is injured."[24] That such feelings of self-condemnation—much like those usually termed "existential guilt"—should be experienced by the *victims* of a nuclear disaster is perhaps the most extreme of its many tragic ironies. Faced

with the task of dealing with this form of guilt, with the problem
of re-establishing trust in the human order, and with the continuing
sense of encounter with death, the survivor of a nuclear disaster
needs nothing less than a new identity in order to come to terms
with his post-disaster world. And once more extending the principle
beyond the victim's experience, it may not be too much to say
that those who permit themselves to confront the consequences of
such a disaster, past or future, are also significantly changed in
the process. Since these consequences now inhabit our world, more
effective approaches to the problem of human survival may well
depend upon our ability to grasp the nature of the fundamentally
new relationship to existence which we all share.

References

1. Studies of the effects of ionizing radiation were instituted by Japanese medical and civilian teams within days after the bomb was dropped, with Dr.
   Masao Tsuzuki of Tokyo Imperial University, playing a leading role.
   American medical groups began their work in early September of 1945, and
   became consolidated in the Joint Commission for the Investigation of the
   Effects of the Atomic Bomb in Japan. Studies of longer-term effects of
   radiation have been conducted at the medical departments and research
   institutes of Hiroshima and Nagasaki Universities. The largest research
   program on delayed radiation effects is being carried out at the Atomic Bomb
   Casualty Commission, in both Hiroshima and Nagasaki, an affiliate of the
   United States National Academy of Sciences—National Research Council,
   under a grant from the U.S. Atomic Energy Commission, administered with
   the cooperation of the Japanese National Institute of Health of the Ministry
   of Health and Welfare. Much of the extensive literature on radiation
   effects has been summarized in the following: Ashley W. Oughterson and
   Shields Warren, *Medical Effects of the Atomic Bomb in Japan* (New York:
   McGraw-Hill, 1956); J. W. Hollingsworth, "Delayed Radiation Effects in
   Survivors of the Atomic Bombings," *New England Journal of Medicine*, 263
   (1960), pp. 381–487; "Bibliography of Publications Concerning the Effects
   of Nuclear Explosions," *Journal of the Hiroshima Medical Association*, 14
   (1961); and in the series of Technical Reports of the ABCC and the various
   issues of the *Proceedings of the Research Institute for Medicine and Biology*
   of Hiroshima University, and of the *Hiroshima Journal of Medical Sciences*.
2. There has, however, been some preliminary sociological and psychological
   research in these areas. See S. Nakano, "Genbaku Eikyo no Shakaigakuteki
   Chosa" (Sociological Study of Atomic Bomb Effects), *Daigakujinkai Kenkyu-
   ronshu I, Betsuzuri* (1954), and "Genbaku to Hiroshima," (The Atomic Bomb
   and Hiroshima), in *Shinshu Hiroshima Shi-shi* (*Newly Revised History of
   Hiroshima City*) Hiroshima Shiyakusho, 1951; Y. Kubo, "Data about the
   Suffering and Opinion of the A-bomb Sufferers," *Psychologia*, 4 (1961), pp.

56–59 (in English); and "A Study of A-bomb Sufferers' Behavior in Hiro-
shima: A Socio-psychological Research on A-bomb and A-energy," *Japanese
Journal of Psychology*, 22 (1952), pp. 103–110 (English abstract); T.
Misao, "Characteristics in Abnormalities Observed in Atom-bombed Survivors,"
Journal of Radiation Research, 2 (1961), pp. 85–97 (in English), in which
various psychosomatic factors are dealt with; Irving L. Janis, *Air War and
Emotional Stress* (New York: McGraw-Hill, 1951), particularly chapters 1–3.

3. Robert J. Lifton, "Youth and History: Individual Change in Postwar Japan,"
Daedalus, 91 (1962), pp. 172–197.

4. Robert J. Lifton, *Thought Reform and the Psychology of Totalism* (New
York: Norton, 1961).

5. *Hibakusha* is a coined word which has no exact English equivalent but means:
one (or those) who has (have) experienced, sustained, or undergone the
(atomic) bomb. It conveys a little bit more than merely having encountered
the bomb, and a little bit less than having experienced definite physical injury from it. *Higaisha*, another word frequently used, means "one who
has sustained injury" or simply "victim." But the words are frequently
used more or less interchangeably, and both in translation are sometimes
rendered as "victim(s)" or "sufferer(s)" from the atomic bomb. Thus, the
English word "survivors" is in no sense an exact translation of either
hibakusha or *higaisha*, but rather a means of designating in a single word
persons who fit into the category of *hibakusha*. While *hibakusha* has come
to convey many things in popular usage, it also is employed to represent
the four groups of people covered by the official legislation on medical
benefits for those exposed to the effects of the bomb: those who at the time
of the bomb were within the city limits then existing for Hiroshima, an area
extending from the bomb's hypocenter to a distance of 4000 (and in some
places up to 5000) meters; those who were not in the city at the time, but
within 14 days entered a designated area extending to about 2000 meters
from the hypocenter; those who were engaged in some form of aid to, or disposal of, bomb victims at various stations then set up; and those who were
in utero, and whose mothers fit into any of the first three categories. For
studying physical aspects of delayed radiation effects, such factors as distance from the hypocenter and degree of protection from radiation (by
buildings, clothing, etc.) are crucial, and from this standpoint a large number
of those designated as *hibakusha* had little or no exposure to significant
amounts of radiation. For psychological and social effects, these factors—
and particularly that of distance from the hypocenter—are also of great
importance, but one cannot make the same relatively sharp correlations
regarding what is, or is not, significant exposure. In this paper I shall
emphasize general psychological themes which apply, in greater or lesser
degree, to virtually all *hibakusha*.

6. It was, of course, inevitable that, after 17 years, elements of selectivity and
distortion would enter into these recollections. But I was impressed with
the vividness of recall, with the willingness of people, once a reasonable
degree of rapport had been established, to express themselves quite freely
about painful, and often humiliating, details; and with the overall agreement contained in these descriptions, with each other and with various
published accounts, concerning what took place generally and how people

behaved. For corroborating published accounts, see, for instance: M.
Hachiya (Warner Wells, ed., trans.), *Hiroshima Diary* (Chapel Hill: Uni-
versity of North Carolina Press, 1955); T. Nagai, *We of Nagasaki* (New
York: Duell, Sloan and Pearce, 1951); H. Agawa, *Devil's Heritage*, (Tokyo:
Hokuseido Press, 1957); A. Osada (compiler), *Children of the A-Bomb* (New
York: Putnam, 1963); Robert Yungk, *Children of the Ashes* (New York:
Harcourt, Brace & World, 1961); John Hersey, *Hiroshima* (New York:
Bantam Books, 1959); Robert Trumbull, *Nine Who Survived Hiroshima and
Nagasaki* (Tokyo and Rutland, Vermont: Charles E. Tuttle, 1957). (S.
Imahon, *Gensuibaku Jidai* (The Age of the A- and H-bomb) (Hiroshima,
1959).

7. For estimates of damage, casualties, and mortality, see Oughterson and
Warren, *op. cit.*, *Hiroshima Genbaku Iryō-shi*, *op. cit.*, M. Ishida and T.
Matsubayashi, "An Analysis of Early Mortality Rates Following the Atomic
Bomb—Hiroshima," ABCC Technical Report 20-61, Hiroshima and Nagasaki
(undated); S. Nagaoka, *Hiroshima Under Atomic Bomb Attack* (Peace
Memorial Museum, Hiroshima, undated); and "Hiroshima: Official Brochure
Produced by Hiroshima City Hall" (based largely upon previously mentioned
sources). Concerning mortality, Oughterson and Warren estimate 64,000
believed to be accurate within ±10 per cent; K. Shimizu (in *Hiroshima
Genbaku Iryō-shi*) estimates "more than 200,000," the figure which is accepted by the City of Hiroshima; Nagaoka estimates "more than 240,000";
the official estimate is usually given as 78,150; and one frequently sees estimates of "more than 100,000." Contributing to this great divergence in
figures are such things as varying techniques of calculation, differing estimates of the number of people in Hiroshima at the moment the bomb fell,
the manner in which military fatalities are included, how long afterward
(and after which census count) the estimate was made, and undoubtedly
other human factors outside the realm of statistical science. The obvious
conclusion is that no one really knows, or, considering the degree of disorganization interfering with collection of accurate population data, is the
problem ever likely to be fully solved.

8. These "fireballs" have no relationship to the fireball of the atomic bomb
previously mentioned, and are here being compared with ordinary fires caused
by the bomb.

9. In such profound emotional experiences, feelings of shame and guilt become
intermixed and virtually indistinguishable. In cases like this one, the guilty
inner fantasy is likely to be, "I am responsible for their (his, her) death,"
or even, "I killed them." The shameful fantasy is likely to be, "I should
have saved them, or at least done more for them." But these are closely
related, and in mentioning either shame or guilt in the remainder of the
paper, I assume that the other is present as well.

10. See Oughterson and Warren, as well as other sources mentioned in reference
1. Oughterson and Warren demonstrate statistically the relationship between incidence of radiation effects and distance from the hypocenter—the
great majority of cases occurring within the 2000 meter radius—but these
scientific distinctions were, of course, completely unknown at the time, and
even after becoming known they have not eliminated survivors' fears of later
effects.

11. See Hollingsworth, *op cit.*, and other sources mentioned in reference 1 for discussions of delayed radiation effects and bibliographies of work done on the subject. Concerning the problem of leukemia, see also A. B. Brill, M. Tomonaga, and R. M. Heyssel, "Leukemia in Man Following Exposure to Ionizing Radiation," *Annals of Internal Medicine*, 56 (1962), pp. 590–609, and S. Watanabe, "On the Incidence of Leukemias in Hiroshima During the Past Fifteen Years From 1946–1960," *Journal of Radiation Research*, 2 (1961), pp. 131–140.
12. The most extensive work on these genetic problems has been done by James V. Neel and W. O. Schull. See their "Radiation and Sex Ratio in Man: Sex Ratio among Children of Atomic Bombings Suggests Induced Sex-Linked Lethal Mutations," *Science*, 128 (1958), pp. 343–348; and *The Effect of Exposure to the Atomic Bomb on Pregnancy Termination in Hiroshima and Nagasaki*, Washington, D. C., National Academy of Sciences—National Research Council (Government Printing Office, 1956). Belief in the possibility of an increase in various forms of congenital malformations in offspring of survivors has been stimulated by the work of I. Hayashi at Nagasaki University, reported in his paper: "Pathological Research on Influences of Atomic Bomb Exposure upon Fatal Development," *Research in the Effects and Influences of the Nuclear Bomb Test Explosions* (in English, undated), though Dr. Hayashi, in summarizing his material, cautions that "one hesitates to give any concrete statement about the effect of the atomic bomb radiation (upon) the growth of fetal life, based on the data available in this paper."
13. These borderline complaints, as detected by the Cornell Medical Index (T. Misao, *op. cit.*) are consistently more frequent in *hibakusha* that in non-*hibakusha*. The cultural concern with bodily symptoms is no more than an intensifying influence, and generally similar psychosomatic anxieties would undoubtedly be manifest in other cultures under similar conditions.
14. Censorship on matters relating to the atomic bomb and its various effects was imposed almost immediately by the American Occupation; fears of retaliation were undoubtedly an important factor, though it is likely that over the years other concerns and influences affected this policy. Reviewing Japanese perceptions of the censorship one gains the impression that its implementation was often inconsistent but sufficient to be felt keenly by writers, and even to interfere with adequate dissemination of much needed medical knowledge about the A-bomb; that descriptions of the A-bomb experience—reportorial, literary, and ideological—nonetheless made their appearance during the early postwar years; that restrictions diminished sufficiently during the last two years of the Occupation for writers to deal freely with the subject; but that the full revelation of the horrors associated with the atomic bomb did not occur for the majority of Japanese until the end of the Occupation in 1952 with the circulation of a now famous issue of the *Asahi Graphic* (a weekly pictorial of Japan's leading newspaper) in which these horrors were vividly depicted.
15. Leukemia, despite its disturbing increase in incidence, remains an infrequent cause of death (Hollingsworth, quoting Heyssel, reports that, up to 1960, 122 cases of leukemia had been discovered in Hiroshima residents); and where death is caused by other conditions it is extremely difficult to assess

the influence of radiation effects. But the individual survivor will often automatically associate the A-bomb Hospital with radiation effects, and the situation is further complicated by the medical and legal complexities already mentioned, and by the generally sensitive psychological atmosphere of Hiroshima.

16. Survivors often marry each other, and frequently feel that by doing so they are likely to be best understood. But some express a strong preference to marry a non-*hibakusha*, and claim that by marrying one another they increase their possibilities for giving birth to abnormal children; they also here reflect an urge to transcend through marriage, rather than intensify, the *hibakusha* identity.

17. I have in this section barely suggested the Japanese cultural influences—particularly the tendency toward a sense of continuity with the dead—which affect survivors' reactions. I believe that the close identification with the dead which I have described, like the psychosomatic patterns discussed in the previous section, should not be thought of as exclusively "Japanese"; rather I would claim that it is also related to the nature of the disaster, although expressed in a particular (Japanese) cultural style. For Japanese attitudes about purity, see Lifton, *Youth and History, op. cit.,* and for relationship of attitudes toward death and purity, see Robert N. Bellah, *Tokugawa Religion* (Glencoe, Ill.: The Free Press, 1957).

18. These attitudes are related to Japanese cultural tendencies to stress human considerations, including apologetic sympathy where this is felt indicated, rather than more abstract determinations of right and wrong or matters of individual conscience. But again it is by no means certain that in similar circumstances, even in cultures with a reverse emphasis, similar hostilities might not occur.

19. Complications of the general literature on disaster are to be found in: George W. Baker and Dwight W. Chapmen, *Man and Society in Disaster* (New York: Basic Books, 1962); Martha Wolfenstein, *Disaster* (Glencoe, Ill.: The Free Press, 1957); "Human Behavior in Disaster: A New Field of Social Research," *The Journal of Social Issues,* 10 (entire issue); *Field Studies of Disaster Behavior, An Inventory* (Disaster Research Group, National Academy of Sciences—National Research Council, Washington, 1961); and L. Bates, C. W. Fogleman and Vernon J. Parenton, *The Social and Psychological Consequences of a National Disaster: A Longitudinal Study of Hurricane Audrey* (National Academy of Sciences—National Research Council, Washington, D.C., 1963).

20. It is to those who were several thousand meters from the hypocenter, including many beyond the outskirts of the city, that the term "illusion of centrality" and its psychological mechanisms (as described in the literature on disaster) apply. Those who were closer, in terms of effects experienced, were sufficiently central to the disaster for the term "illusion" to be inappropriate

21. As in other recent disaster studies I did not (from discussions with medical, psychiatric, and other authorities) have the impression of a large increase of severe mental illness, such as psychosis, at the time of the disaster or immediately afterwards; in view of the limited available statistical data it would be extremely difficult to study this problem, and I did not attempt

to do so. My findings differ, however, from those of other disaster studies in the extent of the psychosocial consequences I encountered which, although emotionally profound, are not of a variety classifiable as "mental illness." This important difference stems mainly, I believe, from special features of the atomic bomb experience, but may also be related to variations in approach and method.

22. I have in this paper dealt only with Hiroshima as it was there that I conducted the research, although I did have the opportunity to make briefer observations in Nagasaki as well. In both cities there is a widely held impression that general reactions to the atomic bomb—mass media dissemination of its effects, peace movements, and even fears and concerns of *hibakusha*—are considerably more intense in Hiroshima than in Nagasaki. I believe this is true, but only in degree, and not in the more or less absolute sense in which it is sometimes depicted. There are a number of factors which have contributed to this difference in intensity, and to Hiroshima's assuming more of a symbolic role for both *hibakusha* and outsiders: Hiroshima was the first to be struck by the new weapon; the bomb fell in the center of Hiroshima, a flat city made up almost entirely of flimsy structures, so that the entire city was virtually devastated, while in Nagasaki the bomb fell at some distance from the center and destruction was limited by the hilly terrain so that the greater part of the city (including a somewhat larger number of concrete structures) was left standing, and casualties and general effects were not so great despite the fact that the Nagasaki bomb was of greater explosive power; Nagasaki could therefore more readily resume some of its previous identity as a city—which included a unique history of having served for several centuries as Japan's main contact with the Western world —while Hiroshima had to recreate itself almost entirely, and without the benefit of a comparable tradition; and Hiroshima is closer to Tokyo and more sensitive to intellectual and ideological currents stemming from Japan's dominant city.

23. For discussions of symbolization of the self see Robert E. Nixon, "An Approach to the Dynamics of Growth in Adolescence," *Psychiatry*, 24 (1961), pp. 18–31; and Susanne Langer, *Philosophy in a New Key* (New York: Mentor Books, 1948), p. 111. For the relevance of shame to this kind of process, see Helen M. Lynd, *On Shame and the Search for Identity* (New York: Harourt, Brace & Co., 1958).

24. "Guilt and Guilt Feelings," *Psychiatry*, 20 (1957), p. 120. In attributing guilt feelings to Japanese, here and elsewhere in this article, I am following recent critiques of the concept of "shame cutures" and "guilt cultures": Gerhart Piers and Milton B. Singer, *Shame and Guilt* (Springfield: Charles C. Thomas, 1953); and more specifically in relationship to Japan, George DeVos, "The Relation of Guilt Toward Parents to Achievement and Arranged Marriage Among Japanese," *Psychiatry*, 23 (1960), pp. 287–301. See also Erik H. Erikson, *Childhood and Society* (New York: Norton, 1950), pp. 222–226. Feelings of shame and guilt, at their most profound level—their psychological meeting ground—as I suggest below (following Buber, Lynd, Erikson, and my own previous work) can be overcome only through a change in one's relationship to the world, and can be under certain conditions creatively utilized on behalf of achieving such a change.

But my impression regarding the atomic bomb experience was that this constructive utilization was the exception rather than the rule, since there was so much that tended to block it and to cause feelings of shame and guilt to be retained in their negative, unresolved form.

Franz Borkenau

The Concept of Death

The thesis tentatively outlined in this paper is that the self-contradictory experience of death is a basic element in shaping the course of human history; that the conflicting attitudes towards death traceable in the individual are equally at work within every human culture, and in the relationships between historic civilizations; that changes in the popular attitude towards death mark great epochs of historical evolution; and that their study can serve as a guide to some problems of the philosophy of history.

We shall start with a few remarks about prehistory, and here an observation on the character of our material will be in place. The fear—more widespread perhaps in earlier periods of research into prehistory than at present—that our understanding of religious origins may be affected by the chance disappearance of material witness to spiritual processes is, I think, validly countered by the statement that purely spiritual developments do not occur. Whatever is basic in human existence has left some trace in tools or implements. Man is a toolmaker, and there cannot have been any human activity which left no material trace. If the remnants of the clearly palaeolithic do not include any evidence of cult or worship, we are free to conclude that man was then exclusively concerned with the satisfaction of his bodily needs. But by the middle palaeolithic the first signs of a new attitude appear: graves. Until this happens we may assume that men's minds floated vaguely between a dim awareness of death and the hope to escape it. The emergence of burial rites clearly suggests a sharpened consciousness of mortality. For burial rites are techniques designed to satisfy the sense of immortality by securing some form of survival postmortem. To this new phase of human development a purely materialistic approach is no longer adequate. True, the effort to secure a life for the dead beyond the grave springs from the same urge

Reprinted from *The Twentieth Century*, April, 1955, by permission of the publisher.

to survival as does the daily struggle for existence; yet the two diverge from the start. If the cult of the dead were derived from the material needs of the living, the phases of its evolution would have to be demonstrably connected with the course of material and technical development; as we shall see, this is not the case. Neither a materialist nor an idealist explanation will serve. Each is one-sided and consequently futile. We must assume two or more basically separate, though frequently interacting, lines of development.

Burial rites in primitive society—and to some extent in higher types of culture too—are directed towards a twofold goal: to keep the dead alive, and to keep them away. These incompatible aims reflect the basic contradiction in the human attitude towards mortality: the rites intended to put the dead "to rest," to console them, to propitiate them, to avert their wrath, the numerous stringent taboos regarding contact with them and their graves, all presuppose that the dead are really alive and dangerous. /On the other hand, such ceremonial actions as the application of paint to the bodies of the deceased, the provision of nourishment and tools for enclosure in the tomb, preservation of the bodies by certain techniques culminating in mummification—all suggest an effort to preserve life in the dead, on the assumption that otherwise this spark would die. There is no strict dividing line between these two aims, and there are rites (such as sacrifices performed at the tomb) which, being propitiatory and preservatory, combine both functions. This shifting character of the attitude behind the rite of burial reflects a continuing uncertainty about the relation of death to life, a carryover from the old palaeolithic mentality, though qualified by clearer insights. One may ask: is the practice of ochre-painting the dead characteristic of certain burial rites intended to symbolize the continued biological existence of the departed? Or is it a means of depriving death of its victory over life? There certainly is no clear answer to this question in the minds of those performing the ritual. In primitive tribal society we seem to be confronted with an infinite variety of burial rites, but also with an infinity of shades of meaning, not merely as between one culture and another but also as between individuals, and even as between individual occurrences of death and burial. Much of the later palaeolithic ritual appears to reflect a somewhat firmer grasp of the inevitability of death, and consequently a growing elaboration of ideas concerning another life beyond the grave. But side by side with customs expressive of such ideas one frequently encounters what amounts to an assertion that man need not die.

Where this latter view prevails it tends to convert tribal society into a madhouse. Every death is then regarded as the effect of black magic, and the life of the tribe centers not so much upon the procurement of the necessities of existence as upon the search for witches who appear to threaten life much more than do famine and disease. It is proposed to describe such an attitude—the most extreme form of conscious option for the unconscious sense of immortality—as "death-denying." It invariably goes with a socially organized persecutory paranoia, and while it rarely occurs in a pure form it is hardly ever completely absent from primitive cultures, since it corresponds best to the unconscious sense of immortality. Residues of such an attitude are to be found even in the burial rites of higher civilizations. Its important, though hidden, role in history will be discussed further on.

The emergence of the first type of higher civilization in the great river valleys of the Middle East does not mark the end of death-denial, but it does correspond to significant changes in the underlying assumptions. The burial rites disclosed in the Pyramid texts still imply Pharaoh's direct ascent to heaven without passage through death. But Pharaoh, although human, is also a god, and genuine immortality is now vouchsafed only to demi-gods, such as rulers and heroes. The paranoic witch hunt of the death-denying tribe has now become superfluous, for Pharaoh is certain of direct immortality (and so are, though somewhat less explicitly, his Sumerian royal opposites), while all his subjects are equally certain of extinction. Mortality is socially stratified—perhaps the only point where religion and society are wholly merged. In part this stratification relates to the more powerful "mana" of the ruler, in part to his greater material means for achieving adequate burial. The aristocracy, too, although excluded from direct immortality, can through mummification achieve a species of immortality after death. Only the fellah, unable to arrange for adequate burial and unknown to the gods, is denied all hope of an after-life.

Popular dissatisfaction with this state of affairs, and a consequent democratic insurgence against the class privileges of immortality, occurs (as Breasted has shown) a good deal earlier than any corresponding movement for social leveling in the material sphere; thus the class struggle manifests itself first on the plane of religion. The popular deities who gradually encroach upon the royal house-gods derive their credit from their power to provide immortality for all. In the course of a gradual transition the belief in direct immortality dies out—and with it the solar tombs of the Pyramid type. In its place there arises a more and more elaborate image of a better world beyond the grave. Ritual remains the precondition of survival in the beyond—man can still die an absolute death where due ritual has been neglected—but with the growing democratization of belief, insistence upon right moral conduct in this world becomes a requirement for "positive" immortality, while the concept of a "negative" kind of immortality—hell—now appears for the first time. The new prayers for the dead, like the old Pharaonic rituals of the Pyramid texts, are based on the solemn assertion of immortality, but now take account of the fact of death. Side by side with a qualified death-denial there arises a qualified acceptance of physical death—anterior to the choice between heaven and hell. These later Egyptian rituals thus represent the first sharply accentuated attempt at a synthesis between the two basic contradictory attitudes towards mortality. Out of the mutual limitation and qualification of death-denial and death-acceptance there arises a new concept which one might d scribe as "death-defiance," in that it accepts death but also aims at transcending it.

Yet the synthesis proves unstable. The moral requirements treated as prerequisites of "positive" immortality are really quite extraneous to the basic idea. The myth concerning the after-life and the rituals attached to them consequently degenerate into scurrilous attempts to deceive the gods as to the deceased's immoral conduct on this earth. The ritual itself loses prestige with the growth of rationalism; the religion and the arts bound up with it grow shallow. No wonder then that the process culminates historically in a revolution against the death-defying cults: the short-lived but portentous attempt by Pharaoh Akhnaton to abolish all the death cults and to replace them by the worship of the Sun—not the actual physical sun which rises and sets, but a fantastic ever-shining Sun. Obsessed with the struggle between monotheism and polytheism, which is central to Christianity but was hardly so relevant to Egyptian thought even at this late stage, modern research has tended to minimize the attitude to death-defiance implicit in the Akhnaton revolution: a revolution which tried to turn defeat in the struggle against death into the basis of a new form of worship.

This cycle is not by any means limited to Egypt, or even to Egypt and Mesopotamia. It appears to be generally true of civilizations that they terminate with a concept of death opposed to that with which they started. This is hardly surprising. Every culture attempts some synthesis between the two extremes sketched earlier, but no synthesis lasts forever, because no solution can do away with the simultaneous presence of two incompatible inner experiences. Now when a particular synthesis breaks down, the pendulum, having in the meantime swung from one extreme (e.g., death-denial) to a compromise with the other (death-acceptance), does not return to its starting point. In our above example such a return would have involved a revival of the old Pharaonic death cults which had in the interval become wholly incompatible with new forms of social life. The tendency is rather for the pendulum to swing wholly to the opposite extreme—in this case to the abortive experiment of founding a new religion exclusively upon acceptance of death as final.

Notwithstanding the wide range of phenomena under discussion, this formula appears fairly satisfying, save for one weakness: the term "civilization" is still insufficiently defined. What is the historical unit to which the cycle just described really applied? Is it the kind of civilization which Spengler and Toynbee have in their various ways attempted to describe and analyze, or should one look for a different kind of unit? This is a question to which we shall have to return.

In an essay published some years ago in *Horizon*, under the title "After the Atom," I ventured to offer some tentative generalizations upon the subject of terminal phases in the life cycle of a culture. One suggestion was that there seemed to be two different types of such end phases, characterized by a choice between ossification and disruption. The first need not concern us here, since it involves merely the "ghost," as it were, of an archaic religion which has lost its original meaning. Disruption, that is, the advent of a "dark age," is more to our point. Egyptian civilization may be said to have ossified—its "archaistic" period brought back the gods and the rituals of the Pyramid age, now emptied of content and misunderstood in the bargain. On the contrary, the civilizations of Mesopotamia and the string of smaller cultures forming a hemicycle from Crete to the Persian Gulf were disrupted and a "dark age" ensued over that wide area. In respect of our problem it may be remarked that, in contrast to higher civilizations which offer a wide variety of responses to the problem of mortality, the various dark ages resemble one another in their prevalent attitude to death. This need not surprise us. The psychological attitudes characteristic of a high civilization are unstable, as the present generation has discovered to its cost; certainly a great deal less stable than the "archetypes" inherited from more primitive epochs. Higher civilizations tend to submerge these archetypes, though not without granting them an indirect representation in the official symbolism. When the higher forms disintegrate, the archetypes re-emerge and rise to the surface. But not unchanged! One may draw some consolation from the thought that in history nothing is ever completely lost. Civilization is deceptive in denying the continuing power of the archetypes—*there* is the everlasting limit of progress! But the archetypes in their turn cannot reassert themselves completely once civilization has done its work. A "relapse into barbarism" is something different from a reversion to the primitive level. The first is a regular occurrence in the story of mankind, the second an idle hope or an idle fear.

In regard to our special problem we may assume that the denial of death is the most deeply rooted of the archetypes, since it is structurally, and in all probability chronologically, tied to the awareness of human mortality. The collapse of a higher civilization therefore regularly entails a partial return towards death-denial. Not a complete one. Civilization has brought an awareness that man must die. Dark ages do not blot out this awareness—what they remove is rather the sum total of those highly spiritualized beliefs which go with the death-*defying* religions at their highest point of development. The dark age which descended around the middle of the second millennium B.C. was incapable of assimilating either the defiance of death or its acceptance by the Akhnaton creed; it took several centuries for the germ then planted by Moses to bear fruit. The interval must be pictured as a kind of religious vacuum. This devaluation of all religion, be it primitive or exalted, is characteristic of every dark age, but it is equally characteristic of such epochs that they cannot dispense with certitude of some kind. The consequence is an influx of magic. Thus amulets and rituals, shorn of their meaning, are utilized exclusively as magical safe-guards against danger, an attitude capable of bearing a religious meaning only in the context of belief in the possibility of escaping physical extinction. The concomitant of this relapse into a mechanical adoption of magical practices is the universal fear of *black* magic which causes men to see in every neighbor a potential murderer; thus every mode of death-denying conduct is present, with-

out the satisfaction of a death-denying faith. Dark ages therefore tend to be paranoiac ages, until they are driven out of their
paranoia by the contradition between their magical pursuits and
their awareness of the inevitability of death. In this, and in much
else, they resemble each other more closely than do the higher
civilizations.

At the moment when—to return to recorded history—the
Hellenic civilization emerges from the dark age following the collapse of the great river-valley civilizations, its culture is primarily
distinguished by a revolutionary change in the ritual of burial:
the physical preservation of the body (by mummification or other
devices) is replaced by its destruction through fire. Concurrently,
the elaborate imagery of survival characteristic of the old river-
valley religions is superseded by the concept of Hades: the shadowy
notion of a realm of shadows, symbolizing not a fuller but an
infinitely less complete existence than the life of the living. Here
we have no more than a grudging concession to the inner certitude
of immortality. Again, the gods, which in the river-valley civilizations were of inhuman shape and led a transstellurian existence,
are now closely identified with human life on the planet—their
immortality as questionable as that of the shadows in Hades. It
is not without significance that the other seminal culture to emerge
from the preceding dark age—that of Israel—though in other respects sharply distinguished from the Hellenic, shares these essential
attitudes. There is no substantial difference between Hades and
Sheol, unless it be the attribution of markedly negative magical
properties which have no counterpart in Greek religion. Immortality is in both cases reserved for a few heroes (the concept of
death opposed to the official one is never *completely* absent), although the Jews did not adopt cremation. If Hellas is more closely
associated in our minds with the acceptance of death as final, the
reason is that classical antiquity has vanished, while Jewry has
survived into an entirely different epoch and, though hesitantly,
adopted its basic beliefs, including that in immortality. The real
creed of ancient, and to a large extent of medieval Jewry, of course,
was not immortality but the future glory and worldly dominance
of Israel. The particular Jewish solution of the problem, that is
to say, was the transference of immortality from the individual
to the community. The parallel Hellenic solution was the extolling
of the individual's undying glory, the hero surviving death
through his own fame. The underlying attitude is basically identi-

cal—as the contrasting one was basically common to Egypt and Mesopotamia.

It would thus appear that a particular attitude towards the problem of mortality is not peculiar to individual civilizations, but rather to a group of them. Civilizations forming a group of this kind may be regarded as being, in a very rough sense, contemporaneous, but what really matters is the identity of their respective positions in the *sequence* of cultural epochs. (The terms "culture" and "civilization" are here, as throughout, used interchangeably.) Thus the death-defying group of river-valley civilizations and their minor kindred represents the first layer of "higher" cultures emerging directly from the neolithic. The subsequent Judaeo-Hellenic group is characterized by its position as heir to the death-defying civilizations. The cycle of cultural units definable in terms of their attitude to death is thus wider than the culture-cycle of individual civilizations identified by Spengler and Toynbee. Secondly, the swing of the pendulum from one attitude towards death to the other, which takes place between the rise and the fall of one and the same civilization, also applies to the relationship between one group and the next. The river-valley cultures were "death-defying," while the Judaeo-Hellenic group was characterized by "death-acceptance," just like the Akhnaton religion, as though no dark age (more pronounced in the case of the Hellenes than in that of the Hebrews) had intervened. The second group starts where the earlier one left off, and thus begins its march with a set of beliefs the exact opposite of those of its predecessor in the corresponding early period. In consequence, its own life-cycle, so to speak, proceeds in the reverse direction. Thus Greek and, albeit in a different manner, Hebrew society tried to encompass all the glory and fullness of life within the limits of an existence confined to what is discernible to direct human experience. But the search for perfection within these limits suggests that a gnawing sense of imperfection and a yearning for something unattainable within mortal life, was never absent. And thus, one can see Hebrew and Hellenic civilization running the full course from the elaboration of a crude belief in earthly perfection—though they held different notions as to what such perfection implied—through a gradual loss of faith in this solution, and in the end to its precise opposite: a firm belief in immortality; at which point the division between the Jewish and the Hellenic world is obliterated by the rise of Christianity.

The story is too well known to need recounting. The point

that matters is the transition from death-acceptance to a new phase of death-defiance without the intermediary of a fully developed dark age. This at any rate seems true of the eastern Mediterranean, where the fundamental transition occurred. But a full-blown collapse *did* take place at the western and north-western end of the geographical area in question. Both circumstances must be considered separately.

If the phenomenon we have called a "dark age" arises from the collapse of a death-defying culture into death-denying and paranoiac barbarism, it would seem logical that the reverse process gives rise to a different conclusion. Loss of faith in survival leaves a void which must be filled; on the contrary, where such a belief asserts itself, there is no void and no room is left for paranoiac retrogression. Yet the emergence of a genuine dark age in the Roman world, similar to that of the second millennium B.C., suggests that our formula is still inadequate. It would appear that two distinct forces are typically at work: loss of faith on the one hand, and a barbarian invasion of the higher culture on the other. There is no need to labor the point that such an invasion occurred both in the case of the pre-Hellenic world of the second millennium B.C., and in that of the Roman world in the first few centuries of our era. I should like to venture the suggestion that the second of these two invasions was facilitated by the failure of the Christian response to disintegration to take full effect in the western half of the Mediterranean world: here the precondition of Christianity's full impact—the fusion of the Hebrew and Hellenic traditions—was lacking, and the new metaphysical message came through, as it were, only very faintly. Thus, instead of transforming itself into defiance of death, the old attitude of accepting human life as finite disintegrated into something very like the barbarism mentioned earlier. The spiritual energy which enabled the Christianized East to ward off the German invaders (and the Mazdaan Persians into the bargain) was absent in the western half of the old Roman Empire. Here, therefore, the barbarians infiltrated without encountering much resistance, destroying in the process both the civilization of their victims and their own tradition-bound way of life, and thus establishing the necessary conditions for a genuine "dark age."

What follows is written on the assumption that the group of Christian civilizations (plus their Islamic counterpart and appendix) have by now completed so much of their course that their development can be viewed as a whole.

It is hardly necessary to emphasize that defiance of death is at the core of the Christian message. The Gospels and St. Paul are at one on this subject. "Oh death, where is thy sting!" One catches an echo here of the old river-valley religions, separated from Christianity, as it were, by the Hellenic interlude. Western scholarship since the Renaissance and the fashionable neo-classicism of the eighteenth and nineteenth centuries has done less than justice to this theme, but a good many obscurities have recently begun to vanish, and the gaps in our understanding are being filled: the abyss separating Christianity from the Hellenic mind is becoming clearer. In essence, we now see, the Christian attitude towards death harks back to that of the ancient Near East. This suggests a qualification of Toynbee's well-known views concerning the relationship between a new culture and its predecessor: in addition to "affiliation" among cultures contiguous in space and time, there seems to be something like a return to more ancient models, separated from the present by a whole interval, in which the most ancient stratum is temporarily buried and lost from sight. But the phrase "return," too, needs qualification, for the intermediate phase—in this instance the seemingly harmonious, actually tragic, death-acceptance—has left profound traces. There could be no simple return to the almost light-hearted treatment of mortality in the religions of the ancient Near East, where death seemed reduced to the status of a disagreeable *contretemps*. The deepening awareness of finality had indeed, as we have seen, produced a gradual insistence upon making the after-life available to all, but it was left to Christianity to place defiance of death at the center of its perception of the human situation.

St. Paul, as we know, still believed in the integral assumption of the faithful after the impending end of the world. It was the decisive achievement of the second generation of Christians that faith in victory over death was preserved, although belief in the imminence of the "kingdom" had waned. Thus the doctrine of the Fall, which was far from being central to Judaism, became the core of the new faith: death being the "wages of sin," salvation was conditional upon a thorough experience of, and victory over, death. There is no need to dwell upon the decisive importance of this concept in relating death-defiance to moral effort, and in promoting a theology based upon the substitute sacrifice of the Lamb of God. Death, in this context, is no longer an incident, hence no longer a stumbling block to faith. On the contrary, it is firmly integrated into the belief in salvation and ultimate

triumph. A partial relapse into a simpler, quasi-Egyptian, form
of death-defiance is not excluded—we have the example of
Islam—but the step once taken, there could be no complete going
back.

Yet the swing of the pendulum has been felt even in the history
of Christianity. By integrating morality more profoundly into metaphysics than any previous creed, the new religion went farther
than any other in establishing a genuine synthesis instead of an
alternation of extremes; but it can hardly be said to have solved
the problem altogether. The swing of the pendulum in our own
age is all too clear, and it is a mistake to date it only from the
nineteenth century. Leaving aside the question whether a complete
synthesis is conceivable at all, the fact remains that the new faith
had scarcely triumphed when its foundations were already beginning
to come under attack.

The late George Orwell, in his nightmare vision *1984*, displayed
remarkable insight in describing one of his three "barely distinguish-
able" totalitarian civilizations—the Japanese—as "death worship."
Such an attitude is indeed characteristic of some Asian cultures.
It has also manifested itself in our own age.

If there is an alternation of "death cultures," the disintegration
of the Christian faith in immortality should give rise to a revival
of the attitude prevalent in classical antiquity. And in fact this
has, since the Renaissance, been the solution favoured by
free-thinking humanists. But we have seen that simple revivals
of the past do not occur. Just as Christianity, in returning to
the death-defying concepts of the ancient Near East, was compelled
to synthesize them with the death-acceptance of Hebrew and
Hellenic religion, so *our modern post-Christian attitude* has somehow had to come to terms with the ingrained Christian belief that
life without immortality is nothing. This conviction, once the concomitant belief in an actual after-life is abandoned, results in
despair, which indeed has increasingly colored the more recent
phases of Western—and latterly of Eastern—Christian history.
There is an obvious tendency for the Christian concept of personal-
ality to follow the Christian belief in immortality into limbo. In
consequence modern secularism is patently about to end in nihilism,
i.e., in denying the relevance, almost the existence, of personality.
This appears to be what Orwell had in mind in speaking of "death
worship."

The denial of personality finds its original expression in the quest for some higher unit, to which mortality would be less relevant. The individual is advised to find satisfaction by merging himself in some group—social, national, or racial—endowed with semidivine attributes: absolute value and virtual eternity. But this solution remains largely verbal until tested by the final proof of self-abandonment; death for the sake of the community. And, since personality is a stubborn thing, even death does not nullify it, as long as it has the character of deliberate martyrdom, freely accepted or even consciously sought. Only where physical extinction is preceded by the total crushing and abandonment of personality has real proof been achieved that the individual is null, mortal, and the community the only real (and undying) entity. Thus the phase in which individuals yearn to be consumed by the fire of their collective belief is succeeded by one in which the community feels the urge to sacrifice to its absolute claims the largest possible number of its own members, against their personal inclination. Koestler, in *Darkness at Noon,* has described the first of these two phases; he was mistaken, however, in treating it as the "higher" one, in believing that the "real" Communist, in contrast to the unwilling victims of the regime, is the man who by his own free will chooses not only death but also self-abandonment in the service of the party. This is still an echo of the Christian point of view. Orwell saw that there is no "real" Communist in this sense, for to be a "real" Communist one must first be a full and real human being, which is precisely the thing "death-embracing" abhors. In this system all must be equally crushed, and there is no torturer who would not at the same time be a victim. As to accepting this willingly, it would be the most subtle and effective form of resistance to the new religion. In this final stage all are equally deprived of freedom and no one is allowed to retain even the right to choose suffering willingly for the sake of the larger whole. Indeed, as Orwell has demonstrated, this free acceptance of martyrdom becomes the ultimate heresay! Self-inflicted suffering in the service of the cause is in effect still an echo of an earlier attitude. The genuine full-fledged totalitarian system is bound to dispense with it. This culture, as it were, embraces death, and thus stands at the extreme remove from the naïveté which denies it.

In searching for early historical examples of such an attitude incorporating itself in a full-fledged civilization, one can hardly fail to be struck by the evidence offered by the great Far Eastern and (pre-Columbian) early American cultures. Indeed, in the latter case one is able to discern two different and yet interrelated models on the same plane. Inca civilization was based on the complete merging of the individual with the community, and may thus be described as an early forerunner of our modern totalitarian experiments. Aztec culture seems to have worshipped death more directly. Both were, however, shot through with what appears to have been a remnant of faith in immortality, rather reminiscent of Egyptian religion. As to the civilizations which have issued from India, they can serve as a memento for all who regard belief in immortality as ordinary wish-fulfilment. Every form of Indian belief since the Upanishads has treated metempsychosis, hence immortality, as both a certainty and a curse! Indian thought and its Buddhist derivates in China, and even more so in Japan, are occupied with the problem of liberation from this curse, be it by dissolving the individual in the absolute, be it by vouchsaving him eternal death, on condition of the faithful performance of certain ascetic techniques. Among certain Japanese sects the final outcome has been a veritable religion of suicide, an active search of death. Thus death-worship need only shed its materialist hue to become a kind of faith.

The fully developed modern totalitarian regimes, however, lack consistency. In contrast to the ancient death-embracing faiths, they hide their real visage behind the tattered rags of nationalism, racialism, Communism, and other nineteenth-century creeds. This is presumably because their true image would be too terrifying for the believers themselves; or rather, genuine belief is impossible where no freedom is left to anyone, and the priestly caste itself loses the distinctive status required for the functioning of a religious system. The upshot is an abrupt transition from the total self-sacrifice demanded from everyone to the total hypocrisy actually practiced by those living under the system, where on pretence of saving the community each individual in fact tries to save his own skin and to demolish someone else. The resulting social paranoia does not differ materially from the witch-hunt of the tribe.

If we may dismiss totalitarianism as an aberration, can we look further into the future? Is the worship of death the end of the story—in every sense, since mankind now disposes of the means to achieve the total self-destruction implied by some of its creeds? Or is it merely the prelude to another dark age and thus eventually to a fresh attempt to solve the problem at a higher level of existence?

No one knows, but there is ground for thinking that we are

all caught up in a process which will usher in a world vastly different from the one we knew in the past. There is a meeting of East and West—the East in this context signifying Asia—from which fresh light may be expected upon our problem. Here a hint must suffice: for all the recent advances of depth psychology in our culture, there is still a stubborn refusal to accept the evidence of the unconscious concerning death, to which reference has been made in the first section of this paper. The great stumbling block in this matter appears to be the absence—in contrast to the physical sciences—of all means of empirical verification. But this may be a parochial attitude. There is evidence that Eastern psychology has evolved stringent and critically tested techniques which allow direct access to the disembodied mind and even to a metapersonal sphere of existence. These techniques have doubtless been impaired by their close connection with a death-embracing culture, and in any case have ossified together with the civilization which gave rise to them. Like every *caput mortuum* of a defunct society, they need the kindling spark of contact with a living culture to come to life again. One need not believe that they allow absolute cognition of anything, but they do seem to hold the key to hitherto unknown spheres of inner experience. They will not provide "evidence" for immortality, but they may make it more intelligible. Will Western thought prove capable of utilizing them and bringing them up to date?

Once it is recognized that belief in immortality is part of the innermost core of personality, it is arbitrary to opt, like Freud, in favor of mortality. For the last three centuries it has been generally admitted that a testing of the validity of sensual and rational cognition must precede metaphysics. Recently, a new dimension of cognition has been opened up by the science of the unconscious. Needless to say, this new dimension has no reference to our knowledge of the external world, and in this respect its contents must indeed be regarded, unless otherwise verified, as dreams and fantasies. But does that also apply to what the innermost core of personality knows about itself? Such an attitude was quite appropriate to a materialistic age which treated as foolery everything that could not be tested in the outside world; but after all psychoanalysis won its triumphs in criticizing these assumptions.

There have been philosophers who claimed absolute validity for the senses, and others who denied all validity to them; similarly with regard to reason. Now we have progressed much farther in understanding nature, and the testing of our capacities is much more of a practical than of a metaphysical kind. What has been the result? In our physics we have drifted away from the direct witness of the senses. We know for certain that not a single piece of objective reality is "similar" to the witness of our senses which, in consequence, should be thoroughly discredited. Actually, of course, the contrary is the case and modern science is one long and glorious vindication of the empirico-mathematical method, the only method capable of providing the knowledge we have gained—and, incidentally, of leading us, through the senses, to cognition of a cosmos no longer material in the old meaning of that term. I do not see why something similar should not in principle apply, in its own sphere, to the witness of the unconscious.

As experimental techniques had to be evolved before it was possible to discuss the real nature of the physical universe, so all our talk about the non-material world is presumptuous until an adequate technique for testing it has been established. We are merely on the threshold. Descartes, concerned to justify the validity of human knowledge of the external world, held that "surely God cannot deceive us" by giving us faculties leading inevitably into error. Such an argument, of course, is technically valid only for those who accept his particular interpretation of the divine. But may it not be adapted to our predicament? Surely mankind could not survive if any of its basic intuitions were radically misleading—and the despair which goes with the intellectual denial of our inner certainty of immortality is a case in point. If we believe that our deepest feelings are in harmony with the nature of the universe, we may gladly bear our ignorance, gladly enjoy a sense of curiosity about the beyond, borne up by the faith of Spinoza, who was not given to superstition; *scimus et sentimus nos immortales esse.*

Charles W. Wahl

The Fear of Death

Physical man, silhouetted against the backdrop of the passing centuries, is largely a static figure. Paleoanthropologists tell us that the bodies of our remote ancestors in structure and function almost

Reprinted with permission from the *Bulletin of the Menninger Clinic*, 22, pp. 214–223. (Copyright 1958 by The Menninger Foundation.)

exactly resemble our own. Social and sapient man, however, is a very different creature from his Cro-Magnon ancestor. For he has learned to pit his brain rather than his brute strength against the opposing forces of nature and so has made his way from cave to penthouse.

In all this complex progression, no attribute more clearly differentiates present from past man than does his steadily increasing ability to control and manipulate his physical environment. This is his hallmark. Today, more than ever in his history, man is the undisputed master of his physical world. Indeed, his successes in the physical and biological sciences have been so many and so remarkable that we have come in consequence to accept as an almost certain and established thing that man, through science, is equal to the solution of any problem that may confront him. Success has become a habit of the species.

But there is a glaring exception to this paean of man's conquests, one problem where all his assurance, ingenuity, and wit avail him nothing; an area which stands in bold contrast to the rest of nature which is so malleable to his will. I refer, of course, to the phenomenon of death. Here man, with all his cleverness, is powerless. He may postpone death, he may assuage its physical pains, he may rationalize it away or deny its very existence, but escape it he cannot.

Yet, by its fearful and unwelcome nature, the inescapable fact of personal death impels a solution. And if it does not yield to science and to rationality as does the rest of the physical universe, then we are perforce impelled to employ the heavy artillery of defense, namely, a recourse to magic and irrationality; and we employ these in this area on a greater scale and in a more massive fashion than in almost any other area of human experience.

The massive extent to which we employ magic in the handling of death is often underestimated by us without a deliberate reflection. Consider the lengths to which we go. Firstly, the word death is itself taboo, instead, cumbersome and elaborate euphemisms such as "passed on" or "departed" are employed. This, however, has been true at all times and in all cultures. The very word "perish" has its origin in the Latin "to pass through," i.e., a denial, even in those days, of life as terminative and finite. We maintain at immense expense an entire industry whose sole purpose is to shield us from the crasser realities of death's existence by attempting to preserve and prettify the corpus, creating an illusion of momentary sleep. Moreover, the vast majority of us identify ourselves with religious and philosophical systems of belief which asseverate that death is not death at all, but is rather a fictive experience, a brief transition between one more important existence and another. Most of these purport to guarantee the existence of an immortal state, and propose to supply in return for credence and adherence to their system a means of avoidance of death and its supposed sequelae. We flee from the reality of our eventual death with such purpose and persistence and we employ defenses so patently magical and regressive that these would be ludicrously obvious to us if we should employ them to this degree in any other area of human conflict.

It is not my purpose here either to discourage or condemn these practices and beliefs, but only to describe them; for by their very ubiquity and massive acceptance we are prone not to see their defensive purpose and paradoxical character.

It is clear, however, that in this respect modern man has not advanced very far beyond his primitive ancestors. He shares with his skin-clad forebearer the belief that death is a fictive experience and does not truly exist. Furthermore, he maintains this in the face of the absence of any slightest shred of evidence of a type which he prefers to collect for the solution of his other problems. Here he remains obdurately immune to reality-testing. But this pell-mell dash of mankind from the central and inescapable fact of existence, *viz.*, its finitude, is not the matter to which it is my intention to address myself here. Rather it is to point out that any heavy reliance upon magical thinking and delusion formation, even when collectively shared, raises problems of emotional sickness *and* health both for the individual and society which are directly germane to the field of psychiatry.

Psychiatry, by the very nature of its field, has always been concerned with the investigation and elucidation of those aspects of human character and symptom formation which the average man is prone to shun. And yet it is a surprising and significant fact that the phenomenon of the fear of death, or specific anxiety about it (thanatophobia), while certainly no clinical rarity, has almost no description in the psychiatric or psychoanalytic literature. Could this suggest that psychiatrists, no less than other mortal men, have a reluctance to consider or study a problem which is so closely and personally indicative of the contingency of the human estate? Perhaps they, no less than their patients, would seem to confirm de la Rochefoucauld's observation that "One cannot look directly at either the sun or death." It is interesting also to note that anxiety about death, when it is noted in the psychiatric literature, is usually described solely as a derivative and secondary phenomenon, often as a more easily endurable form of the "castration fear." There is good clinical evidence that these kinds of displacement occur, but it also is important to consider if these formulations also subserve a defensive need on the part of psychiatrists themselves.

Study of the fear of death and the predominantly magical defenses against it are extremely important. For it is the consistent experience of psychiatry that any defense which enables us to *persistently* escape the perception of any fundamental internal or external reality is psychologically costly. To employ a physical model, this concealment or displacement uses up energy which must be drawn from other sources, leaving us less for the business of living in an unhampered, free, and creative way. There is an advantage in seeing ourselves, as well as life, clearly and wholly, and the greater economy with which we can employ dereism, delusion, magical thinking or defense-formation in the solution of our problems or the formation of our beliefs, in general the happier and richer will be our lives. We have yet to determine if the fear of death, because of the realistic and uncontrollable nature of its referent, must remain a solitary exception to this axiom. As yet, we do not know, because this phenomenon has not been sufficiently studied. But indicative answers, if not certain ones, are available, and it is evident that the fear of death and the irrational methods of its reduction present a paradox which can be investigated by the same methods which the behavioral sciences employ in the study of any other paradoxical aspect of human function or adaptation.

The psychiatrist, when presented with an irrational paradox in human life, turns to many sources for its elucidation. The first of these is in the person of himself and takes the form of a detailed personal psychoanalysis. A second major avenue of exploration is the field of psychopathology, the study of persons evincing neurotic or psychotic behavior. In each instance of mental and emotional illness different aspects of the human psyche are magnified and hypertrophied. Just as the microscopist and histologist use the microscope to magnify cell structure, and from many such views piece together a composite picture of the total physical structure, so each psychotherapeutic case throws into bold and magnified

relief some different aspect of psychic function, enabling the psychiatrist in time to piece together an accurate composite of the
normal psychical structure.   He sees the normal man thereby "writ
bold," a picture which could not be obtained from the normal person
for the very good reason of the proper functioning of his psychical
apparatus.

Study of dreams is another avenue into the recondite land of
the unconscious mind, and one to which the psychiatrist constantly
has recourse.   Study of primitive races and of the "fossil thought"
condensed in pictographic languages such as used by the ancient
Egyptians or the Chinese, are still other ways.

But the *via magna* to the study of the unconscious is the study
of children.   Here in the child we are able to look upon our primordial selves naked of the overburden of years and of the thick
layers of repression and acculturation which make us all strangers
to the arcana, lost land of our own childhoods.   It is the child who
holds the secrets, and if we are to understand death and its fear,
we must understand the mind of the child, which is the place
where the fear of death first manifests itself.

It is only recently, however, that we have been able to learn
from this source.   It was formerly thought that children had little
concern with, or fear of, death.   Freud, himself, said that to the
child, death means little more than a departure or journey, and
he felt that there was no unconscious correlate to be found for
the conscious concept of death.   If a fear of death was evidenced,
it was expected to appear subsequent to the Oedipal period, and
was to be explained as a symbolic product of the fear of castration
attendant upon the improper resolution of the Oedipus complex.
Present-day experience does not altogether support these views.
Thanatophobia is a frequently encountered fear in children.   One
may see it in evidence as early as the third year.   Its appearance
seems to be contiguous with the development of concept formation
and the formation of guilt, both of which greatly antedate the
Oedipus complex.   It is found to be associated with many different
types of intrafamilial stress.   The only factors which these seem
to have in common is that they all may act as inducers of intense
frustration, rage or anxiety, or may threaten in some way parental
loss.   Still, many children go through this entire early development
with no apparent fear of death.   How may we account for this
seeming paradox?

To understand the conflict in the child's mind at such a time we must take into consideration two aspects of his developing sense of causality. The first is the incapacity of the child of one to four years of age to perceive cause and effect sequences in any complete fashion. He initially is even unable to realize that the fulfillment of his bodily needs is related to and dependent upon the ministration of outsiders. For since the needed satisfactions usually follow his wishes for them, he concludes that there is a causal nexus between the two events and that he omnipotently controls his outside environment by his powerful wishes. He makes, as we would say with an adult, a *post hoc* fallacy. This omnipotence is not invincible but is rather quickly modified as he finds that gratification does not invariably succeed wishes.

Nevertheless, a precipitate of this propensity for narcissistic omnipotence appears to persist throughout life in all persons and, if governed and subdued, has many useful subsequent by-products. One of these is its role in the development of individual feelings of security and adequacy. For by this mechanism and by the mechanism of parental identification, the child is able to conceive of himself as a confident and adequate person in the facing of new situations in which he has had no prior experience of successful solution. In other words, part of this confidence is "borrowed" magically from his parents by identification with their adequacy and strength, and another moiety is formed from the residue of his feelings of omnipotence. This development occurs, however, in this form only in the *loved* child. The feeling of benignant omnipotence is almost completely extinguished if the child has been prematurely or excessively exposed to a nonsuccorent environment or when parents have been absent, unloving, or nonnurturent to him.

Hence, the well-loved and nonrejected, nondeprived child is more likely to retain in his unconscious throughout life a quintessence of this infantile omnipotence. It is this proclivity which the average person is able to put to use in the handling of the death anxiety. It enables one to effectively isolate the possibility of eventual death from ourselves. We can then look upon death as did the psalmist David, who said, "A thousand shall fall at thy right hand and ten thousand at thy left, but it shall not come nigh thee." This persistent feeling of personal invulnerability is puissant enough to enable the majority of mankind to remain relatively untroubled in the face of the vast array of facts which should convince us that death is the inevitable end of all men, even ourselves.

If, however, our magical feelings of omnipotence are our main
defense against death anxiety, it is an ironic paradox to note that it
is also this very same factor which is most responsible for its presence.
For the characteristic feature of the thought of the child, *viz.*, that
his wishes have magical power to influence events, is a double-edged
sword. It lends, as we have just seen, a comforting illusion of
credence to our wishes for invincibility and immortality, but it also
forces the child to take responsibility for his hating, annihilating
and destructive thoughts, which he also regards as magically ful-
fillable wishes. Not only does he consider his benevolent wishes
to be magically fulfilled, but the malevolent ones as well.

The child, no less than the savage, is alien to the concept of
chance. All motivation is to him personified. And any unseen
or unwanted eventuality is conceived of as having been the result
of the malignancy of some person or agency. This child reifies
or hypostatizes thought. He equates the symbol with the thing
symbolized, and does not differentiate between objective causation
and wishful causation.

Of course, no child can avoid experiencing in the course of his
maturation a considerable amount of frustration, often of a pecul-
iarly severe and painful kind, and this is not necessarily undesirable. All education is, in effect, frustration based. It is true, however, that the child's characteristic pristine response to frustration
or annoyance is a banishment wish of the frustrating agent or
person, or a reversal wish of the frustrating act. Early in his
life these wishes become equated with "death wishes" towards frustrating objects. This equation of banishment with death is easily
accomplished, since death is not at that time conceived of as an
infinite or permanent state, as the games of children clearly show
us. In the game "Cowboys and Indians," players are shot dead
but quickly come to life again.

It is interesting to note that this theme, violent death and its
magical undoing and reversibility, runs like a leitmotiv through
the folk tales and fairy stories of all generations and cultures. This
wish to undo death is a classic theme in the literature of children,
and should suggest to us the importance and immediacy of this
matter to the child. Only later, when the time sense becomes more
fully developed, does the child begin to learn that death is neither
casual nor reversible, and he then becomes frightened and concerned
about his death wishes towards his ambivalently loved, significant
persons. He attempts then to suppress these or to undo them by

the use of words, using these much as the primitive does in the formation of rite and spell.

Reflect that the most ancient and popular of children's prayers, the origin of which is lost in antiquity, contains a plea against the fear of death ("If I should die before I wake"). And one of the earliest symptoms manifested by the thanatophobic child is his obsessive blessing of persons at the end of this prayer. He will often clearly show his fear that these persons would surely die if he forgot to mention their names in benison or failed to repeat this blessing the proper number of times. These destructive, hating thoughts are doubly frightening, since the child not only fears the loss of his parents through the operation of his death wishes, but also, since he reasons by magical thinking and the law of Talion (to think a thing is to do that thing: to do a thing is to insure an equal and similar punishment to the self), he becomes fearful of his own death.

It must be remembered that the socialization processes for all children are painful and frustrating, and hence no child escapes forming hostile death wishes towards his socializers. Therefore, none escapes the fear of personal death in either direct or symbolic form. Repression is usually so immediate and effective that we rarely see this process in its pristine form.

This process is greatly accentuated, however, if the frustrations naturally implicit in socialization are magnified by circumstances which operate to increase the frequency or intensity of the usual frustrations which the child has had to endure, such as, punitive rejection of the child by unloving, vacillating, or capricious parents, strong sibling rivalry, or the actual experience of parental loss by separation or death. The first two strongly induce the formation of death wishes towards the frustrating figures (and Talion law death fears for the self), and the latter is perceived by the child as proof-positive via the *post hoc* principle that his thoughts have magical power which can kill and destroy. The individual, therefore, lives in expectation that the same Talion punishment will be visited upon him by a malignant or wrathful divinity or fate.

In addition, the child conceives of a parental death or separation as a deliberate abandonment of him by the absent parent, a hostile act on their part for which he is, again, responsible, and for which he will have to pay.

In summary, we see that the child's concept of death is not a single thing, but is rather a composite of mutually contradictory paradoxes. Firstly, death is not conceived of as a possibility in relationship to the self; but conversely, if strong adults die, how can the weaker child survive? Secondly, death is never conceived of as resulting from chance or a natural happening. Causation is personified and the child feels guilt subsequent to a death, as though he were the secret slayer. Yet, paradoxically, he simultaneously experiences rage toward the decedent, as though he had been deliberately abandoned by that person. Consciously these contradictory views would be mutually exclusive, but we must remember that in the unconscious these types of paradoxes can endure in juxtaposition without contradiction.

We see, therefore, that death is not only a state of physical cessation, but is also a complex symbol, the significance of which will vary from one person and culture to another, and which is also profoundly dependent upon the nature and vicissitudes of the developmental process. We also see that death, as a cessation of being, involves aspects of reality inadmissible to the omnipotent and narcissistic self, and for this reason strong defenses are developed against its recognition.

There is a third aspect of the child's interest in causality which serves often to intensify his fear of death. This is concerned with his inability to obtain direct factual data about this problem. Sigmund Freud once described the child's curiosity about the nature of the universe as "the riddle of the Sphinx." He centered his attention upon the child's need to gain meaningful answers to the age old question "Whence came I?," or in the form in which the child grapples with it "Where do babies come from?" And he described at great length the extensive personality deformations which result from the repression of the sexual curiosity which ensues as the child discovers from his parents and from his culture the forbidden nature of this tabooed area.

Modern parents, thanks to Freud and to the generation of educators sparked by his genius, are now able, for the most part, to approach the problem of the child's sexuality in a rational and sensible manner, and as a result there has been a steady diminution during the last fifty years of neurotic formations such as conversion hysteria, whose main etiology is massive sexual repression.

There is a second half to the riddle of the Sphinx to which we have not addressed ourselves. I refer to the complement of "Whence came I?" *viz.*, "Whither go I?" or in the child's language, "What is it to be dead?" Again, clinical experience abundantly proves that children have insatiable curiosity not only about "where people come from" but also "where people go to." In his efforts to find an answer to this conundrum he is met today, as his questions about sexuality would have been met in the 1890's, with evasion and subterfuge. He encounters the same embarrassed prudery and frightened withdrawal which he would have encountered fifty years ago in his efforts to find out about sex. Due to our own gnawing anxieties about death (which the child emphatically perceives, just as he perceives parental embarrassment about sex), the average parent is of little help to the child in his search for answers to these pressing and exigent questions. And the answers which are supplied are as straining to his credulity and faith in his parents as were the "stork" and "baby-in-the-basket" stories which were proffered to him three decades ago in response to his sexual questions. This should make us seriously consider if there may not be an equal risk to the rendering taboo of that opposite end of the question on origin and procreation posed by the child, *viz.*, the nature and the end of man. The classic adult defense against coping with these anxieties in our children is the assertion, maintained even by professional persons, that children cannot conceive of death in *any* form, and, hence, do not need to be reassured about it. One is reminded again of the certainty of a generation ago that the child *has* no sexual feelings, and hence there cannot be a problem about childhood sexuality.

Some excellent research by Sylvia Anthony,[1] as well as a wealth of clinical experience, belies this view. My own psychotherapeutic work with children and adults convinces me that many anxieties, obsessions, phobias, and other neurotic symptom formations are genetically related to the fear of death or its symbolic equivalents, and that these symptoms are, just as in the sexual repressions, symbolic substitutive attempts to bind death anxiety. These relationships are particularly clear in study of the phenomenon of suicide.[2]

Are we then justified in our relegation of this phenomenon of death to the area of tabooed mysticism, as we do with no other phenomenon in modern life?

In parenthesis, let me again cite the earlier analogy of sexual repression, particularly the form in which it appeared fifty years ago. Reflect on the general incredulity and distrust which would have met any statement which advised imparting to children sexual knowledge as a basic part of their learning of the scheme of things.

These critics would have been certain that lust and depravity would have inevitably resulted. Experience has belied that fear.

The fear of death, like the fear of sexuality, when deeply repressed is heavily and expensively symbolized. When we fear death intensely and unremittingly, we fear instead, often, some of the unconscious irrational symbolic equivalences of death. A steadily increasing body of clinical evidence shows us how manifold these may be. While the state of our knowledge is not such as to allow us to say what death *is* with absolute certainty, it is a great help to know what it is *not*. The child who is strongly dependent upon his significant adults for his security and his conception of himself as a worthy and adequate person is capable, if they meet these needs, of integrating the concept of "not-being" if his parents can do so, and he is solaced by the thought that his demise (and theirs) is yet far away. Spinoza has said that the adult who sees death as a completion of a pattern and who has spent his time, unfettered by fear, in living richly and productively, can integrate and accept the thought that his self will one day cease to be.

And in this resolve we have no better example than that given us by the Olympian of our profession, Sigmund Freud. Exploration of the phenomenon of death is not usually done by dying men. Its very propinquity to the old prevents them from forming the necessary detachment which makes scientific investigation possible. Freud is one of the few exceptions to this rule. This old man, who was to live for sixteen years with the daily reality of a malignant cancer, pointed out, while his own sons faced death on the battlefield,[3] that it might be well for us to realize more fully the true nature of our attitudes toward death, an attitude which we are all too willing to distort and suppress. He said, "To deal frankly with the psychology of death has the merit of taking more into account the true state of affairs and in making life more endurable for us." This may be an austere and Spartan hope, but it is on just such a hope, rather than on the promises of the mystics, that the progress of mankind depends.

References

1. S. Anthony, *The Child's Discovery of Death* (New York: Harcourt Brace, 1940).
2. C. W. Wahl, "Suicide as a Magical Act," *Bulletin Menninger Clinic*, 21, pp. 91–98, May 1957.
3. Sigmund Freud, "Thoughts for the Time on War and Death," *Collected Papers*, 4, pp. 288–317, 1925.

Robert Fulton and Gilbert Geis

Death and Social Values

The cultural context within which death is experienced in the United States and the institutionally sanctioned response to it have changed dramatically within the last few decades. Death, in America, is no longer exclusively a matter of religious concern, but has increasingly become a subject of scientific investigation. Theological explanations of the nature and purpose of human life are explicitly and implicitly challenged by medical and social science. So-called wonder drugs, modern hygiene, birth control, and other discoveries and public welfare programs have not only extended the span of man's life but have also caused him to question its meaning anew.

Traditionally, the attitudes of a society toward death have been a function of its religious emphasis. To the extent that theological or sacred doctrines prevail within a society, death generally does not constitute an important challenge to man's conception of himself. The individual comes to regard his demise as natural and preordained. Those who are subsequently forced to accept and to understand their death do so within a prepared metaphysical system which serves to assuage the shock of death through the promise of a renewed or continued existence. Thus the Greeks spoke of a paradisical existence in the Elysian Fields, the Hindus of Nirvana, the Scandinavians held out the prospect of Valhalla, the Persians of an Abode of Song, and the American Indian sought to pass on to the Happy Hunting Ground.

The reality of death, its inevitability, was also treated with characteristic honesty in traditionally oriented societies, and it was often employed as rebuke or warning to individuals who might momentarily have appeared to have forgotten its omnipresence. In this vein Marcus Aurelius gave death its due in his *Meditations:* "It is the duty then of a thinking man to be neither superficial, nor impatient, nor yet contemptuous in his attitude toward death, but to await it as one of the operations of Nature which he will have to undergo."

In Christian religion, the concept of Heaven and Hell promised

Reprinted from the *Indian Journal of Social Research*, 3 (1962), pp. 7–14, by permission of the authors and publisher (Copyright 1962, *Indian Journal of Social Research*).

an uninterrupted existence; death became a gateway to an eternal future of joy or torment. Death was a matter between God and man. To die was to pay the penalty for birth. Shakespeare expresses this idea succinctly when, in *Henry V*, he says, "We owe God a death." Since death was a part of God's plan, the price of original sin could be dealt with openly, discussed freely in church, and treated as a natural phenomenon.

Death-oriented cultures today, such as those found in Italy, Spain, and Mexico, continue to center much attention on subjects that strike persons in other types of cultures as macabre. Skeletons are passed about on All-Soul's Day, and cemeteries are the focal point for much community and familial activity. Cakes are decorated with skulls and crossbones and candies are turned out in the form of cadavers. The cemetery stands in close proximity to the church. For these societies the recognition of death is a prime requisite for life.

Modern studies of death tend to reflect emerging secular attitudes. For the secularly oriented individual death has become a taboo subject to be avoided or disguised. Death suppression is co-terminous with temporal-mindedness and scientific scepticism. In an early statement, Margaret Mead reported that Americans, in contrast to Samoans, tried to protect their children from direct contact with and observations of death and the dead. In Samoa, "all children had seen birth and death" and "had seen many dead bodies" besides having "often witnessed the operation of cutting open any dead body to search out the causes of death."[1] The same uninhibited attitude toward death is found generally in African tribes. For them, ancestors are seen as functioning members of the family, lineage, and clan, and the respect for seniority is extended to the deceased, for whom death has not been so much a departure from the world of the living as a change of status within the social group.[2]

In Western societies, however, attitudes toward death tend to reflect emerging secular emphases which transpose it into an event of awesome dimensions which must perforce be disguised. Avoidance is seen in the practice of relegating the duties and ceremonies attendant upon death to individuals trained and paid to regard it impersonally. By assigning professional functionaries the responsibility for traditional familial roles, contemporary society not only avoids direct and disconcerting contact with death itself, but also, more important, permits its members to avoid close and disturbing confrontations with the inconsistencies inherent in the traditional theological explanations and emerging secular viewpoints. In current secular societies death is not considered an open or polite topic of conversation, except among the aged, and the dead are hidden from view as quickly as possible and removed to a funeral home at the first opportunity.

This pattern of avoidance is clearly shown, furthermore, in a perceptive content analysis of American motion pictures as these deal with the subject of death. Two psychologists, Wolfenstein and Leites, found that the films characteristically refused to allow the audience to build up any emotional identification with a character who would subsequently die or be killed. In pictures dealing with murder, the slain individual was never deeply mourned; rather someone close to him would doggedly pursue his slayer, oblivious to the normal impact of the prior death. Death became only a convenient catalyst for other forms of action, never an emotional reality in itself.[3]

Characteristic of American society also is the use of humor and euphemisms regarding death which serve as another manifestation of a general reluctance to accept its inevitability. Digger O'Dell, a droll funeral director, is an unending source of mass communications humor. Linguistically, a person "passes away," instead of dying, and installment buying of funerals is referred to in some instances as "sunrise plans" rather than, perhaps, as "lay away plans."

Empirical work in the social sciences concerning death was quite fragmentary until the period of the Second World War, though anthropologists accumulated great amounts of data on death rites and funeral practices. Emile Durkheim, the French social anthropologist, saw the funeral complex as a series of ritualistic reconfirmations of the value structure of the society and a reintegration of the group's cohesiveness. In totemic societies, Durkheim believed, where the emphasis is on the omnipotence of deity, death, inexplicable in naturalistic terms, served to call attention to the absolute nature of theistic control.[4] Anthropologists, however, have never integrated their ethnographic data into verifiable general statements concerning divergent social patterns and their relationship to death.

Prompted by Freud's theory of a universal death instinct (thanatos) which in opposition to the life principle (eros) carried on the dialectic of human existence, psychologists and psychiatrists have been stimulated to investigate the phenomenon of death.

While some American analysts, notably Karl Menninger, have attempted to explain suicide and other behaviors in terms of the dominance of death instincts over life impulses,[5] Freud's successors have tended for the most part to reject this bleak dichotomy. Horney, for example, objects to Freud's biological basis for the death instinct, though she concedes the brilliance of the hypothesis.[6]

The major psychological focus in the United States in the 1930's was placed on conscious awareness of death, and served to illustrate the transition of death from an overt, actual phenomenon to an eventuality well repressed from immediacy by a combination of socially constructed curtains.   Thus, Schilder, Bromberg, and Middleton, examining different groups, both those who would apparently have strong feeling about death, individuals such as murderers and psychoneurotics, and those who might not, such as college students, uniformly reported only minor concern among all groups with this theme.[7]   Middleton, for instance, found from a questionnaire study on attitudes toward death among 825 college students that 93 percent reported that they thought only very rarely or occasionally about death.   Sixty-three percent denied having dreams of death or dying, and of the remaining 37 percent only 2 percent reported having such dreams more than very rarely.[8]   Summing up the psychological studies, Alexander and Adlerstein note that: "The material from empirical sources reveals that on a conscious, verbal level people in (American) culture do not seem to be seriously concerned with thoughts of death."[9]

The immediacy and the extent of death during the Second World War, combined with the continuing attrition of the sacred orientation toward human existence, served to focus more compelling attention on the subject.   Nonetheless, social scientists, despite massive research efforts on other aspects of human behavior under stress, singularly neglected to exploit the unique aspects of war to acquire data on human reactions to the possibility of personal or group extermination.   Here was an opportunity to determine how patriotism and theology interacted in affecting attitudes toward death. Innumerable questions suggested themselves: What is the significance of Roman Catholic dogma which opposes the cremation of the body for the soldier who must face a flame thrower?   What is the importance of the manner of dying, for the young man or for the old?   What is the significance of disfiguration of the genitals or of the face in acts of bravery or of cowardice under fire?

What effect does the viewing of hundreds of mutilated bodies have upon the morale of men who in peacetime rarely see or discuss death? Is the soldier who is able to reject for himself the likelihood of death a more effective fighter, or is effectiveness tied to a calm acceptance of the statistical probabilities of survival? The nearest approximations to answers to these questions could be found only in fictional and autobiographical accounts of war.[10] By the end of the war, it was apparent that homefront morale, a new dimension in warfare, might have been better sustained had governments accumulated reliable information about the effects of military deaths on civilian survivors.

In the immediate post-war period, attempts to fill these research gaps and to provide pragmatic information of operational relevance were apparent in a number of studies of disaster areas, studies sponsored by the federal government.[11] The impetus to secure reliable information on reactions to death has also been heightened by the threat of nuclear holocausts and by the large number of individuals surviving beyond the traditional three score and ten years. With mandatory retirement, aged persons were able to concentrate, often to brood, on their inevitable demise. The political importance of the aged, as well as their increasing proportion in the population, led to scientific responsiveness to their problems.

Both the growing interest and the present immaturity of research on death was clearly shown in papers presented at the 5th Gerontological Congress in San Francisco during 1960. Using divergent samples and varying techniques, investigators were unable to reach any consensus on correlates of attitudes toward death. *A priori*, the majority of investigators assumed that the intensity of religious belief would be related in some manner to death fears. There was little agreement, however, on how to define "religious belief" with any integrity, and considerable difficulty in distinguishing between the stated belief of an individual that he did not fear death because of the promise of an idealistic after-life and his actual feelings. Particularly notable in the papers was a failure to perceive that attitudes are most basically a function of the society's interpretation of death. As a discussion of the papers noted: "Modern industrial America with its emphasis upon long cars, long vacations, and longevity has struck a new note in the minds of man. Given the emphasis upon individualism and the inviolability of the person coupled with the relative decline of traditional views, death becomes an infringement upon our right to life, liberty, and the pursuit of happiness. . . . As never before, we chose to disguise it and pretend the meanwhile that it is not the basic condition of all life.[12]

The changing interpretation of death in secularized societies can be most clearly seen from an examination of the structure and function of groups most intimately connected with death and its ordering. Research has shown that the Protestant clergy, for instance, believe that their major task at a funeral is to attend to the living and their needs rather than to the dead.[13] This modern orientation of pastoral psychology is seen also in a memorial issue of the *Register* of the Chicago Theological Seminary. Its entire contents is devoted not to a theological discourse on death or divinity but to the practical essentials of "Religion and Social Work" containing, among other things, down-to-earth hints for ministers on how to counsel and guide most effectively communicants with personal problems. The advice is not to recommend faith in the Divine, but to establish contact with a family casework agency, a mental hygiene clinic, or similar agencies, all of which can provide "expert help for the person."

The interaction between ministers and funeral directors serves to illustrate the relationship between shifting social values and the phenomenon of death in secular societies. In the United States, the funeral director is a private businessman who is commissioned to take charge of the rites and ceremonies connected with the disposal of the body. With the exception of the funeral eulogy, which is the responsibility of the clergy, the modern-day funeral director is prepared to assume all activities associated with death, even to the point of providing "chapel" facilities for the holding of the service.

The funeral director, however, is caught between ambivalent demands: On the one hand, he is encouraged to disguise the reality of death for the survivors who do not possess the emotional support once provided by theology to deal with it; on the other hand, he is impelled to call attention to the special services he is rendering. Thus he both blunts and sharpens the reality of death. The blunting occurs in terms of the atmosphere provided for the funeral and the vocabulary which is employed in connection with it. Funeral homes are delicately lit and sedately appointed. The procession to the cemetery is marked by modern, expensive automobiles, painted in unobtrusive colors. Funeral home employees are rehearsed to transmit dignity both in terms of dress and demeanor, while their particular argot is replete with the euphemisms of denial: the body lies in state in a "slumber room," death is "passing away," having "gone beyond," or "gone home." In addition, the dead man is referred to as if he were still alive (e.g., "Mr. Smith is in Room 214"), while cards and flowers destined for the funeral are addressed to the deceased.

At the same time, the funeral director, if he is to justify his role as an important functionary in death, must focus attention upon the body. Display of the corpse, of course, forces attention upon death itself, but also allows a society with a growing repression of it to deal more comfortably with reality by presenting it in the most favorable form available. Funeral directors are considered successful when, by virtue of developed skills in cosmetic arts, they are able to present a "life-like" corpse to grieving and disbelieving survivors. "Water-tight vaults," air mattresses, and formal dress also contrive to support the image of the living dead. To complete the illusion, cemeteries are landscaped in impeccable and expensive taste, while the living are encouraged to use certain of them for picnics, marriages, and other expressions of viability. Thus, modern society rejects death is the most formidable and paradoxical fashion possible, by embracing casually and joyfully the delicately designed accoutrements of the grave. We find therefore both in death and life-oriented societies the same indifference to death, but stemming in these divergent instances from quite different roots and social needs.

Conclusion

The subject of death has only recently come under the scrutiny of social scientists. Before now, death has been avoided as a subject for research both because of its religious overtones, which were presumptively beyond secular investigation, and because of the general morbidity implicit in such research.

As societies throughout the world have become secularized, there has arisen a growing need to put forward rational explanations of social and psychological phenomena that were previously viewed and interpreted as sacred in nature. Some of these areas have yielded to the overtures of scientific endeavor; others promise to become explicable by means of expanding knowledge and improved research techniques. Still other matters, however, by their very nature, will never be understood through the offices of science. They are, in their most basic sense, extra-scientific. Medical science may very well put forth a naturalistic explanation of human mortality in terms of organic processes and their cessation, but it cannot provide verifiable data on the intrinsic meaning of those processes. As a consequence, human beings find themselves increasingly caught up in the debate on the meaning of death.

The contribution of social science to this dialogue, of course, is in the attempt to comprehend the dimensions of the problem of death for society and the implications death has for human behavior. The social scientific study of death, however, is still in its most nascent form. The social and psychological correlates of varying attitudes toward death remain to be established. Autobiographical data on individual experiences in regard to death is lacking, and the relationship between this material and the individual's perception concerning the death of other persons and his own potential demise needs to be investigated. Cross-cultural data, as yet ungathered, would prove extremely valuable for providing insight into a phenomenon that is basic to and significant for all human beings, and would also provide a testing ground for the psychoanalytical, sociological, and psychological theories which are emerging in this area. It would be interesting, for example, to determine whether societies which are currently undergoing industrialization and secularization will respond in a manner comparable to that found in the United States in regard to the phenomenon of death.

References

1. Margaret Mead, *Coming of Age in Samoa* (New York: William Morrow, 1928), p. 93.
2. Simon and Phoebe Ottenberg, Eds., *Cultures and Societies of Africa* (New York: Random House, 1960), pp. 60–65.
3. Martha Wolfenstein and Nathan Leites, *Movies: A Psychological Study* (Glencoe, Ill.: Free Press, 1950), pp. 233–242.
4. Emile Durkheim, *The Elementary Forms of Religious Life*, trans. by J. W. Swain (Glencoe, Ill.: Free Press, 1947), *passim*.
5. Karl Menninger, *Man Against Himself* (New York: Harcourt, Brace, 1938).
6. Karen Horney, *The Neurotic Personality of Our Time* (New York: Norton, 1937), p. 74.
7. Walter Bromberg and Paul Schilder, "Death and Dying," *Psychoanalytical Review*, 20 (1933), pp. 133–185; also, "The Attitudes of Psychoneurotics Toward Death," *Psychoanalytical Review*, 23 (1936), pp. 1–25; W. C.

Middleton, "Some Reactions Towards Death Among College Students," *Journal Abnormal and Social Psychology*, 31 (1936), pp. 165–174; Paul Schilder and D. Wechsler, "The Attitudes of Murderers Towards Death," *Journal Abnormal and Social Psychology*, 31 (1936), pp. 348–363.

8. Middleton, *op. cit., pp.* 172–174.
9. Irving E. Alexander and Arthur M. Adlerstein, *Studies in the Psychology of Death*, in Henry P. David and J. C. Brengelmann (Eds.), *Perspectives in Personality Research* (New York: Springer Publishing Co., 1960), pp. 65–92.
10. Oddly enough, the most esteemed novel in the United States on the psychology of the soldier facing death is the *Red Badge of Courage*, a Civil War novel by Stephen Crane, an author who never fought in any war.
11. See, for instance, Rue Bucher, "Blame and Hostility in Disaster," *American Journal of Sociology*, 42 (1957), pp. 467–475.
12. Robert L. Fulton, "Attitudes Toward Death—A Discussion," *Journal of Gerontology*, 16 (1961), pp. 405–406.
13. Robert L. Fulton, "The Clergyman and the Funeral Director: A Study in Role Conflict," *Social Forces*, 39 (1961), pp. 317–323.

Part 2.

*Attitudes and Responses
toward Death*

INTRODUCTION

The number of people in the United States who have passed their 65th birthday now totals more than 17,000,000, and this number is increasing at a rapid rate. By 1975, there will be more than 25,000,000 persons past the age of 65. Such a large, aged population means that within the decade we can expect the number of people who will die each year to double. At the same time the present generation in America can be said, in a manner of speaking, to be the first in the history of the world never to have experienced death. The period of time that a family can expect not to have a death occur within its ranks, statistically, is now a generation or approximately twenty years. How will this relatively death-free generation, brought up in a society which attempts to disguise or deny death, greet the death or dying of its elders? And what of the dying person himself? How is he to view his death in the face of a society that increasingly seeks to avoid the reality of it?

The answers to these and similarly pertinent questions are highly complex, but the research reported in this section provides instructive and suggestive clues based upon studies in the United States.

79

For the most part the studies reflect a concern for particular groups within the population, such as college students, mentally-ill patients, and the aged. The diverse techniques for eliciting responses, verbal and nonverbal, conscious and unconscious, and the differences in the sampling procedures used by the studies reported sometimes leads to apparently contradictory conclusions. For instance, Swenson, one of the contributors to this book, reports a positive relationship between religiosity and one's attitudes toward death with the religious person showing the least fear. Christ, on the contrary, in another contribution, reports that the fear of death is not affected by religion or religiosity. All groups, he reports, are equally afraid of death. Rhudick and Dibner, who hypothesize that death-concerns are a function of personality factors *per se*, found in their study a correlation between good health and a positive attitude toward death. Swenson, however, reports that those people reporting poor health most often looked forward to death in a positive manner, whereas those reportedly in good health are most actively evasive or defensive in their responses. Jeffers *et al.*, on the other hand, concur with Swenson and disagree with Christ and Rhudick and Dibner.

Again Adlerstein and Alexander in their study on the affective response to death in children and young adolescents concluded that death had a greater emotional significance for people with less stable ego-structures than for those with an adequate conception of themselves. Diggory and Rothman on the basis of their research reach the opposite conclusion. Their findings suggest to them that a person's fear of death depends on the role he has or expects to have and therefore ultimately on his life goals. They reason that a person who values himself highly should be more afraid of death than one whose self-esteem is low because death is the limiting case of loss or destruction of the self. Not all researchers disagree, however. Strut's finding that elderly subjects living in familiar, non-institutional surroundings have a less apprehensive attitude toward death is complemented by Fulton's report that most of his respondents preferred to remain at home or in a family setting when they knew they were going to die. In this instance it is not the researchers but the culture that is in disagreement for the evidence at hand points heavily in the direction of greater institutionalization and isolation for the dying person in America.

For the most part, however, the contradictory nature of these findings is often more apparent than real and reflects rather the employment of different conceptual referents as well as diverse research instruments applied to a gross admixture of groups and subgroups. For instance, Jeffer's study is based upon 260 volunteer adults who overwhelmingly (94 per cent) were persons with close church affiliations, whereas Christ's study is based on the expressed attitudes of 62 people admitted to a psychiatric ward who did not know the true purpose of the questions asked. Swenson, on the other hand, studied a group of 210 persons recruited from Golden Age Clubs, rest homes, and organizations employing the aged. His sample is three-quarters female, all volunteers, with no follow-up of those who failed to cooperate in the study. For the rest homes, Swenson reports that only 40 per cent of the residents were willing to take part in the study. Again, Rhudick and Dibner base their conclusions on the replies of 60 normal adults, members of an Age Center who volunteered to participate in their study.

These studies, despite their methodological shortcomings, provide intriguing clues to attitudes toward death. It appears, for instance, that religion plays a dual role in a person's attitude toward death. Religion for the deeply devout person may be "functional" and supportive or it may be "dsyfunctional" with the threat of judgment day and eternal damnation overwhelming his hope for Heaven and eternal bliss. It might also be suggested on the basis of the reported research that on a verbal conscious level few people fear death, think about it, or dream about it. On a nonverbal or unconscious level, however, the evidence suggests that the thought of death or experience with words or pictures associated with the idea of death may provoke a strong fear reaction. Further, available studies indicate that death is coming to be seen as an "accident," something to be avoided or prevented, rather than "natural" in a religious sense. In this regard our attitudes seem to approximate those of the Ovimbundu of West Africa and other preliterate societies who believe that death is due to the malevolence of others or to some untoward occurrence.

It further appears that the act of dying rather than death itself is of greater concern to many people in this society. Responses to questions regarding where, and how, and under what conditions one would prefer to die suggest that people prefer to die quickly, painlessly, and with as little fuss or inconvenience to their families or friends as possible. In this regard it is of interest to note that separate studies by Feifel and Fulton show a preference for home as the place to die and a desire by the dying patients to be surrounded by family and friends. But last year in the United States 53 per cent of all deaths occurred in hospitals which typically prohibit children from visiting patients or at best permit their visits in specific areas and only at designated times. In terms of these findings and Weisman and Hackett's concept of an "appropriate death" such a discrepancy between the wishes and needs of people for a dignity in their deaths and the actual practices of our medical institutions suggests that a critical review of our thinking and behavior is needed in this area.

A growing hostility toward the functions and functionaries associated with death is also indicated by research. In two studies Fulton has shown that attitudes toward the rites and practices surrounding death as well as those toward the funeral director are in part negative and critical in nature. Recent books and exposé-type articles and commentaries in the mass media confirm these findings and lend further credence to the earlier comments by Borkenau regarding a cultural shift in attitudes toward death. These criticisms appear to be reflective however of deeper and more complex issues than merely those of economics or ascetic Puritanism. They would seem to mirror basic fears and anxieties on the part of certain segments of our society regarding death itself.

Several studies also report that the phenomenon of repression is associated with current social hostility toward death and reminders of death. Discussion of death with children, in particular, appears to be difficult for adults. This is especially so for certain selected professional groups in America.

In a society in which parents appear to strive to deal realistically with many of the former taboos of parent-child conversation, such as sexual matters and items of authority, the subject of death not only remains unspoken, but appears to be, by comparison, increasingly avoided and disguised.

*Irving E. Alexander, Randolph S. Colley,
and Arthur M. Adlerstein*

Is Death a Matter of Indifference?

Despite a wealth of conjecture and concern about death in philosophy, religion, literature, biology, the arts, and anthropology,

Reprinted from *The Journal of Psychology*, 43 (1957), pp. 277–283, by permission of the authors and publisher.

psychologists have remained rather aloof and have neglected death as a subject for study. In the last half-century, the psychological literature yields relatively few reports dealing with this concept. Psychological theory has also reflected this neglect. Except for some psychoanalytic and existentialist doctrines[1] one can find no reference to the general importance of the idea of death for human functioning.

The few studies that have appeared may be summarized very briefly. Normal people show very little conscious concern about death.[2] Children, old people, and those in psychopathological or socially marginal states express somewhat more conscious interest in the problem.[3] This is where the matter rests. It seems rather strange that the evidence from other disciplines would indicate that man is anything but indifferent to the problem of death, while the evidence from psychology would relegate concern to special states.

There are many possible explanations for the apparent discrepancy. A very likely one involves the methods psychologists used to gather the data. Most of the above studies utilized questionnaire or interview techniques. Perhaps with regard to death one does not always say what one feels. Or perhaps what one is expected to say differs from what one feels.

The present study is designed to assess concern or "affective involvement" with the concept of death by measuring less conscious aspects of man's responses.

Method

A method was sought that would be simple, direct, physiological, psychological, quantitative, and repeatable. The word association task was felt to be most appropriate for obtaining such information and thus the response time, psychogalvanic response, and response word were recorded for a list of stimulus words. The basic procedure was first described by Jung and his students.[4]

The composition of the word list was predicted on the following logic. In order to test "affective involvement," the list should contain words related to each other by superordinate concepts that would, by general agreement, be affect-laden for the subjects. In our subject population the concepts chosen were sex and school. As a base line against which to measure, the list should contain "basal" words, that is, words with no apparent general relationship to other words on the list. As a final step there should be included words related to one another under the heading of our critical variable, the concept of death.

The list finally employed consisted of 27 words selected from the Thorndike and Lorge Teacher's Word Book of 30,000 Words.[5] It contained 18 "basal" words, three "sex" words, three "school" words, and three "death" words. These subgroups were balanced with respect to frequency of their usage in the language, length, and number of syllables. The position of a word in the list was determined by a random procedure with the following restriction— no critical word was allowed to follow any other critical word. Some examples from the list follow: *Sex:* romance, maiden, lover. *School:* college, lecture, scholar. *Death:* funeral, death, burial. *Basal:* sunset, insect, criminal, etc. It is to be noted that "basal" words are by no means affect-free. They are samples from the language, each of which can have affective meaning for any subject. Our concern is whether the critical words are more affectively charged than those we have designated as "basals."

SUBJECTS

The subjects used in this study were 31 male Princeton under- graduates, all of whom were volunteers. Although the subjects were known to one of the experimenters, it was felt that they represented a typical sample of the undergraduate population. They were not known to have had psychiatric histories and were all naïve with respect to the purpose of the experiment.

PROCEDURE

The subject was told that he was helping to determine whether the Sanborn Recorder was an adequate instrument for measuring the psychogalvanic response. After placing his head in a fixed position, the subject was instructed to respond into a telephone receiver with the first word that came to mind after the presentation of the stimulus word. The telephone receiver was used as a voice key to interrupt an electric timing marker which was initiated manually by the experimenter upon presentation of a stimulus word. Measurements were taken of the difference in voltage gener- ated between the palm and the dorsal surface of the hand using the wet electrode and initial rubdown technique described by Bitterman.[6] The response time and *PGR* readings were continuously and automatically recorded on heat sensitive paper on the Sanborn Twin-Viso Recorder Model 651-42. The time interval between word presentations varied between 45 seconds and one minute depending upon the rapidity of the subject's return to a resting level. A short, preliminary word group leading right into the regular list was given to settle the subjects in the apparatus.

Results

Analyses are available for two separate sets of measurements: the latency of response time and the magnitude of the *PGR*. Both distributions, originally skewed, were normalized by the use of a logarithmic transformation. Means were determined for each subject on each of the three sets of words, "basal," "affective" (sex and school), and "death." Differences were assessed by the analysis of variance technique. The results are presented in Table 1.

The *F* ratios indicate that on both sets of measurements there were significant differences in response to the several word groupings and further that there was significant variation among the subjects responding. People react differently to these three sets

Table 1

Analysis of variance of PGR and response time scores

| | PGR | | | | Response time | | | |
Source	Sum of squares	*df*	Mean square	*F*	Sum of squares	*df*	Mean square	*F*
Total	12.30	92			4.25	92		
Between word groups	.2	2	.1	8.55	.07	2	.035	4.86*
Between individuals	11.4	30	.38	32.48	3.75	30	.125	17.36†
Discrepance	.70	60	.0117		.43	60	.0072	

* $p < .05$.
† $p < .01$.

of words and in a manner that differs from one individual to another.

The more pertinent analysis among word groups was made by deriving distributions of differences and evaluating these differences by use of the t-test. The results are found in Table 2.

Table 2

T values for word group comparisons on both response measures

Comparison	PGR	Response time
"Basal" vs. "affective"	4.60*	2.73*
"Basal" vs. "death"	3.85*	2.66*
"Affective" vs. "death"	.09	.61

* $p < .01$.

The logic of our experiment dictated that the first comparison be made between the *a priori* "affective" words and "basal" words. This was a check on the adequacy of the measuring instrument. For both indices the probability of obtaining such difference distributions by chance alone is less than 1 in 100. The technique of measurement seems appropriate for our purposes. The direction of these differences was consistent in both instances. Longer time and greater *PGR* magnitudes were generally noted for sex and school words as opposed to "basal" words.

The comparisons between responses to "death" words and "basal" words also yielded t's beyond the 1 per cent level of confidence. This population of college students responds in the same way to words relating to death as they do to other words involving affect. Again a longer time was needed to respond and the magnitude of the psychogalvanic response increased for "death" words when compared with "basal."

The third comparison, between the *a priori* "affective" category and the "death" words, indicates that on both sets of measurements these distributions differ very little and in a manner that could be attributed to chance fluctuation.

Discussion

The results of this experiment are clear-cut. A population of normal subjects, in a period of life that is characterized by activity and vigor, responds to words related to death with greater emotional intensity (indicated by *PGR* magnitudes and latency of response time) than to equivalent words drawn from the general language sample. This finding is somewhat at variance with the conscious expressions of relative indifference and lack of concern about death indicated by earlier investigators.[7] The differences, however, are not difficult to rationalize. It is likely that we are dealing with two levels of functioning with regard to the death concept. The one involves overt consciously communicated attitudes, the other less conscious processes that can be inferred from response time and *PGR* measurements. In some individuals there is agreement between responses on both levels, in others a wide discrepancy may exist. For example, we might speculate that good accord should be found between verbal report and our measures in certain psychopathological states but at intense values of involvement. This same agreement between measures might obtain for people in states of good mental health but at much more attenuated values. Psychotics may show high concern on both types of measurements, normals very little. In our culture, where death is not an ordinary topic of conversation as it may be in some southern European and Asian countries, e.g., Spain, China, Japan, it is perhaps more usual to find a discrepance between the two levels of response. Our cultural values are generally negative to expressions of fear and awe about death and dying; consequently overt attitudes may tend toward indifference. An extreme of the culturally supported view was made evident to us in a preliminary phase of our study. A trial subject whose *PGR* and response time scores were unusually deviant was interviewed informally and at length. During the discussion he presented quite freely his views about various subjects, including his attitudes and feelings about death. The general picture was one of little concern. This was an area that did not seem to occupy his conscious thoughts. In the last moments of the discussion, and then apparently by chance, it was revealed that he was a diabetic and, we may add parenthetically, one whose very existence depended on a dose of insulin administered each morning. While it is an inference that the extreme test responses and the medical condition are linked to one another, it is one that can be checked by further empirical work.

The observations reported in this study point to the fact that perhaps we have overlooked a significant motivating force in human functioning. In effect they lend support to the speculations gleaned

88   *Attitudes and Responses toward Death*

from the work of the "existentialists" and from many of the "depth" psychologists, see especially Caprio[8] and Moellenhoff.[9] The concern with death would appear to be a force that has a continuing effect and is not confined solely to instances of childhood, old age, and psychopathology. It may be that at these critical times in the life history man is more conscious of his mortal nature and engages in serious efforts to provide some solution to the apparent conflict created between his wish to continue life indefinitely and the knowledge that he must eventually die. In less critical times this struggle may be going on less consciously and may be reflected in a constant search for the meaning of life in such things as religious doctrine, philosophy, and science and may determine to some extent the Weltanschauung of the individual. . . .

References

1. See, K. R. Eissler, *The Psychiatrist and the Dying Patient* (New York: International University Press, 1956). See also, S. Freud, *Beyond the Pleasure Principle* (London: Hogarth Press, 1950); C. G. Jung, *Two Essays on Analytical Psychology* (New York: Pantheon Books, 1953); and G. Zilboorg, "Fear of Death," *Psychoanalytic Quarterly,* 12 (1943), 465–475.
2. See, W. Bromberg and P. Schilder, "Death and Dying," *Psychoanalytic Review,* 20 (1933), 133–185; and W. C. Middleton, "Some Reactions Towards Death Among College Students," *Journal of Abnormal and Social Psychology,* 31 (1936), 165–173.
3. See, S. Anthony, *The Child's Discovery of Death* (New York: Harcourt, Brace, 1940). See also W. Bromberg and P. Schilder, "The Attitudes of Psychoneurotics Toward Death," *Psychoanalytic Review,* 23 (1936), 1–25; M. Nagy, "The Child's Theories Concerning Death," *Journal of Genetic Psychology,* 73 (1948), 3–27; P. Schilder, "The Attitude of Murderers Towards Death," *Journal of Abnormal and Social Psychology,* 31 (1936), 348–363; P. Schilder and D. Wechsler, "The Attitudes of Children Towards Death," *Journal of Genetic Psychology,* 45 (1934), 406–451; C. A. Scott, "Old Age and Death," *American Journal of Psychology,* 8 (1896), 67–122; C. L. Stacey and K. Marken, "The Attitudes of College Students and Penitentiary Inmates Toward Death and a Future Life," *Psychiatric Quarterly (suppl.),* 26 (1952), 27–32; and C. L. Stacey and M. L. Reichen, "Attitudes Toward Death and Future Life Among Normal and Subnormal Adolescent Girls," *Exceptional Children,* 20 (1954), 259–262.
4. C. G. Jung, *Studies in Word Association* (London: Heinemann, 1918).
5. E. C. Thorndike and I. Lorge, *Teacher's Word Book of 30,000 Words* (New York: Teacher's College, Columbia University, 1944).
6. M. E. Bitterman, J. Krauskopf, and W. H. Holtzman, "The Galvanic Skin

Response Following Artificial Reduction of the Basal Resistance," *Journal of Comparative and Physiological Psychology*, 47 (1954), 230–234.
7. Bromberg and Schilder, *op. cit.*, 133–185; and Middleton, *op. cit.*, 165–173.
8. F. S. Caprio, "A Study of Some Psychological Reactions During Pre-pubescence to the Idea of Death," *Psychiatric Quarterly*, 24 (1950), 495–505.
9. F. Moellenhoff, "Ideas of Children About Death," *Bulletin of the Menninger Clinic*, 3 (1939), 148–156.

Robert Fulton

The Sacred and the Secular: Attitudes of the American Public toward Death, Funerals, and Funeral Directors

This paper reports a study of the attitudes of the American public toward death, funerals, and funeral directors. As it has been proposed previously, the rites, customs, and beliefs surrounding death can be viewed as a culture complex and, as such, present rich research possibilities for the sociologist.[1]

Recently, criticism of the funeral ceremony and of the funeral director among the American public has intensified. Funeral reform recommendations in the press, in national magazines and on television, as well as the growth of the funeral reform movement itself, give ample evidence of this. The first national convention, moreover, of funeral reform societies, or of memorial societies as they are called, was held in 1962, and serves to testify to the vitality and extent of this impulse to funeral reform.

It was the intent of this study to determine as far as possible the nature and degree of the public's attitude toward the funeral ceremony and the American funeral director. In so doing the question could be answered whether these criticisms of the American funeral program reflected the opinions of an active and articulate minority or whether they did in fact reflect a common concern or a basic attitudinal shift among the majority of the American public toward contemporary funeral procedures and mourning rites.

By providing answers to the questions: "By whom are these attitudes held?" and "Why are they held?," valuable clues and

A revised and condensed version of the monograph, *The Sacred and the Secular: Attitudes of the American Public Toward Death* (Milwaukee: Bulfin, 1963).

insights into mans' present-day orientation toward himself, religion, and society could be obtained.

The Procedure

A questionnaire was mailed to 10,000 householders across the United States who resided in major urban centers. Their names were chosen at random from the most recent telephone directories available. The householders were selected on a proportional basis from the nine census areas of the United States to insure adequate regional representation. In order to elicit a response from the reluctant or forgetful householder, an additional 1600 questionnaires were mailed to this original sample. In addition, eleven memorial societies participated in this study and altogether 893 questionnaires were mailed. To insure anonymity the selection of memorial society names was done by the societies themselves.

As a check for representativeness, an additional 360 individuals were selected and personally interviewed by graduate students and/or the faculty of 26 departments of sociology throughout the country.

Questions were asked concerning the meaning of death, ideas of God, thoughts of death, fear of death and dying, the purpose and function of the funeral, the duties of clergymen and funeral directors, areas of tension, need for changes, and so on.

In addition, personal information was solicited from the public regarding their religious affiliation, age, education, number of funerals attended, their average income, etc. Space was also provided for additional comment. A letter was included with the mailed questionnaire or was mailed prior to a personal interview explaining the nature of the study. In addition to the request to participate in the study the letter assured the recipient that the questionnaire was anonymous and directed him not to sign his name.

In all, 1722 questionnaires were returned, coded, tabulated, and analyzed. Of this total, 1264 were returned by the general public and 458 by members of the 11 participating memorial societies. In addition, 315 personal interviews were completed.

A word about the selection of the sample. Because most suggested changes, and because most of the unfavorable comments about funerals appeared primarily in urban areas, it was decided that a survey of rural attitudes would add little to the purpose of the study.

Somewhat more than half of the interviews completed were with individuals originally chosen from our sample; the remainder were replacements, due to such normal events as moving, absence from the city, death, or to the refusal of many to participate in the study. These refusals occurred mostly on the east and west coasts. Given the subject matter of the study, we can well appreciate the problem many people could have in being confronted with such a questionnaire. However, the fact of refusal itself is of particular interest as well as the concentration of refusals on the east and west coasts. The data contained in this report contribute to an understanding of the refusal to cooperate with the study. It might be mentioned here that in several instances householders refused to be interviewed because they firmly believed that the study was another device for selling a funeral or cemetery plot.

In order to differentiate clearly among the three groups of respondents, it is proposed to refer to the members of the memorial societies as *the memorial group,* the respondents from the general public *as the householders,* and those personally interviewed as *the interview group.*

Major Findings

A comparison of the householder and memorial group replies showed significant differences in attitude toward the issues raised in this study. With the question on Divinity, for instance, 69% of the householders reported they believed in God or a Creator, compared to 22% of the memorial group. Conversely, 69% of the memorial respondents "believed in a power greater than themselves," believed in the "worth of humanity," or in "natural law." Twenty-six per cent of the householders responded in similar fashion. The remainder of both groups, 9% and 5% of the householders and memorial groups respectively, reported they were atheists or were unsure of what they believed.

An atheistic response by the memorial group is considerably more pronounced, however, with the question on the meaning of death. Fifty-three per cent responded to this question with such replies as "nothing," "finish," "end of life," and "termination of ego."

This compares to 19% of the householders who responded in this way. Contrariwise, 53% of the householders compared to 22% of the memorial group gave religious responses, that is, reference was made to Heaven, salvation, judgment, eternal life, beginning of a new or spiritual life, etc. Other responses such as, "the body decays," "sorrow," "loss of loved one," "peace," "sleep," "release, from trouble," made up approximately the fourth quarter of the responses.

In response to the question of what happens to us after death the replies are consistent for the two groups. That is, the householders gave religious replies in 58% of the cases compared to 19% for the memorial group. Atheistic replies show the two groups reversed with the memorial group reporting this type of response in 50% of the cases compared to 18% for the householders.

Similarities between the two groups were found to exist. Both groups seemed to experience a greater fear of dying than they did of death itself and they agreed in the majority of cases that they would like to die at home.

The questions about thinking about dying and thinking about death also showed a similarity in replies. About 40% of the respondents of each group reported they rarely or never thought about dying or death. In contrast, 12 to 14% of the members of both groups thought about death frequently and/or all of the time.

The householder and memorial group replies showed that in general both groups viewed the purposes of the funeral similarly. For instance, a plurality (about 30%) of both groups indicated that the funeral allows individuals to pay their last respects to the deceased. A lesser number of both groups (about 20%) reported that the funeral provides a situation where the bereaved may be comforted by friends and associates. Further, both groups said they would prefer burial to other means of disposing of the body. Of significance, however, is the fact that 16% of the memorial group viewed the funeral as no longer having any purpose at all. Combined with the fact that only 12% of the householders and 7% of the memorial group indicated that the prime function of the contemporary funeral was religious, these findings demonstrate the secular nature of the attitudes growing up around this traditionally religious ceremony.

A basic difference of opinion was expressed by the two groups. The majority of the householders believed that the funeral ceremony served adequately those purposes and functions previously noted.

The majority of the memorial group, on the other hand, reported that the funeral failed in its function and purpose. In this connection, the majority of householders felt that the funeral assisted in meeting the emotional needs of bereaved families, whereas the majority of the memorial members disagreed and challenged its efficacy as a sociological or psychological aid.

The study showed that more than three-quarters of the memorial group believed changes were needed in the funeral ceremony. Such comments as the following were common: "the funeral should be shortened," it "should be simpler," it "should be less expensive," and it "should be less ostentatious." Criticism was also registered in answer to the question as to the adequacy and value of the funeral. Recurring in the replies were comments that the funeral today is "too formal," "too impersonal," "too long," and "too emotional." Similar criticisms were made even by some of those who felt the funeral did meet human needs and was adequate. About one-third of the householders concurred with the majority opinion of the memorial group.

In pursuing reactions and opinions concerning the funeral ceremony, it was found, as would be expected, that the majority of the memorial group wanted a memorial-type funeral and/or a simple, inexpensive burial. In contrast, approximately half of the householders reported a preference for the traditional funeral with the remaining responses divided between the memorial-type service, and what was termed a simple, inexpensive funeral.

The replies to the question regarding the specific duties of the funeral director were consistent with the information exterior to the study regarding the opinions of the memorial group. For instance, almost two-thirds of the memorial respondents indicated that the funeral director should attend to the specifically physical and service aspects of the funeral such as embalming the body, and taking care of the legal and social notices. In the majority of cases, the householders concurred in this opinion, but much in the manner of the Catholic clergy of a prior study they also suggested that the funeral director had a role as comforter to play.[1] The remainder of the memorial replies ranged from seeing the funeral director relieving the families of details as requested to expressing the belief that the funeral director had no function whatsoever in the funeral. Of importance here is the fact that almost one-quarter of the householders failed to reply to this question.

With respect to the status of the funeral director, the study showed that exactly one-half of the householders viewed him dualistically, that is, as a man who combines a professional service with a business service. Approximately one-quarter of the householders saw his status beyond that, as high or almost as high as a doctor or lawyer. Twenty per cent of the group saw him as having the status of a businessman, while 3% considered his status in the community lower than that of a businessman.

The memorial group, on the other hand, reported in almost half of the cases that they saw the funeral director as a businessman. Approximately one-third reported that they believed that the funeral director combines both the professional and businessman role. Nine per cent viewed him as someone whose standing in the community was not as high as a businessman's, while 7% saw him professionally as high or almost as high as a doctor or lawyer.

The study showed that among the householders there was a more favorable attitude toward the funeral director than toward the funeral ceremony. For instance, slightly less than half of the group reported that they were favorably disposed toward present-day funerals, compared to 60% who viewed the funeral director favorably. This tendency is also observed among the memorial respondents, even though they, in the majority of cases, are unfavorably inclined toward both the funeral and the funeral director.

Another important aspect of the study concerned the matter of funeral costs and judgments as to what constitutes a reasonable price for funerals. As it turned out, there was a notable lack of information among most of the participants of this study concerning the actual costs of funerals. The question of reasonable price was as difficult to answer for these groups of respondents as it was for the clergy of the previous study. The query on the questionnaire asked: "What do you consider a reasonable price to pay for a funeral?" Following this question there was a statement which read: "Please check each service and/or expense this sum would include." The list provided included these items: funeral director's services (including casket), flowers, grave opening and closing expenses, and, finally, a monument or marker. In recording the replies to this question the attempt was made to find out exactly what a "reasonable price" indicated by the respondent included. Thus, in the analysis, reasonable price was broken down for each particular item or combination of items indicated by the respondent. Differences are so great between the two groups, however, that such a detailed analysis need not be presented here. Rather a general statement will suffice. Forty-two per cent of the memorial group considered a reasonable price for a funeral to be something under $300 regardless of what it included. This price may include funeral directors services or it may include every item or expense that would normally be involved in the burial or disposition of a body. Altogether, 68% of this group considered a reasonable price to be under $600. Members of the householder group, however, responded differently. While 32% indicated a reasonable price to be less than $600, 14% checked a price over $600, but under $900. Twenty-seven per cent quoted as reasonable funerals costing more than $900.

Of particular significance, especially in the light of publicized charges of so-called exploitation, and the presumed public concern over funeral costs, is the fact that when the respondents were asked: "What would be the average price for a funeral in your community?" "in your state?," or "in the United States?" we found that 78% of the householders gave no answer with respect to the community, 90% gave no answer with respect to the state, and 91% gave no answer with respect to the United States. To a lesser extent the same held true for the memorial group. Forty-three per cent failed to answer the question with respect to the community, 78% with respect to the state, and 83% with respect to the United States. The implications of these findings will be discussed later in this report.

This study showed like that of the previous clergy study that more people think the funeral director exploits or takes advantage of a family's grief than say they have personal knowledge of such incidents. As can be expected the memorial group leads with the highest percentage of those who feel there is such exploitation, but even many of them indicate no actual knowledge of such.

The dual role the funeral director plays in American society was shown by the large percentage of individuals who did not believe it unethical for a funeral director to advertise his services, but yet felt, many of them, that he should not advertise his prices.

With the question of funeral arrangements we found that people in general think little about doing something about that which will follow their own death. Except for the memorial group, very few reported they had made plans with a funeral director for their own funeral. However, a considerable number replied in the affirmative when asked whether they liked the idea of someone arranging and financing a funeral in advance of death.

Finally, in this regard, the question, "Would you prefer to see funeral arrangements handled through a representative of a government agency?" elicited a "no" response from a large majority of all who participated in the study.

Regional Comparisons

Another part of the study dealt with a regional comparison of the attitudes of the householders. That phase of the study showed that with two exceptions, the Pacific region, i.e., Oregon, Washington, and California, and the East North Central region, i.e., Illinois, Indiana, Michigan, Ohio, and Wisconsin, there were no important differences in attitude among the regional replies of the householders and certainly no consistent pattern in the differences that did occur as is the case for the two regions excepted.

An analysis of the responses to all of the major questions showed a pattern of replies which for the East North Central area is more favorable toward the modern funeral and the funeral director than is the case for all the other Census regions.

On the other hand, the study showed that the Pacific region, in sharp contrast, was almost without exception more critical of modern-day funeral practices and the funeral director than the various regions, either alone or taken together. For example, in the East North Central region many respondents said it was unethical for a funeral director to advertise his prices. They described the practice in such terms as "unprofessional," "mercenary," "undignified," "barbaric," and "in poor taste." On the other hand, most of the Pacific region respondents believed it proper for a funeral director to price advertise. In the minds of this latter group such practice not only supposedly eliminates exploitation but also is proper because funeral service is regarded as "just a business."

The differences in the replies between these two groups of respondents seems to suggest to some degree a difference in attitude toward people as well as toward the funeral and the funeral director. Many more people in the Pacific region were favorably inclined toward the prefinancing of funerals than in the East North Central area. But most important, those individuals who rejected the idea of prearranged, prefinanced funerals gave such reasons for their reply as "the living know what to do," or "the family may wish to do it," or "the family should do it."

How do we account for these contrasts by region? An analysis of the demographic characteristics of the sample by region hinted at a partial answer. The analysis showed that while there were no differences of a statistical nature between the two regions regarding age, sex, or employment, there were significant differences with respect to education, income, and religious affiliation. The analysis showed that the residents of the Pacific region reported higher educational accomplishments on the whole than their counterparts from the East North Central region, particularly at the college graduate level. Income for the respondents of the Pacific region showed graphically a peculiar U-shaped curve with an unusual number reporting average incomes below $6000 per year and above $12,000. The East North Central respondents, to the contrary, were clustered in the $6000 to $12,000 income range. It was with religious affiliation, however, that the attitudinal differences between the two regions were most clearly explained and the significance of the data made apparent. Religious affiliation or its absence was from the analysis of all the data collected, the pivotal factor around which the attitudes expressed in this study revolved. The East North Central region, for example, reported religious affiliation as follows: Catholic 36%, Protestant 54%, Jew 3%, Unitarian 0.8%, nonaffiliated 6%. For the Pacific region, on the other hand, religious affiliation is reported quite differently: Catholic 18%, Protestant 55%, Jew 5%, Unitarian 2%, and nonaffiliated 20%.

The study as a whole showed that favorable responses toward funerals and funeral directors varied strongly with religious affiliation, with Catholics most often reporting favorable replies followed by Protestants, Jews, nonaffiliated, and Unitarians, in that order. As then could be expected, most critical attitudes were expressed by the Unitarians with the percentage lessening in the following order: nonaffiliated, Jews, Protestants, and Catholics.

Before concluding this point, caution should be observed from arriving at too ready an explanation for the differences in attitude between the two regions. Although compensation can and should be made for the differences in education, income, and religion, these factors are not sufficient in themselves to explain the pronounced differences found. We must be prepared to look elsewhere—to the funeral practices of the two areas as well as to the regional variation in the function and activities of the funeral director himself—if we are to understand the significance of these findings.

It is well to comment at this point on the representativeness of the opinions expressed in this study. When we look at the social and personal attributes of the memorial group and householders who make up the sample, two very different and distinct profiles emerge.

Briefly, the householders are, on the whole, younger than the memorial respondents. Forty-six per cent of the householder group are 39 years of age or younger, while 40% of the memorial group are 60 years of age or older.

Seventy-three per cent of the householders are men, compared to 59% of the memorial group.

Seventy-five per cent of the memorial group report occupations of a professional, managerial, technical, or proprietary nature, compared to 45% for the householders.

Although both groups, in approximately a quarter of the cases, reside in cities of 1,000,000 or more, 56% of the memorial respondents, compared to 22% of the householder group, show residence in cities of less than 100,000. In contrast, approximately half of the householders live in cities with populations ranging between 100,000 and 1,000,000.

Forty-nine per cent of the memorial group report residence in the Western and Pacific regions of the United States, with another 38% showing residence in the North Central area. In contrast, the householders are distributed somewhat evenly throughout the country.

The results for the question on education show that 65% of the householders reported no education beyond high school. This compares to 50% of the memorial group who reported a graduate degree.

The contrast in the social characteristics of the two groups is seen further with the question of religious affiliation. The percentages are: Catholic, memorial 1%, householder 25%; Protestant, memorial 36%, householder 56%; Unitarian, memorial 37%, householder 2%; Jew, memorial 4%, householder 7%; nonaffiliated, memorial 22%, householder 10%.

With the question on how religious a person are you, the statistical differences in the replies shown thus far in our analysis are continued. While approximately 23% of both groups fall into the category "very religious," only 38% of the memorial group, compared to 59% of the householders reported being "somewhat religious." On the other hand, 22% of the memorial group reported "no religious affiliation" compared to 6% for the householder group.

Finally, these differences are continued into the question on church attendance with the householders indicating attendance at church "once a week" or more in 46% of the cases. This compares with 32% of the memorial membership. At the other extreme, 15% of the memorial respondents reported no church attendance whatsoever, compared to 7% for the householders.

Only 1% of both groups reported never having seen a dead body.

The analysis showed that 55% of the householders had attended a funeral within the year, as compared to 43% of the memorial group. Of particular interest and significance is the fact that 13% of the memorial group reported not having attended a funeral in more than ten years, compared with only 4% for the householder group. Given the range of social contacts that can be assumed for the members of the memorial group by virtue of their professional status, and the fact that they have a much larger proportion of people over the age of 60 than do the householders, this finding suggests that some attitudes toward the modern funeral expressed here are based on something other than personal experience.

Interview Group

In this study, in order to probe more deeply and to talk personally with people, personal interviews were conducted around the country. When the replies from these interviews were compared with the householders' responses and looked at overall, the statistical differences found between them gave way before a pattern of agreement. That is, the differences found were essentially those of degree rather than kind. The interview group were more traditional in their views and less critical in their assessment of funerals and funeral directors than were the householders; however, compared to the replies of the memorial group, the differences between the householders and interview group were indeed slight.

A brief look at some national statistics is sufficient to tell us that the memorial group membership, which reported the most extreme and critical attitudes toward modern funeral practices in this study, is indeed a select minority in the areas of income and education.

The Bureau of the Census reports that the average national income for 1960 was $6900. The study showed an average income for the memorial group of $14,117. Census statistics show also that the average number of school years completed for the American population is 10.5 years. This compares with 16.5 years for the memorial group.

And what of the householder and interview groups? The study showed that these groups, too, can report more school years completed, 12.1 years, and 13.2 years, respectively, and higher average incomes, $9719 and $7244, respectively, than reported by the census for the American population as a whole. Moreover, the statistical comparison of the householder and interview responses showed that while we were dealing with the same general population, the householder respondents represented, on the whole, a group more critical of the modern funeral program, excepting, of course, memorial society members, than would be found generally in any community. This is indicated by the nature and direction of the replies of the householder and interview groups to the questions asked them, and by the analysis of their demographic data.

Discussion

Death in such a secularly oriented society as ours is no longer the wages of sin; the medical insinuation is that it is the wages of loose living. The fear of death no longer is the fear of judgment but, psychiatrically, the expression of a neurotic personality. Modern America with its emphasis upon youth, health, sports cars, long vacations, and longevity has come to view death as an infringement upon the right to life and upon the pursuit of happiness. And how do we cope with death? As never before we choose to disguise it and pretend the meanwhile that it is not the basic condition of all life. There is no doubt that along with this temporal-mindedness and scientific scepticism in America is the suppression of the idea and presence of death.

Examples of death as taboo are readily cited: except among the aged, death is not considered an open or polite topic of conversation; some newspapers segregate it by devoting special pages to it while seeing to it that no mention of death appears in the society column; the dead are hidden from view as quickly as possible and removed to a funeral home as soon as a funeral director can be summoned; children are protected from direct contact with, and observations of, death and the dead.

Euphemisms and techniques of avoidance, however, are not the sole prerogatives of the general public. On the contrary, those very professional groups—doctors, nurses, and funeral directors— who occupy sensitive if not strategic positions in both the attitude formation and crisis situation of death, also practice the art of disguise in the observance of their professional ministrations. Medical practitioners tend to make death seem unreal by referring to it with such phrases as "the death stimulus," "catastrophic diseases," and the "terminally-ill patient," while the funeral director will invite you to view a "life-like" body resting peacefully in a "slumber room."

Complementing these evasions and euphemisms is society's expectation of stoical acceptance of death. The expression of grief or sympathy for a death is limited to time and place. The dramaturgy of death moves inexorably and expeditiously to a conclusion—often only three days. Within a week one is expected to be back on the job.

Within such a context the funeral director finds himself caught between conflicting demands: on the one hand, he is encouraged to mitigate the reality of death for the survivors who may no longer receive the emotional support once provided by theology to deal with it; on the other hand, he is impelled to call attention to the special services he is rendering. If he is to justify his role as an important functionary in death he must focus attention on the body. In so doing, however, he invites the anger and hostility of a society that is experiencing a growing need to repress death.

A significant development paralleling certain of the attitudes expressed in this study is the vigorous assault upon all sacred and traditional ceremony. There is an increasing tendency for modern man to believe that sacred ceremony is out of date. It is, he believes, empty, artificial, and wasteful of time and money.

However, if we look beyond ritual and rite for a moment, we see that ceremony traditionally not only related man to his God or to the sacred in the way of a sacrifice but also to his fellow man in the form of a gift—to be given and received. Ceremony is the link between the sacred, society, and the individual. For whatever else it does, ceremony permits man not only to reestablish the purity of the relationship between himself and the sacred but also between himself and his fellow man. With the exchange of gifts on such ceremonial occasions as Christmas, Easter, Halloween,

New Year's, a birthday, or wedding, graduation, Bar Mitzvah, or a funeral, man declares his love for his fellow man.

One has only to cite a few instances of this principle of the gift to establish its reality. Traditionally, New Year's is not only a time of stock taking but also a time for the payment of past debts. Christmas, the wedding, and the funeral are characterized not only by the exchange of gifts but also by the setting aside or resolution of old quarrels and hostilities. Halloween, for instance, has traditionally allowed children to express their anger and hostility toward adult authority just as Mardi Gras or Carnival held each year throughout many parts of the world permits a time for man to vent his anger and frustrations toward society as well as toward his fellow man with little fear of retaliation.

We must appreciate that our traditional ceremonies have, and can, serve two social-psychological functions; one, the controlled expression of anger and hostility and two, the lessening of guilt or anxiety.

Freud, Klein, Lindemann, and others have commented upon the presence of anger and guilt in the face of a death and the difficulty the individual faces in unburdening himself of these deep-seated emotions. But if our traditional ceremonies for dealing with death are relegated to the ashcan of history as modern society threatens through its denigration or commercialization of them, what ways does modern man have to alleviate his guilt? In the case of death, Lindemann suggests, it will make its appearance in the form of duodenal ulcers and chronic colitis, or, express itself outwardly in aggressive and hostile acts toward society, as Shoor and Speed have proposed.

However, our society offers still another alternative solution to this problem of grief and guilt, that is, the retirement city. Complementing the memorial society movement which seeks to remove the body from the funeral, the retirement city movement promises to remove those most likely to die from our communities before they do so. Such a development in modern life allows us for the first time to avoid almost entirely the grief and anguish of death. Familial and friendship ties blunted by time and separation are loosened and thus, as we are emotionally separated from the aged members of our family or group, we are freed of the anguish and shock we would otherwise experience when they die.

The findings of this study show that the memorial group in American society exemplifies the trend toward the rational and pragmatic control over one's life and environment. Thus, we found that, of the three groups polled, they were the most extreme in their desire to eliminate or reduce funeral costs and to preplan their funerals. They approved of price advertising, offered their bodies for scientific research, advocated cremation, and avoided the ritual and ceremony of the funeral. Since this group reported such high educational attainments, the greatest percentage of professional occupations, and an annual income twice that of the average American family, as well as the least traditional religious affiliation, they could well represent a new image of modern man.

However, rational thought and scientific scepticism are confounded by death, so we found that this same group was the most anxious of the three groups to avoid or disguise its presence or possibility. This is demonstrated by such findings as their desire to eliminate the body from the funeral, their greater avoidance of funerals, and their greater reluctance to permit their children to attend a funeral ceremony. It is worthy of note that such a finding as the latter is inconsistent with all that characterizes the style of child rearing of professional and progressive groups such as this. Typically, families of the social, professional, and intellectual level of the members of the memorial group strive to bring their children up in a world of reality through the discouraging of such phantasies as ghosts, hobgoblins, Santa Claus, and the bogies of sex. Nevertheless, in this setting they appear to behave contrary to form and seek to shield the ultimate truth from their children.

The recommended absence of flowers at funerals and the appeal that substitute gifts of money be made to charities, research foundations, and so on, suggests a second break with the rationale, and gives added weight to the discussion earlier regarding the need to exchange gifts on such an occasion as death.

What must be recognized here is that whether one offers flowers, food, money, or whatever to the dead or in the name of the dead, he is still behaving irrationally from the point of view of his own best interest. While a church or charity might benefit from such an offering, the most rational and practical thing for a modern functional realist to do would be to make no offering or gift at all, but to keep his money. That such substitute gift giving is recommended by memorial societies and their members suggests that death creates powerful emotions within us that need be vented or calmed.

It is with this finding that we come upon the recognition that the funeral itself is a gift—both given and received by the deceased and by his survivors. Once this is understood it is possible to account for the fact that over half of the cremations in this country every year take place on the Pacific coast. Cremation in America could well be the result of anger, rather than of philosophy or economy. When we reflect upon the fact that some of the aged in this country are no longer welcome in the homes of their children and are no longer secure in the belief that with age comes respect, we can appreciate why they would uproot themselves from their families, friends, and their established place in the local community and flee in unprecedented numbers to retirement cities and other locales on the Pacific Coast which are literally as well as figuratively on the edge of American society. By denying their children or other relatives the opportunity to give them the gift of the funeral at their deaths, they give vent to their hostility and resentment toward a society that has rejected them.

The responses indicating a belief that funeral directors overcharge for their services may be attributable in part to the fact that the so-called practical man in modern secular society, detached from his traditional past, no longer accepts the value of sacrifice or the virtue of a nonutilitarian gift. It is of interest here to mention that statistics suggest that people are prepared to pay for a wedding, on the average, twice what they pay for an average funeral, and this without benefit of "wedding insurance." We know of only one published statement condemning the uneconomical behavior of parents at this festive occasion and know of no charges publicly made of exploitation by the dressmaking industry, catering industry, or Brewers Association of America in connection with the wedding.

Further, the public may feel hostile toward the funeral director because of the role he plays. The guilt generated by desire on the part of the bereaved to rid themselves quickly of the body and by the death itself, the possible confusion and anxiety in the selection of the "right" casket, and the attitude toward the funeral director as the constant reminder and associate of death, prompt the public to lash out at him.

The fact that the criticism expressed here has taken this form in particular is in no little part due to the contradictory nature of the pricing policy observed among funeral directors as they emphasize one or the other of the two roles accorded them by the public.

Professional service is historically "the laying on of the hands" by a person "wrapped in the cloak of a sacred office," such as the priest, doctor, professor, and lawyer. His "blessing" is the same for all. There are no distinctions. Extreme unction administered by a priest is the same for a prince as for his retainer; so, too, the ministrations of the doctor or the counsel of the lawyer. One pays according to his ability to do so. Thus, the concept "noblesse oblige" refers to the duty that the superior person must observe in extending succor, charity, or protection to his inferior. The wealthy man knows that the fee charged him by the doctor permits the doctor to extend his skills to the poor. Other employment, such as that of the laborer, plumber, or mechanic, is quite different. It is on a *quid pro quo* basis—a time and item accounting is demanded and the rich man expects to pay no more for labor or similar services than the poor.

Funeral service is caught today between the pricing policies that reflect these two rationales. This can be observed, on the one hand, with the practice of many funeral directors quoting a minimum-priced funeral for the general public while making special arrangements for the poor or indigent. On the other hand, a *quid pro quo* service is found where funeral services are offered in every price range ("ninety-nine dollars and up" advertising).

The troubles presently experienced by medicine, law, and dentistry, as well as by funeral service, in this regard, reflect the confusion that these two pricing policies create in the public mind and serve to point up once more the dialogue of conflict between the sacred and secular traditions in America.

References

1. Robert Fulton, "The Clergyman and the Funeral Director: A Study in Role Conflict," *Social Forces*, 39 (1961), p. 320.

Wendell M. Swenson

Attitudes toward Death Among the Aged

We, in America, proudly label ourselves a youthful nation; but within our structure there exists an interesting and somewhat paradoxical fact—we are a rapidly aging population. Man's life span

Reprinted from *Minnesota Medicine*, 42 (1959), pp. 399–402, by permission of the author and publisher.

continues to increase in a spiral fashion. At the time of Christ, human life expectancy was said to be about twenty years. During the American Colonial period that expectancy had increased to thirty-five years. In 1850 man could expect to live about forty years, and now we hold hopes for a seventy-year life span. Today about 9 per cent of our U.S. population is over the age of sixty-five. This problem is obviously significant from the point of view of the medical sciences—especially when one discovers that 72 per cent of individuals over age sixty-five report at least one chronic illness.

The gerontic population with all its complexity and variability does have one common experience to be anticipated—death. The temporal aspect of life is perhaps one of the most empirically tested scientific facts known to man. A half-century ago death came earlier in the human race, and the death process was experienced mostly in a sudden or traumatic manner by individuals gainfully employed or otherwise functioning well in society. Now, in the middle of the twentieth century, death commonly comes to individuals who have long since been retired from active social participation and are physically or psychologically incapacitated—presumably giving them considerable time to contemplate death as an impending experience. This development poses a number of rather stimulating questions—What are some of the characteristics of this "death contemplation"? Does it exist in all individuals? If so, can it be measured? Do millions of gerontic individuals all have the same ideas concerning death? In what manner do they deal with the problem? As they grow less and less productive in our society, do they have less and less a desire to live?

The medical sciences seem to have a singular goal or aim which cuts across lines of both research and clinical medicine—to preserve human life as long as possible. Hospitals of many types are now devoting wards or even buildings to the collocation of elderly people who, by present standards, have no useful place in our culture, but still do not die.

As the general practitioner begins to spend more time with the care and treatment of the geriatric patient, he no doubt becomes more sensitized to this problem area. A number of queries here would seem pertinent. How much does the geriatric patient think about death, if he thinks of it at all? Does he tend to fear the death experience, look forward to it, or repress it completely from his conscious thought? What role should the family physician play in discussing the possibilities of death with either the patient or his relatives? Should the physician assume that his geriatric patient is suffering from a relatively intractable fear of the death experience or can he conclude that elderly individuals have resolved the problem of death? Just how much is anxiety of death related to either vague or well-defined psychosomatic complaints of the patient?

In an attempt to answer these and many other related questions, this investigator recently set out to measure the attitudes about death of a large number of gerontic individuals. . . .

Method

The present investigation, described here, involves an attempt to obtain an objective measure of the death attitudes of a reasonably good cross section of aged individuals. A brief description of the procedure follows.

1. Thirty-four individuals, over age fifty, were asked to place their immediate thoughts concerning death into the form of a brief essay. This material was methodically screened for descriptive statements about death. Thirty-five of these descriptive statements evolved from the screening process and were used to measure the death attitudes in the larger group to be studied. The descriptive statements in this thirty-five-item check list fell rather clearly into three major categories describing death: first, a group of *positive or forward looking* attitudes exemplified by such statements as "it will be wonderful," "promise of a new and better life," and "all troubles will be over"; second, an *evasive* attitude toward death exemplified by such statements as "don't think about it," "have nothing to do with the subject," and "feel fine and no reason to think about it"; and third, a *fearful* attitude toward death exemplified by such statements as "the end of everything," "terror overcomes me," and "dread the thought of it."

2. This Death Attitude Check List was presented to more than 200 individuals, all over the age of sixty years. The subjects were obtained from three separate sources: (*a*) homes for the aged, (*b*) so-called golden age clubs, and (*c*) a number of industries and companies employing individuals over the age of sixty years.

3. On the basis of their responses to the Check List the subjects were divided into three rather well-defined groups—those looking

forward to death positively, those avoiding any thought of death, and those fearing the death experience.

4. These derived groups were analyzed to determine the relationship, if any, between attitude toward death and certain measurable physical and social characteristics. One general assumption was made—the closer the proximity of death through age, illness, loss of relatives, and so forth, the more acceptant or positive would be the individual's death attitude, that is, the more he would welcome or look forward to death. Some specific predictions are implicit in this general statement.

Age. The older the individual, the more positive and acceptant will be his attitude toward death.

Physical Condition. The poorer the individual's physical condition, the more positive will be his attitude toward death.

Home Living Conditions. The more solitary a man's home situation and the less his financial security, the more he will look forward to death.

Religiosity. The more fundamental one's religion and the greater his religious activity, the more positively he will look forward to death.

Results

Tabulation of the results revealed the following general breakdown of the subjects with regard to their death attitudes.

1. Almost half the group (45 per cent, admitted to a positive or forward-looking attitude toward death.

2. Also almost half the group (44 per cent) were distinctly evasive in their attitudes, indicating they preferred not to think about death.

3. Only a small and relatively insignificant number (10 per cent) admitted to having any fear of the death experience.

Some specific predictions were made with regard to the relationship between death attitudes and age, physical condition, home living conditions, and religiosity. Using accepted statistical techniques, the significance of these relationships was determined. A brief résumé of the results follow.

By far the most significant relationship was found in the individuals' religious beliefs and activities and their death attitude.   Persons engaged in frequent religious activity or demonstrating a fundamentalist type of religion evidenced a very positive or forward-looking death attitude, whereas those with little religious activity or interest either evaded reference to death or feared it.

The second most significant relationship occurred with regard to the subjects' living conditions and their death attitudes.   Individuals residing in homes for the aged commonly looked positively toward the death experience.   Individuals living with spouse or alone tended to evade the issue of death.   There was some evidence to suggest that a fear of death was found most commonly in those individuals who lived alone outside a rest home.

The relationship between death attitude and level of education, and condition of health, was of much less intensity and showed only suggestive significance.   The more educated subjects (college trained) either looked forward positively toward death or feared it, whereas the less educated (grade school) were evasive and preferred not to think of it.   In other words, the educated individual faced the problem of death—either looking forward to it or fearing it, and the less educated individual avoided considering it.   With regard to the relationship of general health to death attitude, the evidence suggested that those individuals admitting to good health were actively evasive in the consideration of death, whereas, those indicating poor health tended to have a positive or forward-looking attitude.

No relationship could be demonstrated between type of death attitude and sex, age, occupational status, or source of income.

Discussion and Implications

Let us now re-examine the essential results of the study with a consideration of more practical conclusions to be drawn from the data, especially with respect to their possible application to the practice of geriatric medicine.

1. The first and perhaps most significant result of this investigation is that it has demonstrated that death attitudes can be objectively measured with a structured psychometric device.   It now seems neither necessary nor scientifically practical to attempt to determine a person's attitude toward death by devious or indirect

methods—through the "tapping of the unconscious." It is apparent that to obtain a "death attitude" from an individual, one need merely ask some direct questions about it.

2. Fear of death tends to be relatively nonexistent in the conscious thought of the aged. At least the average gerontic individual does not consciously admit a fear of death. He either looks forward to it or evades any reference to it. For the physician treating the geriatric patient, this problem of conscious fear of death, then, need not necessarily be considered as serious. It is reasonable to assume that the average geriatric patient has either developed a philosophy of life which makes death a fairly pleasant positive experience, or he has repressed beneath the level of consciousness any concern about it.

3. Religion and religious activity apparently play a very intrinsic role in the gerontic individual's concept of death. Positive or forward-looking death attitudes were found most frequently in the actively religious group. The obvious conclusion here is that the person of firm Christian beliefs or convictions has a more positive religious orientation and therefore looks forward to the experience of death. This facet of the problem seems pertinent in the practice of geriatric medicine—a knowledge of an individual's religious convictions and habits may well give the physician distinct clues as to the amount of conscious fear of death existing in his patient.

4. Individuals living in homes for the aged look forward positively to death much more than do certain noninstitutionalized gerontic people, whereas those living alone tend to fear the prospect of death. It is apparent that living a solitary existence in old age is associated with a more negative or fearful concept of death. Fear of death, then, seems to be related to solitude. One can infer from these results that older individuals living under relatively normal circumstances, that is, with husband, wife, or other relative, do not concern themselves with the process of death and therefore neither look forward to it nor fear it. Avoidance of death contemplation seems to be associated with the more normal type of social environment.

5. The possible implications of the slight relationship between educational level and death attitudes are of interest. As has been indicated, the individual with relatively little education seems to give less concern to the problem of death (perhaps not understanding its complexity), and, therefore, wants no part of discussing it. The educated person, having confronted the problem directly,

has either resolved it through some sort of religious or philosophic adjustment, or has become frustrated in dealing with the concept and has yet met with no solution—thereby fearing the death experience.

6. One final observation with regard to the discovery of positive relationships. It is apparent from the data that individuals in poor health tend to actually look forward to death more than fear it. It seems reasonable to infer, then, that the physician treating the terminal geriatric patient need not assume any predominant fears in his patient, but rather expect the existence of rather well-organized, positive, forward-looking attitudes toward death. The fact that individuals in good health avoid contemplation of death no doubt reflects the obvious fact that they have simply not yet found the immediate necessity of perusing it.

7. The negative results of this study are also of some significance. Chronologic age, itself, seems to have no value in predicting thoughts concerning death, and there is no evidence of a sex-difference in contemplation of death.

References

1. K. R. Eissler, *The Psychiatrist and the Dying Patient*, (New York: International Universities Press, 1955).
2. J. P. Warbasse, "The Ultimate Adventure," *Geriatrics*, II (1956), 468.
3. P. Williamson, "Fear in elderly people," *Journal American Geriatrics Society*, 1 (1953), 739-742.
4. W. G. Klopfer, "Attitudes toward Death in the Aged," Unpublished M.A. Thesis, City College of New York, 1947.
5. H. Feifel, "Older Persons Look at Death," *Geriatrics*, 11 (1956), 127-130.

Irving E. Alexander and Arthur M. Adlerstein

Affective Responses to the Concept of Death in a Population of Children and Early Adolescents

The child's concern with death has been a part of most parents' experience. Several psychologists, in recording various aspects of development in children, including their own, have discussed this

Reprinted from *The Journal of Genetic Psychology*, 93 (1958), pp. 167–177, by permission of the authors and publisher.

topic briefly.[1] More controlled observations on the subject of the child and death are very scarce in the psychological literature both in this country and abroad.

Perhaps the most comprehensive piece of work was done by Sylvia Anthony. In an excellent and much neglected book[2] she summarizes a series of investigations carried out in prewar England over a two-year period. Children between 3 and 13 years of age were studied with a variety of techniques, including parents' written accounts of their children's spontaneous interest in death, a story-completion test, and an intelligence test in which material relevant to death appears.

Anthony found that death thoughts are frequent in children's fantasies. Roughly 50 per cent of the children tested on the story completion task made reference to death in completing their stories, although the concept did not appear in the story stem. Five stages in children's thoughts about death were distinguished. These ranged from ignorance of the meaning of the word to clear definition in logical or biologically essential terms. By the fifth or sixth year there is meaning attached to the word but rarely in terms of the latter criteria. By the eighth or ninth year causal-logical explanation is being used to some degree by almost all children. These findings parallel those of Piaget on the development of the concept of causality.

Some years previous to this work Schilder and Wechsler[3] published the results of a study on the attitudes of children towards death. Their techniques included observations of play, spontaneous stories given to pictures, and direct questioning. The population observed consisted of 76 children between the ages of 5 and 15. Diagnostic categories included organic hyperkinetics, epileptics, mental defectives, behavior problems, and schizoids. The findings were not evaluated quantitatively, but rather were given in general statements based on the observations of the younger and approximately normal children.

These observers concluded that children deal with death realistically—in a matter-of-fact way. They do not want to die, yet they rarely express fear. They are ready to believe that others can die but do not believe their own deaths probable. The child connects death with deprivation and aggression. These latter concepts are the substructure upon which actual experience with death and dying is built. The authors offer this framework in opposition to the philosophical speculation of Heidegger that death and time are intimately related. For the child this relationship does not seem essential.

Nagy's study,[4] completed in the late 1930's in Budapest, has recently appeared in the American literature. The written compositions, drawings, and recorded discussions of children between 3 and 10 years of age were analyzed. The aim of this work was to investigate the child's *theories* concerning the nature of death. Replies to the question "What is death?" were categorized into three stages. In children under 5 death is reversible and not final. The youngest children are likely to interpret death as sleep or departure, while the 5 year old modifies this distinction by making death gradual and temporary. In the second stage, from the fifth through the ninth year, death is most often personified. It is also thought of as an aggressive event contingent upon the actions of others. The third stage, which follows, brings with it the recognition that death is a process dependent on natural laws, one which is characterized by the cessation of vital bodily activities.

Nagy's findings are similar to those of Cousinet,[5] who also distinguished three stages in children's thinking about death: (*a*) the refusal to accept the idea, (*b*) the substitution of severe but curable illness for death, and (*c*) the disappearance of death as a troublesome concept. According to this author the last stage may precede an understanding of the concept in naturalistic terms.

Several writers have been concerned with the *fear of death* in children and its origin. Anthony[6] relates it to the fear of retaliation (talionic law)—a fear of the aggression of others. In her study two kinds of anxiety about death were differentiated: chronic and critical. The first refers to a reaction from one's own aggressive impulses and is not dependent on a clear conception of the idea of death. Such a state is found in children under five. Critical anxiety is a later phenomenon appearing when the child recognizes the fact that he is an independent being and consequently can die. Schilder and Wechsler[7] state that the fear of death is rare. The child is not concerned with dying, but rather with being murdered. Chadwick[8] questions the orthodox psychoanalytic belief that the fear of death is a derivation of castration anxiety and offers the possibility that the converse may be true. Infantile separation anxiety is given as a root of death fears which serve the purpose of masking the basic wish to return to the mother. Other relationships are drawn between fear of death and conditions of physical restraint, masturbation guilt, and fear of the dark.

Harnik[9] postulates that the fear of suffocation arising from difficulty in breathing in early infancy is a possible basis for the fear of death. Caprio[10] traces neurotic death fears to early fears of the dark, intense emotional experiences at funerals, and the influence of adults with morbid superstitions about death. Rosenzweig and Bray[11] point out an interesting fact for the hypothesis that fear of death relates to extreme guilt about aggressive death wishes towards others. They found that schizophrenics experienced sibling death more often than normals in the population they studied.

Other ideas on the fear of death appear in sources not easily available. Kotsovsky[12] designates several influencing factors: fear of pain, fear of the unknown, the external unpleasant experiences associated with death and burial, and the disappointment and guilt concerning unfulfilled potential. Kotsovsky speaks of both a conscious and an unconscious fear of death. Osipov[13] calls intense fear of death a neurological symptom. It is a product of the transitional stage between the naïveté of the child and the maturity of the adult.

There seems to be reasonable agreement in these studies that the child's thinking about death progresses from a state of nonawareness of the meaning of the concept through a series of intermediate steps to a point where death is considered in logical, causal, naturalistic terms. The degree of affective involvement that children have with death is not quite so clear. On the one hand there are the statements of indifference shown by children: matter-of-factness, reality orientation, and lack of fear. At the same time there are reports of denial (in the defensive sense), morbid concern, and undue stress in fantasy production. With regard to affective arousal, the indicators used by the above investigators were gross. They were mainly clinical judgments of play, fantasy, and discussion. The data did not lend themselves easily to quantification, or to reliability or validity checks. How do children of various ages respond affectively to the idea of death? This question was the focal point of our investigation. It was our intent to approach this question with quantitative methods.

Method

1. TECHNIQUE AND RATIONALE

The essentials of the method have been reported previously. It consisted of a word association task to which response times, galvanic skin responses (GSR), and response words were recorded.

The stimulus words, 27 in all, were taken from a manual for the teaching of spelling published by the Board of Education of the City of New York.[14] The word groupings in this manual were based on word frequency counts of written English for elementary and high school children. Our final list was composed of three sets of words. Each set was equivalent to every other in terms of mean frequency of usage in the language, mean length, and number of syllables. One set was designated as "*a priori* affective," that is, words that would by general agreement be likely to arouse affect in children. These words were drawn from two general concepts, sex and family. There were six such words in all: mama, papa, child, love, married, and kiss. A second set was designated as "basal" words, that is, words with no apparent general relationship to each other or to other words on the list. These are samples from the language against which to measure our critical words. Examples of "basal" words are dress, brave, happy, star, deep, speak, animal, penny, flat etc. The third set, and critical to this experiment, were words related to one another under the superordinate heading of "death." These were buried, kill, and dead. They appeared in positions 6, 15, and 24 on one list and were preceded and followed by two "basal" words.

The rationale is as follows: the difference between response to "*a priori* affectives" and "basal" words gives us a test of the validity of our measuring technique. The crucial test is between responses to "death" words and responses to "basals." It is to be emphasized that "basal" words were by no means chosen to be affect-free as inspection will reveal. They are samples from the language, each of which can have affective meaning for any subject. Our concern is whether "death" words are responded to with greater latencies and increased GSRs than are "basal" words.

2. SUBJECTS

The subjects used in this study were 108 males between the ages of 5 and 16. The age distribution is given in Table 1.

The children were all summer campers at the Grand Street Settlement Camps, Craig's Meadow, East Stroudsburg, Pennsylvania. For the most part they were from low income families. Both Negroes (12 per cent) and whites (88 per cent) were represented in the group. None of the children were known to have psychiatric histories nor was there any reason to believe that intelligence was

Table 1

Age-frequency distribution of subjects

Age	Number
5	1
6	5
7	10
8	13
9	10
10	17
11	12
12	9
13	10
14	10
15	10
16	1

distributed atypically in any of the age groupings. Aside from trying to get a representation of children at all available ages, the only other selection criterion was willingness to serve as a subject. The selection procedure was as follows: an entire group would be scheduled for testing during one of the activity hours in a special room not used by the campers for any other purpose. The experimenters spoke to the group about the alleged purpose of the experiment—to see whether a recording machine (the Sanborn Twin-Viso Recorder Model 651-42) was adequate for measuring changes that went on inside the body. Comparisons with the stethoscope, EKG, etc., were made depending upon the experience level of the children. Following the preliminary explanation and discussion a group demonstration was held. The group counselor was used as a subject and the children observed how the Sanborn recorded and how the time record was made. In all groups great enthusiasm was displayed for being given the opportunity to be "guinea pigs." The demonstration served to allay undue anxiety about the nature of the procedure. After the demonstration volunteers were solicited and the day's testing schedule set up. The volunteer rate was roughly 95 per cent.

3. PROCEDURE

In the individual testing the subject was seated at a table opposite the experimenter. His right hand, both palm and dorsal surface, was rubbed vigorously with electrode jelly to reduce basal skin resistance.[15] The hand was then placed in a foam rubber rig that encased two zinc-plated electrodes, one attached to a wooden board secured to the table, the other to an adjustable webbed strap secured to the board. Contact between the hand surfaces and the electrodes was mediated by two foam rubber inserts dipped in a salt water solution. The advantage of this particular rig was to immobilize the hand without discomfort. A Western Electric telephone receiver housed in a sound-proofed wooden box ($6'' \times 14'' \times 6''$) was then placed close to the mouth of the subject. He was reminded to respond into the telephone receiver with the first word that came to mind when a stimulus word was presented. During this time the subject's basal resistance was gauged and balanced by use of a Wheatstone bridge technique. Four balance levels were used: 5000, 10,000, 15,000, or 20,000 ohms. Roughly 90 per cent of the subjects performed at a basal resistance level of 10,000 ohms or less. Resistance was added in series to that of the subject to bring him up to the closest balance level. This procedure allowed for the measurement of change in skin resistance from a known basal level. In the analysis of the data all responses were transformed by appropriate constants to units relative to 5000-ohm basal resistance.

The telephone receiver was employed as a voice key to interrupt a Standard electric precision timer (Model S1). This instrument, accurately read to the nearest one-hundredth of a second, was initiated manually by the experimenter upon presentation of a stimulus word. One experimenter recorded response times while the other motivated the continuous recording of the change in skin resistance. A practice word list leading into the regular list was given to settle the subjects in the apparatus. The time interval between word presentations varied between 20 seconds and one minute, depending on the rapidity of the subject's return to a resting level after responding.

Results

For purposes of analysis our subject population was divided into three subgroupings: age 5 through 8 ($N = 29$), 9 through 12 ($N = 48$), and 13 through 16 ($N = 31$). This particular division was prompted by several considerations. It seems to be one that violates least the observations that have been made about the development of logical thought in children. Piaget places the beginning of this event between the seventh and eighth years and its consistent utilization in everyday action at age 12. Anthony[16] says that between 5 and 6 children first begin to have some understanding of death. However, it is not until 8 or 9 that reference is made to logical and biological essentials in discussing the concept. Nagy[17] also distinguished the period between 5 and 9 as being a unique one in which death is usually personified. This division also corresponds roughly to parts of Sullivan's[18] developmental scheme, the stage of peer group importance (5-8), sophilic love (9-12), and the development of the lust dynamism (13). The break at 13 is in line with physical notions about adolescence, in particular the maturing of secondary sex characteristics.

Response data orginally in millisecond and millimeter units were skewed. A logarithmic transformation served to normalize the distributions. As a rough check on the validity of the technique for measuring affective arousal, difference t's between responses to "*a*

Table 2

Analysis of variance of GSR and response time scores*

| | GSR $N = 88$ | | | | Response Time $N = 108$ | | | |
Source	Sum of squares	df	Mean square	F	Sum of squares	df	Mean square	F
Treatments	.41	1	.41	4.1†	1.62	1	1.62	14.73†
Age Groups	2.69	2	1.35	.54	20.48	2	10.24	15.28†
Treatments × Age Groups	1.74	2	.87	8.7†	.21	2	.11	1.00
Subjects	213.35	85	2.51		69.93	105	.67	
Treatments × subjects	8.85	85	.10		12.01	105	.11	

* The treatments × subjects variance is used as the error term for treatments × age groups. The subjects variance is used as the error term for age groups. See Wilk and Kempthorne.[19] The N's differ for the GSR and response time measures. In 20 cases GSR records are either not obtainable or not scorable. No one subgroup contained a preponderance of these people. Individual subject means for "basal" and "death" words were based on different numbers of observations (18 and 3). This difference was handled by a weighting technique in the analysis.

† $p < .01$.

priori affective "words and "basal" words for all subjects were assessed. For both indices these differences were significant ($P_{gsr} < .01$, $P_{time} < .05$). We may therefore dispense with the "*a priori* affective*" category from further consideration. The remaining data were analyzed by the analysis of variance technique. Table 2 represents the results.

From this table it is clear that the treatment variable is significant on both response indicators. "Death" words are responded to by the total group with increased latency and decreased skin resistance. On the GSR measure the several age groups respond differently to the treatment variable, while on the response time measure the several age groups respond differently to words as a whole independent of treatment. This latter statement reflects the common observation that response time in a word association task decreases as a function of age (at least for childhood and early adolescent years). These results indicate that death is associated with an increase in affect in our total population. Now let us see how this phenomenon operates developmentally. Table 3 presents difference t's ("basal" vs. "death") for the age subdivisions.

Table 3

*t Values for word group comparisons by age groups
on both response measures‡*

Age group	GSR	Response time
5–8	1.65*	4.74†
9–12	.10	3.17†
13–16	3.47†	2.80†

* $p < .05$.
† $p < .01$.
‡ Significance values for t are estimated on the basis of a one-tailed hypothesis.

This analysis discloses that in all age groups children respond with greater latencies to "death" words than to experimentally equivalent "basal" words. For skin resistance changes the picture differs. In the youngest age group there is a significant decrease ($p < .05$) in skin resistance to "death" words and this same change is also in evidence in the adolescent group ($p < .01$). The 9 through 12 group, however, shows no reliable difference.

Discussion

In this population "death" words generally elicit indications of increased emotional response. This increase we shall attribute to both individual and cultural factors, each of which is represented differentially in our measures. There are, however, wide individual differences in response both among children and among age groups.

Of the two response indicators, the time measure is probably much more sensitive to cultural influence and this is why all groups that we have tested show longer response time to "death" words than to "basal" words. That is to say, death is not welcomed as a conversation piece in our culture regardless of one's attitudes towards the subject. It would seem that increased latency could either reflect one's own distaste for the subject or the awareness of the impact of this topic upon others. In any case the combined possibilities could account for the fact that test latency differences are found throughout the age range tested.

The GSR measure, we feel, is more sensitive to the inner feeling states of the individual, to the immediate emotional value that the stimulus has for him. One would then have to turn to both theory and observation in developmental psychology to account for the differences in response among the several age groups on this measure. What we must explain is the similarity in response for the 5 through 8 and 13 through 16 groups, and the difference between these two and the 9- through 12-year group. The most general statement we would make is that death has a greater emotional significance for people with less stable ego self-pictures than for people with an adequate concept of the self. The period from 5 through 8 has been pointed out as a trying one by many theorists. In the Freudian scheme it is the time of the resolution of the Oedipal situation, and the consequent search for a more permanent and acceptable identification figure. The superego is born and with it comes the attendant grief for the ego in learning how to cope with this harsh master. For Sullivan it is the stage in which peers become important, when new authority figures emerge, when the parental figures lose some of their omnipotence. Piaget indicates that the change to logical-causal thinking becomes evident during the seventh or eighth year. More generally this period can be seen as a time of great unheaval. In our culture it is the beginning of formal education, the emergence from the family cocoon. The changing demands are likely to put the existing self-picture to severe test and as a result the concept of nonself or death is more apt to be responded to with increased emotional intensity.

The interval from the ninth through the twelfth year has been labeled the preadolescent period, a time of latency. Measured in terms of psychological stress it is generally regarded as being a rather benign age. Roles are well defined. Aggressive outlets are sanctioned by the culture in games and activities. Complex skills develop. In short no great new demands calling for marked change in response patterns are introduced. It is, as life goes, a "Golden Age." During this period questions about death disappear from the conscious repertoire as though this matter is no longer of interest. Children at this age seem to be too much involved in the routine of life and its attendant pleasures to be concerned with the concept of death.

The adolescent years in western culture have been written about as a period of "storm and stress." The individual is called upon to be an adult at one moment, a child in the next. There is little consistency in what the culture expects of the individual. Biologically he is an adult with no social status to match. This age (our 13 through 16 group) is characterized by the search for identity. The changing and often conflicting demands made on the adolescent provide the occasion and necessity for reorganization of the self-concept. As in the 5 through 8 age period we may consider adolescence a nodal or crisis point in the life history, a time of a less stable self-picture and consequently a time when death has a greater emotional impact on the individual. This same argument, we hold, would apply to other "critical" points throughout life: marriage, menopause, old age, and states of pathology. In all these instances radical changes are demanded and death is likely to assume increased importance in the psychology of the individual.

What we are saying is that there is nothing peculiar to childhood *per se* that calls forth increased emotional response to death. It is rather that some periods of childhood are subjected to rapid and massive increases in psychological stress, and as a consequence the decrease in ego stability is likely to be reflected in increased affective responses to death.

Summary

Affective responses to "death" words were measured in a population of males from 5 through 16. A word association task was employed in which response times and changes in skin resistance were used to indicate affect. Three age subgroups are defined: 5 through 8, 9 through 12, and 13 through 16. The population as a whole shows increased emotional involvement with "death" words on both response measures. All subgroups showed significantly increased response time to "death" words. On the GSR measure, two subgroups, 5 through 8 and 13 through 16, shows significant decrease in skin resistance. No reliable differences on this measure are found in the 9 through 12 group. The results are discussed in terms of cultural expectations and ego stability.

References

1. I. E. Alexander, R. S. Colley, and A. M. Adlerstein, "Is Death a Matter of Indifference?" *Journal of Psychology*, 43 (1957), 277—283. Also see D. Katz, *Gespräche mit Kindern* (Berlin: Springer, 1928); J. Piaget, *The Language and Thought of the Child* (London: Routledge, 1952); Rasmussen, *Child Psychology*, Vol. 11 (New York: Knopf, 1922); J. Sully, *Studies of Childhood* (New York: Appleton, 1914).

2. S. Anthony, *The Child's Discovery of Death* (New York: Harcourt, Brace, 1940).

3. P. Schilder and D. Wechsler, "The Attitudes of Children towards Death," *Journal of Genetic Psychology*, 45 (1934), 406–451.

4. M. Nagy, "The Child's Theories Concerning Death," *Journal of Genetic Psychology*, 73 (1948), 3–27.

5. R. Cousinet, "L'idee de la mort chex les enfants" ("The Idea of Death in Children"), *Psychological Abstracts*, 14 (1940), 499 (*Abstract*).

6. S. Anthony, *op. cit.*

7. P. Schilder and D. Wechsler, *op. cit.*

8. N. Chadwick, "Notes upon the Fear of Death," *International Journal of Psychoanalysis*, 10 (1929), 321–334.

9. J. Harnik, "One Component of the Fear of Death in Early Infancy," *International Journal of Psychoanalysis*, 11 (1930), 485–491.

10. F. S. Caprio, "A Study of Some Psychological Reactions during Prepubescence to the Idea of Death," *Psychiatric Quarterly*, 24 (1950), 495–505.

11. S. Rosenszweig and D. Bray, "Sibling Deaths in the Anamnesis of Schizophrenic Patients," *Archives of Neurology and Psychiatry*, 49 (1943), 71–92.

12. D. Kotsovsky, "Die psychologie der todesfurcht" ("The Psychology of the Fear of Death") *Psychological Abstract*, 13 (1939), 134 (*Abstract*).

13. N. W. Osipov, "Strach ze Smrti" (Fear of Death"), *Psychological Abstracts*, 9 (1935), 534 (*Abstract*).

14. Teaching Spelling: Course of Study and Manual, Board of Education for the City of New York, Curriculum Bulletin, 1953–54, Series No. 6.

15. M. E. Bitterman, J. Krauskopf, and W. H. Holtzman, "The Galvanic Skin Response Following Artificial Reduction of the Basal Resistance," *Journal of Comparative and Physiological Psychology*, 47 (1954), 230–234.

16. S. Anthony, *op. cit.*
17. M. Nagy, *op. cit.*
18. H. S. Sullivan, *The Interpersonal Theory of Psychiatry* (New York: Norton, 1953).
19. M. B. Wilk and O. Kempthorne, "Fixed, Mixed, and Random Models," *Journal of the American Statistical Association,* 50 (1955), 1144–1166.

Paul J. Rhudick and Andrew S. Dibner

Age, Personality, and Health Correlates of Death Concerns in Normal Aged Individuals

The aim of the present study is to investigate the relationship of death concerns in a normal aged group to various sociological, psychological, and health variables.

The specific hypotheses of this study are as follows: (1) death concerns in an aged sample are related to personality factors rather than to demographic factors such as age, sex, marital status, and occupational status, in that high death concern in older persons is associated with neurotic tendencies; and (2) death concerns in an aged sample are related to attitudes about health, in that older persons who are concerned about death are concerned about their own health.

Subjects

The sample was taken from the research population of the Age Center of New England which is located in Boston, Mass. The 58 subjects can be described as healthy, well-motivated individuals who live independently in the community and who serve as voluntary participants in various research projects. The group includes both sexes, married and unmarried, working and nonworking. Table 1 presents characteristics of the sample in terms of age and education. In this group there are 30 females and 28 males. Twenty of the subjects are married and 38 are unmarried, widowed, or divorced. Thirteen members are currently employed, while 45 are retired.

Reprinted from *Journal of Gerontology,* 16 (1961), pp. 44–49, by permission of the authors and the publisher.

Table 1

Age and education of the sample

		Age (in years)		Education (in years)	
Group	N	Range	Mean	Range	Mean
I	20	60–69	65.9	9–20	13.7
II	28	70–79	74.8	5–20	13.4
III	10	80–86	82.6	6–18	13.0
Total	58	60–86	73.1	5–20	13.4

Method

Each subject completed the Minnesota Multiphasic Personality Inventory (MMPI) and the Cornell Medical Index (CMI) as a part of a "core program" of data collection at the Age Center of New England. These two questionnaires were used to assess personality factors and attitudes toward health.

Inasmuch as some investigators have alluded to the strong tendency of denial of death in questionnaire situations, the Thematic Appreciation Test (TAT) was used to minimize the possibility of such defensive behavior. In this projective test the subject is presented with a series of moderately ambiguous picture cards and is asked to make up a story about each picture. The rationale for use of fantasy productions is that the more unconscious, not readily reportable aspects of personality can be more easily expressed in story constructions than in answers to direct questions.

Twelve standard cards from the TAT were administered in the manner recommended by Murray (1943). Both sexes received cards 1, 2, 3BM, 6GF, 4, 10, 13MF and 15. In addition, the females were shown cards 7GF, 12F and 18GF; while the males were given cards 7BM, 8BM and 12M. Inasmuch as statistical analysis revealed that there were no significant differences in death concerns reported between males and females as a result of the three additional cards for each sex the findings reported in this study are based on analyses of all twelve TAT cards responded to by each subject.

In this study death concern operationally refers to the introduction of a death in the story-response to a TAT card. The reasoning is that mention of death as an integral part of the story production has some personal relevance to the respondent, and may serve as the basis for a measure of his death concern. Two judges agreed 90% in scoring for death content in a story, indicating the reliability of this measure.

It has been noted in a pilot study on a similar sample at the Age Center that certain cards frequently elicited death stories while others seldom did. It was therefore reasoned that mention of death in response to a card in which death is rarely associated must mean a greater concern with this topic than is the case where death is mentioned in response to a death-relevant card, and should be weighted accordingly. Utilizing the pilot data on 47 cases, it was determined that on cards 15, 3BM, 8BM, 13MF and 18GF death was a frequent theme or outcome. Cards 4, 6BM, 10, 12M and 12F elicited considerably fewer death references, while cards 1, 2, 6GF, 7BM and 7GF rarely prompted such responses. Accordingly a three-point scale was derived in which a rating of "1" was recorded if death was introduced on one of the first-named group of cards, and "2" and "3" respectively for the second and third groups.

The total score for a subject was simply the numerical sum of the weighted death references totaled for all twelve cards. On this basis, the lowest possible score was "0" and the maximum score was "24."

All TAT stories were rated without knowledge of the age, marital status, or occupational status of the subject. The only variable known to the rater was the sex of the respondent.

While measurement of the amount of death concern was the principal aim of the research, an additional judgment was made to indicate the extent of appearance of three types of affects in the TAT stories, *viz.*, anxiety, guilt, and depression. These measures were rated simply on a two-point scale. A rating of one was recorded if the affect was mentioned; zero if it was not. The criteria used by the raters to evaluate these affect states were the commonly accepted manifest clinical indices used in clinical evaluation of TAT protocols. Correlations between two raters in scoring for affects were .81 for anxiety, .79 for guilt, and .77 for depression, all of which are statistically significant. Two scores on each affect dimension were determined for each individual, one of the sum of affects across all cards presented to a subject, and the second the sum of affects only on those cards to which the subject responded with a story involving death. The first score is thus an indication of the general intensity of each affect for the individual, and the second score indicates which affect is associated with death concern for him.

Results

Table 2 presents characteristics of the distribution of death-concern scores for the three age groups. For the purpose of comparison of the death scores with other variables, the Median Death Score of "4" was used to separate the subjects into groups of high and low death concern.

Table 2
Distribution of death concern scores

	Death Score		
Group	Range	M	Median
I	1–10	4.9	4
II	1–12	4.2	4
III	1–8	3.6	4
Total	1–12	4.4	4

PERSONALITY FACTORS

The hypothesis relating to the importance of personality factors in relation to death concern was tested by comparing scores on certain selected scales of the MMPI with death concern scores by means of the chi-square test. The results appear in Table 3 and may be summarized as follows: (1) higher death concerns were exhibited by those subjects who also scored significantly higher on these MMPI dimensions: Hypochondriasis, Hysteria, Dependency, and Impulsivity; (2) a suggestive but not significant relationship appeared between high death concern and high score on the Depression scale; and (3) no significant relationships appeared between death concern and any of the other MMPI scales. Thus high death concern seems to be related to certain neurotic tendencies, but unrelated to the tested demographic variables.

HEALTH ATTITUDES

In order to test the hypothesis relating death concern to health attitude, the death concern scores were compared with CMI scores by means of the chi-square test. The scores on the CMI were the number of "yeses" checked in each section. For sections A-L the median was 12; for sections M-R the median was 3; and for all sections, the median was 19. (The median was used to differentiate high and low scorers.) Results showed that (1) those individuals who report a multitude of physical symptoms (CMI sections A-L) exhibit significantly more death concern than those who admit to fewer somatic complaints; (2) those subjects who list more psychiatric complaints (CMI sections M-R) manifest more death concerns than those who check few or no psychiatric symptoms; (3) those subjects who admit both to more physical and psychological disturbance show higher death concerns significantly more than those who list fewer such health complaints.

AFFECT STATES

Ratings of affects across all cards for a subject (general affect-tendencies) were compared with affect ratings on only those cards in which the subject mentioned death. These sets of ratings were almost perfectly positively correlated. There were no statistically significant differences as to the kinds of affects that accompanied the TAT productions, whether or not a death was mentioned.

The type of affective state most frequently appearing was depression. Guilt and anxiety occurred approximately equally, and about half as frequently, on the average, as depression in that order. These proportions remained constant for the different age groups and for the two sexes.

Tests were then made of the relationship between death concern and affect. The findings are shown in Table 3. Concern about death in these older persons seems to be accompanied by depressive affect rather than by anxiety or guilt.

Table 3
Relationship of death concern to MMPI personality measures,
health attitudes and affect states

Variable	N^*	Significance Level of Chi-Square Tests†
Demographic Factors:		
age	58	N.S.
sex	58	N.S.
occupational status	58	N.S.
marital status	58	N.S.
education	58	N.S.
Personality Factors (MMPI):		
Hypochondriasis	47	$P < .01$
Depression	52	$P < .10 > .05$
Hysteria	52	$P < .05$
Psychasthenia	52	N.S.
Paranoia	48	N.S.
Schizophrenia	47	N.S.
Hypomania	47	N.S.
Ego Strength (Barron)	47	N.S.
Social Introversion	47	N.S.
Anxiety (Welsh)	47	N.S.
Repression—Denial (Gough)	47	N.S.
Dependency (Navran)	47	$P < .05$
Impulsivity (Gough)	47	$P < .05$
Neuroticism (Winne)	47	N.S.
Health Attitudes (CMI):		
sections A-L (physical)	58	$< .005$
sections M-R (psychiatric)	58	$< .05$
all sections (physical and psychiatric)	58	$< .025$
Affect States:		
anxiety	58	N.S.
guilt	58	N.S.
depression	58	$< .05$

* Not all subjects received all the MMPI scales because the population at the time of study was utilized simultaneously for other research projects which precluded administration of all the scales.
† One-tailed.

Discussion

These findings tend to corroborate some of those of Swenson (1958) who reported no demonstrable relationship between type of death attitude and sex, age, and occupational status. On the other hand, the results of this study suggests some relationships to certain MMPI scales which Swenson's investigation did not. Further, while Swenson suggested that more educated aged individuals face death more readily than the less educated, this research reveals no significant differences in respect to education.

Some of the inconsistencies may be resolved by reference to the difference in measuring techniques. Swenson relied on responses to questionnaire items, while this study used ambiguous projective stimuli, i.e., TAT cards. The subjects in this study were uninformed as to the particular area being studied, while Swenson's subjects were confronted with direct questions about death. Certainly some defensive behavior can be expected in the latter situation.

The lack of demonstrable relationships between death concerns as operationally defined in this study and certain demographic variables requires comment. It might have been predicted, for instance, that females would express more death concern because they tend to be more expressive in fantasy than males (Lindzey and Goldberg, 1953). While this observation may apply to certain areas which carry special social restrictions for the females, e.g., sex, it apparently does not include the concerns over death.

When the findings in relation to personality variables are examined more closely, several important suggestions emerge. The high scorers on the dimensions of Hypochondriasis (Hs), Hysteria (Hy), Dependency (Dp), and Impulsivity (Im), demonstrated significantly more death concerns than low scorers. At the same time, there were no significant relationships between death concern and the measures of hypomania, paranoia, schizophrenia, anxiety, and psychasthenia. The implication is that the profile of those subjects with high death concerns tends more to be like the neurotic than the psychotic. As May (1950) stated, "It may be that whenever concern about death arises, it is best to work first on the assumption that neurotic elements may be present. . . ."

The type of neurotic constellation suggested by these findings is that of preoccupation and withdrawal into body symptoms, dependence, affective lability, and depression. The lack of relationship of high death concern to anxiety and psychasthenia suggests that those who have preconscious death concern do not have anxiety of the free-floating or obsessive variety; rather, the anxiety tends to be attached to bodily symptoms. This statement seems to be partly corroborated by the finding on the CMI data, i.e., the more frequent the reporting of physical symptoms, the higher the death concern. It is important to note that the CMI elicits attitude toward health, not necessarily the actual physical status of the respondent. The strongest relationships are suggested by the subjects who admit to many physical symptoms on the CMI and also score high on the Hypochondriasis scale of the MMPI.

The finding that those persons who report more psychiatric symptoms on the CMI evidence more death concern than those who check fewer symptoms tends to be consistent with the neurotic pattern exhibited on the MMPI scales.

The examination of the data in relation to type of affect introduced tended to substantiate some previously reported work (Busse, 1955). The most prominent affect, of the three measured, both in cards which had death as an outcome and in those which did not, was that of depression. The fact that anxiety occurred less frequently than depression points to several possibilities: (1) it corroborates, at the projective level, the relative lack of anxiety exhibited on the MMPI; (2) it indicates that death concerns do not necessarily mean the arousal of anxiety; rather, concern over it is accompanied by some somatizing and withdrawal tendencies.

The findings suggested no variation with age in predominant kind of affect. In part this may be due to the simplicity of the measuring device, for Busse (1955) observed in his elderly subjects reported changes with age in the frequency and depth of depressive feelings.

The findings of this study are based on intragroup differences among a normal, apparently healthy, aged population. The amount and type of death concern can be inferred only from these comparisons. Further research should include a younger sample to test age differences in a longer time context than afforded by this study, perhaps aiming at some kind of developmental explanation. In addition, institutionalized aged samples might be studied because such a population could be expected to manifest different attitudes toward death, perhaps as a response to their institutional setting or as a reaction to more pathological health states. Finally, both young and old persons who are in the actual process of dying from terminal-type diseases might serve as a focus of study to assess the handling of death concerns as it is influenced by knowledge of impending death. Ideally, a study with strict controls for age, health, and mental status is needed to ferret out the kinds of complex interactive factors that contribute to death concern.

Herman Feifel

Attitudes of Mentally Ill Patients toward Death

Death themes and fantasies are especially prominent in psychopathology.[1] Ideas of death are recurrent in some neurotic patients and in the delusions and hallucinations of many psychotic patients. The stupor of the catatonic patient, for example, has sometimes been likened to a death state. Caprio[2] thinks that all nervous and mental disorders can be regarded as forms of "psychic death." Also, a number of psychoanalysts[3] are of the opinion that one of the main reasons that shock measures produce positive effects in many patients is that these treatments provide them with a kind of death-and-rebirth fantasy experience.

The major purpose of the present exploratory study is to augment the limited available data regarding the conscious attitudes toward death of mentally disturbed patients. Examination will also be made of the relationship between the adjustment level of the patients and their attitudes toward death.

Method

Hospitalized mentally ill patients were asked to indicate when they thought "people in general" were most afraid of death. They were told to rank this aspect among eight age periods ranging from childhood through old age. The life span was divided into the following categories: childhood (up to 12 years); adolescence (from 13 to 19 years); the age span from 20 on was divided into decades, the last category being 70 years and over. Directions and method of presentation were as follows:

Reprinted from *Journal of Nervous and Mental Disease*, 122 (1955), pp. 375–380, by permission of the author and publisher.

Directions?   People are more afraid of death at certain times in their lives than at others. After that period in life when you think people are most afraid of death, write the number 1; after that period which takes second place in this respect, write the number 2; until finally you write the number 8 after that period when you think people are least afraid of death.

Up to 12 years ———
13 to 19 years ———
20 to 29 years ———
30 to 39 years ———
40 to 49 years ———
50 to 59 years ———
60 to 69 years ———
70 years and over ———

With regard to the instruction to rank fear of death with "people in general" rather than themselves in mind, one of the findings of Bromberg and Schilder is pertinent. These authors discovered little difference between subjectively held attitudes toward death and those generally attributed to other persons.

The patients were also requested to (*a*) answer the question "What does death mean to you?" (*b*) draw a picture of or represent death in any way they wanted to on an 8 by 10 1/2 inch, blank sheet of paper, and (*c*) respond to the following hypothetical situations (4) concerning death: (1) If you were told you could do only one more thing before dying, what would you select to do, disregarding cost, time, effort, etc.? (2) If after death you had to return to earth in a nonhuman form, what would you choose to be? (3) If you had a year to live and $50,000 to spend, how would you spend it?

Subjects

The subjects comprised two groups of mentally disturbed patients in a Veterans NP Hospital. One group consisted of 38 acutely disturbed, closed ward patients in partial remission; the other, of 47 open ward patients diagnosed as psychoneurotic and character and behavior disorders. Patients diagnosed as schizophrenic reaction, paranoid type (79%) and schizophrenic reaction, unclassified (14%) dominated the closed ward population. Patients characterized by anxiety (20%), somatization (15%), and depressive reactions (15%) constituted the major subgroups among the open ward patients. Both groups of patients were well matched on the variables of intelligence, age, education, and occupational background. They were slightly above average in intelligence (mean I.Q.'s 104; 108), with mean ages in the middle 30's, and had completed close to three years of high school. Skilled and clerical job backgrounds prevailed in both groups. A more detailed description of both populations can be found in Feifel.[5]

Results and Discussion

FEAR OF DEATH

To determine when the patients felt people most fear death, mean ranks were computed, for both groups of patients, for each age period. Since it was thought that age might be an influencing variable, comparison was made between the ranks given the various age periods by patients under and over 35 years of age in both groups. In neither were reliable differences found. Total group average rank determinations, therefore, are reported.

Table 1 shows that both closed ward and open ward patients consider the 50's to be the time of life when people are most afraid of death. This is followed by the age period of the 40's. Death is least feared in childhood, followed by adolescence. Both groups view fear of death as increasing gradually from childhood on, reaching a peak in the 50's, and then subsiding somewhat in the 60's and 70's. The drop in the 60's and 70's may be accounted for by the feeling that some resignation or adjustment to the inevitable takes place after the 50's. It is interesting, in this regard, to note that studies of suicides[6] indicate their peak as occurring between the ages of 45 and 54 years. The incidence drops sharply thereafter, becoming rather small among persons 65 years and over.

Another way of analyzing the data is to consider the age periods ranked one (most favorable) and eight (least favorable). In this focus, Table 2 indicates that the patients in both groups rank the

Table 1

*Mean ranks of age periods when people most fear death
by closed ward and open ward patients*

	Mean Rank of Age Periods							
Group	Up to 12	13–19	20–29	30–39	40–49	50–59	60–69	70 and over
Closed ward patients (N = 38)	5.9	5.2	4.9	4.3	3.7	3.5	4.1	4.5
Open ward patients (N = 47)	6.2	5.1	4.2	4.1	4.0	3.7	4.2	4.4

Note: A mean rank of 1.0 would indicate *most* fear of death

period of the 70's and over as the time of life when people are most afraid of death, followed by childhood. The open ward patients rank adolescence and the 20's on a par with childhood in this respect. A majority in both groups select childhood as the age period when people are least afraid of death. The 70's and over age period is ranked second. Old age and childhood apparently dominate the thinking of both groups as to when people most fear and least fear death. No reliable differences exist between the groups with respect to their rankings on this score.

Table 2

*Per cent of closed ward and open ward patients ranking each age period
when people are most afraid and least afraid of death*

		Per Cent Ranking Each Age Period as Most Favorable and Least Favorable							
Group	Choice	Up to 12	13–19	20–29	30–39	40–49	50–59	60–69	70 and over
Closed ward patients (N = 38)	Most	21	5	5	8	8	8	8	37
	Least	52	5	5	3	0	0	3	32
Open ward patients (N = 47)	Most	13	13	14	6	9	11	4	30
	Least	60	2	0	2	6	0	0	30

The frequent choice of childhood as a time when people most fear death is rather surprising. Some investigators[7] hold that attitudes toward death are formed chiefly by experiences derived from the early life of the individual. Also, that children's connotations of death revolve around the idea of deprivation. Since evidence from several directions suggest that, more than average, mentally disturbed patients come from homes where they experienced early affectional deprivation and rejection, it is conceivable that in many such persons impact of the fear of death comes to the fore earlier than in most people. Another possible contributing factor is suggested in the psychoanalytic thinking that anxiety concerning death is in essence a repetition of previous childhood castration fears.[8]

Selection of the 70's and over by a good number of the patients as a time when people are least afraid of death is also somewhat unexpected. It seems related to feelings that, by that time, people know they have to die and accept the idea without much compunction; in addition, life offers older people so little, why fear death. The notion was entertained that some relationship might exist between these rankings and a specific outlook on death. Analysis of the data along this line revealed no significant relationship. There was little correlation, for example, between patients ranking the 70's and over as the time of life when people most feared or least feared death and their conception of death as representing either "peace" and "preparation for a new life," or viewing it as "the end" and "you're through." Actually, there was a slight trend for those regarding death as "the doorway to a new life" and "bringing rest" to more often rank the 70's and over as a period when people were most afraid of dying. If the rankings reflect subjective feelings to any large degree, a future investigation might concern itself with the implication that certain individuals who fear death strongly attempt to master their anxiety in this area by perceiving death as the precursor of a new kind of life.

MEANING OF DEATH

Table 3 indicates that the greatest number of patients in both groups view death with a kind of philosophic rationalization, as the inevitable, final process of life. The next predominating outlook is of a religious nature. Death represents only the dissolution of bodily life and, in reality, is the doorway to a new life. This is followed by the conception of death as a time of rest and peace,

Table 3

*Significance of the differences between response category percentages
of closed ward and open ward patients to question "What does
death mean to you?*

Category	Per Cent of Closed Ward Patients	Per Cent of Open Ward Patients	Significance of Differences between Closed and Open Ward Patients
The end; time to go; you're through	50	49	N.S.*
Preparation for another life	21	23	N.S.
Rest and peace	13	17	N.S.
Don't know anything about it; don't think about it	16	11	N.S.
	100%	100%	
Number of cases	38	47	

* Not significant at the .05 level.

a supreme refuge from the turmoil of life. It is noteworthy that
16 per cent of the closed ward patients and 11 per cent of the
open ward patients found thinking about death so anxiety-provok-
ing that they denied having any ideas at all about it. No significant
differences were found between the groups for any of the response
categories.

Reliability of the categories was determined by having an independent judge score the answers. Agreement was 91 per cent,
indicating that response classification was carried out with a high
degree of consistency. Agreement on the responses categorized in
Tables 4, 5, and 6, which are to follow, ranged from 87 per cent
to 93 per cent.

The patients' concepts of death as evidenced through their drawings were essentially similar to those indicated in Table 3. One
aspect, however, is worthy of comment. This was the frequent
depiction, in both groups, of death occurring by means of some
traumatic event, e.g., being run over by a tractor, crashing in a
plane, being shot, etc. Bromberg and Schilder have also noted this

fear of death via mutilation and dismembering in neurotic children. It is quite likely that violent conception of death mirrors self-held feelings of aggressivity toward others as well as oneself.

HYPOTHETICAL SITUATIONS

Table 4 shows how the patients respond to the hypothetical situation of doing only one more thing before dying. In both groups, most chose to do something to benefit others, e.g., "give my belongings to charity," "stop war if possible," etc. The next choice was activity of a religious nature, e.g., "to know more of God," "give my heart to God," etc. Of similar response strength was the desire to see again close family relatives and friends before dying, e.g., "I'd like to see my wife and children once more," "I'd want to be with my girl and tell her how much I really love her," "visit my uncle—he was a father to me," etc. Next was

Table 4

Significance of the differences between response category percentages of closed ward and open ward patients to hypothetical situation of "Doing only one more thing before dying"

Category	Per Cent of Closed Ward Patients	Per Cent of Open Ward Patients	Significance of Differences between Closed Ward and Open Ward Patients
Benefit others	30	34	N.S.*
Activity of religious nature	18	21	N.S.
Reunion with family, close friends, etc	18	20	N.S.
Travel	16	17	N.S.
Live better economically	13	8	N.S.
Achieve something	5	—	N.S.
	100%	100%	
Number of cases	38	47	

* Not significant at the .05 level.

Table 5

Significance of the differences between response category percentages of closed ward and open ward patients to hypothetical situation of "Returning to earth in a non-human form after death"

Category	Per Cent of Closed Ward Patients	Per Cent of Open Ward Patients	Significance of Differences between Closed Ward and Open Ward Patients
Bird	27	36	N.S.*
Domestic animals	18	29	N.S.
Tree	18	11	N.S.
Wild animals	16	2	2.3†
Nature	3	11	N.S.
Fish	—	2	N.S.
Don't know	18	9	N.S.
	100%	100%	
Number of cases	38	47	

* Not significant at the .05 level.
† Significant at the .05 level.

the wish to travel and encompass new experiences, e.g., "I'd like to see the whole country," "travel to Europe," "fly around the world," etc., followed by the desire to live better economically, e.g., "live in a new home," "spend more money on myself," etc. Last was the expression of the open ward patients to achieve something, e.g., "be a good musician," "a successful farmer," etc.

Here again there are no significant differences between the groups on their category choices. Both give priority to activities of a social and religious nature rather than to more personal pleasures. This is in marked contrast to the results reported on essentially normal adult subjects. Although the groups are not quite comparable to the patient population, the sharp difference is suggestive. The responses of the normals, to how they would act if they knew they had to die soon, emphasized self-interest and personal gratifications much more than religious and social activities. Because of their strong guilt feelings and desire for "peace of mind," mentally sick patients may have a greater need than most people to make amends to others and atone for supposed sins before dying.

Table 5 indicates the nonhuman forms in which the patients would prefer to return to earth after death. A "bird" was the major choice of both groups of patients. This was followed by the category "domestic animals," i.e., dog, horse, etc., and then by a "tree." Most of the patients selecting a bird stated they did so because "a bird can fly where it wants to—it's free," "it can soar high in the heavens," and for "long distances." It is interesting that, in a similar context, major choice of a bird was also characteristic of normals.[10] A significant difference at the five per cent level occurred in the selection of "wild animals," i.e., lion, tiger, etc. The closed ward patients selected this category reliably more often at the 5 per cent level than did the open ward patients. It appears reasonable to assume that this reflects the comparatively intenser aggressive promptings of our schizophrenic patients. In addition, there was a trend for the open ward patients to select the "nature" category, i.e., mountain, lake, etc., more often than did the closed ward patients.

Table 6

Significance of the differences between response category percentages of closed ward and open ward patients to hypothetical situation of "Spending $50,000 with only one year to live"

Category	Per Cent of Closed Ward Patients	Per Cent of Open Ward Patients	Significance of Differences between Closed Ward and Open Ward Patients
Help intimates	31	34	N.S.*
Charity	27	22	N.S.
Personal pleasures	19	20	N.S.
Travel	17	17	N.S.
Achieve something	3	7	N.S.
Pay off debts	3	—	N.S.
	100%	100%	
Number of cases	38	47	

* Not significant at the .05 level.

Quite a few of the patients in both groups blocked on this hypothetical situation, responding with "I don't know." Although the difference was not significant, twice as many closed ward as open ward patients avoided directly answering the question. To some extent, this probably reflects greater difficulty dealing with future events on a symbolic level. Two patients of the Catholic faith felt the question was "blasphemous" and stated they could not answer it. They were included in the "don't know" category.

With regard to how the patients would spend $50,000 with only one year to live, the data in Table 6 generally reinforce the results in Table 4. In both groups, helping members of their immediate family and giving philanthropic assistance to others were ranked ahead of personal pleasures and self-gratifications. Again, this differs from the reported data on normals who rank traveling and hedonistic activities above assistance to intimates and charitable endeavors. Noticeable again is the implicit theme of the patients' need to relieve guilt feelings by paying off debts to others as a sort of atonement before permitting themselves self-pleasures.

Summary

1. The patients, generally, felt that old age was the time of life when people most feared death and childhood the period when they were least afraid.

A substantial minority in both groups of patients, nevertheless, ranked childhood as the time when people *most* feared death. It was thought that this might be related to experiences of severe emotional deprivation early in life by some of the patients and possibly connected with childhood fears of castration. A good number of the patients also ranked old age as the time of life when people were least afraid of death. The consideration was that this reflected the thinking that many older people fear idleness and uselessness more than death. The hypothesis was also entertained that a correlation might exist between religious outlook and rankings of fear of death in old age, but no significant relationship was evident.

2. Most patients perceived death as the natural end of the life process. This was followed by the religious view that it was actually a preparatory stage for another life. Many patients depicted death as occurring through violent means. The conjecture was that this

was allied to intense aggressive impulses with which these patients were contending.

3. When faced with hypothetical situations suggesting the imminence of death, the characteristic choice tendencies of both groups of patients highlighted activities oriented toward benefiting others and stressing religious values. This was in contrast to the reported findings for "normals" whose activities, in similar situations, emphasized personal gratifications.

4. The *degree* of mental disturbance *per se* in the patients had little seeming effect on their overall attitudes toward death.

It should be kept in mind that the data secured in this study pertain to conscious and "public" attitudes more than they do to the "deeper" layers of the personality.

References

1. A. Boisen, R. L. Jenkins, and M. Lorr, "Schizophrenic Ideation as a Striving toward the Solution of Conflict," *Journal of Clinical Psychology*, 10 (1954), 389. See also W. Bromberg and P. Schilder, "The Attitudes of Psychoneurotics toward Death," *Psychoanalytical Review*, 23 (1936), 1; and J. D. Teicher, "Combat Fatigue or Death Anxiety Neurosis," *Journal of Nervous and Mental Diseases*, 117 (1953), 234.
2. F. S. Caprio, "A Psycho-Social Study of Primitive Conceptions of Death," *Journal of Criminal Psychopathology*, 5 (1943), 303.
3. O. Fenichel, *The Psychoanalytic Theory of Neuroses* (New York: Norton, 1945).
   M. Grotjahn, "Psychiatric Observations of Schizophrenic Patients during Metrazol Treatment," *Bulletin Menninger Clinic*, 2 (1938), 142.
   P. Schilder, "Notes on the Psychology of Metrazol Treatment of Schizophrenia," *Journal of Nervous & Mental Diseases*, 89 (1939), 133.
   I. Silbermann, "The Psychical Experiences during the Shocks in Shock Therapy," *International Journal of Psychoanalysis*, 21 (1940), 179.
4. G. F. J. Lehner and B. Saper, "Use of Hypothetical Situation in Personality Assessment," *Journal Personality* 21 (1952), 91.
5. H. Feifel, "Psychiatric Patients Look at Old Age: Level of Adjustment and Attitudes toward Aging," *American Journal of Psychiatry*, 111 (1954), 459.
6. S. Levy and R. H. Southcombe, "Suicide in a State Hospital for the Mentally Ill," *Journal of Nervous & Mental Diseases*, 117 (1953), 504.
   U.S. P.H.S., National Office of Vital Statistics. *National Summaries, 27* (1948), 48.
7. W. Bromberg and P. Schilder, "Death and Dying: A Comparative Study of the Attitudes and Mental Reactions toward Death and Dying," *Psychoanalytical Review*, 20 (1933), 133.

P. Schilder and D. Wechsler, "The Attitudes of Children toward Death," *Journal Genetic Psychology*, 45 (1934), 406.
8. M. Grotjahn, "About the Representation of Death in the Art of Antiquity and in the Unconscious of Modern Men." In *Psychoanalysis and Culture*, Wilbur and Muensterberger, Eds. (New York: International University Press, 1951).
9. Lehner and Saper, *op. cit.*
10. *Ibid.*

Frances C. Jeffers, Claude R. Nichols, and Carl Eisdorfer

Attitudes of Older Persons toward Death: A Preliminary Study

Scheler has said that death is viewed by mankind merely as the end point of aging. It may be hypothesized, however, that attitudes toward death may have a direct effect upon adjustment and upon attitudes toward life. The first step in research undertaken to test this hypothesis will necessarily be an exploration of methods to determine attitudes toward death; the second, an attempt to see what these attitudes may be; and the third, an investigation of the other factors to which these attitudes may be related.

As part of a two-day series of examinations involving a variety of disciplines, a biracial group of 269 community volunteers, 60 years of age and older, were asked, during the course of a two-hour social history interview, "Are you afraid to die?" and "Do you believe in a life after death?"

FEAR OF DEATH

Answers to the first question were distributed as shown in Table 1.

Fear of death was explored in relation to 52 other variables; demographic (race, age, sex, marital status, education); physical (functional rating, cardiac status, symptom count); psychological (taken from three WAIS and four Rorschach ratings); psychiatric (classification, subjective emotional reaction, hypochondriasis); and social (activities, attitudes, self-health rating and concern, religious items, adjustment ratings). Analysis by chi-square yielded the statistically significant associations shown in Table 2.

Reprinted from *Journal of Gerontology*, 16 (1961), pp. 53–56, by permission of the authors and the publisher.

Table 1

Percentages of answers to "Are you afraid to die?" (N = 254)

Yes		10
No		35
No, but want to live as long as possible	13	
No, but dread pain of dying	2	
Mixed feelings (balanced ambivalence)	16	
		31
No, but don't want to be sick or dependent a long time	4	
No, but it's inevitable	17	
No, other elaboration	3	
		24
Total		100

Since many of the older subjects answered the question, "Are you afraid to die?" in religious terminology, an analysis of these answers yielded associations as follows (χ^2 significant at the .001 level):

(1) The *unqualified* "No" answers were associated with religious terminology.

(2) The answers suggesting *ambivalence* were associated with an absence of religious connotations.

Table 2

Fear of death in relation to other variables

	χ^2 level of confidence
Fear of death is associated with:	
Less belief in life after death	.01
Less frequent Bible reading	.01
Feelings of rejection and depression	.05
Lower full-scale IQ	.05
Lower performance IQ	.001
Fewer number of Rorschach responses	.02
Fewer leisure activities	.10

(3) The answers *admitting fear of death* tended to have no religious connotation.

It therefore appears that the factors associated with *no* fear of death include a tendency to read the Bible oftener, more belief in a future life, reference to death with more religious connotations, fewer feelings of rejection and depression, higher scores on full scale and performance IQ, and more responses on the Rorschach (with the suggestion also of more leisure activities).

BELIEF IN AFTERLIFE

The inquiry on belief in life after death revealed that very few of the subjects denied such a belief outright. Only 2 per cent said "no"; 21 per cent said "not sure"; and 77 per cent said, "yes, sure of it."

Belief in life after death was examined in relation to 37 demographic, physical, psychological, psychiatric and social variables. Statistically significant associations were obtained for 10 of these variables (Table 3).

Religious activites and attitudes appear to be the most important variables associated with belief in the life after death, but depression, intelligence, and socioeconomic status are also probably associated.

Table 3
Belief in life after death in relation to other variables

	χ^2 level of confidence
Belief in life after death is associated with:	
Less fear of death	.01
More frequent church attendance	.01
More frequent Bible reading	.001
Greater number of religious activities	.001
Stronger religious attitudes	.001
Feeling that religion is the most important thing in life	.001
Less depression (psychiatric rating)	.001
Lower scores on full scale IQ	.02
Lower socioeconomic status	.05
More women than men	.05
Less high level of education	.10

Clinical Impressions

The clinical impressions and experience of the present investigators, who have had extensive study and contact with not only the 260 community volunteer subjects in the present group but also with other groups of older persons during the past six years or more, may be useful in interpreting the empirical data.

(1) As Schilder has suggested, there may be no common human idea of death, but it may be an extremely individualized concept. He hypothesized that individual experiences become the determining factors for the picture which one develops of death. Gardner Murphy, in his discussion of the contributions to Feifel's book, concludes that, "It is apparent that fear of death is not psychologically homogeneous at all, even in a narrowly defined cultural group."

(2) The technique of direct questioning may be inappropriate for reaching the real feelings of the subject, even though in the present study the questions were asked near the end of a social history taken in an informal setting, and even though the interviewer was previously known to the subject and good rapport had been established. In addition, in all such inquiries, a semantic factor which needs clarification is that of differentiation between the words "death" and "dying."

(3) Bearing in mind that the subjects were community volunteers living in their own homes and neighborhoods, and following Shrut's finding that those older persons having less institutionalized living arrangements show less fear of or preoccupation with death, it is perhaps to be anticipated that only a small proportion of the present sample should express fear of death.

(4) Religion is a very great part of community life in the North Carolina region in which the study was carried out. Only 6 per cent of these older subjects had no church membership. It is accordingly to be expected that most of them would think of death in religious terminology.

(5) The distribution of responses to the question, "Are you afraid to die?" (Table 1) confirms the clinical impressions of the Duke geriatrics research group that denial is a very important mechanism for dealing with anxiety in old age. The mental mechanism of denial may be among the most common adaptive techniques employed in personality adjustment by persons beyond the fifth decade of life. Its use may be promoted chiefly by three factors:

(1) perceptual distortions during the later period of life due to concomitant changes in cortical and receptor processes; (2) changes in body image with age and chronic disease; this parallels the frequent utilization of this same regressive maneuver by younger persons who have devastating chronic diseases; and (3) gradual deterioration of the central nervous system, which causes reversal of the mental processes toward those of early childhood, when the denial mechanism of unacceptable reality situations is quite universally utilized . . . .

Adolph E. Christ

Attitudes toward Death among a Group of Acute Geriatric Psychiatric Patients

This is a pilot study to determine how a group of geriatric psychiatric patients felt about the topic of death. The data are based on interviews of 100 consecutive patients admitted during the last three months of 1959 to the psychiatric wards of the San Francisco General Hospital. Each patient in this group was 60 years or older, had lived in San Francisco for one or more years prior to his hospitalization, and had not required psychiatric treatment prior to the age of 60.

Of the 100 patients, 62 were questioned and were able to respond about their attitude toward death. The death questions used are as follows.

1. Have you had any friends or relatives who have recently been in the hospital, and what happened to them?
2. How old do you wish to get, and how old do you expect to get?
3. How is your physical health?
4. Have you talked about death with anyone before? If not, why not? If yes, what was said?
5. What is your feeling about death?
6. Have you made any plans for the future? Do you have a will, a burial plot, or any plans following your death? What are they?

Reprinted from *Journal of Gerontology*, 16 (1961), pp. 56–59, by permission of the author and publisher.

7. How do you feel about capital punishment, about mercy killing?

8. If a patient is going to die soon, should the doctor tell him? Would you want to be told? Would you want . . . (nearest relative or friend) to be told if he were going to die soon?

9. If you had the choice of dying tomorrow or being bedridden for the next three years, which would you choose?

10. If you had the choice of dying tomorrow or being in severe pain for a year, but knew you would be O.K. at the end of that time, which would you choose?

11. How did you feel about our talk about death? Do you think doctors in general should talk about death with their patients?

With regard to the other 38 patients, the interviewer was first fearful that a discussion of death would upset the more severely disoriented, disorganized, or delusional patients. As the study progressed, however, if was found that those patients who could respond at all to the question about death gave meaningful answers. Therefore, more and more seriously disturbed patients were drawn into the sample, until in the last half of the group only the deaf, aphasic, or comatose patients were excluded. None of the patients became so upset consequently that the hospital staff noticed an adverse behavioral change. To obtain more meaningful responses, the death questions were introduced in as personal and unstructured a way as possible during the course of a psychiatric and neurological examination. One-third of the patients, however, fell asleep, became delusional, became markedly irritable or angry, became more disoriented, or attempted to leave the interviewer, so that it was necessary to explain the research nature of the death questions before the examination was completed.

While discussing the topic of death with this group of psychiatric patients, the interviewer wanted to gather data on the following four questions: What is the physician's subjective impression of patients' reactions to a discussion of death? Would a more objective test, such as the word association test, substantiate the interviewer's subjective impression? Are there any factors such as age, religion, or schooling, which may be associated with the patient's adjustment to the inevitability of his own death? What is the expressed opinion of these patients on various questions dealing directly and indirectly with death? The findings will be given as answers to these four questions.

Findings

Physician's impressions. The interviewer felt that all but two of the patients were considerably upset about death and used denial, suppression, and repression as defenses. For example, a chronic alcoholic woman, whose husband had suddenly and unexpectedly died five days before her admission, required hospitalization because of severe intoxication. When asked her feelings about her husband's death, she seemed perplexed. She then spoke of the settlement of his estate. Although the interviewer attempted to bring out her feelings about the impact of her husband's death on her future, she could not discuss it. She stated she had not thought or talked about death before this discussion. In contrast, a woman with a large fungating necrotic carcinoma of the breast spoke quite freely and with relief that she was in a situation where she could speak about death. She discussed the pros and cons of having a radical mastectomy, saying she seriously wondered whether she should prolong her life—probably only to live in pain.

Since 55 of the 62 patients were judged to require supervision at least at night because of physical illness or incapacitation (although all had been hospitalized for psychiatric reasons), and because five of the 62 died within a few days of the examination, one can speculate that their psychiatric symptoms might in part have been an outgrowth of this marked conscious denial of death.

Word Association Test. Half the patients were asked to respond to the words:

Food	Family
Sleep	Doctor
Water	To Leave
Sickness	Milk
Hospital	Dying

The interviewer postulated that longer association time to the death words than to the other words is correlated with great anxiety about death. With these patients the association time to the word "dying" was longer than the association times to the other nine words. (Statistically, using the t test, the difference obtained could occur by chance alone less than five times out of one hundred.)

With the second half of the patients the word "grave" was substitued for "sickness" and "death" was substituted for "to leave." The average of the association times to the three death words was also longer than the the average of the association times to the seven other words. (Again, this difference could occur by chance alone less than five times out of one hundred.) The associations to the death words were often more bizarre and produced more blocking. Also, these words were more often than the other words not heard by the patient. These findings would substantiate the subjective impression of the examiner that these patients were anxious about death.

Background factors. To determine whether there were any factors in the patients' backgrounds that might have decreased their anxiety about death, the patients were first grouped into those who were more and those who were less afraid of death. To do this, four clinicians (two psychiatrists and two clinical psychologists on the teaching staff of the Langley Porter Neuropsychiatric Institute) were asked to rate the death questions as to their validity as a test of fear of death, and a scale was devised, as follows.

FEAR OF DEATH SCALE

1. The patient has some plan following his death, such as a will: yes, rated 0; no, rated 1.

2. During the talk about death the patient made one or more spontaneous statements about death and showed appropriate affect, rated 0. If he made no spontaneous statement or treated the topic blandly, he is rated 1. If he gives one-word answers or shows anger or resentment at being questioned about death he is rated 2. If he becomes abusively angry or markedly suspicious he is rated 3.

3. In the word association test used with the first half of the patients, if the word "dying" was the longest of the ten, rated 2: if it was the second largest word, rated 1; otherwise, rated 0. With the second half of the patients where "death," "dying," and "grave" were used, if the average association time of these three words is longer than the average association time of the other seven words, rated 1. One additional is given if one of the three death words had the longest association time of all the words. If neither of these is the case, the patient is rated 0.

4. The patient has talked about death or dying before this interview: yes, rated 0; no, rated 1.

5. The patient wants to be told of his own imminent death by a physician: yes, rated 0; no, rated 1.

6. The patient would want his relative or friend told if the relative (friend) were terminally ill: yes, rated 0; no, rated 1.

7. The patient is asked, "How is your physical health?" If he says good, and his health is judged by a physician as "can live alone or needs assistance only at night for physical reasons," rated 0. If he says good, but is judged by a physician as needing almost full time assistance for physical reason, rated 1. If he says good, but is judged by a physician as needing full-time assistance for physical reasons, rated 2.

Scores were computed for 60 patients; and the group was then divided into those with "less fear of death" ($N = 26$) and those with "more fear of death" ($N = 34$).

A series of contingency tables were then constructed to investigate the relationship between fear of death and each of six variables; and the distributions tested for significance by use of the χ^2 test. The variables were: (1) health (good vs. poor); (2) age (60–69 vs. 70 or more); (3) religion (Catholic vs. Protestant); (4) religiosity (religiously staunch vs. religiously indifferent or atheistic); (5) schooling (up to eighth grade vs. high school or higher); and (6) sex (male vs. female). Of the six variables, only the first proved to be significantly related to fear of death; those patients with better health were less afraid of death than those with poorer health. The negative findings with regard to the other five variables do not agree with the findings from other studies. For instance, Feifel states, "The religious person, when compared to the nonreligious individual, is personally more afraid of death," but this was not borne out in the present study. Later Feifel states, "Women tend to think more about death than do men" (although "we should not forget that there is no necessary relationship between thinking about death and fear of death"). The present study indicates that in this group of geriatric psychiatric patients, men and women are equally afraid of death.

Patients' expressed opinions. Of the 62 patients, 54 had never talked to anyone about death or dying before this interview. This agrees with Feifel's statement, "It is noteworthy that in all the groups, particularly the terminally ill patients, some find thinking about death so anxiety provoking that they deny having any ideas at all about it." This is particularly striking in the present study because most of the patients came from homes or hotels with a large population of older people; and many had had friends or relatives who had recently died. One patient did state, "Oh yes, but my family immediately say, 'Why do you have to talk about such a morbid topic? You should be grateful to be alive.' "

One-third of the patients stated they had a will, or some other plan for the disposal of their effects after their death; one-third had no interest in discussing this; and one-third stated, "The state will take care of that."

Of 48 patients, 23 favored capital punishment, 4 were noncommital, the rest were against it. The patients favored mercy killing, about half of them making a restriction, one said, "Yes, but you should have a priest, a lawyer, the patient, and three doctors there at the time of the decision." Most of those who were against euthenasia were markedly angry and agitated; for example, one said, "The doctor should be put to death!"

To the question, "If a patient is going to die soon should the doctor tell him?" Twenty-three of 47 patients said "yes," and all said they personally would want to be told. A few volunteered that they only wanted to know a few days or hours beforehand. . . . "So I could get myself ready, but not too long, or I would get too upset." Those who did not want to be told were often defensive; one said, "There are too many times when the doctor is wrong." This one question aroused the most anxiety, and with about 30 per cent it was necessary to explain that the question was part of a research project and did not refer to them personally. When asked, "would you want—(closest relative or friend) to be told if he were going to die soon?" Seventeen of 35 said "no," 4 refused to commit themselves, the rest said "yes."

When asked to choose between being bedridden for the next three years or dying tomorrow, 15 of 32 patients chose dying, 8 refused to say, and 10 chose living. When asked, "If you had a choice of dying tomorrow or being in severe pain for a year, but knew you would be O.K. at the end of that time," 14 of 32 chose living, 10 refused to commit themselves, and the rest chose dying.

When at the end of the interview, it was explained that the questions were for research and had nothing to do with their specific situation, almost all the patients showed signs of decreased anxiety. Asked how they felt about the questions on death, and whether doctors in general should discuss death with their patients, 15 of 57 stated they had enjoyed the discussion, or had been grateful or proud to have been asked these questions. Another 17 stated they did not mind talking about it, or had accepted talking about

it in a bland, emotionally uninvolved way; and 23 ranged from
saying that they were fearful of the questions to stating that they
disliked talking about death. A very few of these 23 became frankly
suspicious or abusively hostile.

Summary and Discussion

One hundred acute psychiatric geriatric patients consecutively admitted to the San Francisco General Hospital were examined in
this pilot study. Sixty-two could give relevant answers to most
of the questions on their attitudes towards death. The patients
were fearful of death, but as a whole were willing, and in some
cases were relieved to discuss it. Even some physically terminally
ill patients with severe psychiatric symptoms were able to discuss
the topic, at times with evident relief.

It has been said that the topic of death is a taboo today as
the topic of sex was during the nineteenth century. Since the
direct outcome of many diseases in this age group is death, it would
appear that it is the physician's duty to acquaint his patients with
this fact and to help them deal with the attendant fears. Eighty-
nine per cent of the patients in this study needed supervision at
least at night because of physical illness, and 87 per cent stated
they had never talked about death or dying before. One can speculate that at least some of their psychiatric symptoms, which often
included fear of being poisoned, killed, or thrown out of their homes,
as well as frank, somatic delusions, may be symptoms of marked
denial of death. It could seem that with this marked denial of
death it becomes incumbent on the physician to broach the topic
with his patient, and not to wait for the patient to raise the question
of his approaching death.

James C. Diggory and Doreen Z. Rothman

Values Destroyed by Death

There are two questions about fear of death. First, does everyone
always fear death more than anything else? Second, exactly what
is it about death that is feared?

Reprinted from the *Journal of Abnormal and Social Psychology*, 63 (1961),
pp. 205–210, by permission of the authors and publisher.

In answer to the first question, expressions of attitude and overt acts often indicate that other things are more feared than death. College students reported they feared snakes, cancer, and death of loved ones more than their own death (Means); some children do not fear death very acutely, perhaps because they believe its probability is low (Schilder and Wechsler); men risk their lives or lose them to save others or to advance some cause; in the reality or prospect of grievous loss, some commit suicide; martyrs have expired to retain their principles or to gain some future reward; and some aged persons are said to long for death (Challaye). So it seems that death is not always the object of everyone's greatest fear.

The answer to the first question increases the importance of the second: knowing what, specifically, is feared about death. First, some ways of dying are more feared than others, according to Means and some unpublished data of our own. We do not know yet why this is so, but the fact that it is so suffices for the present discussion. Second, suicide often follows receipt of an insult or loss of status so extreme as to make it impossible for the person to function comfortably or effectively in the future (Bunzel, Malinowski, Mead). Though his skills and abilities may be un-damaged, he has lost the opportunity to use them. Suicide also occurs when the person's ability or skill has deteriorated to the point where he cannot function even when he has the opportunity (Freuchen). Whether a person chooses to die because death attracts him or because he fears it less than other alternatives is of no consequence for the present argument. What interests us is that reduction in fear of death may be associated with loss of utility of the self.

Following the value theories of Dewey and von Ehrenfels (*cf.* Eaton), we assume that utility of the self corresponds to the proba-bility that a person, by his own efforts, can achieve objectives that are important to him. The larger the number of important objec-tives for which one's probability of achievement is high, the greater his self-esteem. Loss of ability or skill reduces probability of achieve-ment, and with it, self-esteem. Elimination of opportunity for the exercise of skills or abilities makes them, in effect, worthless, even though they are undamaged. We try to preserve or extend objects we value highly, but those of low value are treated with indifference or destroyed. Thus a person who values himself highly should be more afraid of death than one whose self-esteem is low, because death is the limiting case of loss or destruction of the self. The specific goals important to one person may differ from those important to another. We may value ourselves because we have achieved objectives important only to us or because we take pride in our ability to help others gain their ends. But regardless of the specific content of his goals, what one would lament most about his own death is loss of the specific activities in which he is most involved or feels to be most important. To the extent that the goals a person values highly depend on his social status, his fear of various consequences of his own death should vary with his status or role, whether defined by age, sex, social class, religion, or marital condition.

Procedure

With these considerations in mind, we developed a list of "consequences of one's own death":

   A. I could no longer have any experiences.
   B. I am uncertain as to what might happen to me if there is a life after death.
   C. I am afraid of what might happen to my body after death.
   D. I could no longer care for my dependents.
   E. My death would cause grief to my relatives and friends.
   F. All my plans and projects would come to an end.
   G. The process of dying might be painful.

These were arranged for paired comparisons and included as part of a larger questionnaire on various aspects of attitudes toward death. Respondents indicated the member of each pair that they regarded as worse or more distasteful than the other.

In selecting respondents we made no systematic attempt to draw a sample representing the general population, or did we use a strictly random method. The questionnaires were handed to groups or individuals wherever we had opportunity: in college and high school classrooms, offices, social clubs, fire houses, and union halls. Many respondents are the older or younger relatives of students whom we asked for help. About two-thirds of the questionnaires were returned, including 563 usable responses dealt with in this paper. Figure 2 gives the number of respondents in each category.

Respondents are classed by: Age in years (15–19, 20–24, 25–39, 40–54, and >55); Sex; Marital status (Single, Engaged, Married,

Widowed, or Divorced); Religious affiliation (Protestant, Catholic, Jewish, or Other-None); and Social class (upper, middle, or lower). Social class was judged by combining reported amount and source of annual income and the general educational level of the family.

Results

The curves in Figure 1 were arrived at by the following process. First, from the paired comparisons data a ranking of the seven items was determined for each respondent, with the highest rank (1) assigned to the most frequently chosen, and lowest rank (7) to the least frequently chosen item. Ties were resolved by assigning the average of the appropriate ranks to each of the tied items. Second, frequency distribution tables were constructed showing the number of respondents in a given category who assigned a particular rank to any item. From these tables we constructed tables of the cumulative proportions of respondents assigning an item to a given rank or higher. The curves in Figure 1 are plotted directly from these cumulative proportion tables. The figure shows how we derived the median rank of each item for all respondents. The rank scale on the abscissa of Figure 1 is reproduced in Figure 2A. The other scales in Figure 2 were derived in the same way.

The distribution of cumulative proportions permitted the use of the Kolmogorov-Smirnov test for significance of differences among the various respondent categories. Thus, for any consequence of death, we can find whether the sexes differ significantly in the median rank they assign it, and similarly for the social class, age, marital status, or religious categories. Hereafter, a "significant difference" is understood to mean rejection of the null hypothesis of the Kolmogorov-Smirnov test at $p < .05$. The meanings of such differences in terms of the median rank of the items can be determined from Figure 2.

Dissolution of the body. Item C ("I am afraid of what might happen to my body after death") is a good "anchor point" since it is always at the lowest, least avoided rank. No other item holds its rank so consistently in all comparisons. As a matter of interest, note that women fear this consequence of death significantly more than men do. This may be related to the fact that women value themselves more in terms of their physical attractiveness than do men (Cohen).

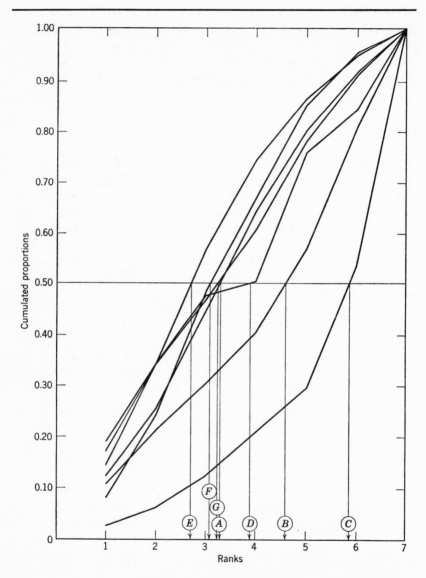

*Figure 1. Cumulated proportions of all 563 respondents assigning each item to
a given, or higher, rank. (The item key is: A, I could no longer have any experiences; B, I am afraid of what might happen to me if there is a life after
death; C, I am afraid of what might happen to my body after death; D, I would
no longer be able to care for my dependents; E, My death would cause grief
to my relatives and friends; F, All my plans and projects would come to an end;
G, The process of dying might be painful. The scale on the abscissa is reproduced in Figure 2 A for comparison with the other scales.)*

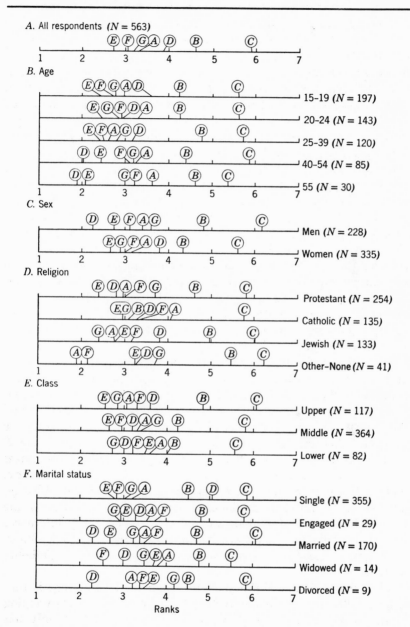

Figure 2. Median scale positions assigned to seven consequences of one's own death by respondents in various categories. (The item key is the same as in Figure 1.)

The purposive activity items. A ("I could no longer have any experiences"), D ("I could no longer care for my dependents"), and F ("All my plans and projects would come to an end") are the most relevant to our main hypothesis. Note that A and F are egocentric as compared with D, and they are less clearly related to any special role. Thus, it is D, rather than A or F, to which we must look for support of our major hypothesis, and the hypothesis is supported. The importance assigned to being able to care for dependents obviously requires that one has dependents or is committed to acquire them. Thus, the progression in Marital status, Single, Engaged, Married, should be accompanied by a marked increase in fear for this item. Since this progression is also a function of age, Item D should increase in importance with increasing age. Also, the sex of the respondents should determine the importance of ability to care for dependents because, in our culture, the modal adult male *has* dependents while the female *is* a dependent. Figure 2—B, C, and F—shows these expectations fully met. In the age category the mean rank of Item D is significantly higher at 40–54 years than at 15–19 years,[1] it is significantly higher for men than for women, and significantly higher for the married group than for the single group.

Items A and F are usually near the top of the scale in all categories of respondents. Moreover, they tend to vary together, only twice being more than one rank apart (*cf.* Catholic and Widowed groups). The least fear of either of them is among Roman Catholics. They are feared most in the Other-None religious group. Outside the religious categories the only significant difference is that Item F is more feared by single than by married persons. This makes sense because married people's plans are not completely egocentric, and are likely to be subsumed under caring for dependents. Clearly, differences in religious affiliation produce more variation in the fear of Items A and F than any other category. All differences among the religious groups are significant for Item A. The Other-None group regards F as significantly more fearful than do Catholics or Jews.

That Items A and F are generally high in the rankings is consistent with our view that actively getting experiences and executing plans are values the loss of which by death would be keenly felt because of their importance to self-esteem.

The fact that loss of ability to have experiences (Item A) is important for the religious groups in the order Jewish > Protestant > Catholic probably reflects differences in their beliefs that death is the end of experience. For Protestants and Jews there are relatively few specific prescribed actions to increase the probability of happiness in the hereafter, but there are many such actions prescribed for Catholics. This difference may mean that life after death is more *real* to Catholics than to Jews or Protestants. Realism in this sense corresponds to Mahler's operational definitions of levels of reality in tasks: real tasks demand and permit concrete manipulations; but unreal ones allow only thinking about the problem solving operations. If this distinction is correctly applied, it is likely that Catholics are less fearful of the loss of experiences by death simply because they do not believe that such a loss is possible.

Possible pain of dying. Item *G* ("The process of dying might be painful") also varies in median rank as a function of religious affiliation, being least feared by Protestants, more so by Catholics, and most by Jews. The position of this item also changes significantly with social class, more feared by upper and middle than by lower class respondents. Also, there is a sex difference: women fear the possible pain of dying more than men do.

Fear of the future. Item *B* ("I am uncertain as to what might happen to me if there is life after death") progresses from greatest to least among the religious groups Catholic > Protestant > Jewish > Other-None. Like the differences in Item *A* discussed above, this doubtless reflects differences in the concreteness of beliefs about life after death. The importance of this item also varies with social class: lower > middle > upper.

Affective consequences of one's own death for others. Item *E* ("My death would cause grief to my relatives and friends") is less important for the Other-None than for any other religious group. The item is also considerably more fearful to upper and middle than to lower class respondents, a somewhat surprising finding in view of the reputed emphasis in lower class groups upon dependence on, and satisfaction in, primary group relations (Bellin and Riessman, Rosenberg, Young and Rosenberg). However, it is entirely possible that the majority of our "lower class" respondents are actually marginal with respect to class membership and espousal of norms.

Conclusions

The general picture provided by these data is that the concomitants, or consequences of his own death which a person fears most, depend on the role he has or expects to have, and therefore, on the goals to which he is committed. The items in this study most relevant to goal striving are *D* (caring for dependents), *A* (having experiences), and *F* (completing plans and projects), the latter two being relatively egocentric compared to the former. The other items are related to ways the person may be passively affected by his own death; *B* (his fate in a life after death), *C* (the fate of his body after death), *G* (he might experience pain while dying), or *E* (the emotional impact of his death on others).

The important factors associated with differences in rank positions of these various items are (*a*) one's adherence to a set of goals defined by his role and (*b*) his devotion (or lack of it) to a religious or social class ideology.

Our hypothesis, that a person fears death because it eliminates his opportunity to pursue goals important to his self-esteem, is supported by the following: fear that one can no longer care for dependents varies systematically with roles defined by marital status, sex, and age; the purposive items of having experiences and completing one's own projects are consistently near the high end of the fear scale, except for people who may be assumed to believe that death is not the end of experience.

References

1. The failure of the significance test between 15–19 years and >55 years is doubtless due to the small number of cases in the latter category.
2. S. Bellin and F. Riessman, Jr., "Education, Culture, and the Anarchic Worker," *Journal of Social Issues*, 5 (1949), 24–32.
3. B. Bunzel, "Suicide," *Encyclopedia of Social Sciences*, 14 (1937), 455–459.
4. F. Challaye, "Psychologie Genetique et Ethnique," in G. Dumas (Ed.), *Traite de Psychologie*, 2 (1924), 725–726.
5. A. K. Cohen, *Delinquent Boys: The Culture of the Gang* (Glencoe, Ill.: Free Press, 1955), pp. 137–147.
6. J. Dewey, "Theory of Valuation," *International Encyclopedia of Unified Sciences*, 2 (1939), No. 4.
7. H. O. Eaton, *The Austrian Philosophy of Values* (Norman: University of Oklahoma Press, 1930).
8. P. Freuchen, "Burying the Mother Alive in a Snow House," in, *Eskimo* (English translation) (New York: Grosset & Dunlap, 1931). Reprinted in Margaret Mead & N. Callas [Eds.], *Our Primitive Heritage* (New York: Random House, 1953).
9. W. Mahler, "Ersatzhandlungen Verschiedenen Realitätsgrades," *Psychologishe Forschung*, 18 (1933), 27–89.
10. B. Malinowski, *Crime and Custom in Savage Society* (London: Paul, 1926).

11. Margaret Mead, *Sex and Temperament in Three Primitive Societies* (New York: William Morrow, 1935).
12. M. H. Means, "Fears of One Thousand College Students," *Journal of Abnormal and Social Psychology*, 31 (1936), 291–311.
13. M. Rosenberg, "The Social Roots of Formation," *Journal of Social Issues*, 5 (1949), 14–23.

Samuel D. Shrut

Attitudes toward Old Age and Death

It was the aim of this study to investigate differences in attitude toward aging on the part of older persons. As an index to this, attitude toward death was chosen on the assumption that attitude toward death is a reflection of attitude toward living.

It was hypothesized that those subjects living under conditions approximating a previous mode of independent residence in the community would reflect a less apprehensive attitude toward death, and generally be better adjusted to the life about them. Consequently, attitude toward death was compared with self-appraisal of health, adjustment in the institutional setting, and claimed participation in activities.

This study compared attitude toward death in ambulatory, currently unmarried, white females in two kinds of institutional living arrangements. Thirty persons residing in the apartment dwellings of the Home for Aged and Infirm Hebrews of New York were compared with a similar population from the same institution's central residential facility (Central House) in which the supervision and regulations are more traditionally instituted. The basic difference in the two modes of residence is that the apartment residents live much like other older people in the community, whereas those in the mass-housing or institutional setting (Central House) are more dependent upon the institutional organization, *per se.*

In each case, the research population consisted of volunteers obtained by means of random selection from a stratified sample, after consultation with the medical and social service departments of the institution. Subjects were well motivated to participate in the study, which was presented to them as having potential beneficial

Reprinted from *Mental Hygiene*, 42 (1958) pp. 259–266, by permission of the author and publisher.

consequences in possibly affecting housing arrangements for older people. Also, respondents were assured that they would remain anonymous.

The experimental design of the study consisted of comparing the two groups by means of a psychological test battery of instruments which, except for the Thematic Apperception Test, were especially devised, along with their respective rating scales, by this investigator. The instruments, in order of their standardized presentation, were as follows: questionnaire on self-appraisal of health, questionnaire for adjustment in the home, sentence-completion test, Thematic Apperception Test and questionnaire on claimed participation in activities.

Some brief statements about the various instruments in the battery are in order.

The health questionnaire was designed to elicit information on past and current medical history for the self-rating of health, on the basis of five categories ranging from "excellent" to "very poor."

The questionnaire on adjustment consisted of seventeen detailed questions relating to food, supervision, rules and general interpersonal relationships of the resident in the institution.

The questionnaire on claimed participation in activities consisted of a series of detailed questions of possible activities involving physical and social pursuits in which the aged respondent may claim to take part.

A sentence completion test and ten TAT cards were also utilized.

Specific rating scales were devised for each of these instruments, each based on a 5-point range. Ratings were made by various categories of judges (a physician, three psychologists, at least three social workers), who rated protocols blind and made pertinent judgments of subjects who were represented by code number to assure anonymity. These ratings were then averaged for the various groups of judges and comparisons were made. However, only the averaged ratings of the three psychologist-judges were employed in evaluating attitude toward death.

Death, whether considered traumatic, or tragic, or "a state of bliss," or a return to Mother Earth, or in terms of the organism's contest between the will to live and the desire to return to the inorganic state, poses a severe problem for most, if not all, human beings. Human response to death has run the whole gamut of emotional possibilities from stalwart indifference to severe and painful apprehension. There is the bracing statement in Shakespeare's

King Henry IV: "By my troth, I care not. A man can die but once; we owe God a death . . . and let it go which way it will, he that dies this year is quit for the next."[1] Then, on the other hand, Gilbert, suggesting an apparent universality of the fear of death, takes pains to stress the importance of working with the aged to help, ". . . prepare the aged person for death, which is inevitable and not too far away, in such a manner as to eliminate fear and help him to achieve serenity and happiness in his remaining years."[2]

Perhaps from the time when man first saw the lifeless form of his companion or enemy he has quite understandably begun to reflect upon death and what, if anything, "happens afterwards," and how this new lifeless state might be related to or concern him. While in the history of literature and mythology there is an abundance of writing, both in prose and poetry, on death, its sorrows and the happy or unhappy life beyond, there is a comparative lack of scientific writing on this subject. This is quite understandable because of its inaccessibility to scientific investigation in spite of its rich speculative possibilities.[3]

As one peruses the wealth of poetic and prosaic utterances that human beings have devoted to the subject of death, dying, and fear of death, one is led to consider the variety of meanings that these words have assumed for different people and different ages. Considering this, it may be useful for the present research to distinguish at least three different concepts of death. The following brief distinctions concerning death concepts may be sufficient.

1. DEATH AS A TOOL

From a psychological orientation, death may be considered a tool with which to attempt to derive certain goals and satisfactions from the present environment. The concept of death as a tool in the psychological economy of the human being is, for example, much more ancient than is the history of suicide. While perhaps only so considered tangentially at times by the layman, death as a tool has increasingly been the subject of scientific inquiry, especially in recent years.

2. DEATH AS PASSAGE

By this expression, reference is made to the circumstance that death not only terminates but also initiates a new phase, transcending life, only to lead to a further state of being. The manner in which the death-initiated new "life" or new state of being is considered is dependent upon the prevalent belief systems entertained by different cultural groups. Death as passage between modes of being or "different worlds," according to the particular belief system, may be represented anywhere in the cultural spectrum from the gruesome to the glorious, or from calm anticipation to tormenting apprehension. Clearly, the particular version of the concept of death as passage directly affects the emotional tone in which death as a biological end is anticipated.

3. DEATH AS AN END

In this manner death is conceived of in strictly biological terms as a terminal ("the eternal void") event in the life span of the organisms. This, as a matter of fact, is singled out by Webster[4] as "the cessation of all vital functions without capability of resuscitation, whether in animals or plants."

Death as an end, it may be added, can never occur as an event to be actually experienced by the organism. As the Stoics held, no human being can ever encounter death, since where one is the other has already departed. As a result, death as an end is an event known to occur to us only by inference from generalizations established with respect to others.

While it is held that the particular beliefs that are entertained about death are reflected in the variations of responses from old people, it is the view of this investigator that the institutional mode of living itself modifies or affects significantly particular death attitudes. It is this hypothesis that will be examined by means of studying aged persons with comparable belief systems, as exemplified by the two groups of the present research population.

In general, the literature reflected that fear of death is universal and that any fear is essentially fear of death. Furthermore, the attitude toward death may be said to cover the spectrum from a seemingly preoccupying phobic reaction to one of complete indifference, with denial figuring prominently in the latter attitude.

Attitude toward death was specifically studied by means of clinical impressions of responses from the sentence completion test and Thematic Apperception Test, along with judgments from the other protocols as well. Here it will be recalled that the other questionnaires (health, adjustment, claimed participation in activities) guided the interviews towards eliciting information in the areas suggested by the titles of the respective questionnaires.

Along with the specific rating scales devised for each of the instruments in the battery, there was an additional "summarizing" scale. The summary scoring of subject's attitude toward death, while not in itself a test, enabled the judges (in this case, psychologists) to combine ratings from all the instruments in the battery. While the various instruments attempted to focus on particular aspects of the respondent's behavior and outlook, ratings on the summary scoring were considered most reflective of attitude toward death because of the comprehensive data on which such ratings were made. For example, a subject's response on the health questionnaire may not have influenced the scoring on that instrument markedly. Or, the subject may have been relatively unproductive on the sentence-completion test, or may have blocked on card 15 ("death card") of the TAT, or may have indicated an indifferent attitude on the adjustment or claimed participation questionnaires, all of which findings are in themselves significant. However, they are not nearly so meaningful as when they are all taken in totality and the responses are seen to dovetail and interrelate, as reflected on the summary scoring.

Table 1 cites the mean ratings of three psychologists on several instruments employed to elicit attitude toward death for subjects of Central House and of the apartment residence.

On the sentence-completion test, the Central House group was judged to give responses more concerned with fear of death, while subjects of the apartment residence revealed an attitude in the direction of equanimity or indifference with regard to death.

The TAT indicated that both subject groups entertained at least mild apprehension with regard to death. While only a slight statistical difference was shown in favor of the apartment residents, a qualitative difference was reflected in that subjects of the apartment residence revealed greater productivity by averaging roughly an additional half-page (double-spaced) more than that obtained in the case of Central House subjects.

Apartment residents obtained higher ratings on the summary scoring, thus being judged significantly less preoccupied with fear or apprehension of death.

Fisher's "t"-test to evaluate mean difference of rated responses between the two groups revealed a difference significant at the 5% level.

Table 1

Judges' mean ratings on several instruments employed to elicit attitude
toward death for subjects of Central House and of apartment residence*

	Mean Ratings on 5-Point Scale		
Instrument	Central House residents	Apartment residents	"*t*"
Sentence-completion test	2.9	3.2	1.3
Thematic apperception test	2.8	2.9	0.59
Summary scoring of subject's attitude toward death	2.9	3.2	2.2†

* The 5-point scale, based on specific criteria, has the following range: (1)
marked dread or preoccupation with death, (2) evident anxiety, (3) mild
anxiety, (4) attitude of equanimity or indifference, and (5) philosophic
acceptance.
† Significant at 5 % level and beyond.

The results indicated that subjects residing in the environment
approximating their preinstitutional home or domestic environment (apartment residence) revealed less fear of death. There
is the consequent implication that subjects of apartment residence
enjoy better mental health and are more concerned with planning
for continued living than appears to hold for subjects of the traditional institutional facility (Central House).

The findings on the health questionnaire are shown on Table 2.

Table 2 revealed that Central House subjects' self-ratings of
health were not only higher than the physician's ratings of their
health, but also exceed similar ratings by subjects of the apartment
residence. This marked overestimation of good health suggests that
compensatory mechanisms were operating more prominently with
subjects of Central House.

Table 3 shows the respective mean ratings of social workers and
psychologists for the adjustment questionnaire.

In the study of Central House and apartment residents, the judges
found no differences in ratings of the two research populations.
However, the ratings of the two groups by social workers were
consistently higher than ratings by the psychologist-judges. The
psychologists' ratings suggested that the respondents seemed nearly
satisfied with their adjustment in the institutional setting, while
social workers' ratings indicated that subjects in both groups were

Table 2

Mean of self-ratings* on health for 30 persons from Central House and 30 persons from apartment residence, as compared with ratings by staff physician

	Central House Residents' Self-Ratings*	M.D.'s Rating	Apartment Residents' Self-Ratings*	M.D.'s Rating
Mean Rating	4.3	3.4	3.9	3.3

* Scale points, based on specific criteria, range as follows: (1) very poor, (2) poor, (3) fair, (4) good, and (5) excellent.

quite pleased with their institutional residency. There is the strong suggestion that a "halo effect" was revealed in the ratings of the social workers. This may be accountable in large measure to the tendency on the part of social workers to view ambulatory and active older people in a manner somewhat different from psychologists, whose less optimistic judgments are arrived at by the additional means of projective tests.

Fisher's "t" disclosed no difference in ratings of responses between the two subject groups.

Table 4 indicated mean ratings on the questionnaire for claimed participation in activities for the two subject groups, as scored by teams of social workers and psychologists.

Table 3

Mean ratings* on adjustment questionnaire for subjects of Central House and of apartment residence, as rated by social workers and psychologists

	Residents of		
Raters	Central House (institutional type)	Apartment Residence	"t"
Social workers	4.4	4.4	0
Psychologists	3.8	3.8	0

* The 5-point scale, based on specific criteria, has the following range: (1) very much dissatisfied, (2) dissatisfied, (3) indifferent, (4) satisfied, and (5) very pleased.

Table 4

Mean ratings on questionnaire for claimed participation in activities for
subjects of Central House and of apartment residence, as rated by
social workers and psychologists*

| Raters | Residents of | | "t" |
	Central House (institutional type)	Apartment Residence	
Social workers	3.6	3.3	—
Psychologists	3.7	3.8	0.7

* Scale points, based on specific criteria, range as follows: (1) markedly dis-
interested, (2) indifferent, (3) mildly participating, (4) active, and (5) very
active.

It was revealed that social workers rated Central House subjects
as being slightly more active than the group from the apartment
residence. Yet psychologists' ratings indicated that apartment residents were somewhat more active than the Central House group.
Here again there is the likelihood of factors operating in a "halo
effect" similar to those with the adjustment questionnaire.

The difference revealed with use of Fisher's "t" test was found
to be not significant.

Also the additional hypotheses concerning relationships between
attitude toward death and self-appraisal of health, adjustment in
the institutional setting, and between attitude toward death and
claimed participation in activities were not found to be supported
statistically to a significant degree.

Conclusions

Attitude toward death was evaluated by means of a psychological
test battery on two equatable groups of 30 ambulatory aged, currently unmarried, white, female persons living under the two already specified modes of institutional residency.

The findings from this study yield the following conclusions.

1. Subjects residing under conditions approximating their previous environment of living independently (apartment residence)
show less fear of, or preoccupation with, death than do those persons
in an environment grossly dissimilar to what they were once used
to. Consequently, there may be a basis for the belief that subjects

of the apartment residence enjoy better mental health and are more concerned with planning for continued living than would hold true for subjects of the traditional institutional residence (Central House). This would serve to sustain the hypothesis.

2. Compensatory mechanisms, especially with regard to overcoming anxiety in the health area, were found to operate more prominently with subjects (institutional type) who indicated a less realistic estimate of their health than appeared to hold for the group from the apartment residence.

3. No clear-cut conclusions were suggested by the findings as to adjustment and claimed participation in activities for the two research groups.

4. On the basis of observed behavior and test performance, respondents from the more permissive apartment setting evidenced greater social alertness and greater productivity, and were more responsive, less suspicious, and generally more cooperative than subjects from Central House.

5. The additional hypotheses with regard to relationships between attitude toward death and self-evaluation of health, adjustment in the institutional setting, and claimed participation in activities were not confirmed by the statistical findings in this study.

6. While impressions from the various instruments of the psychological test battery were also taken into consideration, the sentence completion test and the Thematic Apperception Test appeared to be relatively more productive in this study in facilitating psychological judgments of attitude toward death.

7. Both groups of subjects reveal at least mild anxiety with regard to thoughts of death.

Various research recommendations of a contiguous and ancillary nature present themselves for further investigation in the field of gerontology. There is a deeply-felt need for incisive and fruitful contributions to general knowledge about aged persons, and more specifically with regard to the effects of institutional residency, with its implications for planning with, and for, the aged person.

References

1. Part 2, Act III, Scene ii.
2. J. G. Gilbert, *Understanding Old Age*, 401. While it may be said that religion also aims to help people face death, it thus exerts an influence on how a person views life. G. Stanley Hall contends: "The most essential claim of Christianity is to have obviated the fear of death and made the king of

terrors into a good friend, if not a boon companion, by this most masterly of all psychotherapies." G. Stanley Hall, "A Study of Fears," *American Journal of Psychology*, 8 (1896), 472.

The Hebrew religion is comparable to the various denominations of Christianity from the standpoint of its basic morality and religious orientation, and any sociologic and psychologic observations are applicable to the subjects of this research. S. S. Cohen, *Judaism, A Way of Life*, and K. Kohler, *The Ethical Basis of Judaism*.

3. Except for the biological definition of death, there have been comparatively few scientific investigations of the varying meanings and functions of death concepts and attitudes.

4. *Webster's New International Dictionary*, second edition, unabridged.

Richard A. Kalish

Some Variables in Death Attitudes

The present study is an exploratory investigation of attitudes toward different methods of destroying life and the relationships of these attitudes to religious beliefs. The variables selected as methods of destroying life include birth control, euthanasia, abortion, capital punishment, and wartime killing; the religious beliefs included are belief in God, belief in afterlife and religious affiliation: another variable included was overtly expressed fear of death.

The purpose of this study is three-fold: (*a*) to explore the relationships among the variables related to destroying life, belief in God and after-life, and fear of death; (*b*) to determine differences among religious groups for each variable; and (*c*) to determine sex and age differences on each variable.

Method

A form was prepared to measure attitudes toward the six death-related issues and the two religious issues. The total form consisted of thirty-two Likert-type items, sixteen of which dealt with such topics as federal aid to education, segregation, public housing, etc. These items were added to obscure the purpose of the form, which was titled, "Attitude on Social Issues"; none of the *S*s perceived the

Reprinted from *The Journal of Social Psychology*, 59 (1963), pp. 137–145, by permission of the author and publisher.

nature of the attitude survey. The pertinent sixteen items related to Birth Control, Abortion, Euthanasia, Wartime Killing, Capital Punishment, Fear of Death, Belief in After-life and Belief in God. Two items, one worded positively and the other worded negatively, related to each issue, the purpose being to eliminate any effect of response set. The sequence of presentation of the thirty-two items was random.

Each *S* was asked to indicate his feeling on the issue by circling the symbols SA, A, ?, D, or SD to show Strong Agreement through Strong Disagreement. Equal-appearing intervals were assumed, and five points were given for a favorable response, four for a moderately favorable response, etc. A favorable response was considered to be SA when the item was worded positively or SD when the item was worded negatively. The following items were used, the number to the left of each statement being its position among the thirty-two items:

4. In many instances, married couples should be encouraged to use birth control devices.

7. Mercy-killing, assuming proper precautions are taken, will benefit people on the whole.

9. Preventing conception by mechanical birth control devices is as wrong or almost as wrong as taking a human life after birth.

10. Laws which provide the death penalty for crimes are morally wrong.

11. Although my definition of God may differ from that of others, I believe there is a God.

14. Physical or mental illness, no matter how severe or hopeless, should never be the basis for taking the life of the involved person.

16. Killing during war is just as indefensible as any other sort of killing.

18. As unfortunate as it is, killing during wartime may be justifiable.

19. The possibility that God exists today seems very unlikely.

23. If a mother's life is seriously endangered, forced abortion of the fetus may be necessary.

26. Life after death seems an improbable occurrence.

27. I find the prospect of my eventual death disturbing.

29. There is some sort of existence after our present life ends.

30. Forced abortion of the fetus is wrong, regardless of the health of the mother or the social conditions involved.

31. In the long run, appropriate use of the death penalty for crimes will benefit society.

32. I don't think I am really afraid of death.

Following the attitude form, several biographical items were presented. The Ss were asked to state age, sex, religious identification, and racial background.

1. SUBJECTS

The forms were distributed to approximately 220 students in five advanced psychology classes at Los Angeles State College. A total of 210 Ss returned forms sufficiently complete for analysis.

The Ss ranged in age from 18 to 65 with a median of 28. Since four of the five classes were conducted in the evening, the great majority of Ss were involved with full-time positions in the community, and attended college on a part-time basis. Although obviously not a random sample of the Los Angeles area, they probably more nearly represent the community in race, religion, and social class than most college student samples.

A breakdown of Ss by religion shows 93 Protestants, 38 Catholics, 25 Jews, and 35 Atheist-Agnostics (these two groups were combined since observation indicated no real differences in their responses); the remainder (19) gave no classifiable religious preference. Negroes in the sample numbered 24; people of Asian ancestry totaled six; and 163 were Caucasian; 17 Ss did not state racial background. The sample contained 130 men and 67 women; 13 did not supply this information.

2. DATA ANALYSIS

Since each variable was measured by two items on a five-point scale, the possible range of scores was two to 10. This restricted range led to several highly truncated distributions. Also, because of the nature of the items, data were heavily skewed in several instances. Working within these limitations, three types of data analysis were possible. First, a matrix of tetrachoric correlations based on a median split between each combination of variables was computed. The method of computation followed Edwards[1]; the level of significance was established by determining the significance level for product-moment correlations based on less than one-half the number of Ss as suggested in Guilford[2] (the sample N was 210), while the level of significance utilized was established for Pearson product-moment correlations with N's of 100.

Second, each of the four religious groups was compared with each of the others on each variable. The significance of the differences between means in each instance was established by a t-test.

Third, sex differences and age differences in responses to each variable were determined by t-tests.

Results and Discussion

Results may be divided into three sections, data dealing with relationships among variables, data dealing with religious differences, and data involving sex and age differences.

The intervariable correlation matrix is shown in Table 1. Of the twenty-eight correlations computed, ten were significant at the .01 level of confidence and five were significant at the .05 level of confidence. The data were re-analyzed omitting Catholic Ss on the possibility that the relationships were a function of the attitudes of this group. The recomputed correlations showed negligible differences from the initial ones.

Several pertinent observations may be made from the matrix:

1. Approval of birth control, of abortion, and of euthanasia consistently and significantly correlate with each other. This appears to be a factor which might be termed "Social Liberalism."

2. Belief in God, belief in after-life, and approval of capital punishment also are consistently and significantly correlated with each other. They appear to form a factor which might be termed "Religious Justice."

3. Eight of the nine correlations between variables in the Social Liberalism factor and those in the Religious Justice factor are negative, six of them significantly. This would appear to increase the probability of these being reliable factors.

4. Approval of wartime killing and of capital punishment correlate significantly with each other. Approval of euthanasia correlates positively, although not significantly, with both. The latter correlations appear to have importance in view of the fact that they provide the only deviations from the consistently negative correlations of the Social Liberalism variables with all other variables. A common thread in these three variables is that they each favor destruction

Table 1
Matrix of intervariable correlations on death attitudes of 210 adult college student Ss

	Birth control	Eutha-nasia	Abor-tion	Fear	Killing	Capital punishment	After-life	God
1. Approve of birth control	X	.31†	.55†	−.09	−.11	−.28†	−.33†	−.19*
2. Approve of euthanasia		X	.33†	−.05	.11	.14	−.16	−.22*
3. Approve of abortion			X	−.19*	−.24*	−.15	−.41†	−.24*
4. Fear of death				X	.01	−.07	.03	−.16
5. Approve of wartime killing					X	.44†	.17	.02
6. Approve of capital punishment						X	.31†	.34†
7. Belief in life after death							X	.64†
8. Belief in God								X

* Significant at the .05 level of confidence.
† Significant at the .01 level of confidence.

of adult human beings under stipulated conditions. They will be referred to as the Destruction Accepting factor.

5. Fear of death correlates significantly (and negatively) only with approval of abortion, indicating that those who express overt fear of death are opposed to abortion; the author finds this relationship difficult to interpret in light of the remainder of the data. Of all the variables investigated, it seems likely that fear of death was most contaminated by the extensive use of defense mechanisms.

The comparison of death attitudes between religious groupings is shown in Table 2. On the variables constituting the Social Liberalism factor, the Jews and the Atheist-Agnostics are consistently the most accepting, followed by the Protestants and the Catholics in that order. On the Religious Justice variables, the sequence is Catholic, Protestant, Jew, and Atheist-Agnostic on all three variables. On two of the three variables of the third factor (Killing and Capital Punishment), the sequence from favorable to unfavorable was Catholic, Protestant, Atheist-Agnostic, and Jew, which corresponds in general to the sequence for the Religious Justice variables. However, the trend for acceptance of euthanasia corresponds to that for Social Liberalism variables.

On the variables of Birth Control and Abortion, the only statistically significant differences are between Catholics and each of the other groupings. However, in spite of these differences, inspection of Table 2 indicates that the Catholics tend to be favorable to both ideas. A score of "6" would be neutral, and the Catholics are on the favorable side of neutral on both issues. Approximately 50 per cent more Catholics favored each of the issues than opposed them, but the opposition tended to have extreme scores, while those favorably inclined had moderate scores; thus, the means were computed to be only slightly on the favorable side of neutral.

It is readily observable that the Catholics and the Protestants were significantly more favorably disposed toward believing in God and in an after-life than were the Jews and the Atheist-Agnostics. The differences between the two Christian groups and the Atheist-Agnostics is not surprising. Also the fact that the Jewish religion takes no strong stand on after-life could readily account for the difference between Jews and non-Jews on afterlife. The relative lack of an indicated belief in God by the Jewish *S*s may either be a real difference or it may reflect the tendency of Jewish *S*s who were religiously agnostic but identified as ethnic Jews to check

Table 2

Levels of significance between religious groups on selected variables related to death and to religious beliefs

Mean[1] scores on variables by religious affiliation

Variables	Prot-Cath		Prot-Jew		Prot-Ath-Ag		Cath-Jew		Cath-Ath-Ag		Jew-Ath-Ag	
Birth control	8.83	6.34†	8.83	9.12	8.83	9.16	6.34	9.12†	6.34	9.16†	9.12	9.16
Euthanasia	4.95	4.28	4.95	5.12	4.95	6.05*	4.25	5.12	4.28	6.05†	5.12	6.05
Abortion	8.59	6.66†	8.59	9.16	8.59	9.10	6.66	9.16†	6.66	9.10†	9.16	9.10
Fear of death	5.14	5.26	5.14	5.48	5.14	4.95	5.26	5.45	5.26	4.95	5.48	4.95
Wartime killing	6.91	7.54	6.91	6.68	6.91	6.81	7.54	6.68	7.54	6.81	6.68	6.81
Capital punishment	5.55	6.63*	5.55	4.52	5.55	4.60*	6.63	4.52†	6.63	4.60†	4.52	4.60
Belief in afterlife	6.73	7.37	6.73	4.20†	6.73	3.97†	7.37	4.20†	7.37	3.97†	4.20	3.97
Belief in God	8.88	9.28	8.88	6.44†	8.88	5.34†	9.28	6.44†	9.28	5.34†	6.44	5.34

[1] Mean score on possible range of 2–10, with six as neutral. A high score indicates a favorable attitude.
* Difference significant at the .05 level of confidence.
† Difference significant at the .01 level of confidence.

the category of Jew. If the latter is the case, some individuals who are philosophic atheists or agnostics may be contained within the Jewish category in the sample.

No significant relationships were obtained between scores on any of the eight variables and age. In investigating sex differences, men were significantly more accepting of wartime killing than women ($P < .01$). The remaining seven variables, however, showed extremely small sex-differences.

Attitudes toward methods of destroying life appear to be influenced by a generalized attitude toward life, by religious convictions, and probably by other personality variables. Only in the third factor, containing Euthanasia, Capital Punishment, and Wartime Killing, does a consistency toward destruction of life occur; this factor is also partially obscured by the tendency of the Catholics to be high on Capital Punishment and low on Euthanasia, while the Atheist-Agnostics are low on Capital Punishment and high on Euthanasia. A future study might investigate the Destruction Accepting factor with a more homogeneous population.

The variables of Birth Control, Euthanasia, and Abortion are often assumed to be "humanitarian" reasons for causing life to cease; these issues receive their highest support from the Jews, frequently described as belonging to a humanistic religion, and the Atheist-Agnostics, who, lacking a belief in God, often turn to humanism. On the other hand, Wartime Killing and Capital Punishment are punitive bases for depriving individuals of life, but may be considered as necessary and just under appropriate conditions. *S*s who, by virtue of placing their faith in God, need place less faith in man, may be more concerned with justice and less concerned with humanitarianism.

The lack of differences between religious groups in fear of death is worth noting (Table 2). Since results here not only lack significance statistically, but may be contaminated by the extensive use of defense mechanisms, this provides a fruitful area for further research, probably by projective as well as survey methods.

References

1. A. L. Edwards, *Statistical Methods for the Behavioral Sciences* (New York: Rinehart, 1954).
2. J. P. Guilford, *Fundamental Statistics in Psychology and Education* (New York: McGraw-Hill, 1956).

Part 3.

Grief and Mourning:
The Reaction to Death

INTRODUCTION

Complementing the increased awareness of and investigation into the important question of people's attitudes toward death is the burgeoning research into the aftermath of death and the psychological and medical dimensions of grief and bereavement. Although Freud, Eliot, Deutsch, Nagy, Klein, Becker, and others have commented on and carried out research in this area over the last half-century, it was with Lindemann's classic report, "Symptomatology and Management of Acute Grief," published during World War II, that medical, psychological, and sociological implications of separation, grief, and bereavement were brought dramatically to the attention of medical and social scientists. By interviewing and observing 101 patients, including the bereaved survivors of victims of the Cocoanut Grove fire, Lindemann was able to report that grief is a definite syndrome with psychological and somatic symptomatology. This is, common to all patients interviewed was a remarkably uniform reaction including (1) sensations of somatic distress, which included a feeling of tightness in the throat, choking with shortness of breath, need for sighing and an empty feeling in the abdomen, lack of muscular power, and an intense subjective distress described as tension or mental pain; (2) intense preoccupation with the image of the deceased; (3) strong feelings of guilt; (4) a loss of warmth toward others with a tendency to respond with irritability and anger; and finally (5) disoriented behavior patterns. These five characteristics of grief appear to Lindemann to be pathognomic for grief. This syndrome need not appear immediately after a crisis, however, it may be delayed over a period of months or even years.

The duration of this grief reaction and the manner in which a person finally adjusts to his new social environment depends, Lindemann says, upon the success of what is called the "grief work," i.e., emancipation from the bondage to the deceased, readjustment to the environment in which the deceased is missing, and the formation of new relationships. Lindemann noted considerable resistance on the part of his patients to accept the discomfort and distress of bereavement. The patients chose instead, in many instances, to avoid the intense pain connected with the grief experience and to avoid also the expression of emotion necessary for it. Such distortion of normal grief may well be a prelude to a morbid grief reaction which Lindemann and others have documented, and which may run the gamut of response from such psychosomatic conditions as asthma, ulcerative colitis, and rheumatoid arthritis to antisocial behavior and possibly even psychosis. Several of the studies included in this book supplement Lindemann's initial insights and findings.

Two contributors to this section, Shoor and Speed, report on psychiatric consultations with fourteen adolescents in the care of a Juvenile Probation Department in California. All fourteen came to the attention of the authorities because of their extreme delinquent behavior. In each case there had been a recent death of a close family member. Prior to the time of the death, none of the children had shown such behavioral problems. Operating on the premise that these fourteen boys and girls were acting out their grief and were the unhappy victims of pathologic mourning, Shoor and Speed were able to achieve normal mourning processes with some of their clients and effect a return to more acceptable modes of behavior.

A further report by Brewster tells of the reactions of six psychiatric patients to a month's separation from their common therapist. Three of the patients had a neurosis, two had ulcerative colitis, and one had rheumatoid arthritis. He concludes that the reaction to separation bears symptomatic resemblance to the grief of normal individuals.

An additional illustration of the intimate relationship between grief and psychosomatic responses is provided by Stern and his collaborators. They report on the grief reactions of twenty-five subjects attending an old age counselling service. The most striking features observed were: a relative paucity of overt grief and of conscious guilt feelings, a preponderance of somatic illness precipitated or accentuated by the bereavement, a tendency to self-isolation and to hostility against some living person.

Finally, Barry, reporting on the significance of early bereavement in psychiatric patients, concludes that the evidence suggests that maternal bereavement before the age of eight may be a sensitizing factor in the development of subsequent psychoneurosis.

Volkart, in his contribution to this book, "Bereavement and Mental Health," introduces the "culture concept" to our discussion and permits us to view the phenomenon of grief from the vantage point of certain cross-cultural comparisons. In doing so he raises the important question of how much of what Lindemann describes as "normal grief" is human instead of animal, and what in the "grief reactions" reported by him and the other investigators in this section is human instead of cultural.

Volkart's thesis is that man is a social animal. Every society of men has its own distinct culture. Although death is the lot of all men, each society copes with death in terms of its own set of ideas, beliefs, values, and practices. Some societies, for instance, see death as inevitable and an improvement in one's prospects and status. Others do not. Mourning or weeping over the loss of an individual is not everywhere considered appropriate behavior.

How one reacts to the death of another, therefore, is dependent upon one's "status" and "role" in relation to the deceased. In our society the accepted definition of who is "bereaved" or who has suffered the main "loss" includes the parents and siblings of the deceased as well as his spouse and children. Among Trobriand Islanders, however, the emphasis is placed upon persons related to the deceased through his mother. His maternal kin share the status of "bereaved" and it is they who are seen as having suffered the major loss. They are considered to be "closest" to the deceased—more so even than the spouse. Although he or she may "grieve" the death, this response is considered more obligatory and ceremonial than spontaneous in nature. In any case, the spouse is not considered to be bereaved in the same sense as the maternal relatives of the deceased. Again the expression of grief is seen to be a function of the psychological value that one person may come to have for another within the family system itself. Since we as individuals mature and become distinct personalities primarily within the family structure, the number and kinds of identification, emotional or affective involvement, and the degree and strength of dependency on others, will vary according to the range, frequency, intimacy, and quality of the interactions provided by the family.

Volkart points to the Ifaluk, among whom it has been observed that the pain and distress of grief seem to disappear upon conclusion of the funeral ceremony. Following the anthropologist Spiro, Volkart suggests that this behavior can be explained in terms of the family system and the socialization practices that prevail among these people. Among the Ifaluk, child-rearing is not the sole prerogative of parents and older siblings but is shared by many others in the tribe who are as important to a child as are the members of his "own" family. The emotional relationships of the growing child and the mature adult therefore are diffused and dispersed among many persons, rather than focused and centered on only a significant few. The death of a "family" member therefore does not have the same psychological impact it would have if those relationships were more exclusive. With one's emotional investment distributed more widely, the "other" person is not valued as a unique and irreplaceable personality within one's system of relationships. More important, rather, are the "roles" played by the interchangeable others and the functions these "roles" perform for the individual. The death of any one person in the community or family little disturbs the psychological self and grief is mute.

Turning to American society, Volkart takes note of the limited range of interaction possible within our emerging small family system. In contrast to the Ifaluk, self-identification and personal dependency for a child in our society is channeled among the same few persons within the family setting thus allowing for strong emotional attachments to family figures. These few persons become as a result unique and irreplaceable personalities within the family structure. But, Volkart points out, these same figures are not only the source of love and gratification but also mete out punishment and represent frustration to the growing individual. The upshot of this situation is, according to Volkart, the possible danger of increasing a person's emotional vulnerability in bereavement.

In addition, the situation is further intensified by the fact that death in American society is defined as loss with the result that bereavement and loss and/or grief are considered interchangeable terms. We have seen however that grief, as Lindemann would describe it, is not necessarily synonymous with bereavement which is the social proscriptions, injunctions, expectations and demands placed upon one who is designated or assumes the role of a bereaved person. Nevertheless, the expectation in our society is that a person will or should express grief if bereaved. Feelings of ambivalence, fear, and hostility generated in the emotionally intense family setting are ignored at this time by our cultural emphasis on the idea of loss. The possible result of such a contradiction in many instances where little love or grief is experienced, Volkart believes, is the inducement of guilt. Thus paradoxically the cultural directive to mourn may become dysfunctional in that it can generate a set of discomforting feelings and attitudes where what is intended is the mitigation or amelioration of emotional stress.

Similarly, the role of male in our society prohibits the expression of deep emotions. Yet, on the other hand, the role of bereaved demands an expression of loss. The psychic conflict induced in this and other cultural expectations attendant upon a death prompts Volkart to call for a greater understanding of grief and bereavement and the place mourning rites and customs have in meeting the emotional needs of survivors. In this he has not only in mind the expression of love or loss but also the discharge or release of hostility and guilt. In other words, our constitutional patterns of response to death need to be integrated with the social and psychological needs of the survivors. First, however, we must come to recognize the potentially dangerous crisis situation that bereavement presents us and appreciate more fully that the attitude we take toward it and the manner in which we treat it will be reflected in the mental and physical health of the survivors.

The emerging isolation of the individual in American society at the time of his death, as well as the shift in the definition and meaning that death and dying have for us today, is capsuled in the article which completes this section, "Predilection to Death," by Weisman and Hackett.

Reporting on a group of patients who anticipated their own death, Weisman and Hackett distinguish between and comment upon the impersonal, interpersonal, and intrapersonal elements in their patients' experience of death. Although the major thrust of their paper is an appeal to psychiatrists and other medical personnel to help the dying patient achieve what they call an "appropriate death," the paper serves as well to point up the dilemma of our modern existential condition, particularly as it is experienced in the context of the modern hospital. Conceding the point that the entire discussion of death and dying is probably meaningless to adherents of certain religious faiths, Weisman and Hackett try to introduce order and reason into a situation which includes: a rapidly growing hospital population of the infirm and dying patient; a medical philosophy which both accepts and rejects the idea of death; doctors who avoid their dying patients; nurses and other hospital personnel who are untrained and ill-equipped to cope with the psychological needs and requirements of their aged or dying charges; patients abandoned by their families; and hospitals that isolate the terminally ill patient from his family and friends or from other patients when death occurs.

For Weisman and Hackett, any constructive help that might be extended the dying patient in this day and age requires a careful re-examination of our own attitudes toward death. Even though it is true that how each person dies is determined by how he has lived, it would appear to be equally true that a dignified death proclaims the significance of all men.

Erich Lindemann

Symptomatology and Management of Acute Grief

Introduction

At first glance, acute grief would not seem to be a medical or psychiatric disorder in the strict sense of the word but rather a normal reaction to a distressing situation. However, the understanding of reactions to traumatic experiences whether or not they represent clear-cut neuroses has become of ever-increasing impor-

Reprinted from *American Journal of Psychiatry*, 101 (1944), 141–148, by permission of the author and publisher (Copyright 1944, *American Journal of Psychiatry*).

tance to the psychiatrist. Bereavement or the sudden cessation of social interaction seems to be of special interest because it is often cited among the alleged psychogenic factors in psychosomatic disorders. The enormous increase in grief reactions due to war casualties, furthermore, demands an evaluation of their probable effect on the mental and physical health of our population.

The points to be made in this paper are as follows:

1. Acute grief is a definite syndrome with psychological and somatic symptomatology.

2. This syndrome may appear immediately after a crisis; it may be delayed; it may be exaggerated or apparently absent.

3. In place of the typical syndrome there may appear distorted pictures, each of which represents one special aspect of the grief syndrome.

4. By appropriate techniques these distorted pictures can be successfully transformed into a normal grief reaction with resolution.

Our observations comprise 101 patients. Included are (1) psychoneurotic patients who lost a relative during the course of treatment, (2) relatives of patients who died in the hospital, (3) bereaved disaster victims (Cocoanut Grove Fire) and their close relatives, (4) relatives of members of the armed forces.

The investigation consisted of a series of psychiatric interviews. Both the timing and the content of the discussions were recorded. These records were subsequently analyzed in terms of the symptoms reported and of the changes in mental status observed progressively through a series of interviews. The psychiatrist avoided all suggestions and interpretations until the picture of symptomatology and spontaneous reaction tendencies of the patients had become clear from the records. The somatic complaints offered important leads for objective study . . . .

Symptomatology of Normal Grief

The picture shown by persons in acute grief is remarkably uniform. Common to all is the following syndrome: sensations of somatic distress occurring in waves lasting from twenty minutes to an hour at a time, a feeling of tightness in the throat, choking with shortness of breath, need for sighing, and an empty feeling in the abdomen, lack of muscular power, and an intense subjective distress described as tension or mental pain. The patient soon learns that these waves of discomfort can be precipitated by visits, by mentioning the deceased, and by receiving sympathy. There is a tendency to avoid the syndrome at any cost, to refuse visits lest they should precipitate the reaction, and to keep deliberately from thought all references to the deceased.

The striking features are (1) the marked tendency to sighing respiration; this respiratory disturbance was most conspicuous when the patient was made to discuss his grief. (2) The complaint about lack of strength and exhaustion is universal and is described as follows: "It is almost impossible to climb up a stairway." "Everything I lift seems so heavy." "The slightest effort makes me feel exhausted." "I can't walk to the corner without feeling exhausted." (3) Digestive symptoms are described as follows: "The food tastes like sand." "I have no appetite at all." "I stuff the food down because I have to eat." "My saliva won't flow." "My abdomen feels hollow." "Everything seems slowed up in my stomach."

The sensorium is generally somewhat altered. There is commonly a slight sense of unreality, a feeling of increased emotional distance from other people (sometimes they appear shadowy or small), and there is intense preoccupation with the image of the deceased. A patient who lost his daughter in the Cocoanut Grove disaster visualized his girl in the telephone booth calling for him and was much troubled by the loudness with which his name was called by her and was so vividly preoccupied with the scene that he became oblivious of his surroundings. A young navy pilot lost a close friend; he remained a vivid part of his imagery, not in terms of a religious survival but in terms of an imaginary companion. He ate with him and talked over problems with him, for instance, discussing with him his plan of joining the Air Corps. Up to the time of the study, six months later, he denied the fact that the boy was no longer with him. Some patients are much concerned about this aspect of their grief reaction because they feel it indicates approaching insanity.

Another strong preoccupation is with feelings of guilt. The bereaved searches the time before the death for evidence of failure to do right by the lost one. He accuses himself of negligence and exaggerates minor omissions. After the fire disaster the central topic of discussion for a young married woman was the fact that her husband died after he left her following a quarrel, and of a young man whose wife died, that he fainted too soon to save her.

In addition, there is often disconcerting loss of warmth in relationship to other people, a tendency to respond with irritability and anger, a wish not to be bothered by others at a time when friends and relatives make a special effort to keep up friendly relationships.

These feelings of hostility, surprising and quite inexplicable to the patients, disturbed them and again were often taken as signs of approaching insanity. Great efforts are made to handle them, and the result is often a formalized, stiff manner of social interaction.

The activity throughout the day of the severely bereaved person shows remarkable changes. There is no retardation of action and speech; quite to the contrary, there is a push of speech, especially when talking about the deceased. There is restlessness, inability to sit still, moving about in an aimless fashion, continually searching for something to do. There is, however, at the same time, a painful lack of capacity to initiate and maintain organized patterns of activity. What is done is done with lack of zest, as though one were going through the motions. The bereaved clings to the daily routine of prescribed activities; but these activities do not proceed in the automatic, self-sustaining fashion which characterizes normal work but have to be carried on with effort, as though each fragment of the activity became a special task. The bereaved is surprised to find how large a part of his customary activity was done in some meaningful relationship to the deceased and has now lost its significance. Especially the habits of social interaction—meeting friends, making conversation, sharing enterprises with others—seem to have been lost. This loss lends to a strong dependency on anyone who will stimulate the bereaved to activity and serve as the initiating agent.

These five points—(1) somatic distress, (2) preoccupation with the image of the deceased, (3) guilt, (4) hostile reactions, and (5) loss of patterns of conduct—seem to be pathognomonic for grief. There may be added a sixth characteristic, shown by patients who border on pathological reactions, which is not so conspicuous as the others but nevertheless often striking enough to color the whole picture. This is the appearance of traits of the deceased in the behavior of the bereaved, especially symptoms shown during the last illness, or behavior which may have been shown at the time of the tragedy. A bereaved person is observed or finds himself walking in the manner of his deceased father. He looks in the mirror and believes that his face appears just like that of the deceased. He may show a change of interests in the direction of the former activities of the deceased and may start enterprises entirely different from his former pursuits. A wife who lost her husband, an insurance agent, found herself writing to many insurance companies offering her services with somewhat exaggerated schemes. It seemed a regular observation in these patients that the painful preoccupation with the image of the deceased described above was transformed into preoccupation with symptoms or personality traits of the lost person, but now displaced to their own bodies and activities by identification.

Course of Normal Grief Reactions

The duration of a grief reaction seems to depend upon the success with which a person does the *grief work*, namely, emancipation from the bondage to the deceased, readjustment to the enviroment in which the deceased is missing, and the formation of new relationships. One of the big obstacles to this work seems to be the fact that many patients try to avoid the intense distress connected with the grief experience and to avoid the expression of emotion necessary for it. The men victims after the Cocoanut Grove fire appeared in the early psychiatric interviews to be in a state of tension with tightened facial musculature, unable to relax for fear they might "break down." It required considerable persuasion to yield to the grief process before they were willing to accept the discomfort of bereavement. One assumed a hostile attitude toward the psychiatrist, refusing to allow any references to the deceased and rather rudely asking him to leave. This attitude remained throughout his stay on the ward, and the prognosis for his condition is not good in the light of other observations. Hostility of this sort was encountered on only occasional visits with the other patients. They became willing to accept the grief process and to embark on a program of dealing in memory with the deceased person. As soon as this became possible there seemed to be a rapid relief of tension and the subsequent interviews were rather animated conversations in which the deceased was idealized and in which misgivings about the future adjustment were worked through.

Examples of the psychiatrist's role in assisting patients in their readjustment after bereavement are contained in the following case histories. The first shows a very successful readjustment.

A woman, aged 40, lost her husband in the fire. She had a history of good adjustment previously. One child, ten years old. When she heard about her husband's death she was extremely depressed, cried bitterly, did not want to live, and for three days showed a state of utter dejection.

When seen by the psychiatrist, she was glad to have assistance and described her painful preoccupation with memories of her husband and her fear that she might lose her mind. She had a vivid visual image of his presence, picturing him as going to work in the morning and herself as wondering whether he would return in the evening, whether she could stand his not returning, then, describing to herself how he does return, plays with the dog, receives his child, and gradually tried to accept the fact that he is not there any more. It was only after ten days that she succeeded in accepting his loss and then only after having described in detail the remarkable qualities of her husband, the tragedy of his having to stop his activities at the pinnacle of his success, and his deep devotion to her.

In the subsequent interviews she explained with some distress that she had become very much attached to the examiner and that she waited for the hour of his coming. This reaction she considered disloyal to her husband but at the same time she could accept the fact that it was a hopeful sign of her ability to fill the gap he had left in her life. She then showed a marked drive for activity, making plans for supporting herself and her little girl, mapping out the preliminary steps for resuming her old profession as secretary, and making efforts to secure help from the occupational therapy department in reviewing her knowledge of French.

Her convalescence, both emotional and somatic, progressed smoothly, and she made a good adjustment immediately on her return home.

A man of 52, successful in business, lost his wife, with whom he had lived in happy marriage. The information given him about his wife's death confirmed his suspicions of several days. He responded with a severe grief reaction, with which he was unable to cope. He did not want to see visitors, was ashamed of breaking down, and asked to be permitted to stay in the hospital on the psychiatric service, when his physical condition would have permitted his discharge, because he wanted further assistance. Any mention of his wife produced a severe wave of depressive reaction, but with psychiatric assistance he gradually became willing to go through this painful process, and after three days on the psychiatric service he seemed well enough to go home.

He showed a high rate of verbal activity, was restless, needed to be occupied continually, and felt that the experience had whipped him into a state of restless overactivity.

As soon as he returned home he took an active part in his business, assuming a post in which he had a great many telephone calls. He also took over the role of amateur psychiatrist to another bereaved person, spending time with him and comforting him for his loss. In his eagerness to start anew, he developed a plan to sell all his former holdings, including his house, his furniture, and giving away anything which could remind him of his wife. Only after considerable discussion was he able to see that this would mean avoiding immediate grief at the price of an act of poor judgment. Again he had to be encouraged to deal with his grief reactions in a more direct manner. He has made a good adjustment.

With eight to ten interviews in which the psychiatrist shares the grief work, and with a period of from four to six weeks, it was ordinarily possible to settle an uncomplicated and undistorted grief reaction. This was the case in all but one of the 13 Cocoanut Grove fire victims.

Morbid Grief Reactions

Morbid grief reactions represent distortions of normal grief. The conditions mentioned here were transformed into "normal reactions" and then found their resolution.

DELAY OF REACTION

The most striking and most frequent reaction of this sort is *delay* or *postponement*. If the bereavement occurs at a time when the patient is confronted with important tasks and when there is necessity for maintaining the morale of others, he may show little or no reaction for weeks or even much longer. A brief delay is described in the following example.

> A girl of 16 lost both parents and her boy friend in the fire and was herself burned severely, with marked involvement of the lungs. Throughout her stay in the hospital her attitude was that of cheerful acceptance without any sign of adequate distress. When she was discharged at the end of three weeks she appeared cheerful, talked rapidly, with a considerable flow of ideas, seemed eager to return home to assume the role of parent for her two younger siblings. Except for slight feelings of "lonesomeness" she complained of no distress.
>
> This period of griefless acceptance continued for the next two months, even when the household was dispersed and her younger siblings were placed in other homes. Not until the end of the tenth week did she begin to show a true state of grief with marked feelings of depression, intestinal emptiness, tightness in her throat, frequent crying, and vivid preoccupation with her deceased parents.

That this delay may involve years became obvious first by the fact that patients in acute bereavement about a recent death may soon upon exploration be found preoccupied with grief about a person who died many years ago. In this manner a woman of 38, whose mother had died recently and who had responded to the mother's death with a surprisingly severe reaction, was found to be but mildly concerned with her mother's death but deeply engrossed with unhappy and perplexing fantasies concerning the death of her brother, who died twenty years ago under dramatic circumstances from metastasizing carcinoma after amputation of his arm had been postponed too long. The discovery that a former unresolved grief reaction may be precipitated in the course of the discussion of another recent event was soon demonstrated in psychiatric interviews by patients who showed all the traits of a true grief reaction when the topic of a former loss arose.

The precipitating factor for the delayed reaction may be a deliberate recall of circumstances surrounding the death or may be a spontaneous occurrence in the patient's life. A peculiar form of this is the circumstance that a patient develops the grief reaction at the time when he himself is as old as the person who died.

For instance, a railroad worker, aged 42, appeared in the psychiatric clinic with a picture which was undoubtedly a grief reaction for which he had no explanation. It turned out that when he was 22, his mother, then 42, had committed suicide.

DISTORTED REACTIONS

The delayed reactions may occur after an interval which was not marked by any abnormal behavior or distress, but in which there developed an *alteration* in the patient's *conduct* perhaps not conspicuous or serious enough to lead him to a psychiatrist. These alterations may be considered as the surface manifestations of an unresolved grief reaction, which may be classified as follows: (1) *overactivity without a sense of loss,* rather with a sense of well-being and zest, the activities being of an expansive and adventurous nature and bearing semblance to the activities formerly carried out by the deceased, as described above; (2) *the acquisition of symptoms belonging to the last illness of the deceased.* This type of patient appears in medical clinics and is often labeled hypochondriacal or hysterical. To what extent actual alterations of physiological functions occur under these circumstances will have to be a field of further careful inquiry. I owe to Dr. Chester Jones a report about a patient whose electrocardiogram showed a definite change during a period of three weeks, which started two weeks after the time her father died of heart disease.

While this sort of symptom formation "by identification" may still be considered as conversion symptoms such as we know from hysteria, there is another type of disorder doubtlessly presenting (3) a recognized *medical disease,* namely, a group of psychosomatic conditions, predominantly ulcerative colitis, rheumatoid arthritis, and asthma. Extensive studies in ulcerative colitis have produced evidence that 33 out of 41 patients with ulcerative colitis developed their disease in close time relationship to the loss of an important person. Indeed, it was this observation which first gave the impetus for the present detailed study of grief. Two of the patients developed bloody diarrhea at funerals. In the others it developed within a few weeks after the loss. The course of the ulcerative colitis was strikingly benefited when this grief reaction was resolved by psychiatric technique.

At the level of social adjustment there often occurs a conspicuous (4) *alteration in relationship to friends and relatives.* The patient feels irritable, does not want to be bothered, avoids former social activities, and is afraid he might antagonize his friends by his lack of interest and his critical attitudes. Progressive social isolation follows, and the patient needs considerable encouragement in reestablishing his social relationships.

While overflowing hostility appears to be spread out over all relationships, it may also occur as (5) *furious hostility against specific persons;* the doctor or the surgeon is accused bitterly for neglect of duty and the patient may assume that foul play has led to the death. It is characteristic that while patients talk a good deal about their suspicions and their bitter feelings, they are not likely to take any action against the accused, as a truly paranoid person might do.

(6) Many bereaved persons struggled with much effort against these feelings of hostility, which to them seem absurd, representing a vicious change in their characters and to be hidden as much as possible. Some patients succeed in hiding their hostility but become wooden and formal, with affectivity and conduct *resembling schizophrenic pictures.* A typical report is this, "I go through all the motions of living. I look after my children. I do my errands. I go to social functions, but it is like being in a play; it doesn't really concern me. I can't have any warm feelings. If I were to have any feelings at all I would be angry with everybody." This patient's reaction to therapy was characterized by growing hostility against the therapist, and it required considerable skill to make her continue interviews in spite of the disconcerting hostility which she had been fighting so much. The absence of emotional display in this patient's face and actions was quite striking. Her face had a masklike appearance, her movements were formal, stilted, robotlike, without the fine play of emotional expression.

(7) Closely related to this picture is a *lasting loss of patterns of social interaction.* The patient cannot initiate any activity, is full of eagerness to be active—restless, can't sleep—but throughout the day he will not start any activity unless "primed" by somebody else. He will be grateful at sharing activities with others but will not be able to make up his mind to do anything alone. The picture is one of lack of decision and initiative. Organized activities along social lines occur only if a friend takes the patient along and shares the activity with him. Nothing seems to promise reward; only the ordinary activities of the day are carried on, and these in a

routine manner, falling apart into small steps, each of which has to be carried out with much effort and without zest.

(8) There is, in addition, a picture in which a patient is active but in which most of his activities attain a coloring which is *detrimental to his own social and economic existence*. Such patients with uncalled-for generosity, give away their belongings, are easily lured into foolish economic dealings, lose their friends and professional standing by a series of "stupid acts," and find themselves finally without family, friends, social status, or money. This protracted self-punitive behavior seems to take place without any awareness of excessive feelings of guilt. It is a particularly distressing grief picture because it is likely to hurt other members of the family and drag down friends and business associates.

(9) This leads finally to the picture in which the grief reaction takes the form of a straight *agitated depression* with tension, agitation, insomnia, feelings of worthlessness, bitter self-accusation, and obvious need for punishment. Such patients may be dangerously suicidal.

A young man aged 32 had received only minor burns and left the hospital apparently well on the road to recovery just before the psychiatric survey of the disaster victims took place. On the fifth day he had learned that his wife had died. He seemed somewhat relieved of his worry about her fate; impressed the surgeon as being unusually well controlled during the following short period of his stay in the hospital.

On January 1st he was returned to the hospital by his family. Shortly after his return home he had become restless, did not want to stay at home, had taken a trip to relatives trying to find rest, had not succeeded, and returned home in a state of marked agitation, appearing preoccupied, frightened, and unable to concentrate on any organized activity. The mental status presented a somewhat unusual picture. He was restless, could not sit still or participate in any activity on the ward. He would try to read, drop it after a few minutes, or try to play pingpong, give it up after a short time. He would try to start conversations, break them off abruptly, and then fall into repeated murmured utterances: "Nobody can help me. When is it going to happen? I am doomed, am I not?" With great effort it was possible to establish enough rapport to carry on interviews. He complained about his feeling of extreme tension, inability to breathe, generalized weakness and exhaustion, and his frantic fear that something terrible was going to happen. "I'm destined to live in insanity or I must die. I know that it is God's will. I have this awful feeling of guilt." With intense morbid guilt feelings, he reviewed incessantly the events of the fire. His wife had stayed behind. When he tried to pull her out, he had fainted and was shoved out by the crowd. She was burned while he was saved. "I should have saved her or I should have died too." He complained about being filled with an incredible violence and did not know what to do about it. The rapport established with him lasted for only brief periods of time. He then would fall back into his state of intense agitation and muttering. He slept poorly even with large sedation. In the course of four days he became somewhat more composed, had longer periods of contact with the psychiatrist, and seemed to feel that he was being understood and might be able to cope with his morbid feelings of guilt and violent impulses. On the sixth day of his hospital stay, however, after skillfully distracting the attention of his special nurse, he jumped through a closed window to a violent death.

If the patient is not conspicuously suicidal, it may nevertheless be true that he has a strong desire for painful experiences, and such patients are likely to desire shock treatment of some sort, which they picture as a cruel experience, such as electrocution might be.

A 28-year-old woman, whose 20-month-old son was accidentally smothered, developed a state of severe agitated depression with self-accusation, inability to enjoy anything, hopelessness about the future, overflow of hostility against the husband and his parents, also with excessive hostility against the psychiatrist. She insisted upon electric-shock treatment and was finally referred to another physician who treated her. She responded to the shock treatments very well and felt relieved of her sense of guilt.

It is remarkable that agitated depressions of this sort represent only a small fraction of the pictures of grief in our series.

Prognostic Evaluation

Our observations indicate that to a certain extent the type and severity of the grief reaction can be predicted. Patients with obsessive personality make-up and with a history of former depressions are likely to develop an agitated depression. Severe reactions seem to occur in mothers who have lost young children. The intensity of interaction with the deceased before his death seems to be significant. It is important to realize that such interaction does not have to be of the affectionate type; on the contrary, the death of a person who invited much hostility, especially hostility which could not be well-expressed because of his status and claim to loyalty, may be followed by a severe grief reaction in which hostile impulses are the most conspicuous feature. Not infrequently the person who passed away represented a key person in a social system, his death being followed by disintegration of this social system and by a profound alteration of the living and social conditions for the bereaved. In such cases readjustment presents a severe task quite apart from the reaction to the loss incurred. All these factors seem to be more important than a tendency to react with neurotic symptoms in previous life. In this way the most conspicuous forms of morbid identification were found in persons who had no former history of a tendency to psychoneurotic reactions.

Management

Proper psychiatric management of grief reactions may prevent prolonged and serious alterations in the patient's social adjustment, as well as potential medical disease. The essential task facing the psychiatrist is that of sharing the patient's grief work, namely, his efforts at extricating himself from the bondage to the deceased and at finding new patterns of rewarding interaction. It is of the greatest importance to notice that not only over-reaction but under-reaction of the bereaved must be given attention, because delayed responses may occur at unpredictable moments and the dangerous distortions of the grief reaction, not conspicuous at first, may be quite destructive later and these may be prevented.

Religious agencies have led in dealing with the bereaved. They have provided comfort by giving the backing of dogma to the patient's wish for continued interaction with the deceased, have developed rituals which maintain the patient's interaction with others, and have counteracted the morbid guilt feelings of the patient by Divine Grace and by promising an opportunity for "making up" to the deceased at the time of a later reunion. While these measures have helped countless mourners, comfort alone does not provide adequate assistance in the patient's grief work. He has to review his relationships with the deceased, and has to become acquainted with the alterations in his own modes of emotional reaction. His fear of insanity, his fear of accepting the surprising changes in his feelings, especially the overflow of hostility, have to be worked through. He will have to express his sorrow and sense of loss. He will have to find an acceptable formulation of his future relationship to the deceased. He will have to verbalize his feelings of guilt, and he will have to find persons around him whom he can use as "primers" for the acquisition of new patterns of conduct. All this can be done in eight to ten interviews.

Special techniques are needed if hostility is the most marked feature of the grief reaction. The hostility may be directed against the psychiatrist, and the patient will have such guilt over his hostility that he will avoid further interviews. The help of a social worker or a minister, or if these are not available, a member of the family, to urge the patient to continue coming to see the psychiatrist may be indispensable . . . .

Since it is obvious that not all bereaved persons, especially those suffering because of war casualties, can have the benefit of expert psychiatric help, much of this knowledge will have to be passed on to auxiliary workers. Social workers and ministers will have to be on the lookout for the more ominous pictures, referring these to the psychiatrist while assisting the more normal reactions themselves.

Anticipatory Grief Reactions

While our studies were at first limited to reactions to actual death, it must be understood that grief reactions are just one form of separation reactions. Separation by death is characterized by its irreversibility and finality. Separation may, of course, occur for other reasons. We were at first surprised to find genuine grief reactions in patients who had not experienced a bereavement but who had experienced separation, for instance, with the departure of a member of the family into the armed forces. Separation in this case is not due to death but is under the threat of death. A common picture hitherto not appreciated is a syndrome which we have designated *anticipatory grief*. The patient is so concerned with her adjustment after the potential death of father or son that she goes through all the phases of grief—depression, heightened pre-occupation with the departed, a review of all the forms of death which might befall him, and anticipation of the modes of readjustment which might be necessitated by it. While this reaction may well form a safeguard against the impact of a sudden death notice, it can turn out to be of a disadvantage at the occasion of reunion. Several instances of this sort came to our attention when a soldier just returned from the battlefront complained that his wife did not love him anymore and demanded immediate divorce. In such situations apparently the grief work had been done so effectively that the patient has emancipated herself and the readjustment must now be directed towards new interaction. It is important to know this because many family disasters of this sort may be avoided through prophylactic measures.

References

Many of the observations are, of course, not entirely new. Delayed reactions were described by Helene Deutsch [1]. Shock treatment in agitated depressions due to bereavement has recently been advocated by Myerson [2]. Morbid identification has been stressed at many points in the psychoanalytic literature and recently by H. A. Murray [3]. The relation of mourning and depressive psychoses has been discussed by Freud [4], Melanie Klein [5], and Abraham [6]. Bereavement reactions in wartime were discussed by Wilson [7]. The reactions after the Cocoanut Grove fire were described in some detail in a chapter of the monograph on this civilian disaster [8]. The effect of wartime separations was reported by Rosenbaum [9]. The incidence of grief reactions among the psychogenic factors in asthma and rheumatoid arthritis has been mentioned by Cobb, *et al.* [10, 11].

1. Helene Deutsch, "Absence of Grief," *Psychoanalytical Quarterly*, 6 (1937), 12.
2. Abraham Myerson, "The Use of Shock Therapy in Prolonged Grief Re-actions," *New England Journal of Medicine*, 230 (March 2, 1944), 9.
3. H. A. Murray, "Visual Manifestations of Personality," *Journal of Abnormal and Social Psychology*, 32 (1937), 161–184.
4. Sigmund Freud, "Mourning and Melancholia," *Collected Papers IV*, 288–317; 152–170.
5. Melanie Klein, "Mourning and Its Relation to Manic-Depressive States," *International Journal of Psychoanalysis*, 21 (1940), 125–153.

6. C. Abraham, "Notes on the Psycho-Analytical Investigation and Treatment of the Libido, Viewed in the Light of Mental Disorder," *Selected Papers.*
7. A. T. M. Wilson, "Reactive Emotional Disorders," *Practitioner,* 146, 254–258.
8. S. Cobb and E. Lindemann, "Neuropsychiatric Observations after the Cocoanut Grove Fire," *Annals of Surgery,* June, 1943.
9. Milton Rosenbaum, "Emotional Aspects of Wartime Separations," *Family,* 24 (1944), 337–341.
10. S. Cobb, W. Bauer, and I. Whitney, "Environmental Factors in Rheumatoid Arthritis," *Journal of American Medical Association,* 113 (1939), 668–670.
11. N. McDermott and S. Cobb, "Psychogenic Factors in Asthma," *Psychosomatic Medicine,* I (1939), 204–341.
12. Erich Lindemann, "Psychiatric Factors in the Treatment of Ulcerative Colitis," *Archives of Neurology and Psychiatry,* 49 (1943), 71.

Mervyn Shoor and Mary H. Speed

Death, Delinquency, and the Mourning Process

Death, the total and permanent cessation of the vital functions of an organism, is the inevitable consequence of biological existence. With the exception of some psychotic persons, all men everywhere have recognized the reality of this phenomenon of nature and have sought to understand it, and to deal with it, in diverse ways . . . .

Many psychiatrists have become increasingly interested in the problems that may arise in the wake of death. Doctor Harold Searles recently wrote, "The ostensibly prosaic fact of the inevitability of death is, in actuality, one of the supremely potent sources of man's anxiety, and the feeling responses to this aspect of reality are among the most intense and complex which it is possible for us to experience."

Man's responses to death vary tremendously according to his culture and his religion. When his mourning process is integrated with his cultural milieu, it is considered normal—and essential to mental health. When it is not integrated it may become so pathological, so distorted, that it may not even be recognizable as a variant of the mourning process. In adults these variant reactions may take the form of alcoholism, mental illness, depressive states, obesity, or various neurotic manifestations.

In a child or adolescent, the impact of a loved one's death may result in a normal mourning process with resolution, or an immedi-

Reprinted from *The Psychiatric Quarterly,* 37 (1963), 540–558, by permission of the authors and publisher (Copyright, 1963, *The Psychiatric Quarterly*).

ate pathological reaction, a delayed reaction leading to psychiatric problems as an adult, or delinquent behavior. Surprisingly enough to many people, delinquency may be a masking of the mourning process.

The etiology of delinquent behavior has been a focus of considerable research, writing, and discussion in recent years. Many authorities believe such acting-out behavior is correlated with antisocial attitudes, and that these adolescent delinquents are "children who hate." Too often it is assumed that their behavior is due to hostility.

Recent psychiatric consultation with fourteen adolescents, ranging in age from 14 to 17, indicated that such was not the case. These consultations took place in a large Juvenile Probation Department in California where these young people had been sent because their delinquent behavior was so severe as to come to the attention of legal authorities. In each case this behavior, either immediate or delayed, followed the death of a close family member. The boys and girls involved had previously conformed to family and community expectations. When faced with the reality of loss and death, however, they were not able to express their grief in socially acceptable ways and exploded into serious antisocial activity.

As an example, take the case of a boy we shall call Martin. He was fourteen when he was apprehended by the police for a series of burglaries and brought to the Juvenile Detention Hall. He seemed so sullen and so miserable, his probation officer referred him for psychiatric consultation.

Martin was the oldest of three children. His delivery was complicated and for a while he was not expected to live, but gradually developed into a normal, healthy boy. It was acknowledged that he was his mother's favorite and he was devoted to her. He did well in school and conformed to what was expected of him.

When Martin was ten, however, his mother (still a young woman) was found to have carcinoma. Although she was hospitalized periodically, she spent most of the time at home, in bed and in agony. The father stated Martin became "indifferent" to his mother and so "callous to her suffering" that he began running away from home. Shortly after his mother's funeral, the burglaries of neighbors' houses began. He was also failing in school.

Martin stated that he had been so miserable since his mother became ill he couldn't bear to be around the house. He said, "I'm not like my Dad and the rest of the family. I couldn't cry. I just couldn't." As Martin's behavior deteriorated, his father became more resentful and finally "gave up."

The diagnostic impression was that Martin was suffering acutely from the effects of his mother's death, but he was "acting out" his tears instead of shedding them. Efforts were made to improve the understanding between father and son, and the family pastor was called upon for further counselling and guidance. It was suggested that Martin put into words his grief and sense of loss and be helped to redistribute his affectional needs.

His school work began to improve and his delinquent behavior to subside. When last seen in psychiatric consultation, his father had remarried. Martin spoke warmly of his new mother and seemed to have worked through the mourning process in a normal manner.

Another case in point was that of an adolescent girl. Jeannie, a beautiful, intelligent girl of 15 was brought in to the Juvenile Probation Department by her mother because she was "beyond control." She had recently begun acting-out in sexual areas, in a most indiscriminate manner. The probation officer was impressed by the contrast between Jeannie's sensitive nervous demeanor and her extreme sexual misbehavior. She was unresponsive and unable to shed any light on her own activity. Consequently, she was referred for psychiatric consultation.

When she and her mother were interviewed, the mother stated that Jeannie had been a well-behaved, happy child until the age of seven, when she started lying, stealing, and eventually running away. The mother kept reassuring herself that these were "phases of childhood development"; but when she became aware of Jeannie's sexual activity, she became tremendously concerned and sought professional help.

As the psychiatric consultation progressed, various facts became discernible. Jeannie's father was an epileptic, but in some way this had been hidden from her. He died in an epileptic convulsion, but she was never told the cause of his death and was shielded from the very fact of his death by such euphemisms as "Daddy's gone on a long, long visit with God." The whole matter was handled in a mysterious manner that created frightening anxiety and confusion in this little girl's mind. Gradually she began to develop fantasies that perhaps her mother had murdered her father and this explained the mystery surrounding her father's being away and her mother's refusal to discuss it with her.

Jeannie was an only child and had loved her father dearly. Her sense of loss was compounded by her growing resentment of her mother. Her behavior grew more disorderly and culminated in the activity that brought her to Juvenile Hall.

The mother was urged to tell Jeannie the truth about her father's handicap and the reason for his demise. Jeannie, in turn, was given psychiatric assistance about her own feelings and subsequently was helped to learn the correlation between her delinquent behavior and her mourning for her lost father.

Although Jeannie had gained considerable insight, is doing well in school and has reconciled with her mother, she still wears some psychic scars as the result of years of repressing the normal mourning process and diverting it into antisocial channels. Had she received help at the time of the tragedy she would have been spared much suffering.

As a final example of pathologic mourning, let us consider the case of Wallace.

Wallace, a quiet, well-mannered, blonde youth of sixteen, stole four cars before he was finally apprehended by the police and brought to Juvenile Hall.

During the case investigation, the probation officer discovered a prior tragedy in the family which they refused to discuss. At this point referral for psychiatric consultation was made.

Wallace was a boy of superior intelligence who appeared very depressed. He was the son of moderately well-to-do parents and had two younger sisters who had never presented any problems. When Wallace was twelve, however, he and his twin brother got on their tandem bicycle and rode several miles to an isolated beach. This was strictly against parental orders, but the parents were out playing golf that Sunday, and the boys conveniently "forgot" household rules.

While Wallace was dozing on the sand, his twin decided to have a quick swim. No one knows what happened—but Wallace was awakened by a faint, fearful cry. He dashed into the water, calling frantically his brother's name. He dove repeatedly for him until he himself was pulled out, almost drowned, by a passing policeman.

The brother's body, swollen and pallid, was finally brought to shore. Wallace was not allowed to attend the funeral.

The parents blamed Wallace completely for his brother's death and were particularly bitter because he acted indifferent to the tragedy. They though him a callous boy, and he became a stranger in their midst. The parents forbade any mention of the dead child.

In their pain they removed all traces of the drowned son from their home—even his twin bed from the brothers' formerly shared bedroom.

In the psychiatric interview, it was suggested to the parents that Wallace's "phenomenon of indifference" was doubtless only a cover-up for deeply suppressed feelings of anguish and guilt. The possibility of his delinquent behavior developing as a substitutive grief reaction was discussed with them. It was difficult for them to see how mourning could be connected with delinquency, but they slowly began to face some of their own guilty feelings and reluctantly admitted they had, in a sense, made Wallace the scapegoat for their own grief. They were encouraged to adopt a freer attitude in referring to the dead boy and to help Wallace verbalize his feelings. Wallace's probation officer, under psychiatric guidance, discussed the tragedy with him and each discussion would terminate in a release of tears.

There have been no further delinquencies. Wallace is now on the high school swimming team and entering college this fall. His intended major—Marine Biology.

Although some of our cases were more dramatic and some less successful, the three cited above were fairly representative of the adolescents we have seen, and continue to see, who have been blocked in the normal mourning process.

This process itself may take many months. First, there is the actual loss of person. The deceased is no longer there. At the adult level, the absence of a wife connotes the real loss of one who "ran the house." At first the loss is hard to believe. One carries on as if the other were still living. In a child, the demise of a parent may realistically destroy a child's security and well-being. An extreme example would be the loss of the nursing mother in which the literal supply of food has been lost. Also, in a young child, the mother doubtless fed and cared for the child in a particular manner which could not be completely imitated by another. The child's feelings may go unnoticed by adults, since the child is not able to react appropriately.

The work of mourning may even take a year's duration and is frequently characterized by a review of memories of the deceased. These memories recur in a compelling manner and tend to run the gamut of good and bad. Pleasant associations may be followed by intense regret, guilt over real or fancied hurts. Dreams may also take up "the work." The more intense (especially if dependency and hostility are mixed) the relationship has been, the more distress is apt to occur. The final resolution is a "working through" of these repetitive memories. Successful resolution of the mourning process implies that the deceased will remain "a living memory" without the pain that originally accompanies the grief reaction. Some psychiatrists believe that the work of mourning is similar to a depression, although it is apt to be less prolonged and less self-destructive.

Following the normal completion of mourning, the survivor is now able to seek out other persons for his affectional needs. A new spouse may be sought for. The child will accept a substitute mother.

We have seen how pathologic distortions may occur. An intense depression may require psychiatric intervention. An immediate pathologic response, a radical change in the behavior, may take place. One of us saw a woman in her mid-thirties who reacted to her husband's death with wild and guilt-ridden episodes of drinking and sexual promiscuity.

There may be unresolved mourning that is touched off in later years by parallel circumstances, or there may be, in children and teen-agers, delinquencies of many kinds.

There has been some controversy regarding the capacity of children to mourn. Some psychiatrists have taken the position that because children lack sufficient experiences, the ego of a child is not developed enough to permit mourning. On the basis of our experience, however, we are inclined to feel that children are capable of mourning. Our cases lead us to believe that the delinquent behavior of these children is out of character, that death has precipitated this behavior, and that such behavior is a distorted substitute for normal grieving. Had these youngsters been encouraged to mourn, such distortions would not have evolved.

Herbert Barry, Jr.

Significance of Maternal Bereavement before Age of Eight in Psychiatric Patients

In a previous study[1], evidence was presented which indicated that death of the mother during childhood was more likely to be related

Reprinted from *Archives of Neurology and Psychiatry*, 62 (1949), pp. 630–637, by permission of the author and publisher.

to subsequent psychosis than death of the father. The incidence of maternal deaths was three times as great among psychotic persons as among normal controls (15.7 versus 5.3 per cent); the incidence of paternal deaths, on the other hand, was approximately equal among the psychotic and the normal persons (11.1 and 10.0 per cent). The ratio of maternal to paternal deaths is a useful measure, since mortality rates vary widely both from decade to decade and according to social and economic status in any given year. Thus, in the general population the normal expectancy is that two fathers will die for every mother that dies. The reason for the preponderance of paternal deaths is that mortality rates are higher for males than for females at all ages and that husbands are older than their wives. Among parents or psychotic persons it was found that three mothers died during the patient's childhood for every two fathers who died. The disproportionate number of mothers of psychotic persons who died during the patient's childhood (nearly three times the anticipated number) would seem to warrant more detailed investigation.

While there have been numerous studies on the traumatic effect of parental death that are based on the method of individual case studies,[2] and while statistical data have been presented on the frequency of bereavement in relation to such states as delinquency[3] and ulcerative colitis,[4] there have been relatively few attempts to study the precise incidence of parental deaths among psychotic patients. Rosenzweig and Bray[5] have presented some figures. However, their series involved a selective factor, since they were primarily interested in sibling deaths, and they included only cases in which precise data on this point were obtainable. A large number (44 per cent) of their cases were excluded because of lack of information. Since mothers are, in general, the most reliable source of anamnestic information, it is hardly surprising that the percentage of maternal deaths reported in their series of 200 schizophrenic patients was lower than expectation; in the 44 per cent of cases which were excluded because of lack of information, the percentage of maternal deaths would probably be considerably higher. From the standpoint of parental deaths, their series is, therefore, scarcely representative, and the small percentage of maternal deaths (which was presented as an incidental finding) would hardly be comparable to figures presented in other studies.

Since there was evidence that a disproportionately large number of patients with mental disease experience the death of their mothers during childhood, it seemed desirable to determine whether there was any critical age at which maternal bereavement would be more serious as a contributory or predisposing element in subsequent development of a psychosis. While statements have appeared in the literature,[6] based largely on individual case studies, stressing the importance of age at the time of bereavement, statistical studies on this topic have been infrequent. In fact, studies of maladjustment in the armed forces reveal a notable lack of agreement as to the age before which maternal death might be detrimental. Age limits selected by various authors include 18 years (Guttmacher and Stewart[7]), 17 years (Gardner and Goldman[8]), 16 years (Gardner and Aaron[9]) and 15 years (McNeel and Dancer[10]). Other age limits which appear in the recent literature are 12 years (Ruesch and associates[11]) and 6 years (Gardner and Aaron[9]). There is thus a wide discrepancy in the ages considered significant by the authors cited. If parental death, however, is actually more serious at any age or ages, this fact should be susceptible of statistical demonstration. The study which indicated that maternal deaths might be related to subsequent development of psychosis, previously cited, was based on 549 cases; in order to subdivide maternal deaths according to the age of the patient at the time of bereavement, it seemed desirable to enlarge the series to about three times this number.

Methods and Data

The method employed was similar to that described elsewhere.[12] The material included the series previously reported, together with 683 additional patients, also from the New Jersey State Hospital, Greystone Park.[13] The latter, all representing first admissions, were under 40 years of age and entered this hospital from 1939 to 1945 inclusive. The anamneses of these 1683 state hospital patients were inspected to determine whether either of the parents had died and the age of the patient at the time.

Table 1 shows the incidence of parental bereavement for this series for each year from the patient's birth to the age of 20. If the frequency of paternal deaths is analyzed according to the age of the patient at the time of bereavement, two trends appear: (1) A tendency toward a secular rise in frequency of paternal death with increasing age of the patients. This is in accordance

Table 1

Incidence of separation from parents during early life of 852 male and 831 female psychotic patients by death of either parent

Age of Patient at Separation	Maternal Death			Paternal Death		
	Females	Males	Total	Females	Males	Total
0	7	4	11	7	2	9
1	5	8	13	2	9	11
2	6	7	13	6	5	11
3	8	8	16	5	3	8
4	7	4	11	12	5	17
5	10	9	19	5	8	13
6	12	8	20	7	6	13
7	8	7	15	6	7	13
8	7	4	11	6	5	11
9	6	6	12	9	9	18
10	4	7	11	10	6	16
11	8	1	9	10	5	15
12	4	8	12	10	5	15
13	5	3	8	12	12	24
14	11	4	15	7	7	14
15	11	6	17	16	4	20
16	12	5	17	14	12	26
17	5	7	12	6	11	17
18	5	8	13	9	13	22
19	10	6	16	9	14	23

with statistical expectation, since mortality rates become greater with increasing age. (2) Variations from year to year. These are probably chance fluctuations. Final determination of whether yearly fluctuations are meaningful or are due to chance would require a large number of additional cases.

In contrast to the distribution of patients' ages at the time of paternal death, the ages of psychotic patients when their mothers died follow a different pattern. Three trends appear: (1) A relatively high rate of maternal bereavement during infancy and early childhood; (2) a marked decline in the incidence of maternal death during early adolescence; (3) an irregular, but definite rise in the number of maternal deaths from adolescence onward. This is roughly parallel to the rise in paternal deaths at the same ages and presumably has a similar explanation, in terms of greater mortality rates with increasing age.

In the chart, the results are presented graphically. In order to minimize purely incidental variations and to bring out the underlying trends, abscissas are based on three year intervals. It is evident that a disproportionately large number of maternal deaths occurred prior to the time that the patients were 8 years of age;

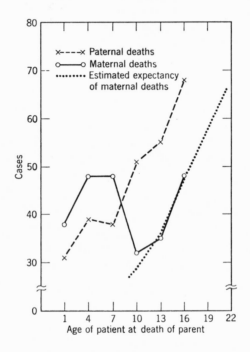

during this period 7.6 per cent of the female patients and 6.4 per cent of the male patients had experienced the death of their mothers. In absolute terms this number is not large; only 1 of 14 female patients and only 1 of 16 male patients had experienced the death of their mothers by the age of 7 years. However, the distribution of parental deaths suggests that the first seven years are critical so far as the presence of the mother is concerned. There is no evidence of a similar trend with respect to the patients' fathers.

Since maternal bereavement seems to be a sensitizing factor in the development of subsequent psychosis if it occurs prior to the age of 8, the question arises whether separation from the mother due to causes other than death might not also have a more traumatic effect if it occurred in early childhood. In a psychotic population, one obvious cause of a disrupted home during the patient's childhood might be the occurrence of a psychosis in either of his parents. While a great deal has been written about the hereditary aspects of mental disease, relatively little emphasis has been placed on the possible trauma to a child in having a parent in an institution for mental disease. For this reason, the ages of patients at the time their parents were committed have been tabulated. It should be emphasized that these data do not represent all cases of mental illness in a parent, but are limited to cases in which the parent was committed to a psychiatric hospital and in which the age of the patient at the time of the commitment was available. The results are presented in Table 2. While the absolute number of cases, when split into four-year intervals, is too small to furnish any reliable conclusions, it will be seen that more mothers than fathers were committed during the first eight years of the patients' lives. During the next eight years, the opposite is true, more fathers than mothers being committed between the time that the patients were 8 and 15 years of age. Though these results are at best

Table 2

Incidence of separation from either parent due to parental commitment or desertion for 1683 psychotic patients

Patient's Age at Separation	Maternal			Paternal		
	Commit-ment at Mental Hospital	De-sertion, Etc.	Total	Commit-ment at Hospital	De-sertion, Etc.	Total
Prior to birth of patient	4	. . .	. . .	1	. . .	. . .
0–3	10	8	18	5	10	15
4–7	9	6	15	10	7	17
8–11	8	1	9	7	9	16
12–15	5	2	7	10	4	14
16–19	7	5	12	3	4	7
Over 20	12	. . .	. . .	5	. . .	. . .
Total	55	. . .	. . .	41	. . .	. . .

only suggestive, and obviously require confirmation with a larger series of cases, they are not inconsistent with the results obtained for parental deaths. The evidence at hand, therefore, suggests that the critical period for separation from the mother is before the age of 8, both when caused by death and when resulting from commitment to a psychiatric institution.

In the same table, figures are presented which show the age of the patient when a parent deserted, or when the patient had been otherwise separated from his parents. Again, there is a trend toward relatively more cases among patients who were separated from their mothers before they were 8 years of age. Although the absolute number of cases, again, is not large, the data indicate that separation from the mother occurred among psychotic patients more frequently before the patient was 8 years of age than after that time, whether this separation was due to maternal death, commitment to an institution, divorce, or desertion.

In order to determine the age distribution of maternal deaths among psychoneurotic patients, it would be necessary to obtain a similar series of psychoneurotic case histories. These should, to

Table 3

Number of psychoneurotic patients who experienced the death of their mothers prior to 16 years of age

	Patient Group			
Age of Patient at Death of Mother, Yr.	Ward (Massachusetts General Hospital)	Private Practice	Riggs Foundation	Total
0–3	2	7	4	13
4–7	3	4	1	8
8–11	1	2	1	4
12–15	2	1	0	3
Total N in each group	(118)	(109)	(103)	(330)
Patients bereaved before age of 8				
Number	...	...	...	21
Percentage	...	...	...	6.4%

be reliable, include at least 1500 cases. However, some clue to the actual distribution may be afforded by a smaller number. Data are therefore presented for 330 cases. These represent three social and economic groups, as represented by (*a*) 118 cases from the wards of Massachusetts General Hospital, (*b*) 109 cases from private practice in which a diagnosis of psychoneurosis was made, and (*c*) 103 cases from the Austen Riggs Foundation, Stockbridge, Mass. The incidence of maternal deaths is presented in Table 3.

It will be seen that 6.4 per cent of the psychoneurotic patients for whom data are available experienced the death of their mothers before they were 8 years of age. While the findings must be regarded as tentative, they suggest that maternal bereavement before the age of 8 years may also be related to later development of a psychoneurosis.

Comment

In recent discussion of psychiatric conditions, there has been an increasing tendency to accept multiple factors as playing a possible role in the causation of mental illness.[14] While various proposals have been made for classifying the causes of psychiatric illness, there would appear to be some advantage in subdividing possible causal factors according to the period in the life history of the patient at which they became operative. The life chart as described by Muncie[15] and developed by Cobb[16] has proved a useful technic in showing the relation between events in a patient's life and the subsequent development of symptoms. In the life chart there are indicated several periods which may assume special significance. These include, first, a prenatal period. Prior to birth many elements may influence the developing organism, such as intrauterine infections, which may result in blindness or other malformations,[17] endocrine imbalance of the pregnant mother, which may adversely affect the developing fetus,[18] and other forces, characterized by Myerson[19] as blastophoria.

Second, after birth, and before the appearance of mental illness, there is usually a period of at least fifteen years. The patient who later becomes mentally ill may often be subjected to numerous traumatic situations during this interval. It has been difficult to determine whether these events actually play a part in the causation of psychiatric illness because of the long period of latency which may elapse between the time of trauma and the actual onset of a psychosis later.

The ideal method of determining whether any factor contributes to the development of a psychosis might seem to involve a comparison of its relative frequency among psychotic patients and normal controls. Unfortunately, it is almost impossible to set up a strictly comparable control group for the study of parental deaths in a hospital population of this size because death rates vary widely according to social and economic status, national origin, date of birth, occupation, and many other factors. However, a comparison of maternal and paternal death rates obviates this difficulty, especially since such comparisons have previously been made by Lotka[20] for large groups of normal persons. The results of such a comparison in a series of psychotic patients reveal a striking preponderance of maternal over paternal deaths prior to the age of 8, followed by reversal to the normal preponderance of paternal deaths after this age. There is a similar tendency for maternal separation, due to hospitalization, etc., to occur more frequently during early childhood than when the patient is older.

A third, and final, period of importance in the life history of psychotic patients is the period immediately prior to the onset of symptoms. Events which occur at this time may be said to precipitate the illness. A study of parental deaths from this point of view is now in preparation.

The question whether the findings presented in this paper are consistent with psychoanalytic theory is not easy to answer. English and Pearson[6] stated that paternal loss is serious, but this does not seem to be true with the psychotic subjects in the present investigation. English and Pearson also stated that death is especially important if it occurs "during the height of the Oedipus situation, i.e., four to seven years of age." The present findings are somewhat ambiguous in this connection because, though there is a tendency toward an increase in maternal deaths in the histories of psychiatric patients between the ages of 4 and 7 years, the increase is not much greater than that which might be anticipated because of increase in age of the mothers at this time. A comparison of maternal deaths among male and female patients does not show any notable differences beyond those which might result from chance variation. On the whole, it would seem to be most likely that the death of the mother may expose a very young child to neglect, hostile step-parents, and other adverse influences. Final judgment on this topic may be deferred until the subsequent histories of patients who experience the death of their mothers during childhood have received further analysis.

References

1. H. Barry, Jr., "A Study of Bereavements: An Approach to Problems in Mental Disease," *American Journal of Orthopsychiatry*, 9 (1939), 355.
2. L. Bender and P. Schilder, "Suicidal Preoccupations and Attempts in Children," *American Journal of Orthopsychiatry*, 7 (1937), 225.
3. S. Glueck and E. T. Glueck, *Five Hundred Delinquent Women* (New York: Alfred A. Knopf, 1934).
4. E. Lindemann, "Psychiatric Aspects of Conservative Treatment of Ulcerative Colitis," *Archives of Neurology and Psychiatry*, 53 (1945), 322.
5. S. Rosenzweig and D. Bray, "Sibling Deaths in the Anamneses of Schizophrenic Patients," *Archives of Neurology and Psychiatry*, 49 (1943), 71.
6. O. S. English and G. H. J. Pearson, *Common Neuroses of Children and Adults* (New York: W. W. Norton, 1937), p. 55.
7. M. S. Guttmacher and F. A. Stewart, "A Psychiatric Study of Absence Without Leave," *American Journal of Psychiatry*, 102 (1945), 74.
8. G. E. Gardner and N. Goldman, "Childhood and Adolescent Adjustment of Naval Successes and Failures," *American Journal of Orthopsychiatry*, 15 (1945), 584.
9. G. E. Gardner and S. Aaron, "The Childhood and Adolescent Adjustment of Negro Psychiatric Casualties," *American Journal of Orthopsychiatry*, 16 (1946), 481.
10. R. H. McNeel and T. E. Dancer, "The Personality of the Successful Soldier," *American Journal of Psychiatry*, 102 (1945), 337.
11. J. Ruesch, C. Christiansen, L. C. Pattern, S., Dewees, and A. Jacobson, "Psychological Invalidism in Thyroidectomized Patients," *Psychosomatic Medicine*, 60 (1947), 77.
12. H. Barry, Jr., "Incidence of Advanced Maternal Age in Mothers of One Thousand State Hospital Patients," *Archives of Neurology and Psychiatry*, 54 (1948), 186.
13. Case histories were made available through the courtesy of Dr. Marcus A. Curry.
14. E. A. Strecker and F. G. Ebaugh, *Practical Clinical Psychiatry*, fifth edition (Philadelphia: The Blakiston Co., 1940).
15. W. Muncie, *Psychobiology and Psychiatry* (St. Louis: C. V. Mosby Co., 1939), p. 38.
16. S. Cobb, *Borderlands of Psychiatry* (Cambridge, Mass: Harvard University Press, 1943), p. 8.
17. C. Wesselhoeft, "Rubella," *New England Journal of Medicine*, 236 (1947), 978.
18. C. E. Benda, *Mongolism and Cretinism* (New York: Grune & Stratton, 1946).

19. A. Myerson, *Inheritance of Mental Disease* (Baltimore: Williams & Wilkins Company, 1925), p. 286.
20. A. J. Lotka, "Orphanhood in Relation to Demographic Factors," *Metron.*, 9 (1931), 1–109.

Henry H. Brewster

Separation Reaction in Psychosomatic Disease and Neurosis

The purpose of the present study was to observe the effect of separation, to compare this effect insofar as possible with that of bereavement, and to compare the significance of separation in a neurosis and in a psychosomatic illness. To this end, six patients were subjected to separation from their psychotherapist, who was the author in each case. Three of the patients had a psychosomatic disease. By way of contrast, three patients were selected who had a neurosis. The diagnoses of the six were: psychogenic vomiting, reactive depression, phobia, ulcerative colitis (in two patients), and rheumatoid arthritis. During the initial period of psychotherapy of each patient, special attention was given to the nature of the patient's dependency upon the therapist. Then the therapist left for a month's vacation. In the course of psychotherapy which followed, observations were made of the nature of the patient's reaction to this separation.

A 13-year-old boy, the son of a teacher, was brought for treatment by his mother, a stiff, quiet, rigorously neat woman of 50. He had been vomiting frequently since he was 4. Examinations showed no evidence of organic disease.

He made a singular appearance at the first interview. His gait was like that of a girl. He spoke quietly and with restraint, lowering his eyes when facing the therapist. His voice was high-pitched and whining. He was shy and appeared scared, guarding his remarks as if to avoid risking the disapproval of the therapist. He sat motionless in a chair, and answered questions asked him.

In the initial interview he indicated that his mother was a methodical and strict taskmaster, whom he and his father

Reprinted from *Psychosomatic Medicine*, 3 (1952), pp. 154–150, by permission of the author and publisher.

feared to cross. She punished him for getting less than B at school, and especially if he vomited his breakfast. He felt helpless to combat her, even when she allocated all his spare time to music lessons.

After two months of weekly interviews, his behavior changed. He walked like a man. He talked vigorously about his vacation plans to go fishing, blew bubble gum, whistled. His mother had been scolding him but he didn't mind. His vomiting had stopped. He was now thinking of the therapist as "an awfully good friend."

Then came the separation of a month from the therapist. Next seen, his behavior had reverted to its original form and he was vomiting. He had been discouraged, sad, and lonely, often angry. He considered running away from home. Often he thought of the therapist, especially when his mother scolded him for not eating. Yet within two weeks of the resumption of treatment, he had regained the state of improvement which had existed prior to the separation.

It is evident that this passive, effeminate boy found in the therapist a more useful model of imitation than in his father. With it, he was able in the course of two months to give up his neurotic symptom of vomiting and to tolerate the aggressive demands of his mother. In that it led to a recurrence of his presenting symptoms, the reaction to separation demonstrated the boy's need to depend upon the therapist. The fact that the boy was angry and sad when he thought of the missing therapist indicates that he felt rejected by the therapist in the same sense as a person in mourning. It should be noted that where it took two months for the original symptom to disappear, the reaction to separation was over within two weeks of the resumption of treatment.

An attractive, 26-year-old housewife came for treatment because, since her marriage of a year's duration, she had been subject to crying spells, sleeplessness, and fears of pregnancy. Her marriage had meant that she move a great distance from her parent's home and live in squalid circumstances.

During a month of weekly interviews, she was much concerned with affectionate memories of her father, an itinerant minister. Her husband seemed unintelligent and unsympathetic by comparison. But she took to working as a mother's helper and she no longer was sleepless or given to crying spells.

After a month of separation from the therapist, she can-
celled her appointment in order to go home and visit her parents.
At the next appointment she was acid and provocative. She
had felt "every way there was to feel, from the highest to the
lowest." She sat behind the therapist, announced that she was
not sure she could continue with therapy. She opened a
camera, snapped a picture, then stated she had no film in the
camera. Subsequently, she was able to express her anger at
the interruption of therapy. Within three weeks, there was
no more evidence of depression or provocative behavior, and
she and her husband had moved from the squalid apartment into
the home of a psychiatrist, who was the son of a minister.

This young housewife, the daughter of a minister, finding
difficulty in adjusting to her marriage, became depressed over her
separation from home, especially from her father. She obtained
relief from these depressive feelings during a month and a half
of therapy, in which the therapist became a substitute for her father.
In response to the month of separation from the therapist, during
which depressive feelings recurred, she returned home to her father.
When psychotherapy was resumed, the therapist met only a display
of anger in the form of bitter remarks and provocative behavior.
Her response to separation appeared to be a re-enactment of her
sense of being rejected by her father. After another month of
therapy, she was no longer depressed and had found a substitute
for both her father and the therapist, i.e., employment in the home
of a psychiatrist whose father was a minister.

A 30-year-old, single woman complained of being anxious,
restless, afraid to be in a crowd, fearful of harming others,
apprehensive she was going insane. Objectively, her body was
in perpetual movement: with her hands she would tear paper
into small bits; her abdomen contracted convulsively; her face
twitched.

From the age of 5, when her father left the home, she lived
under the close supervision of her mother. She shared the
same bed as mother and she reported all her social activities to
her mother. After her father's death (when she was 17), she
developed the above symptoms. But when her mother died
(when she was 20), these symptoms promptly disappeared and
she assumed her mother's job as stenographer to a judge. Subsequently, she moved away to make her home with the family

of her mother's sister. The marriage of her niece and the simultaneous loss of her employer, an older man, caused the recurrence of her symptoms. Her aunt, meanwhile, became an obligatory companion for her. Whenever the aunt would leave the house, she would become either furious or apprehensive that disaster would occur.

During two months of interviews on alternate days, her symptoms in large part subsided. Though she anticipated the interviews with pleasure, she appeared to cling to them with a desperate tenacity. Of her father, she could recall little except that he had left the home. She compared the therapist to her former employer, an older man for whom she was a stenographer and with whom she talked intimately every day (as she had to her mother). Of her mother, she felt: "I was inside of her. I had no personality of my own. I started to live after her death. I was reborn."

Warned of the approaching month's separation from the therapist, she was promptly reminded of her father's leaving home, grew angry, demanded sedation. The therapist now looked to her like her father: she realized they both had the same first names. She became dejected and the twitching movements reappeared. During the month of separation she was subject to bouts of crying. Several times she smashed the contents of her room. It was finally necessary to admit her to the hospital. Next seen by the therapist, all of her original symptoms had recurred. In addition, she was furious at all doctors, fearful she would die, and obsessed with the thought she might choke people. Within three weeks of resuming therapy she was again as she had been before being warned of the month of separation.

This girl's neurosis centered around an ambivalent attachment to her mother. Her human relationships, whether to men or women, were all cut after this pattern. The nature of her life with her mother between the ages of 5 and 20 illustrates the infantile character of such a relationship. At first she was able to tolerate the death of her mother by literally filling her mother's shoes (i.e., incorporating the image of the mother). But it became necessary to find substitutes for the original obligatory companion, first in an employer, then her aunt, and finally the therapist. That the attachments to her mother and mother-substitutes was ambivalent is demonstrated by the fury aroused in her by a separation, no matter how temporary, from her aunt.

During the actual month of separation from the therapist, her neurotic symptoms returned with a vengeance, together with intense loneliness and incapacitating anger with the therapist. The separation, therefore, served not only as a signal that she had been abandoned, but as a trigger for the ambivalent feelings inherent in her attachment to the therapist. Within three weeks of the resumption of interviews after the separation, the storm which had been precipitated by the mention of the therapist's vacation had cleared.

A 33-year-old man, married, and a university graduate student, came for psychiatric treatment of diarrhea. He was having 20–40 stools daily, with tenesmus, anorexia, and great fatigue. Medical examination demonstrated the diagnosis of ulcerative colitis.

He had always been a shy and solitary individual, though a successful student. Subject to inconsolable weeping spells in youth, he felt that his mother was unable to show affection. His father, a civil servant, had a strict code of conduct which he accepted tractably. The one person upon whom he found he could depend was the director of a laboratory, a man he met when he was 7 and for whom he worked when he was 28. It was after leaving this man's laboratory that he developed his first attack of ulcerative colitis. The second episode of colitis occurred two years later when his fiancee's father postponed his marriage. The colitis had recurred again a year before he came to treatment, when his professor told him that he had an undesirable personality.

His colitis stopped after two months of biweekly interviews. In the ensuing eight months, he found that he could concentrate on his work more successfully, though subject to depressions and obsessed by details. Meanwhile, he grew aware of a childlike dependency upon the therapist. At first, he took to reading psychiatric books. Then, he enjoyed the fantasy he was a psychiatrist. Finally, he thought of himself "like a leech without teeth, with a need for attachment to an object" and a desire to monopolize the life of the therapist.

As soon as he was informed of the approaching separation from the therapist, he found it difficult to concentrate upon his work, felt alone. Unable to sleep, he worked longer hours. "I feel I need warm milk to make myself feel right. . . . In my throat, I breathe quietly because I cannot yell. The times I used to cry unrestrainedly, Mother became upset." During the separation he sensed an unknown danger and he grew tense. Then it was as if he withdrew into his own body; nor could he work or speak to anyone. When psychotherapy resumed, he emerged gradually from this emotional state in the course of two months.

The relation of this patient to the therapist followed the pattern of all his significant human relationships: i.e., infantile dependency. He described it in the terms of the dependent parasite sucking on its host, with the aggressive desire to monopolize the life of the therapist. For him, this state was vulnerable. The mere suggestion of separation from the therapist aroused a feeling "like an unwanted child against whom the mother had turned." Faced by the separation itself, he succumbed to a process resembling schizophrenic withdrawal, in which he felt totally isolated and unable to initiate useful action. It is significant that, severe as his response to separation appeared to be, it was possible for him to recover from this emotional state within two months of the resumption of therapy, and to realize that he had often experienced such feelings in the past.

A 40-year-old minister had had progressive rheumatoid arthritis over the course of eight years, involving his knees, hips, hands, and shoulders. He was referred for psychotherapy while under medical treatment in the hospital for pain, stiffness, and swelling of these joints.

He described his youth as a lonely one, lived on a farm with his stepfather and mother. His older sister, a business executive, left the home early due to disputes with the mother. His mother "didn't understand pleasure. Her life consisted of duties to be done and she expected that of me. No love was wasted between us. . . . She nagged my stepfather from morning to night. I felt sorry for him." He became a minister with a militant urge to erase sin and "drive the whole world to Christ." But when he tried to convert his sister, she was insulted and his arthritis commenced. When the sister later stopped communicating with him, he got married. His arthritis grew worse following the birth of a fourth child.

On the medical ward he soon became one to whom other male patients turned for advice. In interviews, despite a sense of sinfulness and a great fear of disapproval, he came to look forward to seeing the therapist. Warned of the approaching separation from the therapist, he grew irritable and aware of feelings of anger at his family, his parish, and hospital personnel. He debated whether to go home for his wedding anniversary or to wait in the hospital for the therapist to return.

During the month of separation, his arthritis, which had become less painful, was intensified. He lay in bed rigidly, out of communication with the other patients, much of the time with his face to the wall. Next seen, he indicated that he had missed the therapist. However, he became quite depressed, his arthritis grew more painful, he dreamed of stuffing a dirty carpet into his mother's mouth, and he anticipated calamities happening to his children and himself. At the end of a month, these symptoms let up. Meanwhile, he succeeded in helping a depressed arthritic patient, who had consulted him and whom the therapist encouraged him to advise. To the therapist he commented: "The parent gives the child guiding principles. I was thinking of you in those terms." Subsequently, he felt in good spirits, stated that he believed he would recover from his arthritis, and became hopeful about his parish and children.

In the initial two months of weekly psychiatric interviews, the arthritic patient found narcissistic approval he had looked for from his parents in the past, and from Christ in the present. There was slight relief in his arthritic pain. With the threat of separation from the therapist, he grew sorrowful and angry. During the month of separation, he withdrew into a shell, physically and emotionally; he lay in bed, encased in a plaster cast, and failed to communicate with persons about him. With the resumption of interviews, he emerged from this shell gradually over the course of a month. During this emergence, it was evident that he regarded the therapist as a mother against whom he was impelled to vent his fury orally. This is illustrated by the dream in which he is lying naked on the floor, speaks harsh words to his mother, then stuffs a dirty rug into his mother's mouth. The dream was followed by severe joint pain and depression and the fear that he was losing control of his children and of his parish. But, at the end of a month, after the arthritic patient whom he had been counseling became well, he was in good spirits and he had no pain in his joints. Able to thus identify with the therapist, he then became aware that he had leaned heavily on this mother in childhood, as he now confessed to be doing with the therapist.

A 26-year-old single girl, a college graduate, had had recurrent attacks of ulcerative colitis for two years. She came for psychotherapy the day after she arrived in this city in which she had no family or friends.

Socially a lone wolf, she had invariably alienated herself from her few friends by her own jealousy and the anticipation that she would be deserted, despite preeminence in studies and athletics at school and college.

During six months of psychotherapy, she worked as an editorial assistant, but spent much time by herself, preoccupied with the memory of an old girl friend. At church she would pray to be "kept a whole person." She anticipated many sorts of calamity happening to her, especially at the hands of a man. From a frequency of 8–10 times daily and nightly, her diarrhea dropped to 3–4 times without bleeding.

Toward the therapist she became aware of tender feelings, but of a tentative nature. Every night she would talk to him, calling him by his first name. He seemed to be inside of her. Then she would feel whole. But at interviews, he seemed different and she felt "broken up and crippled, my mind and part of my intestine."

In the month of separation she slept poorly, felt dejected, worked extra time, and saw little of her few acquaintances. "I felt as if I'd like to tear things apart and beat people up. I thought it would be nice to cry, but I couldn't." In a series of unmailed letters addressed to the therapist, she wrote about herself with an intimacy and tenderness seldom encountered in interviews.

When psychotherapy was resumed, she indicated that her diarrhea had grown more severe. She was disappointed that she could not talk to the therapist as well as to the doctor of her correspondence. She grew angry at the therapist for not understanding her. Subsequently, she grew abusive, accusing the therapist of feeding her only crumbs. Three months after the end of the month of separation, she left therapy precipitously to go to another city in order to find a woman therapist.

This girl with ulcerative colitis demonstrated the impoverished personality of a schizoid character. She came to feel dependent, upon the therapist but in a bizarre way. In the manner of a schizophrenic, she split the therapist into two people. One was the person whom she felt was inside of her and whom she addressed tenderly at night when she felt whole. The other was the doctor whom she encountered in interviews, where she felt cold, broken, and crippled.

The month of separation served only to increase her fears of being harmed and rejected by the therapist of interviews. She became irritated, dejected, fatigued, and more lonely. The process of splitting the therapist she carried further. Toward the doctor of her night conversations she turned her whole attention and addressed letters of great warmth. Toward the doctor of interviews she felt increasing hostility until finally it was necessary for her to seek a woman (i.e., a mother towards whom she felt less hostile).

Discussion

The reaction of these patients to separation bears resemblances to the symptomatic picture of grief described by Lindemann. All the patients experienced a subjective sensation which they defined as missing the therapist. Often striking was the patient's preoccupation with thoughts of or the image of the missing therapist. It was common for the patient to respond with irritability to other people. Finally, there were frequent alterations in the established patterns of the patient's behavior. For example, the two patients with ulcerative colitis lost so much enthusiasm for their work that activities which had been automatic for them were carried on with the greatest effort. The minister with arthritis slipped into complete social isolation by lying in bed with his face to the wall. In the reaction of the man with ulcerative colitis to separation, there was no external evidence of hostility. Instead, he showed a picture of withdrawal resembling schizophrenia, in which, unable to find help in the external world of reality, he retreated in fantasy to the interior of his own body where he could feel nothing except fatigue and the desire to sleep.

Dynamically, the nature of the reaction to separation varied with the nature of the patient's neurotic illness.[1] Both the boy with vomiting and the girl with the reactive depression regarded the therapist as a necessary, paternal figure; the boy still in need of an adequate "father" with whom to identify; the girl, of a "father" as an object of her instinctual heterosexual longings. Both of them were able to tolerate the month of separation with a modicum of discomfort and disappointment in these needs, but without total disorganization of their emotional lives. At the other extreme are the minister with arthritis and the man with ulcerative colitis, both narcissistic personalities whose instinctive drives are still expressed principally in oral terms. For them the therapist represented a guiding or nourishing mother. During separation they succumbed to a vegetative existence, having severed emotional relatedness to everyone about them. The same could be said for the girl with ulcerative colitis, for whom the separation served only to intensify her already hostile feelings for the therapist to such a point as to rupture therapy. The reaction of the girl with the phobia to the separation stands somewhere in between these two extremes. She responded as if she had lost an object of affection but also, as demonstrated by her impulse to be destructive, a target of extremely ambivalent feelings.

Each of these patients assigned feelings to the therapist characteristic of the patient's psychological needs and development. The separation was clearly an interruption of these transference feelings. Grief, too, is a response to an interruption of feelings. But while bereavement, of which grief is the expression, refers to a *permanent* cessation of an interpersonal relationship, separation is only a *temporary* interruption, having the promise of restoration. It is, therefore, not surprising that the recovery from the reaction to separation as described seemed more rapid than might be expected from grief. The reaction to separation resembled grief in that the more infantile and regressive was the expression of the patient's relationship to the therapist. the more severe was the reaction to separation.

Of the six patients studied, the response to separation was far more severe in the three with ulcerative colitis and rheumatoid arthritis than in the three with neuroses. Likewise, the three patients with psychosomatic illness demonstrated a more defective psychological development; they were more narcissistic, more dependent, and prone to instinctual expression in oral-sadistic terms.

Separation has a practical significance that bereavement has not. The separation of one partner of a human relationship from another occurs frequently, whereas bereavement is a less common experience. If a patient can react as vigorously to such a temporary separation from a therapist as described, then any interruption of a physician's relationships to a patient can be looked upon as a stimulus to the development of a reaction to separation. Ferenczi[2] has long since described the "Sunday neurosis," in which the patient developed depression on Sunday, i.e., a day on which the patient did not see the psychotherapist. The ending of the patient's therapeutic interviews with the doctor, or the referral of a patient from one doctor to another, may be in themselves provocative of a separation reaction. As such, these situations may well deserve further study and examination, especially if the clinical improvement by any type of medical therapy is not to be undone by the symptoms of a reaction to separation.

References

1. H. H. Brewster, *Psychiatry and Religion* (ed. J. L. Liebman) (Boston: The Beacon Press, 1946), pp. 183–202.
2. S. Ferenczi, *Further Contributions to the Theory and Technique of Psychoanalysis* (London: Institute of Psychoanalysis and the Hogarth Press, 1926).

Joseph M. Natterson and Alfred G. Knudson, Jr.

Observations Concerning Fear of Death in Fatally Ill Children and Their Mothers

In dealing with a fatally ill child, parents and physicians are frequently troubled by the question of the child's awareness and fear of his impending death. Thus from the clinical standpoint it should be useful to have data on this subject. Furthermore, data on fear of death in children may contribute to the understanding of psychological development.

The relation of fear of death to other fears, such as separation fear and mutilation (castration) fear, remains vague. Rank[1] regarded separation fear as the primal human problem. He implicitly equated it with death fear, and he treated castration fear as a subvariant. It is a commonplace of psychoanalytic practice to regard a fear of death that appears in consciousness or in dreams as a disguised castration fear. Also, a clear and consistent differenti-

Reprinted from *Psychosomatic Medicine*, 22 (1960), pp. 456–463, by permission of the authors and publisher.

ation between castration fear and separation fear is not available, and yet such a distinction is regularly implied. Some psychoanalysts, e.g., Grotjahn[2] and Klein,[3] regard fear of death as the crucial problem in schizophrenia. Other psychoanalysts deny that fear of death plays an important role in the psychology of the individual. It is obvious that further data would be helpful.

Death awareness is defined as the individual's consciousness of the finiteness of his personal existence. The differentiation of awareness of death and fear of death will not be attempted in this study, and the terms will be used synonymously. The possible necessity for such a differentiation should not be overlooked. In this portion of the study, an attempt is made to discern the maturational pattern of death fear.

Setting

The present study concerns 33 children, ages 0–13 years, followed at the City of Hope Medical Center during the period of June 1956 to August 1958, and selected according to the following criteria: (*a*) admitted to the City of Hope during this period, (*b*) followed for at least 2 weeks; (*c*) died at City of Hope during this period, and (*d*) diagnosis of cancer, leukemia, or blood disease. . . .

The following data were recorded on the children:

1. *Age.* Range $1\frac{0}{12}$–$12\frac{4}{12}$ years; 16 children $1\frac{0}{12}$–$4\frac{11}{12}$ years, 12 children $5\frac{0}{12}$–$9\frac{0}{12}$ years, 5 children $10\frac{0}{12}$–$12\frac{4}{12}$ years.

2. *Sex.* 19 boys, 14 girls.

3. *Ethnic background.* 27 Caucasian, 4 Mexican, 2 Negro.

4. *Religion.* 22 Protestant, 10 Catholic, 1 Jewish.

5. *Intelligence.* 2 children superior (IQ > 120), 28 children normal (80–120), 1 child inferior (50–80), 2 children defective (IQ < 50)—both mongoloid idiots. These are gross measurements, since IQ or DQ ratings were not made in all cases.

6. *Behavior.* One child was aggressive and antisocial, another was very withdrawn; the others exhibited relatively normal behavior, in keeping with age and intelligence.

7. *Diagnosis.* Leukemia, 22; neuroblastoma, 3; lymphosarcoma, rhabdomyosarcoma, and aplastic anemia, 2 each; Ewing's sarcoma and agranulocytosis, 1 each.

8. *Research program.* At some time during the course of their illness, most of the children participated in some phase of the medical research program, necessitating, in many cases, hospitalization beyond that usually required for recognized diagnosis and treatment. Participation, 28; no participation, 5.

9. *Distance from home.* This was often a factor in the duration of hospitalization. Only 11 children lived within 25 miles of the medical center; 11 lived more than 100 miles away.

10. *Time at medical center.* The range in time from first visit until death was 18–629 days. The range in time spent in the hospital by a parent was 3–205 days.

The patients were observed during the hospitalization and in the out-patient clinic. The inpatients were in a 15-bed unit consisting of 3-bed rooms. Those children who were well enough ate meals in a communal recreation room. During the morning, the children aged 3 and over attended a schoolroom near the nursing unit, under the supervision of a schoolteacher from the Duarte School District. In the afternoon, the children had a rest period, followed by activities supervised by an occupational therapist, also in a room near the nursing unit. Daily activities often included outdoor play in the playground.

The Pediatrics Unit has a program for the participation of parents in the hospital care of the children.[4] Parents may attend their children on the unit from the hour of rising until bedtime at night. They aid in the dressing, bathing, feeding, and nursing of their children and may observe medical activities in the treatment room.

The children and their parents were under the observation of physicians, nurses, the schoolteacher, the occupational therapist, and the social worker. Observations were either recorded on charts or communicated orally. The social worker kept a central file for such observations. A weekly conference was held with a consulting psychiatrist. All patients were discussed at these meetings, and the discussions were recorded by notes or by tape recorder.

In addition to having illnesses which could cause considerable distress, these children were subject to three stresses of environmental origin, namely, separation from mother, traumatic procedures, and deaths of other children. The observations recorded here concern the behavior of the children in response to these stresses. The observations are partially retrospective, although some were recorded at staff meetings in almost current fashion. Many observations were recorded in the nurses' notes on the medical charts. Some of the children's drawings and written stories had been saved and were available for study.

Observations

The most commonly noted cause of distress in the child was the mother's absence. Whereas some children adapted well to the mother's absence and became very friendly with the nursing staff, others seemed never to tolerate maternal absence. The children in the latter group were irritable and often withdrawn. They frequently showed signs of regression socially. These symptoms were less remarkable when the mother was present, but these children demanded the physical attention of their mothers. When the mothers departed, such children often had tantrums or cried for their mothers. This reaction to separation from the mother tended to improve with time and seemed to have little, if any, relationship to the clinical condition of the child.

Adverse reactions to separation from the mother were present to some extent in virtually all patients. The exceptions may be worth noting. Two children were mongoloid idiots. Another child, an infant, was virtually "adopted" by the ward and seemed very secure with nursing personnel. Another patient seemed remarkably secure because of the almost constant presence of his great-grandmother. Two patients were past the age of 10 years. Of the remaining 27 patients, 18 showed a moderate degree of reaction to separation, whereas 9 showed a severe degree. There was a clustering of the severe reactions in the younger age group, the oldest child making such a response being $5\frac{8}{12}$ years old.

Another cause of distress in the child was his subjection to traumatic procedures, such as venipunctures, and bone-marrow aspirations. About half of the children were passive during these procedures and complained only temporarily about them. Other children were less passive, complained more strenuously, and expressed anxiety about the procedures at times when they were not being done. Four of these children (all boys, ages 6–9 years) actively struggled against the procedures and required restraint. All four were apprehensive, apparently on the basis of their anxiety about the procedures. The mother's presence did not seem to relieve this apprehension.   Such reactions to the procedures clustered in the age group 3–9 years.

A third cause of distress was the death of another child.   When a child died in the hospital, most of the other children knew only that the child was no longer there.   Minimal explanation for such absence was offered, this usually being a statement that the child had gone home.   In some instances this explanation did not entirely suffice, either because the questioning child had fairly direct evidence to the contrary, or because he was unusually suspicious.   The death was not denied in such instances.   Interestingly, however, children who probably knew about the deaths of other children seldom asked questions of the staff.   We are not able to comment on the awareness of particular children of the deaths of other children. At present, we shall confine our remarks to the behavior of children as it related to such deaths, realizing that the behavior of the children was affected partly by such deaths themselves, partly by the effects of death upon the staff and parents, and partly by the death theme generally.

Several children became anxious, depressed, and withdrawn when other children died.   The presence of the mother did not alleviate this tendency, nor did the execution of the procedures seem to intensify it.   Four children actually expressed apprehension about the deaths of other children, and about the possibility of their own deaths.   Two of these discussed with each other the question of which of them would die first.   These children were all in the older age group, 6–12 years.

It can be seen that the oldest children revealed anxiety or apprehension obviously related to death, in some cases involving an openly expressed fear of death.   However, there were indications that anxiety about death may have been present in more subtle form in younger children, even though overshadowed by fear of separation, or fear of the procedures.   Such indications were sometimes found in the drawings and stories of the children.

Discussion

The reactions to separation were most severe in the age group 0–5 years; the reactions to the procedures were most intense in the age group 5–10 years; and the reactions to death were strongest in the age group 10 years and over.   It is evident that the reactions described consisted largely of anxiety. In fact, they seemed to constitute, in turn, fear of separation, fear of mutilation, and fear of death. The observations suggest that fear of death is related to the other fears in a maturational pattern.

Separation fear is the most elemental form of fear, occurs earliest in life, and is obviously related to the dependent necessities of early life. Separation fear requires minimal ego development and minimal cognitive capacity. Separation fear seems, then, to be a function of primary process adaptation, and in this respect it may be the most closely related of human fears to fears in other species. The absence of demonstrable relation of separation fear to the clinical condition of the child suggests that it is not an expression of the awareness and the fear of death.

Fears other than separation fear were not evident below 2–3 years of age. This negative finding indicates that mutilation and death fears are distinct from separation fear and suggests that the former fears require a more highly developed integrative capacity.

Mutilation fear tended to occupy a temporally transitional position in relation to separation fear and death fear. Its expressions were less decisive, and its clinical importance less pressing.

Despite the equivocal nature of the findings concerning mutilation fear, the findings are consistent with the conclusions of Freud and many other psychoanalysts regarding the age of development of mutilation fear, and its age of maximal intensity. Neither negative nor positive findings were obtained which would bear on Freud's views[5] as to the central significance of mutilation fear in normal and pathologic personality development.

The evolution of death fear as suggested by this study is in general concordance with the findings of Maria Nagy.[6] She reports, for example, that in children from 3–5 years of age death is denied, and that it is not permanent and regular, and that it is only a change of some kind and may be temporary. These children cannot distinguish the external world from themselves and hence cannot conceive of lifelessness. From 5–9 years, the children recognize death, but without exception regard it as a person. Only from the ninth year do children achieve a realistic conception of death as a permanent biologic process, according to Nagy.

The realistic fear of death demonstrated by the oldest children seems important for several reasons: (1) In the oldest children fear of death took definite precedence over the other fears. (2) This fear of death seemed to be a function of a highly developed integrative capacity and reality sense. (3) Fear of death in the older children was urgent, pervasive, and persistent, whereas in the younger children manifestations of death fear were vague and evanescent.

Separation fear predominated in the younger children, mutilation fear was the most evident concern in the intermediate age group, and death fear took precedence in the older age-group. It is felt that the evolution of these fears is related to the maturation of consciousness. The child is first aware of his mother, then of his own body, and finally of himself in time (i.e., of life itself). The sequence of dominating fears follows the same maturational pattern, proceeding from separation fear, through mutilation fear, to death fear. . . .

Mothers of children who are victims of slowly fatal diseases were the subjects of the present study. The mother-child relationship is generally regarded as the most reciprocally intense of inter-personal relationships. It is assumed that, because of the maximal intensity of the relationship, identification of the mother with the child is maximal in these cases. Therefore, the threat of death to the child poses a symbolic threat of death to the mother and consequently should elicit reactions to the threat in the mother. In a sense, the mother faces death, experiences it, and survives it. The crucial variables become the mother's acute contact with death, and her knowledge that she herself will survive it. We do not imply that all the reactions of the mothers to the death of her child are to be understood as functions of the mother's symbolic death.

In this study an effort is made to isolate and examine the mother's reactions to the death threat. The reactions of mothers during the course of fatal illness in their children are presented and analyzed below. Patterns of responses are described, and the possibility that death fear is a maturing influence in these mothers is considered.

Setting

The general setting has been described in the previous section on the children. As noted therein, on the Pediatrics Ward parents could attend their children from the hour of rising until bedtime at night. They aided in the dressing, bathing, feeding, and nursing of their children. They could observe medical activities in the treatment room. They received information on the medical problem, and on the research program from the staff physicians, either on an individual basis, or in regularly scheduled parent-physician group conferences. The parents were aided in dealing with personal problems, and in their arrangements for transportation and housing by the social worker.

Data on personal and family variables not noted in the section on the children are as follows.

1. *Age range.* 24–45 years.
2. *Marital status.* Four mothers had been divorced; two of these had remarried, two had not.
3. *Husband's occupation.* Most of the husbands were skilled laborers or white-collar workers.
4. *Other children.* In only three cases was the patient an only child, and in one of these cases the mother was pregnant. In four other cases the mother was pregnant at some time during the patient's illness. In three instances the patient was one of fraternal twins.
5. *Prior knowledge of prognosis.* In only two cases did the mother not know the fatal prognosis before the first visit to the medical center. In one instance, this prognosis was given on the day of arrival, and in the other instance, 164 days after the first visit, when the fatal nature of the illness first became evident to the medical staff. In the remaining cases the range in time between knowing the prognosis and first visiting the medical center was 1–140 days. In only five instances was the interval greater than 6 weeks.

Mothers on the ward were generally very helpful to the staff. They performed a major portion of the more simple nursing tasks for their own children and often helped in the care of other children. They did not accompany their children to the morning schoolroom when the child attended school, but they did accompany them sometimes during occupational therapy activities. They usually fed, dressed, and bathed the children. In the evenings, they read to their children and put them to bed.

They spent variable amounts of time away from their children during the day. They ate their own meals in the regular hospital cafeteria, usually with each other. They had a lounge of their own to relax in, away from the children. At the children's nap time, they sat in the lounge, engaged in occupational-therapy activities in the occupational therapy shop, or performed personal errands.

Parents had regular educational conferences with the physicians in order to learn more about their children's diseases, the program of treatment, and the investigative program. The reception given by the parents was rewarding to the physicians.

The reactions of the mothers were observed by staff members of four categories: (1) nursing personnel, (2) social workers, (3) teachers and occupational therapists, and (4) physicians. The observations, as in the case of the children, were partially retrospective, although some of these were recorded in the patient's charts and in the minutes of staff meetings. In addition, the social worker kept a file in which pertinent data from interviews with the mothers were recorded. Some of these interviews were arranged by the worker specifically for the purpose of gathering information of social research value.

Observations of the mother were recorded throughout the course of the child's illness. However, particular attention was given to the mother's initial reactions, and to her reactions late in the child's course. In this way a longitudinal appraisal of each mother was possible.

Observations

Initially, most mothers (25 of 33) were tense, anxious, withdrawn, and readily inclined to weep. They reacted in a disbelieving manner, tending to deny either the diagnosis of the disease or its fatal outcome. They wanted to be with their children as much as possible, often tending to cling to them physically. This staying with the child was sometimes without much regard for the needs of the remainder of the family. Hope for the child was stressed, but in a nonspecific way—"Something will be discovered." They wanted, often in an irrational manner, to try anything in the way of new treatment that might offer hope for a cure. At this stage, mothers often expressed some degree of guilt about the child's illness, wondering whether they might have done something wrong.

The initial behavior of 8 mothers was atypical. Two mothers were very calm initially. They accepted the diagnosis and prognosis. Needs of the family were considered to be important. Hope was expressed for children more generally. However, unusual factors were present in both cases. In one case the fatal prognosis had been given four months prior to the child's being seen at this institution. In the other case the fatal prognosis had been known for two months, and, in addition, the child had been known since birth to be a mongoloid idiot. The other six mothers demonstrated intermediate reactions initially. In two of these, the fatal prognosis had been given three and a half and five months previously. In two other cases a period of six weeks had intervened. In only one case was an interval greater than two months associated with the "typical" reaction described above. On the other hand, in two cases an intermediate reaction was associated with a very short interval. In one of these instances the child had been known to be a mongoloid idiot. In the other, the mother was a very controlled person emotionally, and it was difficult to evaluate her reaction.

Toward the end of the child's course the most common reaction (19 of 33) of the mothers was calm acceptance of the fatal outcome. There was almost no tendency to weep. In some instances, the mother expressed a wish that the child die so that his suffering would be ended. Hope was expressed for children generally rather than for the mother's own child. The mother was with the child whenever possible, but with adequate consideration for the remainder of the family. There was no expression of guilt. When the children of such mothers actually died, there was a mixed expression of calm sorrow and relief.

Almost half (14) of the 33 mothers did not react in this manner, however. Six mothers were anxious and tense, had a strong tendency to weep and clung to hope for their own children. When the children of these mothers actually died, the mothers reacted hysterically. Eight mothers were not so overtly affected but nevertheless revealed a lack of acceptance. It is worth noting that in only three of these fourteen cases was the interval between fatal prognosis and death greater than four months. In one of these three cases the patient was an only child. In the other two cases, the death of the child occurred suddenly and unexpectedly. Of the group of 19 mothers who accepted their children's deaths calmly, the interval between prognosis and death was less than four months in only three instances. In one of these the child had been known from birth to be a mongoloid idiot.

Of the 14 mothers whose children died within four months after a fatal prognosis had been given, 11 showed reactions of the most disturbed or the intermediate type. There were 19 mothers whose children died more than four months after a fatal prognosis had been given. In this group, 16 showed calm acceptance of the child's death, and in the other three cases one of the children was an only child, while the other two deaths occurred suddenly and unexpectedly.

In the mothers who showed a tense, denying, and irrational initial reaction and a calm acceptance terminally, the change was apparently related to a time interval of more than four months. These mothers gradually became less tense and anxious. They stopped denying the diagnosis or its prognosis. Their hope for the child became more specific, often related to particular scientific efforts. A considerable interest in the investigative program often developed at this time. There was a tendency to see the medical problem in its broader aspects, with the beginning of an expressed desire to help all children. Mothers during this period tended to cling less to their own children, encouraging them to participate in school or occupational therapy activities. They often helped in the care of other children on the ward and were generally more social. They spoke more about fulfilling family obligations. In most instances, this reaction gradually gave rise to the calm terminal reaction described previously.

In summary, the reactions of the mothers whose children survived more than four months manifested a disturbed initial reaction, a more rational interim reaction, and a relatively integrated terminal reaction. An interesting contrast was observed among almost all staff members. Initially, their reactions to a child were not marked, but the reactions at the time of death often were, with depression and guilt in evidence.

Discussion

The mothers whose children survived more than four months from the time of fatal prognosis tended to show a triphasic response—initial, intermediate, and terminal—following the prognosis. Certain ego functions appeared characteristic of each phase. In the first phase, the mothers generally tended to deny the reality. In the second phase, they tended to accept the reality and to direct their energy toward those realistic measures that offered hope of saving the child. In the third phase, the mothers tended to direct their energy away from their respective children, and interests less sharply focused on the individual child and of a less painfully narcissistic type became evident.

Denial is the most prominent ego function of the first phase. The traumatic announcement to the mother of the diagnosis and prognosis in effect constitutes an immediate rupture of the normal mother-child object relationship, and so a deep regression is induced, and the usual modicum of reality testing is abandoned. With reduced ego capacity, the pleasure principle prevails—the immediate internal reality needs become dominant, and external reality demands pale into insignificance. The maternal identification with the child becomes blatant, the pain is intolerable, and the psychologically primitive mechanism of denial is regularly seen to some degree. Psychosis in a few mothers was suspected at this point. Reports by Bozeman, *et al.*[7] and Bierman, on parents of leukemic children include observations which the present authors find characteristic of the first phase.

Active, realistic efforts to prolong the child's life are typical of the mother in the second phase. She has relinquished the conscious denial, but the realistic behavior reveals that the hope of saving the child is retained. Although the pleasure principle has not been abandoned, it has been subordinated to the reality principle. While the mother clings to the hope that her efforts will save the child, the intensity of the expectation is gradually reduced. Emotionally, the mothers are separating themselves from the children. The mourning process, as described by Richmond and Waisman,[8] is beginning. Also, the mothers are not solely interested in those measures which involve treatment of the disease, but are also interested in the child's comfort and general emotional needs.

The final phase corresponds temporally with the crumbling of resistance to the disease and the death of the child. It is rarely observed if the course of the disease from time of diagnosis is less than four months. In this phase there is an acceptance of the death of the child which has hitherto been absent in the mother. Separation from the child is no longer an adaptive problem for the mother. For the first time, wishes for the death of the child may be expressed openly—and in a relatively guiltless way. Certain changes suggestive of sublimation were observed in some mothers;

these included qualitative changes in scientific interest, so that it no longer pertained to the mother's particular child but to children or humanity in general, and changes in the mother's relation to other children and their parents, especially in the direction of providing physical aid and psychological comfort. These and other changes which have been noted all suggest the development of socializing tendencies. In some mothers severe neurotic symptoms observed on admission were markedly improved at the time of the child's death. In general, ego strength and breadth were markedly greater in the third than in the first phase. Whether the mother's general integrative ability was greater in the third stage than prior to the child's illness could not be stated, since no premorbid data were available.

Suggestions of increase in sublimation during the illness were noted, but no comparisons with the premorbid condition can be made. The question of the relation of creative sublimation to mastery of death fear remains unanswered. The socializing tendencies alluded to above suggest a basis for further study.

Whereas the period of maximal emotional disturbances in the mothers occurred in the first phase, the disturbed staff reactions occurred in the third phase. This can be understood in view of the facts that, on admission, the mother and child are strangers to the staff, and that the normal population of the ward consists of fatally ill children. As time passes, and emotional attachments between staff and child develop, the staff becomes increasingly reactive to the child's existential problem. Also, each death among the children represents a thwarting of the goal-directed behavior of the staff. It was regularly noted that depressive, guilty, and self-examining reactions occurred in the staff when a death occurred on the ward.

Summary

1. Observations concerning the behavior of 33 children fatally ill with leukemia or related disorders are presented. The following conclusions are reached:

(*a*) In addition to distress directly due to illness, these children manifested behavioral changes in response to three environmental factors, namely, separation from the mother, traumatic procedures, and deaths of other children.

(*b*) The reactions to these environmental stress are considered to represent separation fear, mutilation fear, and death fear.

(*c*) There is a strong age-dependence of the fully developed forms of these fears, separation fear occurring first and death fear last.

(*d*) The evolution of these fears seems to be related to the maturation of consciousness.

2. Observations on the 33 mothers of these fatally ill children are also presented. The following conclusions are reached:

(*a*) It is assumed that the fatal illnesses in the children constituted death threats to the mothers.

(*b*) The mothers reacted to the illnesses with a triphasic response when disease lasted four months or more.

(*c*) Denial was most characteristic of the initial phase.

(*d*) Calm acceptance of death of the child with improved integration characterized the terminal phase.

(*e*) Increased sublimation was suggested in some mothers during the terminal phase.

(*f*) In contrast to the mothers, the reactions of the staff were least well integrated during the terminal phase.

3. The findings reinforced, but do not prove, the hypothesis that the existential problem of death constitutes an important variable in individual and group development.

References

1. O. Rank, *The Trauma of Birth* (New York: Harcourt, Brace, 1929).
2. M. Crotjahn, "Death Anxiety and Ego Identity," to be published.
3. M. Klein, "The Psychogenesis of Manic-Depressive States" (1934), In *Contributions to Psychoanalysis 1921–1945* (London: Hogarth Press, 1950).
4. H. R. Bierman, "Parent Participation Program in Pediatric Oncology: A Preliminary Report," *Journal of Chronic Diseases*, 3 (1956), 632. Also see A. G. Knudson, Jr., and J. M. Natterson. "Participation of Parents in the Hospital Care of Fatally Ill Children," *Pediatrics*, 26 (1960), 482–490.
5. S. Freud, *General Introduction to Psychoanalysis* (New York: Liveright, 1935).
6. M. Nagy, "The Child's Theories Concerning Death," *Journal of Genetic Psychology*, 73 (1948), 3.
7. M. F. Bozeman *et al.*, "Psychological Impact of Cancer and Its Treatment. III. The Adaptation of Mothers to the Threatened Loss of Their Children through Leukemia: Part I." *Cancer*, 8 (1955), 1.
8. J. B. Richmond and H. A. Waisman, "Psychological Aspects of Management of Children with Malignant Diseases," *A.M.A. American Journal of Diseases of Children*, 89 (1955), 42.

Karl Stern, Gwendolyn M. Williams, and Miguel Prados

Grief Reactions in Later Life

The gerontologic unit within the Department of Psychiatry at McGill University has been running an old age counselling service since 1945. A description of this type of service and the main problems involved has been given on previous occasions. One of the most frequent situations with which one has to deal in this age group is that of bereavement. This is probably accentuated by the fact that the patients seen in the counselling service are members of the indigent population. In such a socially and economically selected group the patient comes to the attention of a social agency for the first time when he or she loses a marital partner or some other family member. In the following study an attempt is made to draw attention to certain features of grief reactions that are particularly striking within this age group and that may differ in character from grief reactions in younger age groups.

Subjects

The present observations were made on 25 subjects, one of whom was male and 24 of whom were female. The age at the time of interview varies from 53 to 70. The problems encountered in old age can only be artificially differentiated from those of the involutional period. Therefore, in this study the age range is greater and the lower age limit is 50.

Method

A social history is taken by the social worker before the psychiatrist sees the patient. A systematic psychiatric history is taken in the first interview, which is followed by a varying number of informal interviews. The first interview has to be kept "free" so that the patient does not have the feeling of a systematic "history taking."

Reprinted from *American Journal of Psychiatry*, 58 (1951), pp. 289–294, by permission of the authors and publisher.

The facts have to be compiled gradually during several interviews, as well as from the history taken by the social worker.

Observations

A composite picture of these cases presents itself as follows. There is a dearth of overt mental manifestations of grief or of conscious guilt feelings. On the other hand, there is a preponderance of somatic illness. In some cases the time relationship between the onset or accentuation of these somatic illnesses and the time of bereavement is quite obvious. The image of the deceased undergoes peculiar changes in the consciousness of the mourner; the idealization commonly encountered during the process of grief sometimes assumes bizarre degrees. In contrast to this there frequently develops an irrational hostility toward living persons, particularly in the patient's immediate environment. Here there is also a time relationship between the onset of the hostility and the time of bereavement in some cases.

The features are best illustrated by some case examples.

A woman of 59 (Mrs. A. C.), who had lost her husband two years before she was first seen, developed arthritis at the time of his death. She had an operation for prolapse of the bladder on the day of the anniversary of his death. "Coming out" of the operation she developed a pain in her right arm that since has "spread all over."

A man of 59 (Mr. J. S.) developed breathlessness and a large amount of sputum within the year following his wife's death, which had occurred six years before the first interview. At that time bronchiectases were diagnosed.

A woman of 63 (Mrs. I. T.), who had lost her husband six years before the first interview, suffered three accidents within four years, always when in domestic employment. On one occasion she slipped and broke her wrist while the family for whom she was working was preparing the house for Christmas.

One woman of 63 (Mrs. I. R.) was admitted to the Allan Memorial Institute with the typical picture of a senile dementia. Interviews of the relatives revealed the fact that her organic cerebral syndrome set in immediately following her husband's death. This time relationship was stated independently by several relatives.

This woman was born in Montreal. Her father died at the age of 84 of cancer. He was an engineer and had emigrated from England. Her mother died of cancer at the age of 80. The patient was the third of ten children of whom six were still living at the time of interview. Two children died in infancy of meningitis, one sister died of typhoid fever, one brother died of cancer, and another brother had been in a mental hospital for the last ten years. After completing high school she took a business course and worked for more than ten years with an insurance company.

At the age of 28 she married, and her husband was approximately the same age. Her relationship with him seems to have been a very dependent one. She said that arguments were her fault because she was "such a little snip." She had very high praise for his thoughtfulness, his ability at the office, and his musical talent: "I don't like to brag but . . . ." The main social activities of their life were centered about the church and the choir, for which her husband was the organist. He was employed by an insurance firm. They entertained friends in their home. She could not have children and said that she now felt inadequate. She treated her nephew "as my son."

According to information obtained from her sister, the patient had never been considered a strong person. Twice she had travelled to England because she felt "terribly worn down" after the death of a near relative. These trips made her feel much better. She had had a gynecological operation many years ago. She had a gastroenterostomy for the relief of an obstructive ulcer. She had had pleurisy and bronchitis the two winters previous to the death of her husband.

In August 1949 her husband died suddenly as the result of an accident; while doing some house painting he fell on a picket fence and his lung was pierced. Following his death she became restless and anxious; at the same time it was noticed that she became forgetful, increasingly disoriented, and negligent in her everyday work. In October 1950 she was admitted to the Allan Memorial Institute.

She was a short, thin, and pale woman, with a mild facial asymmetry. She would move restlessly about the ward, repeating over and over that she was a nuisance to everybody, that she could not understand why people were so kind to her, and that she ought to have her glasses fixed. Physical examination revealed diminished hearing in the left ear, diminished vision in the left eye, a sluggish right pupillary response, an equivocal plantar reflex on the right, bradycardia (50), and retinal arteriosclerosis.

Interview: (What is your name?) "Ivy, a plant . . . . I was the first girl, so they thought they had to give me a flower name . . . . You have a pretty view up here . . . . My husband and I used to go for lovely walks in the fall . . . . Do you have a son? . . . A doctor who examined my eyes had a son here, that's why I thought you might have a son . . . ."

(What is wrong with you?) "Just if I could see, read . . . it's my eyes."

(How long have you had this?) "It dates back to childhood. I think I had a fall when I was a child, I think it's that what causes all the trouble . . . ."

(Is there anything else wrong with you? You would not be taken into this place on account of your eyesight.) "I don't know . . . . They told me to come in here, that's all."

(How do you sleep?) "I sleep fairly well since I got over the shock. It was a month, I don't know exactly."

(How is your appetite?) "Thank you, that's improved."

(How is your memory?) "The first little while after the shock I didn't remember so well."

(What would you say is the date today?) "I don't care . . . . I didn't follow it up. (Looks through the window.) Oh, I *do* know, it's November sixth, my birthday." (Correct)

(What year is it?) "Oh, I don't have any occasion, I didn't write letters . . . . Oh, I give up, I'm half asleep anyway."

(Would you say it is closer to 1948 or to 1938?) "I would rather say it's 1940 something than 1930 something."

(Examiner had introduced himself twice before. "What is my name?") I don't think I heard it." (Examiner repeats his name.) "Oh yes, you told me so. I thought I had only my eyes to be tested."

(What was the shock you mentioned?) "I made a great mistake. My brother-in-law said all the time to keep it up . . . . That's why my side is sore all the time, I feel tight here. I don't get any breath. It's dreadful to be alone in the house. You know we were very near, we had no children.

That silence in the house, how can I stand it? My brother didn't understand me (cries). You see, my husband was musical, we often had the choir in the house. When the accident took place he had three different offers to play the organ."

She gave contradictory reports as to the actual time of the accident. Her retention was severely impaired on counting tests (3). She showed considerable stability in her defects during several examinations within two weeks.

The following examples illustrate the actual attitude toward the lost person; all "dark" features are blotted out and the deceased becomes transfigured in an unreal way.

A woman of 60 (Mrs. E. D.) who had lost her husband three years before the first interview complained of "feeling bad" in a busy or noisy environment. Her sleep was poor, appetite varied, digestion was irregular. "Sometimes I don't feel too bad, at other times I feel like dying." She described her husband as a "wonderful man." Actually he had been an alcoholic who deserted her on several occasions and was cruel when intoxicated. There were notes in the record at the Family Welfare Association to the effect that she had come running for protection and help. In successive interviews she gave a glowing picture of her husband, and when finally confronted with the facts she denied them.

A similar situation existed in the case of a woman of 61 (Mrs. H. W.), who was seen in private practice. She had lost her husband seven years before the first interview. This woman referred to her deceased husband in terms that struck the examiner as almost fantastic glorification. Moreover, she involved his name in connection with any, even trivial, decision she had to make. Remarks such as, "Walter would want me to do this . . . ." or ". . . would not want me to do that," occurred frequently. She had a villa in one of the most beautiful spots of Sweden and spent part of every year there. Several rooms of the villa remained untouched, as if she were dealing with a shrine in his memory. The history taken from her son and her daughter revealed that the husband had been a psychopath with sadistic features. He had retired early in life, around the age of 40, living on his ample income. Every morning he would sit at his writing desk and compose an exact timetable of duties for each member of the family. This included physical exercises, open air walks, etc., even for the Parkinsonian mother-in-law, who frequently pleaded not to have to go for walks on cold days but was forced to do so just the same. He carried on an affair with the children's governess for many years, and would bring well-known dancers and actresses as "guests" into the home. Our informants told us that the patient had not only known about these things, but it seems that her husband made sure that she would know about them.

Another trend observed in our group was toward self-isolation, and of hostility against people in the bereaved person's surroundings. In fact, at times the immediate reason for which the social worker brought the client to the attention of the old age counselling service was precisely because he or she had "turned against" other roomers in the house, or against a member of the family, usually of the same sex as the deceased.

A woman of 61 (Mrs. M. B.), who was first seen two years after her husband's death, complained of insomnia and anorexia. "I've had a sour stomach all my life. Milk, if it is not cooked properly, doesn't agree with me." She said that she had cried a good deal since her husband's death. "If it were not for crying I'd be dead. It's the only thing that relieves me."

At the age of 27 she had married a man ten years her senior. She said that she had known her husband since childhood "because he came into her house." For several years before his death he suffered from "amnesia" (described what appeared to be senile dementia) and she apparently had a difficult time with him. "He wanted to go out all the time. One night he went out in his underwear and with his straw hat on." The last six months of his life he was in a mental institution. They had one child, a married daughter. After his death, our patient had a terrible quarrel with her son-in-law. When asked why, she was rather vague: "I did not like the way he acted . . . . He is rather a nervous man himself."

The private patient mentioned above developed a marked hostility against her son-in-law shortly after her husband's death. She described him as a cruel man who held her daughter in subjugation. Actually the daughter was happily married and, according to the latter as well as her son, the picture she gave of her son-in-law was completely distorted and would actually have fitted her husband.

Treatment

None of the cases described here was psychotic, nor was the depression of such a degree that electric shock treatment or hospitalization was necessary. The mechanisms of transference are largely modified in this age group. In view of the numerous somatic illnesses it must be emphasized that the patient needs to feel that the psychiatrist keeps close track and shows genuine interest in all medical and surgical procedures.

All channels toward sublimation have to be carefully exploited. The private patient (Mrs. H. W.) whose husband had been "idealized" in such an incongruous fashion developed a strong hero-worship of her minister, and began much church activity and community work, and is now on good terms with her son-in-law.

A large part of the therapy in the cases described consists of manipulating the environment. The mechanisms of hostility and self-isolation have to be interpreted to the relatives. Whenever possible the patient himself should be led up the the point of insight. In the cases of irrational hostility directed toward a member of the family the hostility disappeared during the course of the interviews.

Discussion

Reactions of grief and mourning are so important from a clinical point of view that they have been studied intensively.[2] Most of these investigations are based on psychoanalytic concepts. The one persistent trend apparent in all these papers is the one implied in Freud's original study,[3] and best formulated in the observation by Helene Deutsch,[4] namely, that the "work" of mourning must be viewed in the light of the psychoanalytic theory of libido. This theory is based on an analogy between the "conservation" of libido on one hand, and the law of conservation of energy on the other.

From a review of the literature it appears that grief reactions in later life have never been studied systematically. If we look at the most important features observed in our group, namely, the relative paucity of conscious guilt feelings, the tendency toward a replacement of the emotional grief reaction by somatic equivalents, the distortion of the image of the deceased in the direction of some unreal glorification, the tendency to self-isolation and hostility toward surviving members of the family or toward friends, it seems that they all lend themselves to an interpretation along the lines evolved in the psychoanalytic literature. Helene Deutsch[5] explained the absence of mourning in children on the basis of the assumption that the child's ego is too weak to carry out the "work" of mourning. Grief would endanger the ego at that stage to such a degree that the child has an immediate scotoma for the loss. However, she contends that the process of grief must be completed later. Now it has been stated that old age is characterized by a weakening of the strength of the ego; on this basis it has been assumed that involutional depressions are due to the fact that dynamic forces emanating from the superego are relatively prevalent during the involution.[6] This relative strengthening of the superego is made possible by the waning of the ego in the aging person.

If this theory is correct one should, at first sight, assume that conscious guilt, or a tendency toward delusions of guilt, should be found more frequently in old than in young bereaved persons. Our observations, however, seem to indicate the opposite. In order to explain this apparent discrepancy, namely, between a greater tendency to overt guilt in later life melancholias and the comparative absence of guilt in states of mourning, we have to consider the following. Under certain circumstances the older person is more ready to "channel" material that would produce overt emotional conflict into somatic illness. It is interesting to note in this connection Cobb's observation that the correlation between psychogenic trauma and rheumatoid arthritis became greater as the age of the investigated patients increased.[7] Something analogous was observed in the first hundred clients of our old age counselling service.[8] It would be the subject of a special study to decide whether these somatic illnesses represent a tendency toward self-punishment or an expression of the death wish and an identification with the deceased. However, it is safe to assume that the aging organism is biologically more ready for somatic equivalents of depressions. Even the senile dementia observed in one of our cases obviously represented such a flight into the somatic. It is generally known that degenerative cerebral disease can be enhanced or precipitated by emotional factors. Kral[9] showed that in elderly inmates of concentration camps there were not more affective psychotic disorders than would be expected in a control group but there was, under emotional stress, a definite tendency toward precipitation of organic senile psychoses. Incidentally, it is interesting to study the verbal productions of our senile patient from the point of view of the symbolic connotations of the psychogenic factor. She believes that she is in the hospital to have her eyesight tested. This may be interpreted, as in the case of a hysterical blindness, as representing her wish "not to see." Moreover, she thinks that her illness is due to a fall she had during childhood. On another occasion she points at the side of her chest and indicates that it hurts in there. There is little doubt that the "fall" and the pain in her side are associated with the mode of death of her husband who had been killed by falling on a picket fence and pierced his lung.

The most extensive and systematic study on grief reactions[10] was carried out chiefly on the bereaved persons after a disaster with violent death. This kind of death has unconscious symbolic connotations that, for obvious reasons, lend themselves more to the formation of ideas of guilt. In elderly people the death of the deceased has often been expected over a long time; there is frequently a history of nursing the sick person for a long period before death; the bereaved person is at an age at which he is preparing for death—in other words, contrary to situations like those described by Lindemann, there is more opportunity to identify with the deceased rather than feel guilty toward him.

This may also explain the tendency toward distortion. Helene Deutsch emphasized that ambivalence toward the deceased is the most difficult conflict to master during the reaction of mourning.[11] In our cases we saw a tendency to preserve an image of the deceased consisting only of light without shadow. We might say that the shadow is buried, or in those cases in which the shadow is not repressed it is projected onto a living person. This would explain the irrational hostility toward a living member of the family. In fact, the description that the bereaved gives of the relative toward whom he displays hostility may correspond surprisingly to the objectionable features of the deceased. In any case, the ambivalence is handled by splitting the image of the deceased into two. This mechanism is suggestive of an ego defence. To work through the ambivalence on a conscious level would be too great a strain. In purifying the image of the deceased to an unreal degree, the bereaved fulfills narcissistic needs that are urgent at this stage of life and avoids the intolerable stress of overt hostility.

Thus, we can tentatively explain all the phenomena observed here on the basis of defence against dynamic forces that would be destructive to a weakened ego. Apart from this, it is possible that the "somatic equivalents" of grief reactions are facilitated by identification with the deceased and the death wish of the mourner.

References

1. Karl Stern, "Observations in An Old Age Counselling Center," *Journal of Gerontology*, 3 (1948), 48, and "Problems Encountered in An Old Age Counselling Center," in *Problems of Aging* (New York: Josiah Macy, Jr., Foundation, 1950).
2. D. Ewen Cameron and F. Feldman, "The Measurement of Remembering," *American Journal of Psychiatry*, 100 (1944). 7; Sigmund Freud, "Mourning and Melancholia," *Collected Papers, IV*. 10, 152; Helene Deutsch, "Absence of Grief," *Psychoanalytic Quarterly*, 6 (1937), 12; Melanie Klein, "Mourning and Manic-Depressive States," *International Journal of Psychoanalysis*, 21 (1940), 125; Stanley Cobb and Erich Lindemann, Neuropsychiatric Observations after the Cocoanut Grove Fire," *Annals of Surgery*, 117 (1943), 814; Erich Lindemann, "Symptomatology and Management of Acute Grief," *American Journal of Psychiatry*, 101 (1944), 141; Milton Rosenbaum, "Emotional Aspects of Wartime Separations," *Family*, 24 (1944), 337.
3. Sigmund Freud, *op. cit.*
4. Helene Deutsch, *op. cit.*
5. *Ibid.*
6. Gerald H. J. Pearson, "An Interpretative Study of Involutional Depression," *American Journal of Psychiatry*, 85 (1928), 289.
7. S. Cobb, *et al.*, "Environmental Factors in Rheumatoid Arthritis," *Journal of the American Medical Association*, 113 (1939), 668.
8. Karl Stern, *op. cit.*
9. V. A. Kral, "Psychiatric Observations of Chronic Stress," *American Journal of Psychiatry*, 108 (1951), 185.
10. Erich Lindemann, *op. cit.*
11. Helene Deutsch, *op. cit.*

Joseph D. Teicher

"Combat Fatigue" or Death Anxiety Neurosis

Peacetime offers an appropriate opportunity to weigh some of the puzzling phenomena of war. Service in the Naval Medical

Reprinted from *Journal of Nervous and Mental Disease*, 117 (1953), pp. 234–243, by permission of the author and publisher. Copyright, 1953, The Williams and Wilkins Co., Baltimore, Md.).

Corps, and subsequent postwar experience with veterans still ex-
hibiting common psychiatric disability of war termed "combat fatigue," led me to review and re-evaluate the nature of this syndrome. During the recent war, the term "combat fatigue" was
introduced to describe a common disabling syndrome present in
some combatants. Less common, but frequently enough to confuse,
terms like "operational fatigue," "traumatic neurosis," "war neurosis," and "situational fatigue" were also used. More or less sharp
distinctions were made between "war neurosis" and "combat fatigue," depending upon the background and training of the psychiatrist. To complicate matters, while some psychiatrists considered
"combat fatigue," "war neurosis," and "psychoneurosis anxiety"
as different syndromes, others considered them all the same type
of emotional disorder. The variety of terms used by many psychiatrists interchangeably, and the shades of diagnostic criteria used
to reenforce the individual conviction that these terms indicate different syndromes, point up the confusion existing and still present
about these psychiatric illnesses of war. A review of literature
strengthens the impression of a profusion of concepts and a confusion
of basic dynamic mechanisms involved in this emotional disorder.

One of the important considerations of medical survey boards
was to evaluate the degree of disability, as well as to determine
whether this disability had its origin prior to enlistment. The latter
was important inasmuch as the pension which might later be
allowed by the authorities was often heavily based on whether
the disabling emotional disorder had its origin in the personality
development and makeup as it existed prior to enlistment. "Combat
fatigue" was the term often used when there were no "neurotic
determinants," and "war neurosis" or "psychoneurosis anxiety"
applied when there were "neurotic determinants" in the history of
the individual. There were no really sound criteria despite official
attempts to distinguish one category from another clinically. If
one began to investigate the meaning of the terms and questioned
why they were often used interchangeably, and why the sharp
distinctions were frequently made, depending on the psychiatrist,
only one conclusion was obvious. The terms were not clear, and
what was more, the origin of the particular syndrome either not
clearly or superficially understood.

I propose to re-examine the diagnostic term "combat fatigue"
(the most common term used), and to demonstrate its admitted
inadequacy, and, what is more, that it is actually misleading, expeci-

ally in view of the basic psychologic principles behind the emotional disorders precipitated by combat or being in a combat or danger zone.

The usual symptoms considered necessary for the diagnosis of a full blown "combat fatigue" patient are: repeated catastrophic nightmares; a "startle reaction" where the physiologic concomitants of anxiety and even marked fear reactions are produced by sudden loud noises; personality changes in that the patients become irritable, morose, silent, sullen, withdrawn, and often disciplinary problems; and, commonly, a guilt reaction with depression. Fatigue is not mentioned as a diagnostic symptom.

Rather than review here the mass of literature, let us consider two representative viewpoints. Raines and Kolb, with a largely psychobiologic view, consider "combat fatigue" as a syndrome apart from psychoneurosis.[1] Grinker and Spiegel, psychoanalytically oriented, consider "combat fatigue" as a neurotic disturbance.[2] Raines and Kolb, who had extensive experience with Naval personnel, repeatedly stress that "combat fatigue" is not a psychoneurosis but "psychoneurotic symptoms on a previously stable personality."

They established four arbitrary criteria for the diagnosis of "war neurosis" or "combat fatigue" as distinct from the neuroses of peacetime. The criteria were: (a) "a stable personality prior to the appearance of the traumatically determined emotional disturbance," emphasizing there should be no objective evidence of maladjustment in childhood or adolescence; (b) "a combat experience of sufficient intensity to render it feasible as a precipitating agent," stressing that the mere threat of combat "is not enough to produce neurotic symptoms in men other than those specifically predisposed, i.e., the psychoneurotics"; (c) "objective evidence of subjective anxiety," particularly when discussing combat experience—"when a battle description rolls out smoothly, search more carefully for a psychoneurosis or psychosis"; (d) "recoverability": "It is our belief that all true 'war neuroses' will recover in a comparatively short time with even relatively superficial therapy. When symptoms persist in disabling degree beyond two months under treatment, then the treatment is not adequate or the psychoneurosis is simply not 'combat fatigue' and has its roots in a deep-seated emotional conflict which long antedated the traumatic experience."

Precipitating factors stressed in "combat fatigue" are lack of confidence in the leader, poor training, and presence in combat with new shipmates. In the etiology of the syndrome, Raines and Kolb found two personality types as especially predisposed: (1) The emotionally and intellectually immature with a great deal of dependence, usually eighteen years of age or less; (2) the fully matured, independent older men, of thirty-eight or older. However, they recognize that "the psychological mechanisms associated with 'traumatic neurosis' are so fundamental as to be present in all men, and are of concern only in determining the extent of the neurotic response, not its content." In another instance, they state that "any such psychological mechanisms as exist are common to a great majority of men, that their eradication is impossible, and that therefore their importance can be minimized in the prevention and treatment of 'war neuroses' in the present state of our knowledge."

As already indicated, they "believe the traumatically determined emotional disturbance in itself goes no further than these symptoms; beyond lies the true psychoneurotic, easily diagnosed by longitudinal history." "The psychological picture appears to be the product of the individual's attempt to handle severe grades of stress and anxiety." The syndrome is grouped roughly into clinical pictures dominated by anxiety, by anxiety and depression, or anxiety "plus evidence of neuroses, particularly hysteria."

In the symptoms already described, the guilt reaction was not felt to be essential for the diagnosis. In this connection, the following is an interesting passage from Kubie, *et al.*, who studied Merchant Marine personnel. "Perhaps the worst situation occurs whenever a group of men are trapped in a spot from which few can escape. Escape from such a predicament leaves the survivors haunted by the memory of those who are left behind, with a sense of guilt as great as if they had murdered them."[3]

As the war progressed and invasions were more frequent, it was soon apparent that symptoms persisted in disabling degree in larger and larger numbers. The men could not perform even noncombat duty adequately. It was always difficult *not* to find some "neurotic" determinants in all cases of so-called "combat fatigue," as well as in those without "combat fatigue" and yet exposed to the same experience. With larger numbers of casualties, it was increasingly more of a task to determine what combat experience of sufficient intensity was, and many apparently previously stable individuals developed symptoms while merely on continual duty in a danger zone. Not always were there objective signs of anxiety in relating the traumatic experience. It was soon abundantly clear, too, that the symptoms were not limited to any "personality types." In short, the criteria left much to be desired. If one adhered to them rigidly, there were very few cases of "combat fatigue"; if one used them roughly, then they were not criteria at all.

A much more fundamental objection exists to their views. On the one hand, they believe the traumatically determined, emotional disorder goes no further than the symptoms; beyond lies the psychoneurotic. On the other hand, they recognize "the psychological mechanisms associated with 'traumatic neurosis' are so fundamental as to be present in all men, and are of concern only in determining the extent of the neurotic response, not its content." There appears to be a strange schizophrenia, an artificial splitting between the symptoms and the psychologic mechanisms within the individual, as if the symptoms are not the product of the psychological mechanisms. "Combat fatigue" symptoms are psychoneurotic symptoms, rather than "true psychoneuroses" seems to be a forced and artificial distinction.

Psychoneurotic symptoms are an expression of the individual's attempt to master emotional problems. It is recognized that "the psychological picture appears to be the result of the individual's attempt to handle severe grades of stress and anxiety." How can any emotional disorder, however determined, go "no further than the symptoms"? The point is that the symptoms are not, as implied, something superficial, something imposed on the individual, as it were. They are an expression, enhanced and magnified, of the defenses by which the individual attempts to handle anxiety, and the mechanisms involved are fundamental and determine the extent of the response to anxiety. The extent depends upon the individual's early psychologic development and his traumatic experience. The symptoms, an expression of the attempt to master the stressful situation, are intimately, inextricably interwoven with the fundamental psychologic mechanisms motivating the personality.

This allegedly superficial disorder, "combat fatigue," is presumably caused by combat experience of sufficient intensity. Note that in mentioning the clinical features of "combat fatigue," fatigue is not one of the symptoms listed! The psychologic effects of fatigue, which is essentially a protective mechanism, have been intensively studied. Fatigue may serve as a protection from fear, because, in general, stimuli, however violent, tend to lose their effect by continued repetition. Irritability, quarrelsomeness, poor concentration, etc., have been described, but these usually subsided quickly with rest if produced only by physical fatigue. One must conclude that the persistence of these symptoms—the personality changes—is not due to fatigue, but rather is the result and expression of psychologic conflicts within the individual.

Actual strife is an extreme hazard. Why do some combatants develop the disabling symptoms while others do not? In many cases of both categories examination of their civilian life shows good adjustment and their development reveals nothing one would consider overtly neurotic. This is on the basis of the usual histories, not on the basis of psychoanalysis of the individual. One is driven, upon reflection, to conclude that combat is not the cause of the illness. Rather, in combat, fundamental psychologic mechanisms present in all, and probably basic conflicts, are activated in individuals who are predisposed. The personality types suggested by Raines and Kolb are not valid. If psychologic mechanisms fundamental to all are stimulated by combat, then that too fails to explain why some do and some do not develop the symptoms. The probability arises that the answer may be found in the basic conflicts aroused, since the intensity and resolution of a conflict are never exactly the same in two individuals. The conclusion drawn from the above is that "combat fatigue" is neither due to combat nor fatigue.

Grinker and Spiegel, who had a large experience with land and air force troops, quite correctly regarded "war neuroses" as psychoneuroses. They ask, "What do we really mean by war neuroses? Are they temporary reactions to catastrophic events, are they something different from psychoneuroses, and do they justify a special nosological designation?" They conclude that basically the "war neuroses" show the same characteristics as other neuroses, and the same imperceptible gradations into psychotic states, since they "represent more or less successful defenses against the dissolution of the ego characteristic of a psychosis." Every combat soldier reacts according to how his previous psychologic patterns have prepared him. It is only the quantitative features common to most "war neuroses" which give them, as a group, an apparent distinction from all other neuroses. After the initial blow, reaction is internalized and is repetitive according to previous patterns of the personality and like other neuroses.

Grinker and Spiegel do not stress personality types. As to the etiology of the "combat neuroses," they point out that the principal way in which "the combat personality is affected by the specific stress to which he is subjected is in the production of fear and, to a lesser extent, of hostility." The individual develops fear because of the combat situation. How he handles it or "protects against its appearance" is another problem, which includes symptom formation. Grinker and Spiegel afford a more valid and clearer understanding of the problems, "combat fatigue," but they do not go far enough.

In combat, as in other stressful, life-threatening situations, we deal not only with the hazards which produce anxiety and fear, but we must take into account the fundamental psychologic mechanisms present in all men, as well as the individual pattern of personality development. Everyone brings into his adulthood, along with remnants of his infantile sexuality, a certain neurotic potentiality. What is common to all cases, regardless of degree of potentiality, is that the neurotic illness is ultimately due to the unresolved remnants of their respective infantile conflicts. Raines and Kolb echo the old "shock" theory where the defenses against undue stimuli are overpowered, producing a "war neurosis" in previously healthy individuals. Obviously, this view disregards the infantile sexual conflicts of civilized man, and the resultant precipitates.

Let us examine further what fundamental psychologic mechanism is especially activated, what remnants of infantile sexuality and what anxieties once experienced by the child come to the surface in the neuroses of war.

As representative of contributions to the discussion of "combat fatigue," both groups of authors stress the combat hazards as producing anxiety and fear, and that the symptoms and clinical picture are diffused with anxiety. That basic psychologic phenomena present in all are involved in the production of the clinical picture is a view held by both, although Raines and Kolb limit the role of fundamental psychologic phenomena as only determining the "extent" of neurotic response.

There is no dispute that a basic motivation of man is to preserve himself, to preserve his life. The social development of man has overlaid this fundamental drive with all kinds of elaborations and reaction formations. As Zilboorg pointed out, the term 'self-preservation' implies an effort against some force of disintegration; the affective aspect of this effort is fear, fear of death."[4] If this fear were constantly conscious we would be unable to function normally, and hence must be properly repressed. No one is free of the fear of death, not even the most courageous soldier. Behind "the sense of discouragement and depression, there always lurks the basic fear of death, a fear which undergoes most complex elaborations and manifests itself in many indirect ways."

In war, Zilboorg points out, the civilian begins to wrestle with an unconscious sense of guilt about those who have fallen, and with a mounting sense of anger and feeling of hatred for the enemy who kills. Actual fear of death is mastered through a direct form of aggression, "the hatred for the enemy and the enthusiasm for the defeat." It is the degree of conversion of the fear of death into murderous hatred that is the main ingredient of "morale" (indicating how a knowledge of basic psychologic mechanisms *can* be utilized in prevention and treatment of war neuroses?). The murderous destructive drives within us are the only ones capable of maintaining the fear of death in a low state of tension. He goes on to point out that in battle, raw troops become seasoned "as soon as they begin to convert their fear of death into hatred and aggression" . . . "primarily because their anger begins to be aroused after they have lost some of their brothers in combat. It is the mechanism of revenge, or overcoming death by means of murder . . . ."[5]

The war casualties called "war neuroses" are neurotic forms of the fear of death. In these, Zilboorg finds "it is not difficult to discern a certain paralysis of motor aggression." The soldier enters the battle handicapped by a guilty conscience which antedates his military service, and which leads him to profound unconscious compassion (identification with the dead) without corresponding murderous aggressive hatred. His identification with the dead around him is too great; he is unable to fight. He succumbs to a passivity from which he is unable to escape except by the way of fantasy, which is why "so many of these cases are so suffused with anxiety." In passivity "they avoid both death and murder but are unable to escape the fear of either . . . their fear of death is overcharged with a sense of guilt for a fantasied murder committed long before they were called upon to meet the grim problems of combat."

The psychobiologists minimize the basic nature of the fear of death. Whitehorn believes that because physicians are preoccupied with life and death problems they are apt to assume fear of death is the great common denominator of anxiety. "Even in deadly warfare one's greatest apprehension is not of death but of being maimed or failing in one's duty, and that, in large part, because one dreads the reactions of other persons."[6] That view is not supported by the clinical experience on the combat field, nor does it grant the role of unconscious dynamic forces, nor even the unconscious.

To repeat, in the neurotic form of fear of death, the sufferers are afraid to die and afraid to kill; in their illness they avoid death and murder. Their fear is overcharged with guilt for a fantasied murder in the past. Recall that Kubie, *et al.*, stress the guilt of survivors "as great as if they had murdered" (those lost). What, of course, Zilboorg (and Kubie) refers to in the past is the period of infantile sexuality, of the Oedipus complex, which is universal in civilized man.

In the resolution of the Oedipus complex the child feels guilty not only because he wishes for the forbidden mother but primarily because of his murderous hatred for the powerful father whom he fears. He cannot act because he is helpless and because he fears retaliation. For his forbidden desires he fears punishment, i.e., castration, and feels guilty as well. This is sketchy since there are many aspects to the Oedipus complex. If siblings are present, for example, a brother may feel the same murderous hatred toward another brother who is rival with him for the mother. The child's fears and hates are primarily expressed and acted out in a very active fantasy life (largely repressed) and not, of course, in motor aggression. The guilt is a distillate of the Oedipal complex. The prime anxieties of the child in the infantile period are connected with castration (and the fear of being maimed is basically that), and with loss of love which threatens to leave him helpless and abandoned. The extent of damage actually done to the child varies with the attitudes and handling by the parents, and determines the degree of the neurotic potentiality of the adult.

War demands of a good soldier that he kill his, the country's, enemies. He is also exposed to constant, realistic threats of death. If the sense of guilt, the precipitate of his Oedipal complex, is strong, his identification with the dead becomes profound. "This punishment will be mine, because I am guilty" (of the fantasied murder). The threat of death, highly charged by combat, is regarded unconsciously as a punishment for the fantasied crime. Hence, the escape into passivity and fantasy, just as in childhood; hence, the paralysis of motor aggression which is impossible for the child to express although he hates murderously. The hate cannot be actively carried out, because of fear of murder and its consequences, death to the murderer. Thus, later, they avoid both death and murder in their illness, but not the fear of either, the precipitate of the Oedipus complex. "War neuroses" would not exist in the clinical form they do otherwise.

The structure of "war neuroses" is certainly more elaborate than I have indicated. I have wanted to point out what is so commonly overlooked, namely, that the precipitate of the Oedipal situation, i.e., guilt, and the fear of death, present in all, are the fundamental pillars of what is usually incorrectly called "combat fatigue." I have no intention of discussing the technical concepts of "war" and "peace" super-egos, the super-ego as fate, as the successor of the introjected parents, ego conflicts and the abandonment by outer and inner protective forces, the unconscious sadistic trends gratified in the violent loss of human life, and the unconscious reaction of egocentric self-delight ("I am glad it was not I"), to name a few elements which bear upon the problem of "war neuroses" or "traumatic neuroses."

Psychoanalysts in studying the neuroses precipitated by war have pointed out consistently that the structure of these neuroses, in varying degrees, consisted of conversion hysteria manifestations (anxiety converted into somatic symptoms); the traumatic element proper (breakdown of protective apparatus against stimuli and the attempt to build it up again) expressed in the repetitive catastrophic nightmare and startle reaction; manifestations of reactivated anxiety (and guilt) and defenses against this anxiety; and manifestations of ego conflicts, the fear experienced by the ego lest the super-ego abandon it. This latter, Freud called death anxiety.

Summary

In summary, I repeat that the purpose of this paper is to point out that the fundamental basic pillars of the neuroses in war are based on the drive for self-preservation with its affective aspect, fear of death, and on the residues of the Oedipus complex present in all in varying degrees, particularly the sense of guilt deriving from a fantasied murder in the past. Every adult has within him the precipitates of the Oedipal complex, of infantile sexuality, and hence has a certain neurotic potentiality which varies with the individual. These are basic facts. Given these, combat may provoke symptoms of the psychoneurosis called "war neurosis." Other elements in the structure of the neurosis have been indicated to indicate its complexity, and that it is not only as "deep as the symptom."

In view of the fundamental nature of the fear of death present in all, and the considerations pointing out its neurotic structure, it is obvious that "combat fatigue" is totally misleading, that "operational fatigue" is equally so, that "traumatic" and "war neuroses" are closer descriptions of the syndrome. However, I wonder if the neurosis is not more cogently expressed in the term "death anxiety neurosis" which, while not a pleasant term, is nonetheless more completely descriptive and accurate than any of the others.

References

1. G. N. Raines and L. C. Kolb, "Combat Fatigue and War Neurosis," *U.S. Naval Medical Bulletin*, 41 (1943), 923, 1200.
2. R. R. Grinker and J. P. Spiegel, *Men Under Stress* (Philadelphia: Blakiston, 1945).
3. Raines and Kolb, *op. cit.*
4. G. Zilboorg, "Fear of Death," *Psychoanalytical Quarterly*, 12 (1943), 465.
5. *Ibid.*
6. J. C. Whitehorn, "Guide to Interviewing," *Archives of Neurology and Psychiatry*, 52 (1944), 197.
7. S. Freud, *The Ego and The Id* (London: Hogarth Press, 1947).
8. G. N. Raines and E. Broomhead, "Rorschach Studies on Combat Fatigue," *Diseases of the Nervous System*, 6 (1945), 1.
9. E. Simmel, *Psychoanalyses and the War Neuroses* (London: International Psychoanalytic Press, 1921).
10. J. D. Teicher, "Experience with Group Psychotherapy." *U.S. Naval Medical Bulletin*, 44 (1945), 753 and "Disciplinary Problems Among Men with Combat Fatigue," *U.S. Naval Medical Bulletin*, 45 (1945), 6.

Josephine R. Hilgard, Martha F. Newman, and Fern Fisk

Strength of Adult Ego Following Childhood Bereavement

The adult ego, strong or weak, develops out of the experiences of childhood, experiences both traumatic and benign. The death of a parent is potentially one of the most traumatic events that may occur in childhood. How traumatic the loss of a parent will be depends on relationships within the home prior to the parental death and upon the maintenance or reconstruction of the home after the death occurs.

The importance of these relationships was brought to our attention by a study over the past five years of selected patients in a mental hospital, all of whom had suffered parental losses. In

Reprinted from *American Journal of Psychiatry*, 30 (1959), pp. 788–798, by permission of the authors and publisher.

most of these cases the loss of the parent was followed by very disruptive circumstances, which seemed to have contributed to a weaker ego and to the later breakdown in adult life. The investigation here reported is an outgrowth of these conjectures through the study of a random sample of adults from the metropolitan area served by the hospital; we sought to determine whether or not the experiences of these individuals prior to and following parental death differed from those of the hospitalized patients. We have found such differences, and they offer a number of suggestions regarding mental health practices connected with a loss of a parent.

Sampling and Interview Procedures

In order to find an appropriate interview sample, we selected four census tracts within the metropolitan area that appeared to represent a fair cross section of the community according to socioeconomic criteria. Within these tracts we devised a probability sample of residence units, and selected at random all respondents between the ages of 19 and 49 inclusive, an age range which corresponded to our hospital experimental group. The resulting sample consisted of 2377 dwellings visited. Statistical interviews were completed with 1269 who fell within our age ranges; of these 1136 were white and native born, consistent with our hospital group. Thus our final metropolitan sample included 1136 subjects of whom 493 were men and 643 were women. These initial interviews were designed to obtain demographic information as well as data on parent loss in childhood.

They were precoded so as to facilitate study by the usual IBM methods. Whenever a parent-loss case meeting the same criteria as our intensively studied hospital sample (namely, married and with children) was found in this larger population, the interviewer asked for permission to return for a further interview. Sixty-five follow-up interviews were completed, representing two-thirds of this particular pool of parent-loss cases. Of those who were interviewed, 29 women had lost fathers, 19 women had lost mothers, 13 men had lost fathers and 4 men had lost mothers. Women were more numerous as well as more available for intensive interviews than men. These more searching interviews lasted from one to two hours in most cases. The 65 completed interviews permitted comparison with the 256 cases of parent loss studied intensively in the hospital. During the interview a brief social adjustment scale also was administered, the 39-item Edwards Social Desirability Test. A high score on it represents adjustment on a verbal level to social norms of desirable conduct; a low score indicates anxiety, uneasiness in social relationships, and some related signs of acknowledged maladjustment.

While we shall not present the statistical material in any detail in this paper, one figure, the per cent of parent loss in childhood, is of considerable significance. For our age range, contradictory figures in the literature have varied from less than 12 per cent based on census material,[1] (though the census has not asked questions on orphanhood directly), to 25 per cent based on special groups used as controls.[2] We found among our metropolitan group a total of 240 individuals who had lost one or both parents prior to the age of 19. This represents 21 per cent of the total group of 1136 between the ages of 19 and 49. This figure is the best comparison figure we have against which to reflect parent losses in other groups. For example, among 3579 patients in the same age range at the state hospital where we have been conducting our studies, we found 27 per cent loss of parents by death—a relatively small increase over the frequency of parental loss in the general population from which these patients come.[3]

The fact that a relatively small percentage difference exists between the hospitalized and nonhospitalized groups does not mean that parent loss is an unimportant factor in mental illness. It does point up the need to *determine what circumstances* permit such a traumatic event to be taken in stride. We believe that our study on the metropolitan group helps to clarify certain factors. In a paper of this length, however, only a limited number of observations can be reported.

Protection Against the Trauma of Parent Loss

When we consider among our respondents those who seem now, in adult life, to be reasonably well adjusted, i.e., to be living in an intact home where the marriage appears to be satisfactory, where the relationships with the children are adequate, the scores on the Edwards test indicate comfortable adaptation to social life, what do we find about the circumstances surrounding the loss of a parent in childhood?

Let us begin with a group of 29 women who lost fathers in childhood. Of these, 14 (or approximately half) fit our essentially well-adjusted group. What can we say of them?

First, *the home was kept intact.* In ten cases, the mother did not remarry but kept the family together by serving the dual role of mother as homemaker and father as breadwinner. The mother was characterized as strong, rather than as warm or tender, more the stereotype of the pioneer woman, meeting hardships with courage. These mothers were able to assume the dual role with little conflict, the masculine personality components predominating because of the *need* to work outside the home. In the recollection of the now-grown daughters, feminity of the mother is submerged; yet these daughters (now our respondents) became adequate wives and mothers and did not themselves necessarily show masculine role identifications. We believe this arose because the mothers were essentially feminine women, had been feminine mothers during their early years, and took on the social characteristics of masculinity as adequate social responses to an emergency because they were strong enough to meet the challenge. In our hospitalized group there was much less adequacy and much more conflict among the mothers over adopting the new roles required by the emergency.

Let us permit a few of our respondents to speak for themselves, as they describe their widowed mothers:

"She was responsible, hard-working."
"Thoughtful, strict, hard-working."
"Very strong, energetic, with little help from anyone."
"Worked very hard, gave me little in the way of emotion."
"Hard-working, conscientious, strong."
"Hard-working; a big group of relatives made it easier."

Some of these strong mothers could produce a warm image in their daughters' recollections:

"Very strong, gay, and giving; laughing even in great adversity."

"Calm and secure, gave much to her children. Our grandparents also gave to us."

"Worked hard at WPA and laundry to support us; she was strong and giving."

For most of these mothers, however, ego strength did not mean warmth as we usually understand it. The children use statements of hard work and energy far more than they make any mention of affection. Yet the end result was adequate adjustment.

One of the protective factors we see, then, is a strong mother who works and keeps the home intact, engendering a strong ego in her children, both through her example to them and through her expectations of their performance.

To stay with this same group of women who have lost fathers, we note several other positive factors. One is the presence of a network of support outside the home, *and* the capacity of the mother to make use of it. This may be a group of relatives, the church, community resources such as public welfare, and community members. The strong mother in order to use these resources well must be relatively free of conflict over dependency. That is, she must be willing to turn for help without feeling belittled; if she can, these sources of support outside the home become of great help in her emergency.

Other important factors go back to the period prior to the death of the father. Where the childhood years have been spent in a home with two parents who had well-defined roles, so that early identifications were good, the later lives of the children tend to show a high degree of stability. A reflection of this stability lies in the unusually large number of stable and long marriages among our respondents with cordial intrafamilial relationships. This is true whether the father or the mother was lost. Our cases are not enough to establish a critical period, but we note a number of outstandingly good adjustments among those whose parent loss came between the ages of 10 and 15, following a satisfactory home life. One evidence of the compatability in parental relationships is found also in the group of parents who make good remarriages after a while.

We shall not discuss in detail the group of respondents who lost mothers in childhood and whose fathers either assumed, or declined to assume the role of both father and mother. Our observations indicate that a mother was more apt to keep the children with her than was the father so that the threat to the integrity of the family was greater where the mother died. Here are two typical illustrations:

> One woman, happily married for 23 years, with three children of her own told us: "I was ten when my mother died.

the fourth of nine children. Against the advice of all the relatives, my father kept us together. He was father and mother. He taught us to cook and to bake, and each of us girls, in turn, took responsibility for the house as the next older one married. My mother was a wonderful woman but we were a happy family even after she died, and all of us have happy families now."

On the opposite side of the coin is the woman, convalescing at the time of the interview from an injury sustained in a brawl, who told us this story: "There were seven of us. I think my oldest sister was fifteen when Mother died in childbirth. I was seven. We all went to different homes—I, to my godparents. Mine was a good home, but I never saw my family. We all met for the first time—as adults—at my father's funeral. We stood there, strangers, hating the man who could have kept us together, and didn't." This woman was divorced and her husband had custody of her children.

Grief and Mourning

To understand bereavement we need to be aware of more general attitudes in the family, particularly the factor of *separation tolerance*. This is a kind of prepared antidote to separation anxiety. The process of achieving independence in psychosexual development involves a whole series of separations in normal upbringing, and the way in which these earlier separations had been accomplished affected the resolution of the separation trauma produced by the parental death.

A special illustration is provided by the preparation for death in some of the cases in which the parental death followed a long illness, and the parent about to die prepared the children for the event. In some cases a dying mother speeded up the maturing of her daughter by coaching her in household responsibilities, as well as by giving sex instructions that she might otherwise have postponed for a time.

Separation tolerance not only involves more general attitudes of parents toward dependence and independence in their children, but in the emergency created by death, it also involves the reaction by both parents to the approaching irrevocable separation. A dying parent may convey to his child an acceptance of this complete separation and in so doing may help the child to accept it. The surviving parent can provide acceptance of the death without excessive guilt. We found surprisingly few of our respondents who recalled a feeling of guilt or of responsibility for death. This is in contrast to the ideas expressed in the hospitalized patients and, we believe, reflects primarily a difference in home climate.

About a third of our parent-loss cases fell into the chronic death classification, while the other two-thirds were sudden losses. In the sudden loss cases the relatives and the community appear to respond more vigorously to the immediate stimulus. There were no suicides in the metropolitan sample, whereas there were 6.3 per cent in the hospital experimental group. The traumatic effect of loss through a parent's own volitional act such as suicide, in conjunction with the circumstances that preceded it, is apparent in our hospitalized patients. This particular type of parental death may be a specific to alert one to potential maladjustment in later life.

One is naturally concerned with the expression of grief as a way of meeting the emotional crisis of death. What recollections are there of the expression of grief and mourning? Though the number of subjects in each group is small, our observations are indicative of certain trends.

Our study suggests that grief at the death of a parent is recalled only in rare instances when such a death has been experienced prior to the age of nine. Of the women who had been nine or under at the father's death, about half recalled the mother's reaction vividly; the other half recalled occasional fragments of the funeral rituals. None recalled grief of her own. Thus the outstanding memory of women who lost fathers when they were nine or younger concerned the mother's grief and mourning. This extreme sensitivity to the mother's mood overshadowed all else.

We might say that the ages of 9-10-11 are transitional ones, for here there could be either recall of the maternal mourning or recall of the individual's own grief. When the loss had occurred after the age of 11, identification with the maternal grieving ceased and the individual spoke more of her own feeling of loss.

We should like to interject here a brief comment about the significance of our finding that the age of nine years represents a definite shift in the ability to grieve. Some clinicians may raise the objection that the presence or absence of grief reported by adults many years later is due to repression of such feeling. Thus a more accurate account would state that, in the recollection of adults, the presence of grief was unlikely to be remembered when a parent had died before the child was nine. Interestingly, this age of nine also crops up as a significant one in several studies where children's ideas about death were subject to systematic scrutiny. Three studies of normal children in widely scattered geographical areas—Anthony[4] in England, Nagy[5] in Hungary, and Gesell[6] in the United States—stress the presence of a shift in the child's ability to look at death, which occurs at about the age of nine. A child who has first denied the facts of death and subsequently has looked only in a tangential way at them now looks at death directly, realizing both that those he loves may die and that he himself will some day die. Prior to the age of nine, children's attitudes have undergone a series of changes, but such a major shift at nine highlights the importance of the maturational process of the ego as a function of age as well as of experience in coping with concepts such as death.[7] The parallelism of our finding that personal grief over a death can be remembered when the parental death occurred when the child was nine or older and the findings by Gesell, Anthony, and Nagy that children accept death on a different level after age nine suggests significant related changes in the ego.

Only in women whose fathers had died was there an identification with the parental mood over loss. Women whose mothers died did not report their own sensitivity to the father's grief, as such. The responses to mother loss were more varied: some girls took over prematurely the responsibility of running a household, while for some the threat of family disintegration was imminent. In sharp contrast to father death, there was marked recall of the ritual, particularly the funeral. It should be reiterated that the number of cases in these comparisons is very small, but even so the recall in the one type of loss, of grief without ritual, and in the other type of loss, of ritual without grief, deserves further investigation.

Men who lost fathers showed vivid recall of the death or funeral in all cases when they were over nine years of age at the time of the death; men did not, however, identify with the mother's grief as the women did. It turned out that there were only four men in the sample who had lost mothers. All had vivid recollections of the funeral, and some recall of grief, but individual circumstances are too varied to make much comparison in this small group.

What conjectures arise from these differentiated recollections of grief and ritual? The clearest picture is that of women who lost fathers, who reacted primarily to the mother's grief. It may be that adequate grieving by a strong mother is a protection and clears the air, especially if the mother soon starts her new life and keeps the home intact. Our hospital experience leads us to suspect that loss of the mother is a more serious thing for the daughter than the loss of a father in terms of her reliving this tragic event later in life when she has children. In our metropolitan sample, the girls who lost mothers were the ones who remembered the ritual rather than the mourning; it may be that less emotional expressiveness by fathers in our culture denies the child some emotional benefit from a more overt expression of grief by the surviving adult. On the basis of our analysis of the data thus far, it would appear that a freer expression of grief at the time of mother loss might be beneficial, though it must be recalled that most individuals in our sample have made adequate adjustments despite the limited expression or recall of grieving.

Social Pathology Following Parental Loss

The fact that our sample is drawn from the nonhospitalized fraction of the community does not mean that there is no pathology within it. In this section of the paper we propose to indicate some of the consequences of parent loss that have proved troublesome for the members of this "normal" sample.

Continued dependency. In one form of social pathology, the surviving parent becomes so emotionally dependent upon the children that the child finds it difficult to make a normal separation from that parent when he himself becomes an adult.

The group of men whose fathers had died were involved in this type of interdependency to a marked degree, far more than the women. Before describing individual reactions in this group, however, let us remind ourselves that the size of this sample is small. There were only 13 men, 3 of whose mothers had remarried. If we turn our attention to the group of 10 where the mothers did not remarry, we note that only one of the 10 mothers showed a fair degree of independence, while 9 manifested an emotional dependency on their children, particularly the sons. An eldest son of 35, who was a sibling of one of our respondents, was unmarried and still lived with his mother. Both a daughter and a son of another mother managed to marry, but their marriages ended in divorce and they returned to the mother's home, where they appeared contented. In yet another family, three sons who lived with their widowed mother did not marry until after her death. One mother threatened suicide when her son married. In addition, four widowed mothers lived with their married sons; some of these sons were siblings of our respondents. Several men felt as though their mothers had placed them in the position of substitute husband, and in our review of the material it seemed to us that this had frequently been the case whether the son verbalized it or not.

The mother's continued dependency on daughters, though less often indicated by the women than by the men, was in excess of what would be expected in a population with intact parental homes. Occasionally a child had found the close bond intolerable and made an early escape, as in the case of one daughter who was aware that she married at the early age of 16 rather than continue the exceptionally close association demanded by her mother. The mothers felt that they were needed by their grown children, and in some cases this was indeed true, because the mother's continued concern had perpetuated childhood patterns. In any event the mother was able to continue the major role that she had known so long.

Thus in the normal situation where a father has died and a mother has not remarried, the dependency relationships tend to be abnormal when compared with the general population. This continued parental dependency upon growing and grown children with its interwoven and never resolved dependencies in both generations exerts a profound effect on the degree of maturity achieved by the ego in its close interpersonal relationships. We observed that the work ego or intellectual ego among men whose fathers had died attained a superior level, however, as indicated by occupation. Among them there were three Ph.D.'s,* one attorney, one engineer, one stockbroker, two salesmen, two electricians, and a truck driver. Competence in work ranged from moderately successful to very successful.

We may compare men in the metropolitan and hospitalized groups in regard to the variables we have just discussed, namely, dependency needs and work abilities. We observe marked dependency needs in both groups. In the metropolitan sample, these needs frequently continue to be fulfilled especially through

* Possibly consistent with the fact that this was a university town.

nurturing by the mother herself. In the hospital sample dependency needs are meeting current life frustrations; the hospital patients have known a checkered career of unreliable fulfillment from the earliest years. The adequacy of the work ego in the metropolitan sample, compared with its relative inferiority in the hospital group, could arise in part from the gratification of basic needs by the surviving parent. This gratification frequently carries a price tag of immaturity with continued dependency on the mother herself or on a mother substitute.

Hazards of remarriage. Another form of difficulty in social adjustment is created by the widow (or widower) who feels that a new marriage must be made at all costs in order to have an intact household, although, in fact, the choice of marital partners for a man or woman with young children is somewhat limited. Though our cases are too few for adequate generalization, the most difficult period for satisfactory remarriage of a mother appears to be in the 30's. The younger mothers—in their 20's—were apt to remarry adequately, but of seven remarriages between the ages of 30 and 36, five of the stepfathers were rather inadequate. The mothers above 40 who remarried were more apt to find satisfactory stepfathers for their children. One can only conjecture that the very young ones made the typical marriages of young people, the older ones made mature choices with perhaps less romantic considerations, while the in-between ones, caught in the conflicts between a youthful marriage and a more mature type, settled for an unsatisfactory compromise.

Anniversary syndromes. One of the threads that has run through our studies of the aftereffects of parent loss is what we have called the *anniversary* reaction. This is a tendency for reliving the childhood trauma at a specific time, for example, when a woman reaches the age of the mother's death, or when her daughter reaches the age the woman was when her mother died. Sometimes this reliving is of such irrational intensity as to lead to hospitalization, but we have noted that there are similar manifestations in the nonhospitalized population. Within our sample we have several illustrations of events in the next generation that mirror in some ways the events of the earlier one, and are associated with anniversaries.

One of our respondents expected to die at age 25, the age of her mother at death. She was surprised, and relieved, to live out her 25th year. Now she felt destined to live out her mother's life, and this sense of destiny has continued. She did not marry until she reached 25, and, as though the magical reincarnation must continue. Her marriage has been satisfactory for 20 years. This case—the expected death at the mother's death age, and the postponement of marriage until the hurdle is crossed—is similar in these respects to the history of Marie Bonaparte,[8] who has given her own autobiographical account of her fears.

Another one of our respondents expected to die at 14, the age at which an elder brother had died, a few months after her mother's death. Among our respondents there was a total of three hysterectomies and in each case they were closely associated with anniversary dates. We do not have enough evidence to demonstrate that these were engendered by psychological circumstances, but there are fragments suggesting that possibility. The first woman had a hysterectomy at age 39; her mother had died at age 38. The second had a hysterectomy when her son was 6; she was 6 when her mother died. Is the loss of fertility through hysterectomy somehow symbolic of the mother's loss through death? The third hysterectomy case was that of a woman who had lost a father at age 41, when her mother was 39. Her hysterectomy came at age 40; if it has symbolic significance it is probably associated in this case with the mother's loss of the father.

Thus there are many ways in which a childhood trauma may leave scars that can be opened again at a later time. We have demonstrated in earlier studies that sometimes these early wounds end much later in psychotic episodes.[9] Our study of a representative population has shown us that there are also detectable effects, short of mental illness, which show the intensity of the trauma and the earlier problems faced in separation.

Other Mental Health Implications

The clinical material obtained in our intensive interviews of the metropolitan sample corroborates the truism that the mothers and fathers who did the most to protect their children and lead them to normal adult lives were those with ego strength. But ego strength in a widow must not be confused with some idealized picture of the "good mother," warm and dispensing affection. Motherliness and warmth are needed for growth and maturation, but we need to evaluate the other components that make for independence, for a good work-ego, for the separation tolerance that is needed to meet severe losses. Motherliness is not sufficiently defined by endearment and sweetness. The reality-oriented mothers, with strong fiber that enabled them to face the world as substitute fathers, did something to make their daughters satisfactory women. A penalty for a too-long continued orientation toward children was overdependency on the children. This was one of the major problems faced later in life by our respondents.

We feel that one of the significant contributions of this study to us, as a staff, was a reorientation of our thinking toward strengths. Like all clinicians we found ourselves automatically turning first to consider problem areas in the 65 life histories. Naturally, we could detect many such areas among representative members of our culture. When we turned our attention to the present-day adequacies and the correlating positive factors in the early years, we realized the extent to which we had been attuned to illness rather than to health. Actually the very considerable adequacy of the generation we had interviewed reflected the strength inherent in the earlier generation described by our respondents. In comparing the metropolitan sample and the hospital one, we noted that in the former there was more apt to be a parent who had marshaled his resources both personal and external, while in the latter there was usually a parent who for various reasons was unable to meet the emergency. We, of the clinically oriented professions, should be constantly on the alert to see that we are phrasing our traditional query regarding the individual's problems to include also his strengths. .The basic question remains "What strengths does this individual have which we can help him mobilize to meet his problems?" There have been many self-curative experiences of life in the past as there can be in the present and in the future. It is our privilege as therapists to help people build on them.

References

1. Louis O. Shudde and Lenore A. Epstein, "Orphanhood: A Diminishing Problem," *Social Security Bulletin,* March 1955, pp. 17–19.
2. J. E. Oltman, J. J. McGarry, and S. Friedman, "Parental Deprivation and the Broken Home in Dementia Praecox and Other Mental Disorders," *American Journal of Psychiatry,* 108 (1952), 685–694.
3. Josephine R. Hilgard and Martha F. Newman, "Parent Loss Among Mental Patients and the Population at Large," paper given at the Western Psychiatric Association meeting, Los Angeles, November 1957.

4. Sylvia Anthony, *The Child's Discovery of Death* (London: Kegan, Trench, Trubner, 1940).
5. Maria Nagy, *A Gyermak és a Halal* (*The Child and Death*) (Budapest: Budapest University Pázmány Peter, 1936), and "The Child's Theory Concerning Death," *Journal Genetic Psychology*, 73 (1948), 3–27.
6. Arnold Gesell and Frances L. Ilg, *The Child from Five to Ten* (New York: Harper, 1946).
7. Jean Piaget, *Judgment and Reasoning in the Child* (New York: Harcourt, Brace, 1928).
8. Marie Bonaparte, "L'Identification d'Une Fille à Sa Mère Morte," *Revue Francaise Psychoanalysis*, 2 (1928), 541–565.
9. Josephine R. Hilgard and Martha F. Newman, "Anniversaries in Mental Illness," *Psychiatry*, 22 (1959), 113–121.

Edmund H. Volkart, with the collaboration of Stanley T. Michael

Bereavement and Mental Health

One of the crucial problems in all mental health research is to discover why some persons are more vulnerable to particular situations or experiences than are others. A series of situations, or a single situation, which apparently precipitates a severe breakdown in one person would seem to be handled with ease by another.

Knowledge of such differential reactions leads us to assume one or more of several hypotheses: for example, the person who breaks down has a weaker organism, by virtue of defects in heredity or constitution; or the person has weaker psychic defenses; or, perhaps, the presumably same event really had different meanings and thus was not the same psychologically. Regardless of the particular etiological formulation, the search is for that combination of predisposing and precipitating factors which produces the mental health problem in question.

The inquiry undertaken here concerns differential reactions to bereavement situations. Bereavement is usually understood to indicate the emotional state, behavior, and conduct of the survivors immediately following the experience of separation by death from a person who fulfilled dependency needs, especially needs related to emotional interaction. The circumstances of bereavement—the termination of a life and its emotional and social functions—the

Reprinted from *Explorations in Social Psychiatry* (New York: Basic Books, 1957), pp. 281–304, by permission of the authors and publisher.

necessity on the part of the survivors to deal with and adjust to the resulting sense of emptiness, and the drastic changes in the pattern of life experience may create a formidable emotional stress.

Whereas most people everywhere apparently meet and surmount the experience, some do not. At least in the Western cultures, some persons in the wake of bereavement develop extreme and unusual tension; they may perhaps attempt suicide or they may manifest symptoms of physical illness such as ulcerated colitis.[1]

Whatever their particular reactions may be, their distress and disorder are beyond the bounds of "normal grief," and they require medical attention, particularly from psychiatry.

The actual frequency of bereavement disorders is not known, even for our own society. There are no statistics; and we do not know whether the number of cases is increasing or decreasing over time or how our own rates compare with rates in other cultures. But patients with bereavement disorders evidently appear frequently enough to have stimulated the development of a rich psychiatric literature on the subject.[2]

In an often-quoted classic of the psychoanalytic literature, Freud[3] dealt with the dilemma of the difference between the so-called normal depression of ordinary grief and the psychotic depression. Freud maintained that the difference between ordinary grief and psychotic melancholia lies in the manner in which the ego deals with the object.

In grief, there is an actual loss of the object and consequently a feeling of the world being poor and empty. But there is insignificant fall in self-esteem and little self-accusation. In contrast, in psychotic melancholia the external, objective loss may be trivial but the intense feeling of disappointment and loss which the subject experiences is based on internal factors. In melancholia the emotional loss is attributed to an object which had been strongly desired, wanted, or loved. This object had become part of the subject's ego by a process of assimilation, incorporation, introjection, by oral symbolic processes. The emotional loss transpires within the narcissistic ego of the subject and the disappointment, neglect, and hurt over the loss experienced by the subject's ego is a source of hostile, angry feelings. These are then turned against the incorporated object and the ego by the patient's superego, and the patient experiences a feeling of rejection and depression.

Lindemann reported on the symptomatology and management of acute grief in 101 persons who in the process of bereavement were given psychiatric assistance.[4] Lindemann describes five features which he considers "pathognomic" for grief.

1. Somatic distress characterized by sighing respiration, a complaint of lack of strength and exhaustion, and digestive symptoms with lack of appetite.
2. An intense preoccupation with the image of the deceased, occasionally accompanied by altered sensorium in the form of a slight sense of unreality.
3. A strong preoccupation with feelings of guilt, self-accusation, and feelings of negligence in relation to the deceased.
4. A disconcerting loss of warmth in relationship to other people, and a tendency to respond with irritability and anger.
5. A disorganized pattern of conduct which is characterized by restlessness, inability to sit still, and an aimless, searching agitation rather than by retardation in psychomotor activity.

Lindemann also described the symptomatology of morbid grief reactions, which are essentially exaggerations of the patterns described. Surprisingly, agitated depressions represented only a small fraction of the morbid grief reactions.

Recently, special subareas of the general field of bereavement and some related topics have been the subject of investigation. For example, some persons exhibit intense grief symptoms after experiencing separation from another under circumstances other than death. This has led to the concept of "separation reactions" as being the more general phenomenon, in which bereavement reactions would be but one type.[5] In addition, there has been much interest in the long-range impact on personality when a child is separated, by death or otherwise, from a significant other, usually the mother, a sibling, or the father. Thus, the development of schizophrenia in adults has been related to childhood experience with death or separation,[6] and later personality problems of various kinds have been related to the child's separation from the mother, or other emotionally significant figures, during the early years.[7]

The social sciences complement the psychiatric study of bereavement by virtue of their interest in social relationships and social structure. Any concept of bereavement or separation implies at the outset the existence of an established relationship between at least two people. In human societies, relationships involving affect do not often spring up or persist in a random, idiosyncratic fashion. Rather, they are structured by cultural principles and institutional arrangements, and each individual is more or less "placed" or fitted into the kinds of structures that exist. The import of this for present purposes is to emphasize the fact that crucial deaths or separations always involve the severing of social relationships defined by mutual expectations and needs which are, for the most part, learned. Hence, in each case of bereavement or separation there are social and cultural as well as psychological dimensions of the event—whether problems in mental health do or do not arise. In all societies death is, for example, embedded in a number of religious beliefs and practices, and the community, as well as the individual or the family, notes the death-event and participates in the piacular rites, i.e., those "which are celebrated . . . in a state of uneasiness or sadness."[8]

Such considerations suggest that the mental health problems in bereavement and separation are subjects of inquiry that properly belong in the field of social psychiatry. Unfortunately, there is at present no social psychiatry in this area, although some beginnings of one are discernible. Among psychiatrists, for example, Lindemann[9] and Brewster[10] have moved in that direction by their emphasis on bereavement reactions occurring in altered systems of social interaction; but the social scientists (especially sociologists, social psychologists, and cultural anthropologists) have practically ignored bereavement and separation as direct subjects of investigation. Eliot[11] is an exception; there are some brief, but perceptive, references in textbooks[12]; and there are some descriptive data on mourning customs and rites in different cultures.[13]

No summary analysis of the social psychiatry of bereavement and separation can here be made, since none as yet exists. Neither can all the possible phases of these complicated subjects be covered in this chapter. Accordingly, the scope of the chapter is restricted to bereavement and excludes the broader field of separation; more particularly, it is restricted to bereavement as an apparent precipitating factor in the personal distress of more or less mature adults.

The purpose here, then, is to explore the implications of some social science concepts as these seem to apply to problems of bereavement reactions. Such application can only be illustrated, not demonstrated. The general viewpoint expressed is cultural rather than clinical, theoretical rather than practical. The basic assumption is that in the long run it is just as important to understand why bereavement does not always precipitate an acute breakdown as to understand why it sometimes does. As a preliminary venture into social psychiatry, therefore, this chapter is concerned with some social and cultural conditions which tend either to exacerbate or to lessen the force of the intrapsychic elements immediately underlying bereavement distress.

Cultural Perspectives

A convenient place to begin is with the concept of culture, which is often regarded as the most important single concept in the social sciences. Although it may be defined technically in different words and used in slightly different ways, culture refers basically to the ideas, norms, values, practices, and beliefs which are historically shared by the members of an organized group or society. Each society has its own distinctive culture; and, whereas at one level of abstraction there are certain universals common to all cultures, the specific contents of various cultures are amazingly diverse.[14]

The concept of culture is significant in the present connection in that each individual is born into and develops within a specific cultural context. By example, precept, reward, and punishment he learns most of the culture to which he is exposed.

Any sociocultural system may be envisaged as being composed of a series or organized groups of what are sometimes termed "social institutions."[15] At one level of analysis these are specific and local—i.e., a family, a school, a church, and so on; at another level of analysis the specific units are combined into "type" institutions— i.e., the family, the school, the church, and so on, indicating a particular emphasis on the typical features of each.

Each such group, or institutional unit, in turn may be regarded as an organization of "positions" or "statuses." A family, for example, is composed of husband, wife, parents, children, brothers and sisters, each status being identified by its relation to another (i.e., husband-wife, parent-child, brother-sister, etc.). These positions are, of course, occupied by particular persons, but the behavior of the persons in their relation to each other is channeled by the structure of the relationship itself. Mutual expectations arise and the statuses of the relationships come to involve certain "roles" or role behaviors vis-à-vis each other. All of the principal social relationships, in any culture, may be regarded as interlocking roles.[16]

As soon as an individual is born, he begins to be a part of a social relationship (parent-child), in the setting of a particular institution (the family), which is composed, at least in part, of persons who have already been culturally trained. In their behavior toward the newcomer, much of their cultural learning will be manifest; and this is important because the individual *self* will develop primarily in interaction with family members.[17] The individual self, in belief, is a social self, including the "reflected appraisals of others," such roles as have been internalized, and "the residue" of an individual's experiences within his institutional and cultural framework.[18]

From the standpoint of a given individual, his culture is experienced by the way in which his interactions are channeled in social relationships, within institutional settings, and by the various pressures, demands, responses, and expectations of others which make themselves felt in countless life situations. Thus each individual, consciously or unconsciously, comes to adopt most of the prevailing ideas, practices, norms, values and beliefs which parents, peers, and nonfamilial adults introduce to him. In this way he has available, for practically every life-situation, a culturally determined solution.

Thus far, then, culture has been shown to be linked to individual behavior by means of a series of intervening concepts: social institutions, positions and statuses, roles, and the self. At this point some general implications of the concept of culture may be suggested.

In the first place, human death is a universal and recurring event. Every culture has its own values, ideas, beliefs, and practices concerning it. An individual learns the orientations of his culture toward death; and thus when he is faced with bereavement, one factor involved is his conception of the meaning of death. In this connection many, if not most, societies throughout the world do not regard the event of death as being an inevitable fact of life; rather, it is often construed as being the result of an accident, of negligence, or of malice on the part of magicians or sorcerers.[19] Similarly, the cultural orientation of many peoples toward death is that it represents a gain for the deceased, an improvement in his prospects and status, and that mourning for his loss of life is inappropriate.[20] These are in marked contrast to our own prevailing beliefs, for with us death is inevitable, and the fate of the deceased is by no means as clear and as certain as it may once have been in the Christian tradition.

If, then, we assume that beliefs can influence self-perceptions and self-reactions, the kinds of beliefs that are accepted and internalized will condition bereavement reactions. By the same token, the emotional displays of bereaved persons may also be learned responses and may have nothing to do with necessary and inherent feelings of grief. Conventional bereavement behavior varies widely from culture to culture, and whether it is genuine, "natural" emotional expression or mere ritual performance is in given cases often open to question.[21] In some cultures, for example, our conventional sign of grief—i.e., weeping—either is not manifest by the bereaved or is manifest in circumstances that we should regard as strange or is mingled with laughter as we understand it.

All of this raises the question, of course, as to whether the self is entirely social or whether it shares some deep-seated, indestructible fragments of humanity in general. Social scientists tend to hold the former view, whereas some branches of psychiatry tend to hold the latter. The issue cannot now be resolved, but it should be apparent that cross-cultural data can at least provide fresh perspectives on bereavement reactions and present viewpoints concerning them.

Moreover, it may not be amiss to note that cultural considerations may influence any attempt scientifically to analyze bereavement problems. Those who are familiar with, and sensitive to, cultural influences on behavior should first be wary of themselves and their work, i.e., the way in which they perceive, categorize, and explain behavioral events. For various implicit and explicit assumptions, biases, terminology and evaluations, all derived from the culture, can easily intrude upon the task at hand; they cannot all be erased, but they should at least be recognized for what they are: a curious blend of folk knowledge, rationalizations, beliefs, and ignorance. It may even be that some mental health problems we attribute to bereavement, by reason of proximity in time, have other and quite different sources.

The phenomena which we label "bereavement" and "grief" are embedded in a cultural frame of reference. Just as other peoples have their interpretation of death, and appropriate reactions to it, so, too, do we in Western civilizations; but our own implicit interpretation is not easy for us to recognize and make explicit as a cultural rather than scientific orientation simply because we have absorbed that orientation and perceive events accordingly.

Thus, as cultural norm and idea we tend to define a given death as a "loss" to someone, especially to close members of the family of the deceased. Almost any behavior that they then manifest is regarded as "grief"; thus the term "grief" functions, culturally, both as a descriptive label and as a satisfying interpretation based on a presumably known "cause." Moreover, we tend to regard such "grief" not only as natural but also as desirable. A bereaved person ought to show grief, both as a token of respect to the dead and for the sake of his own mental health—expression of grief gets it "out of the system."

It is simply generally assumed that a bereaved person will be grief-stricken; but whether these displays of grief stem from internal compulsions or external demands is not usually a matter of concern. Indeed, the very source of the behavior and the imputed feelings is assumed to lie in what were satisfactory relationships with the deceased other, even though it is often well known that a given relationship, husband-wife or parent-child, fell far short of being satisfactory to one or both of the partners. At least in our culture there is a tendency to idealize the relationship which has been severed by death—and this, too, is culturally encouraged. "Don't speak ill of the dead."

In short, the behavioral phenomena characterized by the words "bereavement" and "grief" are heavily saturated with cultural assumptions. Moreover, any analyst, be he psychiatrist or social scientist, has absorbed many of these premises long before he has professed to be a scientist; to the extent that he has accepted and internalized them, his perceptions of events have therefore been previously structured, thus preconditioning the analysis through the uncritical use of conventional categories.

The point here, of course, is not the validity of the prevailing cultural interpretation of bereavement and grief, which may be correct in part or in whole, as other folk interpretations of events have been correct in the past. The point is that the cultural orientation is a matter for inquiry and verification rather than *a priori*, and often unwitting, acceptance.

Bereavement can be defined with sufficient precision to be useful. "Grief," on the other hand, presents difficulties: the total reaction pattern of a bereaved person may be only partially an expression of grief (in the sense of felt loss), and the amount of grief anyone possesses is always inferential anyway. For these reasons, the phenomena that we usually label as "grief," "sorrow," and "mourning" will here be designated by the more colorless phrases "bereavement behavior" or "bereavement reactions." Such usage will not alter any of the distress of the experience or its poignancy, but it will remind us, perhaps, that more elements than sorrow or grief are involved, and it will also facilitate cross-cultural comparisons. "Behavior" can be observed and recorded, "grief" cannot. And it is essential that as much cross-cultural perspective as possible be gained, else the purported analysis may prove to be nothing more than a technical restatement of prevailing cultural premises.[22]

Bereavement, Family Structure, and the Self

Of all the social institutions, the family and kinship systems are of the greatest importance insofar as the study of bereavement is concerned. Indeed, their structure and the manner in which they emphasize some relationships rather than others supply initial reference points for the concept of bereavement itself. Always and everywhere some persons rather than others are considered to have a special interest in a given death; but who they are, and in what relationship they stand to the deceased, are matters of cultural variability.

In our society, for example, when a married adult dies, the prevailing definition of bereaved persons includes his parents and siblings (i.e., members of his family of orientation) and his spouse and their children (i.e., members of his family of procreation). The emphasis is placed on members of the immediate nuclear families as having suffered the main loss;[23] and if collateral relatives, such as cousins or aunts or uncles or "in-laws" are included, it is by special relationship rather than as part of the system. They are family members nominally, not functionally.[24]

By way of contrast, the Trobriand Islanders have a quite different scheme of family relationships and a correspondingly different concept of who constitute the bereaved.[25] Their emphasis is placed on persons related to the deceased through his mother, that is, his maternal kin of all kinds are considered to have been "closest" to the deceased and to have more of an interest in the event than any of the paternal relatives or even the spouse. A wife, for example, may "grieve" at the death of her husband, but this is usually ceremonial and obligatory rather than spontaneous, and she is not considered by others to be bereaved in the same sense as are the maternal kin.

These brief, contrasting examples of family systems indicate that, regardless of cultural variability, bereavement is an observable condition; it is not inferential; its definition, in cultural terms, can be determined. Further, bereavement is a formal status in which individuals either have or have not legitimate occupancy. It derives from family and kinship structures which place persons in necessary or preferred positions vis-à-vis each other. Thus, in some places a maternal aunt or a paternal uncle may be more important to the individual, socially and psychologically, than are his own biological or sociological parents. When they die bereavement is thrust upon him by the system.

Such considerations are important not only for purposes of initial orientation toward phenomena but also because they bear upon the development of the self in terms of whom the individual will attach himself and in what manner. That is, although different family systems may have the same positions or statuses in the abstract (i.e., mothers, fathers, aunts, siblings, etc.), the psychological value of such positions in interpersonal relations is by no means always equivalent. Some positions may be singled out according to cultural principles of descent as more important than others; and their interpersonal value will also be influenced by the size of the family unit, together with the degree to which intrafamily relations are based on different ideas of authority, punishment, need-satisfaction, and so on.

Thus, since the development of the self takes place primarily within the family context, that process will be influenced by the range, frequency, intimacy, and quality of the interactions provided by the family system. The number of "targets" for emotional attachment will vary accordingly, as will the particular statuses that will become targets. Such factors, in turn, will affect the number and kinds of identifications the self will make, the degree of dependency on others, and the general mode and strength of affective ties.

If, then, the amount of self-involvement with another is a major variable in bereavement behavior, its sources must lie at least in part in the familial conditions of self-development. And if this is true, we should expect typically different bereavement behaviors in societies with different systems. There is some evidence for this interpretation, as the following examples will illustrate.

In his study of the Ifaluk people, Spiro[26] was puzzled by some features of bereavement behavior there. When a family member died, the immediate survivors displayed considerable pain and distress, which behavior was in accordance with local custom. However, as soon as the funeral was over, the bereaved were able to laugh, smile, and behave in general as if they had suffered no loss or injury at all. Their "grief" seemed to disappear as if by magic, and this too was approved by custom.

Several hypotheses might be offered to account for these events which contrast sharply with those we would expect. At one extreme, it might plausibly be argued that the brief, but intense, mourning period was sufficient to discharge all the implicated emotions (such as hostility, loss, guilt, etc.) and thus provided rapid reintegration of the self. This would assume object-relationships of a kind familiar to us but would not particularly account for the efficiency and timing of the observed behavior. At the other extreme (à la Durkheim,[27]) it might be said that the displays were mere conventions, rituals, and, having little to do with emotional experience, could be turned off and on as learned. Or it might be suggested that the grief actually represented intense subjective feelings and that these persisted privately after the funeral but in a manner not easily detected by an observer.

Spiro's analysis, based on his knowledge of the total culture, is along the following lines, which involve the family system and socialization practices that prevail among the Ifaluk. There the developing child forms no exclusive emotional attachments to other family members. Child-rearing is not conducted solely in the home by parents and siblings but involves many other persons who are as important in an individual's life as are family members. The growing child and the mature adult have, therefore, diffused and dispersed their emotional ties among many persons rather than focused them on a few. Accordingly, the psychological significance of any single family member to any other family member is muted rather than intensified.

In terms of the thesis being developed here, the bereavement behavior of the Ifaluk suggests that their family system is such as to develop selves which are initially less vulnerable in bereavement than are the selves we are accustomed to. This can be explained by a consideration of how both social and psychological forces interact.

If we assume that any social relationship, mediated by physical and symbolic interaction, inevitably produces in the partners the feelings and conditions of love, ambivalence, hostility, identification, and dependence, then the Ifaluk develop selves in which these are relatively weak insofar as any given other person is concerned. The family relationships which impinged on self-development are such as to minimize personal dependence on any one person, to make a person's identifications multiple rather than exclusive, and to enable him to distribute his feelings of love and hostility more widely.

Another way of stating this is that in self-other relations among the Ifaluk, the other is not valued by the self as a unique and necessary personality. Functionally speaking, not only are the roles of others dispersed, but the roles themselves are more important psychologically than are the particular persons who play the roles vis-à-vis the self. Multiple and interchangeable personnel performing the same functions for the individual provides the individual with many psychological anchors in his social environment; the death of any one person leaves the others and thus diminishes loss.

In American society, of course, it is not so easy to describe the family system, for there are many subgroup variations. Nevertheless, some sociologists have discerned a trend toward the "small family system," particularly among middle-class urban populations.[28] To relate this system to the present problem involves considerable overgeneralization, yet for heuristic purposes it may be contrasted with the Ifaluk system.

The American small family system has several dimensions. In contrast to the extended family, it is one in which there are relatively few members and these few live together under one roof and somewhat apart from relatives and neighbors.

In terms of self-development, the small family system means a number of things. During a person's early years the range of his interactions is largely confined to his mother, father, and siblings, if any, and especially to his mother. Frequency and intimacy of contact are thereby channeled among the same few persons who become the only (and repetitive) targets for identification and dependency. Moreover, these same few sources provide the person with his most intense gratifications and frustrations, a condition that tends to maximize ambivalence as well as repressed hostility.[29] Guilt-feelings are easily aroused in connection with authority figures—especially since the person knows that he is supposed to love them, yet cannot do so all the time because they punish and frustrate him.

In these circumstances, it is likely that the self develops strong emotional attachments to the family figures and has considerable affective investment in them. These self-feelings are, however, quite complicated. To the extent that one loves his family members (and this is inculcated as a cultural value), he may feel a corresponding loss when they die—a sentiment which is reinforced by the fact that, as a cultural norm, the death of a family member is socially defined as a loss. But, in addition to the love elements and those of dependency and identification, there are intertwined with them the self-feelings of ambivalence and hostility. In bereavement the self, therefore, faces not only the problem of replacing the loss but also the one of managing these feelings of guilt and hostility.

Moreover, the small family system tends to breed overidentification and overdependence. That is to say, intrafamily experiences are such as to make it difficult for the person to separate the parental activities toward him from the particular individuals who engage in those activities. The maternal role, for example, which aunts, older sisters, or other female adults could occupy and enact, is occupied continuously by the same woman, for in the small family system there are no other persons to act as substitutes and thus disperse the emotional investment. Emotional attachments to particular persons are thereby fostered, and the person becomes dependent on their unique personalities in addition to their roles.

Furthermore, other cultural values operate in the development of the self to influence the process similarly. Not only does the child experience the same persons in the roles of father and mother, but he is taught that he can have only one father and mother, that is, the particular persons who are thus labeled. Cultural training and actual experience thus reinforce each other in such a way that specific persons continually appear to be irreplaceable, and no one is psychologically prepared to accept substitutes.

By way of contrast, it is reported of the Murngin[30] that the death of a father creates few psychological problems for his children. All their lives they have called their paternal uncles "father," and their relationships with these uncles have not differed very much from their relationships with their father. When the self develops in such a system, there is less likelihood that it will become closely attached to a particular figure; thus the sense of loss is lessened and the relationship with that figure can be more readily transferred to substitute figures.

The inference to be drawn from all this is that familial systems, by their influence on the development of the self, can enhance or reduce the initial vulnerability of persons in bereavement. This vulnerability is increased to the extent that self-involvements with others are concentrated on a few, thus maximizing their psychological significance; it is decreased to the extent that self-involvements are diffuse, thus minimizing the psychological significance of any one other.

In this connection, one further feature of the small family system should be noted. Typically, a married adult belongs to two families, the one of orientation and the one of procreation. In a sense this dual membership involves a dispersion of affect and self-involvement, for the person simply has more relationships: in addition to being son or daughter, brother or sister, he is now also husband and parent. His roles have multiplied.

But, although membership in the family of orientation is officially retained, residence in a separate household usually diminishes his opportunities for interaction and continued emotional investment in parents and siblings. There simply is not so much intimate association with them as there was when he lived under the same roof. He tends, therefore, to gain some release from whatever self-feelings he had toward them by increasing his physical, social, and psychological distance from them. Thus his vulnerability vis-à-vis these family members tends to be reduced.

At the same time, through marriage, children, and a separate residence, he is again enmeshed in a small family system, but with new personnel. Now his self-involvements tend to be directed toward spouse and children, and, because of the way his self developed in the small family of orientation, his relationships with these "new" persons tend to be of the same order as were the old, i.e., exclusive attachments.

In brief, membership in the two small families does not necessarily have the same psychological effect as continued residence in an extended family may have. Dispersion of affect need not occur. Rather, it is much more likely that one's emotional investments are merely redirected from one set of figures to another; and as vulnerability to bereavement in the family of orientation diminishes, vulnerability to deaths in the family of procreation may increase.

The preceding pages have attempted to sketch some of the ideal-typical relationships between family structure, self-development, and vulnerability in bereavement. From the two polar-type family systems that were used for illustrative purposes it is suggested that the meaning of bereavement to the persons involved can be modified. In one case the degree of self-involvement with others, and therefore vulnerability in bereavement, was minimal; in the other the degree of self-involvement with others, and therefore vulnerability in bereavement, was maximal.

High vulnerability in interpersonal relationships does not, however, mean the inevitable presence of mental health problems in bereavement. Psychic stresses and strains may be multiplied, to be sure, but if these have been fostered by some social and cultural conditions, there may be other social and cultural conditions which can help to ease them.[31] In brief, the course and outcome of high vulnerability in bereavement may be a function not only of itself but also of the requirements and taboos that exist within the bereavement situation. This can best be indicated by considering the importance and utility of the concept of "social role" as this is applicable to bereavement reactions.

Bereavement and Social Roles

It has previously been indicated that the category of bereaved persons, at a given death, is culturally defined. Some relationships in the family and kinship system are included and some are not, and the inclusions and exclusions vary from culture to culture; but whenever a death evokes that category, the persons in it come to occupy a formal, legitimate status in the eyes of others as well as in their own eyes. And as is the case with other statuses, the persons in it have a new social role to play—the social role of the bereaved person.

In cross-cultural terms, the specific content of the role varies widely: weeping; personal preparation of the corpse for burial, gashing one's own body with knives or sharp sticks, protracted seclusion; fasting, wreaking vengeance on those responsible for the death, special religious obligations of prayer or sacrifice, sharp and humiliating alterations in dress and appearance, and so on.

In a given culture, some of these role behaviors may apply to all persons in the bereavement status, whereas others apply only to persons in specified relation to the deceased. For example, the widow may have some obligations which apply only to her, such as not to remarry or not to remarry within certain periods of time; or it may be that she is obliged to remarry with her next partner being culturally prescribed, e.g., a brother or cousin of the deceased husband.

Although there are great variations in the specific content of the social role of the bereaved person, one point is clear: whatever the obligations, proscriptions, or injunctions may be, they exist from his standpoint in the form of expectations, demands, and pressures from others. They are social obligations, immediate and potent, yet to fulfill them in a way that is both psychologically and socially satisfactory is by no means as obvious or as easy as is frequently assumed. Often the role requirements are painful in themselves, and it is also a difficult role to learn because it is not encountered frequently in the course of life and opportunities for rehearsal are scarce.

The import of this is to suggest that the conception of the bereaved person as having a social role to perform provides another perspective from which to examine mental health problems in bereavement. Such problems may be socially induced as well as psychologically induced, i.e., they may have their source in role deficiencies and difficulties as well as in the self-other relationship itself. Such a formulation suggests a number of possibilities that psychiatrists and social scientists might further explore.

The formulation, for example, opens up the possibility that some bereavement problems may be occasioned not by severe loss but by an awareness of one's inability to play the bereaved role properly. If we assume that one of the role obligations is to express grief and loss and that these sentiments are imputed to the bereaved by others, the bereaved person who lacks these sentiments may be in a painfully dangerous situation as the result of guilty fear.

A hypothetical reconstruction, in terms of the present analysis, may illustrate the problem. A given role (husband, wife, mother, etc.) is culturally defined as involving considerable emotional investment in the partner who occupies the complementary role in the relationship. The role, in its ideal sense, is internalized by an individual, but his experience in the relationship contradicts the role. Inappropriate sentiments are developed, e.g., more hostility than love. Fearing the reactions of others, he remains in the relationship which, on the surface, does not deviate too far from the typical; but the hostility must be repressed and guilt over failure to meet the ideal is increased. Then, in bereavement, this individual is supposed to feel loss, and the social role he is expected to enact deals almost entirely with this imputed sentiment. He is expected to express grief. Such expectations and imputations are not congruent with his own self-feelings, and awareness of the discrepancy between self and role increases guilt. There are also no socially sanctioned avenues for the release or displacement of the hostility. There is, in short, an accumulation of pressures which come to a climax in bereavement. In such a case, which is probably quite atypical, the bereavement experience, including the incompatible role that is imposed, precipitates and crystallizes mental health problems that were already incipient. Such a case can indicate the significance of situational pressures to adopt the proper role.

In American culture, it is difficult to consider the social role of the bereaved person in other than very general terms, but it appears to center around ideas of loss and the desirability of expressing that loss and grief. The language makes "bereavement" and "loss" interchangeable terms. Individuals learn to regard bereavement as meaning loss, and this sentiment is attributed to them by others when the bereavement situation actually occurs. Thus, to the extent that this evaluation of the event has been internalized, and to the extent that the self-other relationship as personally experienced makes it possible, the psychological sense of loss will be enhanced. When this happens, the bereaved person can more or less adequately play his required role, i.e., to have some sort of episodic breakdown, express his grief conventionally, and thus behave "normally."

However, this type of role, with its emphasis on loss, grief, and expression of them, may not always be psychologically functional. And here several possibilities appear.

For example, this particular type of role of the bereaved person may conflict with other roles he has, e.g., sex roles. In our society, females are generally permitted and encouraged to be more "emotional" than males in various life situations. To the extent that women internalize this segment of their sex role, it should be easier for them to meet the requirements of "expressing grief" in their social role of the bereaved person; it simply requires a reapplication of a lifelong pattern.

Men, on the other hand, are expected and encouraged to be more stoical and restrained than women in any life emergency.[32] The role of male in our culture does not encourage emotional displays. Thus, in bereavement males may experience a conflict between their lifelong training in their sex role and the immediate situational demand for emotional expression as a bereaved person. It may be, therefore, that when bereaved males exhibit signs of psychic stress, in the form of intensities and distortions beyond expected levels, they are reflecting this conflict in addition to, or even instead of, the sense of loss and grief.

Our cultural emphasis on loss in bereavement, with its social role preoccupied with grief expression, provides still other problems. The social role, by concentrating on the feeling and expression of loss, thereby neglects to provide for other emotions and the needs they create. This can be formulated as follows: The emotions of a bereaved person, vis-à-vis the deceased other, consist of various degrees and intensities of the sense of loss, hostility, guilt, and the like. When these are minimal in strength, the bereaved person has a very low initial vulnerability to any mental health problems. When these are maximal and complicated, the person (unless he has a correspondingly high ego strength) has a high initial vulnerability to mental health problems in bereavement, for the stronger and more complex these self-feelings are, the greater is their tendency to create new personality needs. If a strong sense of loss is involved, there is a need for replacement; if there is much latent hostility, there is need for discharge; if guilt is strong, there is need for release or displacement. If all are present, as our family and cultural system tends to make probable, then the bereaved person is vulnerable unless his social role as a bereaved person adequately meets these needs.

In other words, the character of the self-other relationship conditions the level of initial vulnerability in bereavement. When this level is high, and new personality needs are therewith generated, the social role of the bereaved person may either lessen that vulnerability by meeting the needs or exacerbate it by failing to meet them.

From this standpoint, our preoccupation with loss and grief in bereavement may create special kinds of mental health problems of which we are only dimly aware. For example, as has previously been suggested, the significant other in our culture is significant in terms of his unique personality in addition to, or instead of, the functions he performs vis-à-vis the self. Thus, in bereavement, one loses not merely a role in his whole system of interaction but a particular person in the role. Thus, whereas we stress the sense of loss and recognize the need for replacement,[33] basically the culture creates conditions in which the deceased is irreplaceable because he cannot ever really be duplicated. The social role cannot contain a provision for "automatic replacement" because all our patterns of interpersonal relationships militate against such replacement.

In order for replacements to be accepted and acceptable, the role of the deceased must be regarded, culturally and personally, as at least equal in importance to the person who plays it. Other societies have handled this problem of replacement by the devices of obligatory remarriage[34] or adoption. Such arrangements, though, are not merely *ad hoc*, set up to take care of bereavement problems alone. Rather, they are basic ingredients of the way in which the sociocultural system operates, of the way in which interpersonal relations are perceived, valued, and practiced. Since the expectations of the partners in the social relationship do not come to include the absorption of the self in the other, it is possible for the social role of the bereaved person (i.e., as widow, widower, orphan, etc.) to include replacement of the other without particular psychic stress.

The fact that the social role of the bereaved person in our culture may not easily cope with the problem of replacement is, therefore, a local one. It is bound up in our system of interpersonal relations, the kind of selves we tend to develop, and is exaggerated by our cultural emphasis on loss. In this way the bereaved person has no automatic cultural solution to the problem of replacement.

In the same manner, the social role of the bereaved person in our culture makes no real provision for the other emotions and the personality needs they create, i.e., hostility and guilt and their release, discharge, or displacement. At least, there are no obvious segments of the role which include socially approved devices for handling those residues of guilt, hostility, and ambivalence. With the person left on his own, so to speak, to handle them as best he can, it is not surprising that these feelings and the unmet needs they create appear in cases of "acute" or "distorted" grief in our society.

In many cultures prevailing mourning customs may be interpreted as providing role requirements which do meet some of these emotional needs. Opler,[35] for example, has shown how the ambivalence toward relatives, which is induced by the social structure of the Apache, finds socially sanctioned displacement in mourning rites and customs. Warner[36] indicates how the obligation of the bereaved to avenge the death of the deceased provides sanctioned means of ridding guilt-feelings and hostility among the Murngin. And in anthropological literature there are many examples of the bereaved being required to inflict pain and disfiguration on their bodies—obligations which may be regarded as attempts to fasten the attention of the bereaved upon himself and therefore to hasten his emancipation from the deceased.

Such considerations lend some weight to the hypothesis that different cultures will select, from among all the possible involvements the self may have with the other, one or a few which will be dealt with in the social role of the bereaved person. Thus, if the bereavement problems of a given culture are adequately perceived, functionally adequate social roles for the bereaved may be devised which can blunt such vulnerability to breakdown as may appear. But to the extent that social and cultural conditions encourage interpersonal relationships in which overidentification, overdependence, sense of loss, hostility, guilt, and ambivalence are bred in profusion, and to the extent that the social role of the bereaved person does not take account of these feelings and the needs they inspire—to that extent bereaved persons may often be unintended victims of their sociocultural system. In our case, the sense of loss may be handled satisfactorily by the role which encourages expression of loss and grief; but the role does not, and cannot, adequately provide for replacement when this need is strong, and the added burdens of accumulated and unrelieved guilt, hostility, and ambivalence, when they are strong, can only increase vulnerability to psychic breakdown.

References

1. See, C. Anderson, "Aspects of Pathological Grief and Mourning," *International Journal of Psychoanalysis*, 30 (1949), pp. 48–55; E. Bergler, "Psychopathology and Duration of Mourning in Neurotics," *Journal of Clinical Psychopathology*, 3 (1948), pp. 478–482; H. Brewster, "Grief: A Disrupted Human Relationship," *Human Organization*, 9 (1950), pp. 19–22; E. Lindemann, "Symptomatology and Management of Acute Grief," *American Journal of Psychiatry*, 101 (1944), pp. 141–148.
2. See, for instance, the following: K. Abraham, *Selected Papers* (New York: Basic Books, 1953), pp. 418–501; C. Anderson, *op. cit.*; E. Bergler, *op. cit.*; H. Brewster, *op. cit.*, H. Deutsch, "Absence of Grief." *Psychoanalytic Quarterly*, 6 (1937), pp. 12–22; S. Freud, "Mourning and Melancholia," *Collected Papers*, 4 (London: Hogarth Press, 1925), pp. 152–170; M. Klein, "Mourning and its Relation to Manic Depressive States," *International Journal of Psychoanalysis*, 21 (1940) pp. 125–153; E. Lindemann, *op. cit.* and "Modifications in the Course of Ulcerative Colitis in Relationship to Changes in Life Situations and Reaction Patterns," *Life Stress and Bodily Disease*, (Baltimore: Williams and Wilkins Co., 1950); S. Rado, "The Problem of Melancholia," *International Journal of Psychoanalysis*, 9 (1928), pp. 420–438, and S. Rado, "Psychodynamics of Depression from the Etiologic Point of View," *Psychosomatic Medicine*, 13 (1951), pp. 51–55.
3. S. Freud, *op. cit.*
4. E. Lindemann, "Symptomatology and Management of Acute Grief," p. 143.
5. H. Brewster, *op. cit.*; E. Lindemann, "Symptomatology and Management of Acute Grief," p. 147; and I. D. Suttie, *The Origins of Love and Hate* (London: Routledge, and Co., 1935).

6. E. Hare, "The Ecology of Mental Disease: A Dissertation on the Influence of Environmental Factors in the Distribution, Development and Variation of Mental Disease, *Journal of Mental Science*, 98 (1952), and L. Hepple, "Selective Service Rejectees in Missouri," Unpublished doctoral dissertation, Univerity of Missouri, 1946.

7. S. Anthony, *The Child's Discovery of Death* (New York: Harcourt, Brace, 1940): and J. Bowlby, *Maternal Care and Mental Health* (Geneva: World Health Organization, 1951); P. Hock and J. Zupin, Eds., *Depression*, Chapter 8 (New York: Grune and Stratton, 1954); R. Spitz, "Hospitalism—An Inquiry into the Genesis of Psychiatric Conditions in Early Childhood," *The Psychoanalytic Study of the Child*, 1 (International University Press, 1945), pp. 53–74.

8. E. Durkheim, *The Elementary Forms of Religious Life* (New York: Free Press, 1947), p. 39; and B. Malinowski, *Crime and Custom in Savage Society* (London: Humanities Press, 1926).

9. E. Lindemann, *op. cit.*

10. H. Brewster, *op. cit.*

11. T. D. Eliot, "The Adjustive Behavior of Bereaved Families: A New Field for Research," *Social Forces*, 8 (1930), pp. 543–549. Also see his "The Bereaved Family," *Annals of the American Academy of Political and Social Science, March* (1932), pp. 1–7; . . . "Of the Shadow of Death," *Annals of the American Academy of Political and Social Science* 229 (1943), pp. 87–99; "War Bereavements and Their Recovery," *Marriage and Family Living*, 8 (1946), pp. 1–6.

12. R. Lapiere and P. Farnsworth, *Social Psychology* (New York: McGraw-Hill, 1949); W. Waller and R. Hill, *The Family* (New York: Dryden Press, 1951).

13. See, for instance: A. Hocart, "Death Customs," in E. B. Seligman and A. Johnston, Eds., *Encyclopaedia of the Social Sciences*, 5 (New York: MacMillan, 1931), pp. 21–27; E. Durkheim, *op. cit.*; B. Malinowski, *op. cit.*; D. Mitra, "Mourning Customs and Modern Life in Bengal," *American Journal of Sociology* 52 (1947), pp. 309–311; M. Opler, "An Interpretation of Ambivalence in Two American Indian Tribes," *Journal of Social Psychology*, 7 (1936), pp. 82–116; A. R. Radcliffe-Brown, *The Andaman Islanders*, (Cambridge: Harvard University Press, 1933); W. L. Warner, *A Black Civilization* (New York: Harper, 1937).

14. C. Kluckholn, "Culture and Behavior," in G. Lindsey, Ed., *Handbook of Social Psychology* (New York: Addison-Wesley, 1954), p. 922 and see also his "Universal Categories of Culture" in A. L. Kroeber, Ed., *Anthropology Today* (Chicago: University of Chicago Press, 1953).

15. B. Malinowski, *A Scientific Theory of Culture and Other Essays* (Chapel Hill: University of North Carolina Press, 1944).

16. L. S. Cottrell Jr., "The Adjustment of the Individual to his Age and Sex Roles," *American Sociological Review*, 7 (1942), pp. 618–625; and T. Parsons, *The Social System* (Glencoe: The Free Press, 1951).

17. G. H. Mead, *Mind, Self and Society*, C. W. Morris, Ed., (University of Chicago Press, 1934).

18. C. Kluckhohn, *op. cit.*, p. 922; T. R. Sorbin, "Role Theory," in G. Lindsey, Ed., *Handbook of Social Psychology*, (New York: Addison-Wesley, 1952).

19. L. W. Simmons, *The Role of the Aged in Primitive Society*, (New Haven: Yale University Press, 1945), pp. 217–220.
20. *Ibid.*, pp. 223–224; and W. G. Sumner and A. C. Keller, *The Science of Society* 2 (New Haven: Yale University Press, 1927), pp. 943 *ff.*
21. H. Gerth and C. W. Mills, *Character and Social Structure* (Harcourt-Brace, 1953), pp. 48 *ff.*; and E. Hartley and R. Hartley, *Fundamentals of Social Psychology* (New York: Knopf, 1952), p. 210.
22. C. Kluckhohn, *op. cit.*; and E. Stairbrook, "A Cross-Cultural Evaluation of Depressive Reactions," in P. Hock and J. Zubin, Eds., *Depression* (New York: (Grune and Stratton, 1954).
23. T. D. Eliot, *op. cit.*; and W. Waller and R. Hill, *op. cit.*
24. E. Gruenberg, "Major Disorders," *Epidemiology of Mental Disorder*, (Milbank Memorial Fund, 1950).
25. R. Fraser, *et al.*, *The Incidence of Neurosis Among Factory Workers*, Medical Research Council, Industrial Research Board, Report No. 90 (London: His Majesty's Stationery Office, 1947), p. 26.
26. M. Spiro, "Ifaluk: A South Sea Culture," Unpublished Manuscript, National Research Council, *Human Relations Area Files*, (Yale University, 1949).
27. E. Durkheim, *op. cit.*, p. 397.
28. J. Bossard, *Parent and Child* (University of Pennsylvania Press, 1953); and also A. W. Green, "The Middle Class Male Child and Neurosis," *American Sociological Review*, 11 (1946), pp. 31–41; T. Parsons, "Certain Primary Sources and Patterns of Aggression in the Social Structure of the Western World," in P. Mullahy, Ed., *A Study of Interpersonal Relations* (Nelson, 1949), pp. 269–296.
29. T. Parsons, *op. cit.*
30. W. L. Warner, *op. cit.*
31. L. W. Simmons and H. Wolff, *Social Science in Medicine* (Russell Sage Foundation, 1954); and M. Spiro, "A Psychotic Personality in the South Seas," *Psychiatry*, 13 (1950), pp. 189–204.
32. J. Anderson, "Changes in Emotional Responses with Age," in M. L. Reymert, Ed., *Feelings and Emotions* (New York: McGraw-Hill, 1952), pp. 424–425.
33. E. Lindemann, *op. cit.*
34. W. G. Sumner and A. C. Keller, *op. cit.*, Vol. 3, pp. 1841–1854.
35. M. E. Opler, *op. cit.*
36. W. L. Warner, *op. cit.*

Avery D. Weisman and Thomas P. Hackett

Predilection to Death

Patients who are convinced of their impending death should not be operated upon, according to a familiar surgical tradition. Al-

Reprinted from *Psychosomatic Medicine*, 23 (1961), pp. 232–256, by permission of the authors and publisher.

though many experienced physicians cite anecdotes to illustrate that death in fact is apt to occur in such cases, there is little documentation for this belief. Standard textbooks of surgery, even those which give more than a passing nod to emotional factors, are silent about psychological "predilection" to surgical death. Nevertheless, when patients are extremely fearful of surgery, the usual procedure is to forestall cumulative anxiety by operating immediately. As a rule, this is enough to relieve anxiety completely and the patient recovers uneventfully. Similarly, patients who are profoundly depressed seem to recover as promptly after operation as do other patients, and may even be relieved of their depression for a long time. Even suicidal patients with extensive self-inflicted wounds may be no more predisposed to death following reparative surgery than any patient with comparable injuries. Surgical mortality in modern mental hospitals is not likely to be greater than that occurring in general hospitals, despite the poor nutrition and general absence of subjective complaints of patients in the former.[1] These facts suggest that if there actually are patients with a predilection to death, the cause is other than severe anxiety, mental illness, depression or suicidal wishes.

Validation of the hypothesis that there are certain patients who have a predilection to death and should not be operated upon involves the almost insurmountable obstacle of devising proper psychiatric, surgical, and pathological criteria.[2] This work remains to be done.

The purpose of this paper is to call attention to a group of patients who, without open conflict, suicidal intention, profound depression, or extreme panic, correctly anticipated their own deaths. Psychiatric evaluation of these patients, although necessarily brief, demonstrated some of the factors that contributed to their conviction that death was desirable and appropriate, and not a calamity. How these patients came to terms with death was studied by assessing the psychological significance, for the doctor as well as the patient, of the act of dying and the fact of death.

Material and Method

Preoperative *fear* of dying is different from the *conviction* of impending death, which these patients demonstrated. Patients with intense preoperative anxiety responded readily to psychiatric intervention;[3] not one died following operation, and their apprehension often receded completely. By contrast, this finding helped to define the patient with a predilection to death; namely, one who is firmly convinced of approaching death but regards it as wholly appropriate and shows little depression and no anxiety. As a result, the attitude of predilection patients is unobstrusive and, therefore, they usually are not referred to the psychiatric consultant. That there are probably many such patients who escape detection is indicated by the following case.

A 61-year-old immigrant tailor went into shock upon recovering consciousness after an uncomplicated orchidectomy for a testicular mass. No explanation for the shock was manifest. Suspecting intra-abdominal bleeding, the surgeon performed a laparotomy, but no hemorrhage was found. When the patient's wife was informed of the serious turn of events, she exclaimed, "Then the soothsayer was right—he will die!" The astonished surgeon then learned that over 40 years before he had been told by a fortuneteller that he would die in his sixtieth year. At the time he scoffed because he was more concerned with her immediate predictions about his work and love life.

With the passing of years, he almost forgot about the strange prediction. Although he had been careful to tell his wife of it before their marriage, it was not until his mid-fifties that he began to seek reassurance from her that the fortunetellers were fakes and had no reliable clairvoyance. He passed his sixtieth birthday without mishap, but apprehension was not relieved. Two months after his sixty-first birthday he discovered the testicular mass. Hoping to avoid an operation he consulted a succession of doctors. Only when he was threatened with cancellation of his life insurance did he consent to an operation.

Despite his conviction of being a doomed man, he told the surgeons nothing of his fear. Consequently, no precautions were taken before surgery. After he went into shock, he hovered on the brink of death for 3 days. His survival was due to the diligence of his doctors and the thoroughness of their treatment. No cause for the shock was ever ascribed.

After the crucial incident, the psychiatric consultant found the patient glad to be alive and ready to admit his concern about the prediction. He acknowledged that when all the doctors had recommended an operation he had thought, "This is it," meaning that he was certain now to die, however belatedly. In subsequent interviews, however, as his health returned, he no longer admitted that he had ever been anxious about the fortuneteller's prediction. In fact, when pressed on this matter shortly before his hospital discharge, he adamantly denied any trace of emotional response that could implicate him disadvantageously. He blamed his wife for disclosing the information in the first place and asserted that he had not really been so gravely ill and that the testicular tumor had been removed purely as a precautionary measure.

Had not the patient's wife been an intelligent, perceptive woman the secret he harbored for nearly half a century would never have been disclosed. He spoke to the consultant in only the most succinct terms when he was ill, and presented almost global denial after recovery. Although this patient differed both from patients who fear dying and those who are convinced of death, he does illustrate the gradation of attitudes toward death, in that he was both anxious and felt doomed, without necessarily being committed to death. He did not wish to die, and displayed enough preoperative anxiety to eliminate the possibility that he considered death appropriate.

This patient illustrates some of the difficulties encountered in obtaining information about death and dying from any patient. While many people can discuss death as an abstraction, they are rarely able to talk about their private notions of death. Even when they couch their language in terms of death, psychiatric patients usually are referring to problems of living. Nevertheless, a "death-minded" psychiatrist can detect the influence of death phantasies in many of his patient's communications. It was difficult to interview the predilection patients, who were by no means as responsive to inquiry as the patient with preoperative fears of dying. They had come to terms with life and with people, while anxious patients were in the midst of conflict and reached out for a responsive relationship.

The five cases presented in this study were accumulated during three years of consultation psychiatry on the surgical wards of the Massachusetts General Hospital. During this time, approximately 600 patients (including almost every patient who expressed undue apprehension about a surgical procedure) were interviewed by psychiatrists for various reasons. Only the true predilection patient remained elusive. When experienced surgeons were asked to recall patients who might fit into this category, they readily expressed familiarity with the syndrome but generally could remember only one or two cases.

The interview technique and method of formulation employed in this study have been described in other publications.[4] Since it was possible to see these patients in only a limited number of interviews, additional information was obtained from friends and relatives as well as from all professional personnel.

Case Reports

PATIENT 1

A 71-year-old immigrant Greek farmer had suffered from a duodenal ulcer for 15 years. On two occasions an operation had been recommended, but each time he refused, saying that he preferred suicide to surgery. On his final admission he was in extreme pain, which all attempts at medical management failed to alleviate; surgical treatment was mandatory. In view of his previous recalcitrance a psychiatric consultation was requested.

The consultant found a pleasant, cordial man with grey hair and stark, weather-beaten features. He complained of having to use narcotics, but expressed neither concern about his pain nor aversion to surgical intervention. With a faint smile he simply stated he would die if an operation was performed. He offered no explanation for this and spoke casually, as though his conviction was commonplace knowledge.

He talked of his past life easily and pointed out how the recent exacerbation of ulcer pain had followed a crop failure. Just before this had happened, however, his last enemy had died. In speaking of this his manner suddenly changed. He appeared to forget the consultant's presence and spoke in the present tense of an episode that had occurred 20 years before. Rapidly talking in fierce tones, using dramatic gestures, he re-enacted a fight in the Boston Market, where he used to sell his vegetables. A friend who occupied a neighboring market stall had unfairly accused him. A fist fight had ensued in which the patient's jaw was broken. At that moment, "The joy went out of living." He no longer went to the market and sent his son in his place. Months and years were spent in prolonged,

useless, and costly litigation from which he received no satisfaction—only more pain and humiliation. Although he had
raised a large family and had supported them comfortably, he
lost interest in everything but vengeance. Eventually he
moved away from his family to a nearby town, where he lived
in a room in bitter solitude, thinking only of revenge on those
who had wronged him. Within a few years, one or two of
those who opposed him died. After 10 years, he noted with
grim satisfaction that the names of most of the witnesses and
lawyers and the assailant himself had appeared in the obituary
column. With the passage of even more years the number of
enemies decreased, until finally he found himself the only living actor in a forgotten melodrama. Soon after the vendetta
was thus terminated his crops were ruined by drought. He
believed this to be a sign from heaven that his own end was
now certain.

Once finished with his tale, he again assumed an air of untroubled relaxation. The psychiatrist reviewed and reinter-
preted the patient's reality situation to no avail. The surgeons
made every effort to reassure the patient, but without success.
His conviction of forthcoming death remained unshakable.
He underwent a subtotal gastrectomy from which he recovered
uneventfully. On the third day of an uncomplicated course,
he suddenly became dyspneic, developed atrial flutter, and died
within a few hours. At autopsy there was a large mural
thrombus that occluded the pulmonary valve.

The patient had developed a circumscribed paranoid system in
which everyone associated with his ill-fated lawsuit was his enemy.
By nursing his phantasies of revenge in solitude, the death wishes
for his enemies became confused with the ultimate fact of their
deaths. Only when his last enemy had been buried in the earth
was his unremitting anger appeased. Then, after drought destroyed
his crops, it became an augury that his punishment was imminent.
It is important to compare his violent opposition to surgery on
earlier admissions with his quiet acquiescence on this occasion.
While he previously would have chosen suicide, now there was
neither anger nor depression. His conviction of death could be
interpreted as a resolution of both fear of punishment and wish
to murder. There was no one left to murder; he was almost serene
in his attitude toward death. It is possible to conjecture that this

was his contribution to a pact he had made with fate. He was resigned to his death, which for him was entirely appropriate; struggle was unthinkable.

PATIENT 2

At the age of 41, the patient had undergone an abdomino-perineal resection for carcinoma of the rectum, which kept her an invalid for the next 28 years. She was cared for by a devoted husband who worked as a machinist during the day, then as her nurse and housekeeper in the evening. Through those long years she was convinced that he was repelled by the colostomy, especially by the odor and the occasional accident that soiled the bed. Even though he treated these matters lightly and remained affectionate, she regarded herself as a worthless burden. When she developed chronically draining rectal abscesses, her unhappy sense of being foul and fetid increased. Although at night in bed with him she often longed for death, she did not consider suicide. His unremitting solicitude and tenderness only compounded her self-reproach for having deprived him of happiness. Despite three earlier pregnancies, there had been no children. Each conception had ended in miscarriage because "they bled themselves out." Her inability to bear children gave rational confirmation to the lifelong belief that something was wrong in her. Not only had she sapped the life from her husband, but, in addition, the substance of life had soured and died inside her. This was further substantiated by developing cancer at an early age.

The patient's misfortunes multiplied as the years of invalidism went on. Her favorite brother died from a painful rectal carcinoma, leaving his large family destitute. Ironically, with so much to live for, he died from the same disease that had spared her. In rapid succession, three of her sisters died, one of a debilitating neurological disorder. Finally her loyal husband died of a coronary thrombosis, as had her father when she was a child. Alone now, she spent her days and nights in almost total solitude, tended by a niece who lived nearby, shunning everyone except a remaining sister who visited her on infrequent holidays.

Even before the psychiatrist spoke with the patient, he was aware of a sickening atmosphere of death in her room. In part, it was the offensive and heavy odor of feces which somehow eluded all efforts at hygiene. But more forceful was the leaden expression of anguish on the patient's face, which, in its solemn immobility, resembled a death mask. In a low, monotonous voice, she answered questions without ever changing her expression. Incongruously sanguine, nothing she said suggested that she was depressed. She easily stated her conviction that death would occur in a few days and went on to say she had wanted to die for many years, but had been unable to until now. When asked why she wanted to die, she told of the deaths in her family, of watching through the long, dreary years the death of nearly everyone around her. While they died she lived and grew fat. Indirectly, she indicated that her survival had been at the expense of other lives, even those of her unborn children. She thought of herself as a plump and sickening slug wallowing and feeding on death. Other people gave her the means to live while she could not return the gift.

In speaking of her own death, she did not merely intimate that the long-sought end was near, but avowed that she would be killed by surgery. After a previous operation she had suffered terrifying dyspnea as a result of a pulmonary hemorrhage. She recalled that prompt treatment brought her both relief and regret that she had not bled to death. Now she was certain another lung hemorrhage would recur, except that this time she would certainly die. Eight days after surgery she unexpectedly succumbed to a massive pulmonary hemorrhage.

During this postoperative period she was visited regularly by the psychiatrist. At no time was there any sign of rapport even though she responded compliantly to all his questions There was never a smile, never a protest, never a complaint during any interview. To the very end she remained withdrawn, uncommunicative, and retarded, but not depressed. Her dying words were, "I have no husband . . . I'm all alone."

It would be difficult to conceive of a patient who welcomed death as did this woman. She had survived at the cost of every person to whom she was devoted, and managed to live on with a disease of usually rapid mortality. It was as though she had ironically survived as proof of her conviction that something indeed was wrong with her. The persistent sense of being soiled and repulsive clung to her. Her loneliness in the later years and preoccupation with the fate of those she had lost held her encased in a little room, but still she did not die. The important question is not, however, that she wished to die. She had understood for many years that only death could resolve her difficulties. Why had she survived so long? Had she died at any time, death would have been welcome. Psychiatry cannot conjecture beyond asserting that the patient had been convinced of her own death for the first time when she entered the hospital. The difference between a chronic yearning for death and a conviction that death is imminent cannot be more sharply illustrated. Her emotional status was not that of depression but of flattened affect, a condition more characteristic of the chronically ill than of the melancholic patient.

PATIENT 3

A large, robust, hawk-faced man of 86 was admitted for repair of a femoral neck fracture. He looked much younger than his actual age and quickly captured the attention of the ward by his colorful and expansive conversation, intoned in a theatrical bass voice. Although he flirted with the nurses and quipped with the doctors, he also announced his forthcoming death with firm conviction. At first everyone thought this was part of his histrionic character, but, as the days passed and his conviction remained unchanged, the psychiatrist was called to see him just before the operation for implanting the prosthesis.

The consultant was given a hearty greeting and elicited the facts of the patient's life without effort. The patient stated that he was an illegitimate member of an illustrious New England family, who had left him on the doorstep of an orphanage shortly after his birth. Looking older than he was, he joined the Navy after escaping from the orphanage when he was 14. For the next 20 years he traveled the globe as a sailor and merchant seaman. He had been on the battleship *Maine* when it was sunk and could recall in detail the roster of 34 officers he had served under during the action in Havana Harbor. Away from the sea, he turned his talent to robbery and served a sentence in the penitentiary. While there, he earned the reputation of being an "iron man" for his capacity to be in solitary confinement on bread and water for half a year (sic). After his release, he worked regularly as a railroad man until he was prematurely retired as a result of a coupling accident in which he lost his leg. Unable to work, he moved into a cheap hotel room where he maintained himself on a meager pension.

He was a life-long bachelor who prided himself on being able to live in solitude verging on isolation. All human associations were avoided except those he found among barroom companions and prostitutes. As he grew old, he stayed more to himself and often slept 18 hours a day. Finally, his only source of pleasure was a weekly visit to a burlesque show, followed by a few beers in a nearby tavern. At an undetermined point during his old age he became preoccupied with the wish to die. Instead of committing suicide, however, he thought of ways to be killed. At first he tried bribing parking lot attendants to rig up a pipe from the exhaust of a car. After failing to persuade them, he next tried to hire some local thugs to shoot him. Still unsuccessful, he started the rumor that he carried his life savings in his wooden leg, vainly hoping that a cutthroat would kill him, but *no one seemed to care*. Finally, after being struck by the car, which broke his leg and resulted in his hospital admission, he decided that his assassin was to be the surgeon.

As he listened to the picaresque story, the psychiatrist found it difficult to consider this patient predilected to death. Nothing in his history or manner suggested depression, yet his amiable wish to die remained steadfast. In answer to all persuasions, he simply reiterated that it was time for him to die, and that it was time for his whole prominent family to die because they were all rascals whose fortune had been built by cheating Indians out of land and importing slaves in the early days of the Commonwealth. He considered it strange that anyone should attempt to talk him out of death when everything in his experience pointed to its appropriateness at this point in his life.

He survived the operation easily and was interviewed on the second postoperative day. Undismayed and unencouraged by his survival, he asked the doctor what sense there was in remaining in the world when he had no further interest in it. On the eighth day he suddenly died of a pulmonary embolism.

The most impressive psychiatric findings were (1) a strong counterphobic attitude, (2) an absence of depression, and (3) a wish to be killed by an accomplice. Lifelong isolation and total absence of sustaining human relationships had become an ideal for this aged man, who prided himself on his ability to withstand unremitting deprivation and solitude. Nevertheless, his last years were marked by ever-increasing isolation and withdrawal from even casual acquaintances. While he boasted about being an "iron man" who needed no one, he also romanticized his loneliness by claiming kinship with a prominent family. Whether this alleged relationship was factual or not is irrelevant to its importance in sustaining him in his isolation. Depression or suicidal trends were denied, even though he had tried to find someone who would kill him for money. This suggests that the familiar phantasy of being the offspring of famous parents, who left him on a doorstep as an infant, enabled him to anticipate a final reunion with his family in death: "We are all rascals: it is time to die!"

PATIENT 4

An unusually attractive 14-year-old girl was brought to the hospital because of severe knee pain that had been unsuccessfully treated for 6 months by a combination of rest, reassurance, and analgesics. When, finally, an osteogenic sarcoma was diagnosed by X-ray, it was more of a surprise to her parents and physicians than to the patient who had predicted the findings because she had a friend with identical symptoms who suffered from the same disease. A high thigh amputation of the right leg was performed immediately, after which she began a period of rehabilitation.

From the moment she made her appearance on the ward, this bright and pretty young girl won the admiration of the staff by her intelligence, maturity beyond her years, and an utter lack of self-pity after the amputation. While learning how to use her prosthesis, she continued her school work with a tutor and kept up her interest in reading and music. Her equanimity in the face of mutilating surgery and an uncertain fate moved everyone concerned with her care to an unusual degree of attachment and devotion; even those who ordinarily held themselves above personal involvement became interested in her.

At the rehabilitation center she became acquainted with a boy a year older, who had also lost his leg because of osteogenic sarcoma. He was more adept at using his prosthesis and taught her some of the tricks he had learned. A good-natured competition developed between them. He introduced her to his family, who encouraged her to spend weekends at their house. Before doing so, she first had to overcome the objections of her mother—also a young woman—who worked as a waitress to supplement the meager income of her husband.

An atmosphere of mutual restraint and disapproval had always existed between mother and daughter. Because the patient had usually turned to others for understanding, neither parent could understand her benign acceptance of the amputation, much less the prognosis. As weeks passed, her mother's deceptively calm composure dissolved into near panic as she could no longer ignore what the future held. In contrast, the boy's mother had come to terms with the illness of her son. She had a large family ranging from infants to young adults. Warm and naturally close, this thriving group instantly took the patient into the fold. The boy's mother encouraged the friendship between her son and the girl, and soon there was no family function in which she did not participate.

Instead of resenting her own mother, who had neglected her in some respects, the patient recognized the dismay, confusion, and grief of her parents and seemed to feel only compassion for them. Her own attitude was clearly one of acceptance. Only when an empty reassurance or false hope was offered by either her parents or the medical staff would she become alarmed and angry. When further surgical procedures were needed she endured them, as long as the facts were first explained. However, if she sensed that misguided sympathy concealed the real issue, she lapsed into depression. It was evident that the patient was far less disturbed by her disease than were her parents or her physicians.

For 15 months following her first admission and growing friendship, perhaps romance, with the boy, the patient was completely free of symptoms. It was only when the boy succumbed to his illness after having developed severe chest, stump, and jaw pain, that she too started to ache in the same parts. With his death, which she accepted with unusual ease, phantom limb pain began, along with dyspnea, and hip pain. Radiological examination revealed metastatic lesions in the painful areas.

It was at this time that a psychiatric consultation was requested to determine if a prefrontal leukotomy would help to relieve the pain. The consultant found the patient to be a model of composure. Even though no one had openly told her what the future held, she was aware of what faced her and accepted it with disarming serenity. Without guile, she radiated an unnerving aura of solemn acceptance and joy. In that interview she seemed to give much more than she received. The psychiatrist was by no means alone in feeling that she had imparted something to him, an unspoken lesson for which there was no response. Without tears or nostalgia, she spoke of her boy friend as though he had merely preceded her in death, while she occupied her remaining time in as pleasant a way as possible until she was able to take up with him where they had left off. She was more than content to remain dependent on narcotics to control her pain, and displayed neither anxiety nor depression. On the contrary, she welcomed the inevitable with gracious resignation. At her terminal admission, despite cachexia and pain, she remained cheerful. A large mandibular lesion, along with heavy sedation, made conversation impossible. Had she been able to speak, those who saw her to the end did not doubt that she would have said good-bye with the same equanimity she maintained throughout her tragic, but happy termination.

From the first admission, the patient's unfaltering acceptance of her tragic situation imprinted itself upon those who took care of her. Her unusual charm and enthusiasm only underscored the pain and depredations the disease would later exact. However, she thrived during the initial 15 months after the amputation. She relapsed and developed intractable symptoms along with metastases only after the boy's death. During this period her attitude changed from teen-age vivacity to self-contained serenity, which became more evident by contrast with the growing apprehension of her parents and the professional staff workers, who could barely maintain their own clinical objectivity.

Since death was inevitable, there was no indication in this patient of a "predilection" to death. Perhaps because of her short-lived romance, impending death concerned her little. There were indications that she and the boy had anticipated their own deaths. Since the essence of her relationship with others consisted of frankly confronting facts, there was reason to believe that these two had faced together the interruption in their lives. She had indeed come to terms with death. Only pain and her pain reflected in others disturbed her composure. The theme of *Liebestod* is familiar in legend and occasionally in fact. The star-crossed lovers who are reunited only in death is too often surrounded by pathos. For psychiatric purposes, the important issue is that this young girl was able to face her own death with unmistakable equanimity and without self-pity, depression, anxiety, or regret. At no time was reassurance required, except for the doctors and for her parents.

PATIENT 5

Four years before admission to the hospital, a 54-year-old unmarried secretary had given up her executive position because of deepening depression and paranoid ideas. During her last working year she had become increasingly grandiose and suspicious; she resented inappropriately the appointment of a new vice-president, and spoke obliquely about being followed by a mysterious stranger who had erotic designs. This gradually abated, and profound depression replaced her erotic delusions. She was given electroshock treatment without improvement and for the next 3 years was confined to a mental hospital. Periodically she improved enough to stay briefly with friends, but relapse usually was prompt. At no time was suicide threatened.

About a year before her final illness she began to complain of severe abdominal pain and weakness. A laparotomy disclosed an advanced ovarian carcinoma with many tumor implants in the peritoneum. Although her chronic depression improved slightly after the initial operation, it soon recurred, along with unrelenting weakness and pain. A series of treatments with new therapeutic drugs caused her more distress without benefit, and she was admitted for a colostomy in an effort to prolong her life.

From her first hospital day, the patient spoke openly about wanting to die. She was bitter that so much was being done to preserve her meaningless life when she wanted it over with. In fact, she was convinced that death would certainly occur during this period. She reported to the psychiatric consultant that she was less depressed than she had been for years, now that she realized that her sufferings would not be interminable. Her sole concern was with a speedy death. At each indication that the colostomy might prolong her life, or that there was a possibility of survival, she became alarmed.

After the operation she was bitter, withdrawn, and again depressed. "They have done something terrible to me. But it won't work. I will die tonight. It is worse than being an animal, and yet they call it a good result. Something is wrong and it will never be right. You can take the pain away, but you can't use drugs on the immortal soul of suffering. It is too much for me; I am in agony and this is the end of my life." She died that night of myocardial infarction.

From the patient's previous hospital and social work records, it was learned that while she had been an unusually effective executive secretary for many years, her life was largely one of isolation. She had several married sisters, but had been too competitive with men to attract romantic interest. Her sisters were dumbfounded in the early stages of her illness when she began to hint about a secret lover, an important man, who had begun to follow her.

The sole consolation of this unhappy woman was that her agonies would not be limitless. The immortal soul could not be reached by either cancer or psychosis, by drugs or surgery, and this was all that mattered. Her despair was not altogether brought about by physical pain, but was also due to the burden and humiliation of having first her mind and then her body riddled by disease. During most of her life she had scornfully held herself aloof from most people, shunning intimate friends, and believing herself superior to most men. Her one satisfaction in life had been the effective management of her job. This had been taken away from her by the growing mental illness, and then by the discovery of advanced carcinoma. She was outraged by the prospect of living on with both a damaged body and mind; her remaining wish was to leave an existence that had brought her only sorrow and pain, and to cling to that part of herself, the soul, which had not been violated by disease.

Discussion

In the spectrum of dying patients, there are many nuances in the encounter with death. While it is probably true that death is a symbol with different meaning for different people, according to personality, social orientation, age, and so forth, there is, in addition, a wide range of "differential death attitudes" that is of clinical value, rather than simply of philosophical significance. Cases of "psychic" death have occasionally been reported[5] in which highly disturbed patients have correctly predicted their own deaths, and in which medical examination or autopsy findings have discovered little organic disease to account for the death. In contrast, it is commonplace for the medical examiner to find unsuspected fatal illness in people who have suddenly succumbed in the midst of apparent health. Not infrequently, the cause of death is not evident even after a careful autopsy.[6] At still another extreme are the patients who are about to undergo high mortality surgery with a realistic recognition of the risk, or those people who suffer from terminal illness and gradually approach the end of their lives with full acknowledgment that their survival is measured in hours or days.

The fear of dying is a matter distinct from the anticipation of death. The fear of death, of which so many patients speak, is in fact a specific attitude toward the process of dying, and is not related to the fact of death. It pertains to a sense of imminent disintegration, collapse, or dissolution, and hence is more closely allied to primary anxiety or panic than to the transfiguration that death entails. Some patients experience the fear of dying before an operation, and then, when rescued by the surgeon, quickly regain a hopeful attitude. In other patients preoperative anxiety or fear of dying may, in fatal cases, be succeeded by adaptation to the inevitability of death, often with no significant anxiety or depression. Clinicians have noted that cancer patients rarely talk about death, particularly in the terminal stages. In this respect they differ from the predilection patients, some of whom had terminal cancer, but also wished to die.

Among patients who face certain death, panic is a rare occurrence. Even intractable pain is not common. Osler,[7] Munk,[8] and many other physicians have observed that there is seldom suffering when the patient is at the threshold of death. Whenever there is sufficient time between awareness of impending death and the actual occurrence of death, the distinction between dying and death may become more evident, and the final exitus is made with less suffering and fear. Some of this is, of course, encouraged by physicians who insist upon maintaining even illusory hope by diverting the patients' attention and concern to the secondary complications of their terminal disease. As a result, these patients frequently complain of pain, lack of appetite, impatience with their slow improvement, and so forth. Even though each new symptom, for example, may be an advancement of a malignancy, some patients ignore this fact and regard new symptoms as separate ailments that require individual treatment. A young man who had lost sight in both eyes as a result of a rapidly growing orbital tumor, continued to sit up in bed, staring toward the television screen. He waited until the final day of his life for his vision to return after his "infection" had cleared.

The illusory phantasy of rescue is commonly encountered among prisoners who are serving long sentences (Ganser syndrome). It also has been reported in some suicidal patients,[9] and in patients suffering from fatal diseases, who may maintain an unrealistic attitude of optimism until shortly before death. Among these are patients who refuse to accept an unfavorable diagnosis, who go from one clinic or specialist to another, and make religious pilgrimages. Only in rare instances does the sudden development of acute anxiety herald approaching death.[10]

Patients with predilection to death are not a remarkable group, provided that a distinction is made between the fear of dying and the fact of death. It is their attitude toward death that is remarkable, not the reality of their death. These patients are neither examples of "voodoo" death[11] nor commonplace capitulations of demoralized, debilitated invalids. That some of these patients were aged, suffered from fatal diseases, or had extensive operations, did not account for the psychologically specific attitude they held towards death. Each patient shared the conviction that death was not only inevitable, but desirable. In general, death was confronted without dismay, anxiety, severe depression, or concern about the dying process. For each, death was *appropriate,* as a fact that resolved conflict. In patients 1 and 3, where neither fatal disease nor high-mortality surgery had occurred, each man had for years regarded death as the only means of coming to terms with his individual problems. However desperate or depressed at earlier times, these patients had never seriously considered suicide. With the exception of patient 5, a woman who had suffered from mental disease and could tolerate no further illness, none was profoundly depressed during the terminal admission.

It is of more than theoretic interest that no patient threatened suicide. In some sense the suicidal patient wants to live; his wish is to be free of that part of the ego that is a burden.[12] For the predilection patients, the body was a burden; they were eager for that *resolution by release* that could be achieved only in death. Patient 1 regarded himself as a hostage who awaited God's punishment; patient 2 believed that she was foul and poisonous, surviving only because others had given up their lives; patient 3 looked upon death as a means of rejoining his phatasied family; patient 4 anticipated the reunited love that death would bring; patient 5, a proud woman who had scorned intimate relationships, thought of death as the only means of restoring her dignity as a human being. Instead of depression, there were elements of exaltation in these death phantasies. There was little incentive to live, but death held out a promise.

In his or her own way, each patient was lonely and isolated as death approached. Patient 3 had never known human intimacy; patient 2 had had each member of her family successively leave her by death; patient 1 had bitterly secluded himself from his wife and children; patient 5 had discouraged any friendly relationships, aside from those necessary to her job; patient 4, who was in fact affectionate and responsive, had become isolated following the death of her close friend because the people on whom she was forced to depend had, by their own apprehension of her death, alientated themselves from full communication with her. Thus, each patient had been left emotionally alone to die, whether as a result of primary isolation of characterological attitudes or of the secondary isolation of loss and abandonment.

With the exception of patient 4, these patients were not only convinced of imminent death but expected to be killed. Actually, while patient 4 serenely anticipated reunion in death, she did not explicitly report a conviction of death, even though she was entirely aware of the prognosis. The combination of a conviction of an appropriate death and a wish to be killed suggests that, to these isolated people, being killed is not a phantasy of retribution or hostility, but is a regressive affirmation of a relationship of some kind. In any case, psychiatrists frequently observe that some patients prefer a hostile relationship to none at all, because, as one patient put it, "At least some one cares enough to hate me!"

Dimensions of Death and Dying

From the biological viewpoint, death is the termination of the active processes of living. But to institutionalize death simply as the collective negation of all biological processes is as one-sided as regarding life as a summation of biochemistry and physiology. This concept ignores the human or personal dimensions of life and death and what it means to be alive and to be dead. Life *as it is lived* has more parameters than there are laboratory methods available to use them; death encompasses the human personality as much as life does.

Because death is personified at least as often as is the concept of "life," it lends itself readily to metaphors, mystic abstractions, and lugubrious platitudes. However, it is possible to record some of the panoply of death and still develop principles of clinical value by distinguishing between *impersonal, interpersonal,* and *intrapersonal* elements in the experience of death. The guiding hypothesis is that people's attitudes toward death correspond to their attitudes toward life; how each person dies is determined by how he has lived.

Impersonal Death

In this view, death is an impersonal event, stripped of the human element, and the dead are simply dead bodies classified or discarded according to various categories. Bodies or cadavers are of interest chiefly to the pathologist, who studies their condition at the time of death and finds what the patient died with, not from, or to the statistician who records the number of dead bodies per category. There is no mutual influence or modification brought about by a dead body; we stand in an impersonal and unilateral "I-it" relation to "specimens" whose unique existence does not matter.

Whether or not a wholly impersonal attitude toward death can be consistently maintained probably depends upon the doctor's personality and convictions. However, the impersonal death occurs more often than most doctors realize, for the patient who is an "interesting case" while alive becomes an interesting dead body at autopsy. While this may result from either indifference or irrelevance with respect to the personal dimension of death, sometimes the vastness of the personal element is so overwhelming that the full human impact is beyond comprehension. The death of six million Jews in Nazi concentration camps is too vast and overwhelming; but the *Diary of Anne Frank* tells the story of the death of one adolescent girl among the multitude and so has come to represent these collective deaths for humanity.

Seeming impersonality may also occur among dedicated physicians who acquire "professional" attitudes towards death and disease as the only possible means of coping with disaster daily.

Interpersonal Death

This orientation is concerned with the objective fact of death of the *other one*. Our subjective death is not involved; it is the loss of the other one that affects us. While impersonal death refers to "It is dead," interpersonal death means "Someone else is dead." Much has already been written about objective, interpersonal death from the viewpoint of bereavement, grief, fear of abandonment, or the wish to banish the lost one. However, interpersonal death may be disguised as impersonal death, as in the patient, who, when he saw the body of his dead sister, asked his mother when she was going to get rid of "that thing," or as in another patient who began to laugh and joke involuntarily while serving as a pallbearer for a boyhood friend. While grief is the usual response to death of the other one, there are many less familiar syndromes. A survivor may feel no grief; he may be jubilant when another one dies. Then, years later, the normal grief reaction may erupt in the course of another relationship. More frequently than is usually realized, a survivor may experience a sense of personal triumph in another's death, not because of ambivalence to the dead, but simply from gratification at being spared.

The death of another one foreshadows our own. Interpersonal relations do not cease with death; the deceased may continue to influence the survivor for many years. While such influence may be as obvious as that of regulating the lives of descendants by the conditions of a will, the manners, morals, prejudices, and preoccupations of one person may abide in generations of survivors. The impulses of one generation may be the principles of the next. In the following case, a mother-daughter relationship suddenly changed years after the mother's death.

A middle-aged woman was surprised to find herself dreaming almost nightly of her dead mother when her own daughter reached adolescence. The woman, the youngest of three daughters, had resented the favoritism her mother had shown to her more attractive sisters. She became an argumentative, provocative rebel who deliberately violated the conventions of a middle-class family. After an early marriage she left the family home; although overt controversies gradually abated, she saw her mother infrequently, and their relation was cool and strained. In the 15 years since her mother's death, the patient had thought of her only rarely. Then, a long series of vivid dreams developed in which the mother was far more affectionate, responsive, and appreciative than she had ever actually been; no sisters were ever in the scene. In several dreams the patient rescued the mother from a catastrophe—a fire, automobile accident, drowning—as a result of which they would be closer than ever.

Because the patient's daughter had begun to show some recalcitrance and rebellious behavior, she recognized that her dreams indicated a wish to have a relationship with her daughter different from what she had had with her mother, to avoid a similar catastrophe. Along with this, however, came a belated understanding that her own rebellion was an effort to force a clear demonstration of love from her mother. Now she was in the same perplexing position that her mother once was, and as a result was able to modify her demands upon her daughter, which reduced the need for defiance. Her relation with her dead mother also changed; as she became aware of her identification with her, the hostile component receded and she began to idealize the retrospective image.

Intrapersonal Death

This is the only dimension of death that really matters. The impact of the dead body or death of the other one are important only because of their importance for subjective death: "I am dead." Intrapersonal death has double significance in that it applies both to the *process of dying*, particularly the fear of dying, and to the fact of *subjective death;* each has different psychological aspects.

FEAR OF THE DYING PROCESS

Few human beings are free of the *fear of dying*, but they dread the impairment illness entails far more than they fear death. Extinction is less feared than is the propect of progressive dissolution. Dying is equivalent to dissolution, and the fear of dying assumes many forms. In physical terms, it may be expressed as a fear of disease. Hypochondriasis, for example, usually occurs in withdrawn people who, with heightened preoccupation in their visceral sensations and diminished concern with the world, interpret events within them as portents of fatal illness. The fear of dying may also present itself in psychological terms as a fear of insanity. When patients first experience attacks of acute anxiety they often believe that because their world is no longer connected by familiar ties, and seems to be falling away, they are becoming insane. From the purely biological viewpoint, the process of dying is only the impersonal impairment of physiological functions. But for the patient who experiences it in the vivid, private, intrapersonal world into which no one else can enter, the fear of dying is the sense of impending dissolution or disintegration of all familiar ways of thought or action. The world normally at one with our perceptions suddenly becomes alien, disjointed, and runs along without us. Whether or not unconscious narcissism permits anyone really to believe in the possibility of his subjective death is irrelevant to the immediacy of the fear of dying in states of panic or despair. At such moments, the world *is* all that we fear it to be—we *are* dying; the familiar codes and cues by which we recognize and understand the world break into isolated, meaningless fragments.

The fear of dying is evidently a necessary condition to the fact of living; it emerges whenever the act of living is threatened with disintegration. Fear of dying need not be acute; there is a chronic form that consists of an awareness of progressive erosion of body and mind, depletion of resources, accumulation of regrets, perseveration of the past, obtuseness in the present, and blunted appetite for the future. After a certain age every vague complaint, in the absence of surgically localized disorders, is attributed to either "menopause" or the "infirmities" of old age. These syndromes may be instances of the chronic form of fear of dying, in which the future, usually determined by hope or confidence in the creative possibilities of our own resources, is transmogrified into a recurrent decimal of dwindling value.

Why, then, do not the dying always feel despair? There are instances where patients who have been chronically anxious and hypochondriacal during their lifetime are transformed into uncomplaining, serene stoics after they learn that their illness is fatal. In contrast, highly rational, independent patients sometimes become converted to a primitive religious cult when death seems imminent. Still others, to a varying degree, die as they have lived, with little change in personality. This is by no means as paradoxical as it may seem, because the fear of dying, the sense of blind disintegration that eludes comprehension or control, does not affect every dying person to the same extent. The fear of the dying process is psychologically different from the fear of intrapersonal death. Condemned men have been known to attempt suicide in order to avert the process of dying, which is the period of waiting until the moment of execution. The temporal process of dying is evidently more fearsome than death itself. Conversely, patients on the very threshold of death are not always afraid, once the dying process has about run its course, and scarcely mention death. This does not necessarily mean that such patients are using denial or are repressing awareness of death.

While few patients, save the truly predilected, approach death without despair, it is often easier for the doctor to encourage denial by voicing false optimism, rationalizing symptoms into signs of improvement ("You can expect to get worse before you get better."), displacing attention from the disease onto peripheral manifestations and emphasizing subtle properties of the treatment that does not cure. In the early stages of terminal malignancy some patients will become uneasy about their refractory response to drugs or to their prolonged convalescence from surgery. In an indirect, disingenuous way, their questions will disclose their qualms, if not their conviction, that they suffer from incurable disease. Nevertheless, physicians, as well as others close to the patient, sometimes do not respond to veiled inquiries simply because of their own anxiety.

A 37-year-old executive had been in psychotherapy for about 1 year and had successfully worked out the problems for which he had sought help. During this time he had been closely observed by his internist because of a suspected lung tumor. The diagnosis was not confirmed until after the psychotherapy had been discontinued, and as a result, the medical problem had not been discussed with the patient by either his psychiatrist or internist.

Several months later the patient was admitted to the hospital for "study." His lesion was clearly one of bronchogenic carcinoma, which now was rapidly spreading. Although the original problems that brought him to the psychiatrist had abated, the patient asked to see his former doctor. The psychiatrist anticipated some questions about the carcinoma and the prognosis and discovered that he was reluctant to respond to the invitation. When he finally visited the patient the question of malignancy was not raised. Instead, the patient, who was a highly intelligent and effective man, simply alluded to his progressive weakness and complained that no one had told him why the various remedies were not more effective. He asked abstract questions about the nature of the medicine, but did not ask about his primary illness. He also was puzzled about the altered attitude of his family who, in fact, now treated him as if he were already dead. The psychiatrist found himself mouthing platitudes of reassurance, anticipating the end of the interview, and moving slowly toward the door. The patient, however, started to follow the doctor, asking questions that were impossible to answer without giving him the full prognosis, even though no explicit reference to the lung lesion was made.

The phychiatrist was thoroughly familiar with his former patient's easy use of denial and so was able to support this defense effectively. The real issue, however, was that the doctor himself found the use of psychological artifice more comfortable than facing the ultimate truth with his patient.

Later in the course of fatal illnesses the anxiety of dying may abate, and in some unspoken sense the patient will come to terms with his subjective death. Since this is clinically congenial to everyone concerned, the reasons for it have not been studied. It is possible, however, that several factors are at work. Affect may be blunted by drugs or diseases; denial may be fortified by isolation, displacement, or phantasy. By regression to a simpler level of ego function, some patients are spared their usual conflicts and even develop a transmuted hope that a fatal outcome will be avoided. In any case, it is frequently clear that in the terminal phase the sharp antitheses of living and dying gradually become modulated into a dampened harmonic line.

Subjective Death

The fear of dying process is only one aspect of the intrapersonal dimension of death. The second is the concept of subjective death. What can any man imagine of his own death? Is it possible to conceive of his own utter extinction? Whatever attempt he makes to project himself into the time of death, it results only in seeing the *other one*, and object, not the subjective *one*, the "I," of the here and now. A phantasy of absolute subjective death is impossible to imagine. If there is some meaning or emotion in the phrase, "When I am dead," there is also a trace of psychological survival in which "I" continue to exercise an influence in some form or other. Bromberg and Schilder[13] confirmed that in death phantasies there is not only a continuity of life's problems, but a successful resolution. The notion of "I am dead" is a paradox. In phantasies of eternal survival, some perpetuation of that to which one was committed in life may be detected, even among those who do not profess an elaborate mythology of survival.

If complete obliteration in subjective death is inconceivable, then what does the "fear" in "fear of death" refer to? Death, of course, awaits each of us; it is a rare person who does not fear extinction. However, the simple recognition that we shall all one day be dead has little intrapersonal impact; there is a futile hope that it may be avoided or at least indefinitely postponed. The paradox that finds no one actually believing that he will die coupled with the practically universal fear of death requires closer scrutiny. According to Freud,[14] the unconscious admits no concept of personal death. In our terms, this refers to an *intrapersonal* death. Others[15] have said that the fear of death occurs only to the degree that there has been fear of life, phantasies of death are projected forms of phantasies of life.

Despite the inevitability of death, fear of death is a phantasy of dread that has characteristics of a clinical phobia, rather than that of a fear-avoidance response. There are certain fears so universal that many people have come to regard them as "natural" or "rational." Other less common fears are considered "irrational" because they occur in situations ordinarily encountered without anxiety. The "rational" fears include such fears as that of disease, injury, illness, poverty, disgrace, and so forth; a list that is an inverted image of our value system. Because our society esteems values of health, security, and honor, fears of disease, poverty, and disgrace are strong, and hence contribute to the conviction that it is "natural" to have these fears and unthinkable to feel otherwise. Fear of death is usually included among "rational" fears. In contrast, "irrational" fears commonly refer to phobias, which are interpreted as being displacements of fears that more closely approximate "rational" fears. The distinction between "natural" fears and "irrational" phobias, however, is a demographic, not a psychodynamic decision. Both of these fears differ from a third kind of fear, the conditioned avoidance, which is a response to an anticipated pain on the basis of past experience.

. . . . To cite an example closely associated with the fear of death, a fear of being buried alive is certainly "natural"; as one can readily imagine a state of being entombed and can displace a variety of suffocating sensations experienced at some time. Nevertheless, fear of being buried alive is infrequently seen, except among miners, tunnel workers, submarine rejectees, and so on. This contrasts with the high incidence of claustrophobia. In other words, the realistic fear that can be conceptualized easily is rare, while the symbolic fear is common. This has several implications for the fear of death: (1) universality of a fear is not a criterion for its being "natural"; (2) the inevitability of disaster is not a decisive factor in evoking a chronic state of fear; (3) displacement of fearful associations and phantasies may be the crucial factor.

The fear of dying and of dissolution may be at the root of all fears, but it would be begging the question to assume that the fear of death cannot be reduced further into phobic phantasies that have been displaced forward in time. To preserve the distinction between "rational" and "irrational" fears simply by asserting that it is a matter of degree is to bypass the problem, since "degrees" or "quantities" in psychiatry are only metaphorical entities. The aversion of the intrapersonal "I" to becoming an impersonal "it" in death expresses both a fear of passive dissolution and a projection in time of the phantasy in which a relic of the "I" is interred in the "it." If it were possible to know, for example, that one would die on a Wednesday afternoon at 5 o'clock, the phantasies of death would become more urgent; 5:00 P.M. Wednesday of every week would acquire the characteristics of a phobia as well as of a powerful superstition.

If our concept of intrapersonal death, as well as that of patients, is in fact a condensed or fragmentary phantasy of survival in which the fulfillment of appetites, avoidance of disaster, and resolution of conflict are permanently established, then the inner core of the death phobia is a symbolic equivalent of such problems as abandonment, desertion, banishment, loneliness, dependency, pain, guilt, retaliation, and so forth.

These considerations imply that psychiatric evaluation of death and dying may provide answers to more general questions related to death. Surprisingly, psychiatric studies of this problem have been meager, even though death is a familiar theme in all ages and all literature. Moreover, it is a subject about which even careful workers can readily become tendentious; unless death can be objectively investigated, philosophical prejudices are apt to be disguised as psychological principles. Feifel's research[16] has indicated that mental illness produces no unusual attitudes towards death. Bromberg and Schilder[17] have reiterated this conclusion. A host of factors determines attitudes towards death, quite apart from religious or social orientation. Whether death is regarded as a termination of natural life or as the start of a new existence, it remains an important concern for everyone.

The death phobia is only one of other possible attitudes towards the event. One patient believed that by committing suicide he could reconcile his constantly battling parents, and did in fact attempt suicide several times. The theme of martyrdom thus had great appeal both in his work and in his private thoughts. In the course of psychoanalysis it becomes clear that his attraction to martyrdom was determined by a wish to conceal his revenge phantasies and to find relief through reversal of his hostile impulses. Another patient had a phantasy in which she would be buried while in a state of inanimation. She would then recover consciousness after burial and pound on the coffin lid until people disinterred her. But by then she would be so exhausted from the struggle to be heard that once again she would be considered dead and would be reburied. Her life had been a protracted struggle for recognition and appreciation by her family who periodically banished her because of her provocative assaults and self-imposed exiles. The phantasied cycle of death, revival, death, revival corresponded to this pattern—an effective, macabre device for retaining appreciation and attention from her family. Felix Deutsch pointed out that serene anticipation of impending death occurs when the regressive path to infantile love objects can be followed without guilt or conflict.[18] Euthanasia—death without suffering—will thus be facilitated, according to Deutsch, when subjective death is regarded as a phantasy in which inexorable fate is reconciled by a reunion with lost loves in a longed-for fulfillment.

Concept of An Appropriate Death

Each of the five patients cited as examples of predilection approached death with a minimum of anxiety or conflict. For them, death could be said to have a liberating effect because it seemed utterly appropriate. This suggests that it is the sense of being appropriate that robs subjective death of its terror. Quite apart from the process of dying, the concept of an appropriate death is consistent with the hypothesis that our attitude toward our own death is a phantasy of idealized survival in a condensed or disguised form.

What makes one death appropriate and another death tragic? It is strange that, while medicine presides daily over unnumbered deaths and psychiatrists study the psychopathology of death in its protean forms, death has so universally been regarded as a dark symbol beyond investigation. Psychiatrists do not hesitate to study various types of suicide, but the reverse of a suicidal situation, one in which the prospect of appropriate resolution in death far outweighs the fear of dissolution by dying, is rarely mentioned.

Part of the answer to this is to be found in the aversion among doctors to confront themselves with the fact of their own death and to wonder if death can ever be appropriate for them. Despair wears many masks; a hard shell of materialism may cover a tenderness that shuns exposure. The dedication to forestall death is an indication that the medical profession believes that death is never appropriate.

A death that is appropriate for one person may be quite out of character for another. For most people martyrdom holds little appeal as an appropriate death, nor do we tend to glorify death as did the ancient Egyptians. The death of Socrates is a classic example of an appropriate death for the philosopher, but one that would be incongruous for a military man who, conceivably, might prefer the Viking's death in the midst of action, consumed by flames. In any case, the dramatic context for death, which seems so heroic from a distance, is of little clinical help in determining what an appropriate death is from the intrapersonal and interpersonal viewpoints of the individual patient, who is usually neither a general nor a philosopher.

The concept of an appropriate death is one so alien to most people that it is difficult to obtain an accurate appraisal of the circumstances in which any individual patient would be prepared to die. Although he faces the fact that living comes to an end, he finds it easier to imagine the conditions under which he might commit suicide. What responses would most people make if they were asked to write their own eulogies? Would it be easier to write a proposed suicide note than an obituary? Under what circumstances, for example, would the reader be willing to die? It is as difficult to propose an appropriate personal death as it is to imagine subjective obliteration itself. Simply to cite desirable examples of impersonal death, such as dying for a cause; or of interpersonal death, such as reunion with a lost love; or even of intrapersonal death, such as resurrection, does not adequately define an appropriate death. All three personal dimensions are necessary if this concept is to have meaning.

Our hypothesis is that, whatever its content, an appropriate death must satisfy four principal requirements: (1) conflict is reduced; (2) compatibility with the ego ideal is achieved; (3) continuity of important relationships is preserved or restored; (4) consummation of a wish is brought about. This does not mean, of course, that under the usual circumstances of dying it is possible to attain a death that is as wholly acceptable as it was to the predilection patients. Nevertheless, planning and implementing psychotherapeutic interventions in other patients who are certain to die may be facilitated if these criteria are used as guides, together with the psychodynamic formulation of the patient's private concerns.

Psychotherapeutic Implications

If death is inevitable, of what importance are psychotherapeutic considerations? Although the medical profession is dedicated to survival and health, it cannot indefinitely postpone death. The doctor may regard a dying patient as a challenge to his competence, but the approaching death of the patient is neither evidence of failure nor a cause for capitulation or despair. Among his other tasks, the physician is also committed to help his patient achieve an appropriate emotional world in which to die.

Psychiatric participation extends the range of the physician's care. The aim is not simply to make death "easy," for, aside from the depredation brought about by disease, the patient who faces imminent death often suffers far less than those who will lose emotionally by his death. Many pleas for euthanasia of the incurably ill are designed to relieve the suffering of the survivors, not of the patient. Psychiatric intervention is particularly important in two groups of patients: (1) those who are either afraid of dying or are convinced that death is necessary as a solution for life's problems; (2) those who face certain death. In the first group, the problem is largely psychological; in the second, the task is to render death more acceptable and appropriate.

Fear of Dying and Conviction of Death

Patients who express a fear of dying, a fear of death, a wish to die, or a conviction that death is imminent may differ widely in other respects. The apprehensive preoperative patient who is afraid of dying suffers from his anticipatory phantasies of destruction and disability. In another paper, we have discussed the management of this type of operative syndrome.[19] As a rule, the preoperative patient with "high anxiety" survives the operation without unusual complications. While the hospital course and convalescence of depressed preoperative patients is more uncertain, it must be re-emphasized that such patients are not typical predilection patients. The depressed surgical patient may be hopeless and despondent, but is rarely convinced of certain death.

When a patient develops an acute fear of dying in the absence of serious medical or surgical illness, his management is directed toward primary anxiety itself. Fear of death is an indication of active conflict and is treated like any other phobia. Both fear of death and the wish to die frequently occur together, not only in depressed or suicidal patients but in so-called "masochistic characters" who conceal a hostile or triumphant core inside a shell of defeat and despair.

While these clinical problems undoubtedly arise more frequently in psychiatric practice than in medicine or surgery, the quiet conviction of impending death as shown in the predilection patients is unusual even among physically well patients. The clinical significance of the predilection patients described here is not that they required psychiatric treatment; this would have been feasible only for patients 1 and 3 who did not have mortal diseases. Had these two patients been accessible to psychotherapy, it is even problematical if either patient would have succumbed without the additional stress of operation. Nevertheless, effective or not, psychiatric intervention is indicated when there is a strong conviction of death and little or no somatic disorder to justify it, simply because the psychological factor predominates; these are cases of potential "psychic death" that have been reported in both civilized and primitive communities.[20] Psychiatric management of these patients would, in effect, mean reversing a kind of "voodoo death," whether as a result of an internal conflict or of an externally imposed bone-pointing. The therapeutic aim would involve undermining the image of appropriate death that these patients maintain. The exalted prospect of death as a means of appeasing guilt or enhancing ego function, together with the effect of silence, isolation, and the sanction of death as an appropriate institution, are certain to be important psychotherapeutic considerations.   In order to neutralize these the psychiatrist would have to reaffirm enough hope and motivation through living interpersonal relationships with the patient to justify survival.

Certainty of Death

The appropriate death that predilection patients spontaneously demonstrate suggests that when death is certain, suffering may be reduced for other patients by fostering an image of appropriate death. If a bereaved patient derives benefit from clarifying his attitude towards the death of another[12] (objective death), a dying patient may find value in considering his own death (subjective death). This will mean that both the doctor and patient must face death with frankness and clarity, unfettered by the taboos and emotional conflicts that occur in other situations.   Death is among the many forbidden topics that humanity regulates with euphemism and impersonal ritual.   Many of the restrictions placed upon conversation with a dying patient are determined more often by social convention than by clinical value.   Families and doctors frequently ask whether to tell a cancer patient, for example, about his diagnosis and prognosis.   This query seldom needs to be answered, since patients with fatal diseases usually do not ask if they will die.   In some cases this may be due to denial or isolation, but competent observers agree that many patients would be willing to discuss death, if the doctor were only able to overcome his own guilt or anxiety enough to permit it.

An elderly man had been followed for many months because of carcinoma of the tongue.   Pain gradually became so severe that a dorsomedial thalamotomy was required.   During hospitalization a particularly warm bond had been established between the patient and his doctor.   The patient's general high spirits after the thalamotomy led the staff to assume that the operation had not only relieved pain, but had fortunately spared the patient from any ultimate awareness of his fatal condition. During his final admission, the patient suffered from an ob-

structed airway caused by extensive infiltration of the carcinoma. Speech, of course, was impossible, and the patient
could communicate only be writing. Late one evening his
doctor visited him, and was moved to pity by the futility of his
patient's plight. It was obvious that life could not continue
and that there was little to say except good-bye. As the doctor
sat silently, he sadly put his hand on the patient's shoulder.
The patient glanced at him and wrote on a pad of paper:
"Don't take it so hard, doc!" Within a few hours he was dead.

Despite the superficial air of denial, seeming indifference, and
the thalamic lesion, this simple statement revealed that the patient
had been completely aware of his fate. His doctor's professional
optimism had not deceived him. As a rule, only clergymen have
enough objectivity to face death frankly with patients.[22] The reason
for this is uncertain, except that where death has been institutionalized—i.e., impersonalized—it is somewhat easier to face in the
other one. How the clergyman feels about his own death is another
issue.

For the majority of dying patients, it is likely that there is neither
complete acceptance nor total repudiation of the imminence of
death. To deny this "middle knowledge" of approaching death
is to deny the responsiveness of the mind to both internal perceptions and external information. There is always psychological sampling of the physiological stream; fever, weakness, anorexia, weight
loss, and pain are subjective counterparts of homeostatic alteration.
When prompt response to illness does not occur and, instead, new
symptoms join the old, few patients can fail to perceive a downward
course. If to this are added changes in those close to the patient,
then knowledge of approaching death is confirmed. When a patient
has responded to others under even more subtle circumstances,
he will not ignore the manifold signals now offered to him.

The prospect of death becomes filled with suffering when defeat
and demoralization are added to the deterioration of disease. An appropriate attitude toward death, in contrast, comes about when (1)
there is quiet acceptance that death is a solution to abiding problems,
or that few problems remain at the time of death; (2) superego
demands are reduced; (3) optimal interpersonal relations are maintained; and (4) the ego is encouraged to operate at as high a
level as may be compatible with the physical illness. Some of
these factors the physician can modify; others obviously are beyond

his power. Clearly, however, the physician's responsibility does not end with the decision to or not to inform the patient or his relatives of the hopeless prognosis.[23]

One of the distinguishing features of the predilection patients was the absence of living human relationships during the terminal period, combined with anticipated reunion, resolution, or release in death. Isolation in itself did not evoke the image of appropriate death, but it undoubtedly encouraged the conviction that death was desirable. All showed little remaining interest in the world of living people. In contrast, the dying patient may suffer more from abrupt emotional isolation and deprivation than from his illness. To attribute the dying person's withdrawal of interest in his surroundings to a retraction of libidinal cathexis is a redundant rationalization. Frequently it is the survivors who withdraw interest from the patient. The syndrome of premortem loneliness, *bereavement of the dying*, is partially evoked by the isolation the living force upon the dying. There have been cases where the use of narcotics has been a substitute for diminished human relationships, as well as being a gesture of futility. In an attempt to overcome their aversion to impending death, survivors will carry out certain preparatory rituals. The drawn shades, hushed voices, and unnatural attitudes of visitors and family are indications of complete capitulation, abandonment, and, in fact, premortem burial. The predilection patients did not suffer from bereavement of the dying because they had no one left for whom they cared enough; the phantasied survival provided enough incentive to make death worth dying for. Most dying patients, except the very aged, maintain some emotional attachments and so may suffer from the indulgent isolation of the survivors. It should be understood that abandonment of the dying can occur in many ways—not always as literally as in the following case—and that in most instances it is due to the survivor's uneasy conscience in being alive while the other one dies.

A 68-year-old machinist had suffered from syringomyelia for 8 years. Until then, however, he had worked and provided for his wife and her 6 children from a previous marriage. All of the children had married and established homes of their own by the time he became incapacitated. His wife cared for him until he required more nursing care than she could provide. At this point the patient was admitted to the hospital for evaluation prior to sending him to a chronic infirmary. Although the patient was weak, unable to walk, and suffered from urinary incontinence, aside from a nutritional anemia he was not moribund. It was expected that after blood transfusion, physiotherapy, and dietary supplement he could easily be cared for in a nursing home. When the stepchildren were asked to replace the blood given him, each refused, with one excuse or another. It was then necessary to ask the patient if he knew other people who would give blood and to explain that the children were not able to be donors. The patient did not respond immediately, and then with quiet tears talked of the long years of caring for 6 homeless children and their widowed mother. Finally he turned away from the doctor as if to sleep, without suggesting substitute donors. He was clearly depressed during the next 3 days, responded briefly to inquiries about his health, and died unexpectedly on the fourth day. Only syringomyelia was found at autopsy.

The object of psychiatric intervention is to help the dying patient preserve his identity and dignity as a unique individual, despite the disease, or, in some cases, because of it. The doctor encourages in the patient a self-image of value that will forestall a state of unobstructive, demoralized vegetation. One of the factors contributing to disintegration in chronic illness is the tendency to overlook the patient's individual identity and to concentrate solely on the vicissitudes of the disease. The psychiatrist always asks himself what the patient would be like without the disease, and then tries to produce a therapeutic dissociation of the patient's self-image, ideal and actual, from the disease itself; the alternative is to permit the personality to die before the patient does. Nature herself seems to use this method by isolating diseased organs and impersonalizing painful functions to a degree that often gives them an existence of their own.

Achievement of an appropriate attitude towards death can be implemented in several ways. In addition to preserving and reviving the relationship with the living and the already dead, the patient is required to maintain his effective ego functions on the highest possible plane. This may be done by continuing his major activities or at least engaging his interest. The patient's ego ideal, expressed in unrealistic ambitions and unfulfilled desires, may be discussed in a matter-of-fact way. Strangely enough, when the psychiatrist asks an older patient at what point in his life things might have been different had another decision been made, few patients will acknowledge that a wholly different decision could have been made or that drastic alteration in the course of their lives would even have been desirable. Many people have life-long day dreams of glory, but they also have an implied stipulation that everything else that they have found valuable will remain the same. Since issues of this kind may have evoked conflict in life they may also obstruct the amicable acceptance of death. The interests of the ego and ego ideal may also be served by helping to rectify wrongs whenever possible; reaffirming objectives from a realistic viewpoint; and discussing matters not previously disclosed. Use may be made of the occurrence of the tendency for "unrepression," which some authors have described.[24] Paradoxical as it may seem, the therapeutic dissociation may be strengthened by encouraging the concept that death is a solution, not a catastrophe; indicating that the disease does not affect the patient's value as an individual; emphasizing that he has fulfilled his reasonable aims in life and that, literally, there is nothing more to live for.

If this viewpoint seems too schematic and visionary, then reduction of any conflict is equally implausible. It is our paradoxical attitude towards death, not the fact of death itself, that makes insoluble conflict seem inevitable. This attitude accounts for the conviction that although death cannot be avoided it is always undesirable and that few can even adapt to its approach, let alone welcome the event. These interventions have one simple objective; to modify the patient's attitude towards death so that neither motivations nor ego functions are destroyed before the body succumbs.

By their very nature, phobic components of death are less tractable to direct psychiatric intervention. Hence, open discussion of gross phobic displacements is the only method available for dealing with this problem. The patient's actual anticipations, and expectations are apt to vary with his concepts of survival, punishment, reclamation, and resurrection. In a recent book, Feifel[25] has brought together representative essays that emphasize the research possibilities of the meaning of death. It is likely that for adherents of certain religious faiths, this entire discussion of death and the dying patient is meaningless. Nevertheless, we may conjecture that a patient's church affiliations and professed beliefs are not always a reliable index to his actual attitude towards death. This applies to both devout and agnostic declarations.

The application of these principles is not necessarily beyond the doctor's competence, since it is part of the terminal care of patients. This means that helping the dying patient to achieve an appropriate attitude towards death entails a re-examination of our own attitudes. It is neither mysticism nor pessimism to assert that the purpose of living is to create a world in which we would be willing to die; it is an unyielding fact of existence. Moreover, attainment of an appropriate death without suffering is probably not at all rare. If the physician can successfully reconcile the dying patient to his death, it will be because the image of being an abandoned, impersonal dead body has been replaced by the prospect of the dignified death of a significant individual. It may even help the physician to accept his own death.

References

1. W. Marchand, "Practice of Surgery in A Neuropsychiatric Hospital," *Archives of General Psychiatry*, 1 (1959), 123.
2. H. Selye, personal communication.
3. T. Hackett and A. Weisman, "Psychiatric Management of Operative Syndromes," *Psychosomatic Medicine*, 22 (1960), 267 and 356.
4. A. Weisman, "Psychodynamic Formulation of Conflict," *Archives of General Psychiatry*, 1 (1959), 288.
5. P. "Vom Tode Hussy, und Todessahnungen," *Veska-Z. Schweiz*, 9 (1945), 251, I. Janis, *Psychological Stress: Psychoanalytic and Behavioral Studies of Surgical Patients* (New York: Wiley, 1958); M. Walters, "Psychic Death: Report of a Possible Case," *Archives of Neurology and Psychiatry*, 52 (1944), 84.
6. A. Moritz, and N. Zamcheck, "Sudden and Unexpected Deaths of Young Soldiers," *Archives of Pathology*, 42 (1946), 459.
7. H. Cushing, *Life of Sir William Osler*. Vol. 1. (Oxford: Clarendon Press), pp. 294, 639.
8. W. Munk, *Euthanasia or Medical Treatment in Aid of an Easy Death* (London and New York: Longmans, 1887).
9. V. Jensen, and T. Petty, "The Fantasy of Being Rescued in Suicide," *Psychoanalytic Quarterly*, 27 (1958), 327.
10. J. Beigler, "Anxiety as An Aid in the Prognostication of Impending Death," *Archives of Neurology and Psychiatry*, 77 (1957), 171.
11. W. Cannon, "Voodoo Death," *Psychosomatic Medicine*, 19 (1957), 182.
12. R. Rubenstein, R. Moses, and T. Lidz, "On Attempted Suicide," *Archives of Neurology and Psychiatry*, 79 (1958), 103.
13. W. Bromberg, and P. Schilder, "Death and Dying: A Comparative Study of the Attitudes and Mental Reactions towards Death and Dying," *Psychoanalytic Review*, 20 (1933), 133.
14. S. Freud, *Thoughts for the Times on War and Death*. Collected Papers, Vol. 4 (London: Hogarth Press, 1948), p. 288.

15. H. Feifel, (Ed.) *The Meaning of Death* (New York: McGraw-Hill, 1959).
16. *Ibid.* See also, H. Feifel, "Some Aspects of the Meaning of Death," in *Clues to Suicide*, E. Shneidman, and N. Farberow, (Eds.) (New York: McGraw-Hill, 1957).
17. W. Bromberg, and P. Schilder, "The Attitude of Psychoneurotics towards Death," *Psychoanalytic Review*, 23 (1936), 1.
18. F. Deutsch, "Euthanasia: A Clinical Study," *Psychoanalytical Quarterly*, 5 (1936), 347.
19. T. Hackett, and A. Weisman, *op. cit.*
20. J. Steward, "Tribes of the Montana: An Introduction," in *Handbook of South American Indians*, J. H. Steward, (Ed.), *Bulletin Bureau of American Ethnology*, 3 (1948), 143. Smithsonian Institution. Washington, D.C. See also, W. Cannon, *op. cit.*
21. E. Lindemann, "Symptomatology and Management of Acute Grief," *American Journal of Psychiatry*, 101 (1944), 141.
22. D. Beatty, "Shall We Talk About Death?" *Pastoral Psychology*, 6 (1955), 11; R. Fairbanks, "Ministering to the Dying," *Journal of Pastoral Care*, 2 (1948), 6.
23. R. Bulger, "The Dying Patient and His Doctor," *Harvard Medical Alumni Bulletin*, 34 (1960), 23; P. Chodoff, "A Psychiatric Approach to the Dying Patient," CA: *Bulletin Cancer Progress*, 10 (1960), 29.
24. I. Janis, *op. cit.*
25. H. Feifel, (Ed.), *op. cit.*

Part 4.

Ceremony, The Self, and Society

INTRODUCTION

Death, like birth, puberty, and marriage is a most significant event, not only for the individual but also for society. The responses and reactions engendered by death have a social as well as a personal immediacy. Like most profound events death is universally recognized and set off by ritual and ceremony.

In this final section the three contributors discuss the question of the meaning of the dramaturgical celebration of death in society and its significance for the community as well as the bereaved individual. Approaching the subject of ritual from three widely different perspectives, Mandelbaum, Warner, and Paz provide us with insights and analyses which contribute not only to our understanding of the role of ritual and ceremony in the face of death, but which also assist us to comprehend its place and purpose in our changing American society. Ultimately, Mandelbaum says, the question every society must answer is: "What to do about death?" In examining death rites from five widely separated cultures, he illustrates the great range of ways in which that question is answered.

The funeral, Mandelbaum concludes, serves three "manifest" purposes: (1) the disposal of the body, (2) aiding the bereaved to reorient themselves from the shock of death, and (3) publicly acknowledging and commemorating a death while asserting the viability of the group. He points out, however, that the funeral can have other "latent" functions which are not so readily seen or understood, but which are nonetheless important. These "latent" functions Mandelbaum illustrates by citing the funeral customs of the Kota of South India. The economic and reciprocal social obligations that extend from the immediate family to the village, and from there to the larger Kota society are remembered, re-enacted, and reinforced in the course of a funeral. In this way the role taken by a participant in the funeral not only reflects his position in Kota society, but also reaffirms the social order itself. Further, the obligations placed upon all members of the deceased's family, such as style of dress, demeanor, preparation of food, restricted social intercourse, both identify and demonstrate family cohesion. The extended kinship system beyond the family, moreover, is also acknowledged and affirmed by the funeral. Members of the larger family console the survivors as well as share in the expense of the ceremony itself.

Clan membership and village affiliation and participation in other social groups are acknowledged and represented in the funeral ceremony. Through the participation in the funeral of neighboring peoples and other non-Kotas, an individual is presented with and reminded of the various parts and personnel of his social order. Participation in the ceremony, the procession, the funeral pyre, the feast, the dancing, all add to the sense of being a part of a larger social whole, just as the strict order of precedence in the conduct of the ceremony reminds one that there is structure and order in the social system.

The funeral, finally, is a "rite of passage." As such it not only marks the completion of a life, but also reaffirms the social character of human existence.

Mandelbaum, like our previous contributors, recognizes that bereavement may well be an occasion for extremely complex and contradictory emotions. Love of the dead and loathing for the corpse, the desire to preserve the bond with the deceased and simultaneously to break it, catch survivors on the horns of ambivalence.

Mandelbaum goes further than Volkart and the others, however, and suggests that traditional funeral rites need not always serve to repair the damage to the social fabric or console the bereaved. Mandelbaum cites an instance in a Javanese town where the traditional funeral ceremony merely aggravated the sorrow of the survivors and provoked social discord. The principal difficulty he reports was that the rites and ceremonies appropriate to an agricultural farm community were inappropriate for town dwellers and when performed failed to meet their emotional and social needs and expectations.

Mandelbaum's discussion of the various elements that contributed to the failure of the Javanese funeral affords us a comparison with certain changes occurring in the United States which promise to have their impact upon the traditional American funeral. From what has been discussed previously it is quite apparent that in the United States death in our small urban families has a sharply different meaning from the day of the extended, multigenerational family and the large rural homestead. Following Volkart, it can be said that the death crisis which survivors today face is more profoundly disruptive than ever before. The denial of death and the deritualization of mourning growing apace in America today parallel and reflect other significant changes apparent in family life. These changes can be identified briefly as: (1) from predominance of the religious to predominance of the secular, (2) from a large group to a small group, (3) from a stable to a mobile group, (4) from an adult-centered to a child-centered family, (5) from a communal family-ideology to a democratic one, (6) from an integrated to an individualized group, and (7) from a neighborhood-enclosed family to an isolated family in an urban environment.

Such changes in the structure of American family life mean of course that the role of the bereaved person changes. Bereavement, as has already been pointed out, is not only grief felt and expressed but is also the symbolization and dramatization of the death itself. The funeral, traditionally, has been a part of that dramatization. It would seem that the modern funeral ceremony, if it is to be effective in aiding the bereaved individual cope with his loss and his grief, must be responsive to these new social facts. A ceremony which no longer appropriately symbolizes the understood meaning of death, or fails to dramatize correctly the change that has overtaken the living and the dead, can create confusion and possible anger and frustration on the part of the bereaved. Such concern for the place of ritual in contemporary America can be seen in the emergence of funeral reform societies and their vigorous assault upon the traditional funeral. For them, ritual for the dead is viewed as empty and formalistic, a conspicuous waste of time and money, of little worth to either the quick or the dead. The performance and repetition of ritual is seen as being an end in itself instead of augmenting social unity, serving sacred purposes, or enhancing the sense of self.

Funeral reform movements give expression to this attitude by recommending the donation of one's body to medical science research, or advising private cremation without public services. In this way the advocates of funerary reform believe that what they see as the disintegrating and dysfunctional formalism of ritual can be circumvented.

The ritual of the funeral, however, may be avoided in this country in quite another way. Implicit in the social changes and trends just discussed is the possibility of extensive age-grading and the isolation and depersonalization of those who no longer can cope with the tempo and demands of these changes. Such a development has already occurred in the retirement city movement. Here for the first time is the promise that men might be able to avoid almost entirely the grief and anguish of death. By encouraging the aged members of the society to congregate in segregated communities, familial and friendship commitments can be made fewer by time and distance, and emotional and social bonds loosened. Physically and emotionally separated from those most likely to die, the individual can be freed of the anguish and shock he would otherwise experience from the death of such persons. Herein may lie a form of modern man's "conquest of death."

The social strain and the severe psychological tension that are reported today in connection with mourning and burial rites reflect the conflicts and structural dissolutions and attempted reintegrations that are so characteristic of our changing world. Simply stated: the meaning of a prayer today is lost upon a person who holds no religious beliefs. So too, a ceremony that invites all to mourn a death presents serious difficulties for the person who has come to believe his grief is a private and personal thing. Some young couples today, for instance, see their life as a private affair and choose a civil or nonpublic wedding as a result. Reasons of practicality or economy only partially explain this choice. We must recognize that such a restricted ceremony serves to dramatize for them their perception of a nonreligious or nonsacred world and their place in it. So too can it be said in the case of the funeral. A funeral that attempts to represent relationships, ideas, or values which the individual no longer believes or holds true may thwart and frustrate him rather than achieve its intended end.

This issue of the sacred and secular worlds is most perceptibly drawn by our last two contributors. Warner in his paper, "The City of the Dead," describes the symbolic significance of the cemetery for our traditionally death-defying (religious) society and the part played by the attendant functionaries of death—the clergyman, the doctor, and the funeral director.

The cemetery, Warner points out, expresses as well as reflects the basic beliefs and values of a society, what the persons of men are, and their place in both the temporal and spiritual worlds. The cemetery, like its counterpart the funeral, is a visible reminder of man's fate as well as a symbol of the dual nature of reality, its twin attributes of the spirit and the flesh.

More than 70 million persons in the United States are no longer church-affiliated. This fact is no better illustrated than in the changing patterns of dying and attitudes toward death observed in this country and in the attendant conflict and confusion that presently prevails in regard to these changes. Not the least disturbed are those whose function it is to deal with the dying and moribund. Warner's discussion of the waning role of the cleric, and, most particularly, the Protestant minister, the emerging role of the doctor, and the contradictory place of the funeral director as performing functionaries in this "rite of passage" serves to point up again the change in emphasis and shift in attitude regarding the phenomenon of death.

In his article, "The Day of the Dead," Paz uses the Mexican fiesta to remind us of the emotionally rich content of the world of the sacred as well as to delineate man's perceived place in that world. In the dual reality of the sacred, time stands still, man and society are continually reborn, and the funeral and the fiesta are linked as gifts of regeneration to be given and received. Death in such a world is not the end of finite existence but a phase in an infinite cycle of life, death, and resurrection. As such, death serves to mirror our life, the fiesta announces our identity, and the funeral reminds us of our fate.

In gross contrast, modern death, Paz says, is impersonal. It has no significance that transcends it. Rather, it is viewed merely as the inevitable conclusion of a natural process. As such death lacks meaning, it is merely a fact in a world of facts, and so too,

our lives lose their essence and we must search in vain for our lost
selves.

David G. Mandelbaum

Social Uses of Funeral Rites

Rites performed for the dead generally have important effects for
the living. A funeral ceremony is personal in its focus and is societal
in its consequences. The people of every society have a pattern
for dealing with the death of their fellows. No matter how unpre-
pared an individual may be for the fact of a particular death,
the group must always have some plan of action in the event of
death.

Certain things must be done after a death, whether it occurs
in a very simple or in a highly complex society. The corpse must
be disposed of; those who are bereaved—who are personally shocked
and socially disoriented—must be helped to reorient themselves;
the whole group must have a known way of readjustment after
the loss of one of its members. These things "must" be done in
the sense that they *are* done. When people find that they have
no set pattern for dealing with death—as may occur in newly co-
alesced groups—or when they discover that the former pattern is
no longer a feasible one, they tend quickly to establish some clear
plan for coping with the occasion of death.

These common purposes of funeral rites are accomplished in a
great variety of ways among the different cultures of the world.
Death ceremonies often entail central motifs of a culture; their performance usually helps to bolster the solidarity of the social group.
I shall describe one funeral ceremony, that of the Kota of South India,
in some detail, as an example of rites with complex content and
multiple functions. Funeral rites include both the ritual performed
immediately after the death of a person and also those rites of
mourning, and commemoration which, in many societies, are performed weeks or months after the death. In the Kota cases, our
interest is mainly in the second funeral, the commemorative ceremony staged once a year in a village for all those who have died
in the preceding year.

Reprinted from *The Meaning of Death*, Herman Feifel (Ed.), (New York:
McGraw-Hill), 1959, by permission of the author and publisher.

We shall more briefly examine death rites of other cultures in order to illustrate some general concepts concerning funeral practices. From two American Indian societies come examples showing the possible range in emphasis of death ceremonies. In the one, the Cocopa, the mourning ceremony is the great event of tribal life and one in which tribal wealth—a very meager wealth and therefore all the more precious—is extravagantly expended. In the other society, that of the Hopi, a funeral ceremony is played down and hurried over. From the Hebridean island of Barra, we have an example of funeral rites conducted according to the ritual of the Roman Catholic Church, but performed with significant local characteristics as well.

How funeral rites may reflect psychological ambivalence is indicated in the example of the Apache death observances. An analysis of a particular funeral in a town in Java shows that, under certain circumstances, the performance of a funeral ceremony may rouse social conflict. Discussion of these examples can serve as an introduction to the study of funeral ceremonies, one of the universals of human social experience.

1

The Kotas are a people who live in seven small villages which are interspersed among the villages of their neighbors on a high plateau, the Nilgiri Hills, in South India. The height and inaccessibility of the plateau formerly isolated the tribal peoples who lived on it from the main currents of Indian civilization.

That isolation was first broken during the middle of the nineteenth century, and since then many other peoples, English and Indian, have come to enjoy the cool heights or to work there. As a result of these contacts, the cultures of the indigenous Nilgiri folk have been changed. In many ways, the Kotas are now much like typical villagers of low caste in the surrounding plains, but their funeral rites—though altered in recent generations—still follow much of the ancient form.

The Kotas observe two funeral ceremonies: the first, called the "Green Funeral," takes place shortly after a death and it is then that the body is cremated; the second, called the "Dry Funeral," is held once a year (or once in two years) for all the deaths that have occurred since the last Dry Funeral was celebrated.[1] The terms are an analogy to a cut plant. At the first funeral the loss is green and fresh in the mind; at the second it is dried out, sere.

At the first funeral, a bit of skull bone is taken from the ashes of the pyre and reverently cached away until the second funeral. The Dry Funeral extends over eleven days and comes to a climax when each relic from the year's deaths is carried off to the cremation ground and, after complex ritual acts, the relics are recremated. The first funeral is attended by the close relatives and friends of the deceased. The second funeral is a grand occasion, attended by people from all the Kota villages and by non-Kotas as well.

Why is there a second funeral—why does not the first suffice? The Kotas give two reasons: one religious, the other social.

The religious reason is that the spirit of the dead person does not finally depart for the "Motherland," the Kota afterworld, until the second funeral has been completed. Only then is the spirit purified enough to reach God. The social reason is that the dead man continues to have certain attributes of social personality until his second funeral. Most importantly, a widow is still her late husband's wife up to the conclusion of the Dry Funeral. If she becomes pregnant after his physical death but before his second funeral, the child is his, shares in his name, clan, and property. In this society, biological paternity is considerably less important than sociological paternity. Hence the faithful widow of a man who has died without a son will conscientiously try to become pregnant before the end of his Dry Funeral. The dead man's right to a child of her womb ceases only after her first menstrual period following the second funeral.

In a way, the Kotas endow society rather than nature with the last word on whether a man has really died. The process, to be sure, begins with his physical demise, but it is not until people perform a Dry Funeral for him that his spirit departs from earth and his social status is finally deleted.

The emphasis of the funeral ritual is much more on speeding the departure of the spirit from this world than it is on the "Motherland" beyond. Kotas are not much interested in the other world and have only sketchy ideas about it. They are quite precise about the purification which the spirit and the surviving kin must undergo in order that the spirit may depart for good.

Among the Kotas, as among many of the peoples of India, contact with death is considered to be deeply polluting. A polluted person is debarred from normal social relations until he has been purified by proper and protracted ritual. The spirit of the dead person, too, is polluted in leaving the body, and the dual funeral rites purify the spirit so that it may take up proper relations in the afterworld.

Between the time of the body's last breath and the climactic end of the Dry Funeral, the lingering spirit is dangerous to men, especially to the deceased's closest kin. The climax comes when a pot is smashed, at the proper ritual juncture, in the cremation ground beyond the village. At that signal all who have attended the ceremony—that is to say, most of the villagers and many visitors—run back to the village without looking behind them. The living go one way, the dead another. The rite is always successful, the dead never return to plague the living as occurs in some societies. This says much about Kota self-confidence and cultural assurance.

The Dry Funeral extends over eleven days and involves villagers and visitors in a series of ceremonial roles which they play out in a fixed sequence, like the acts of a play. And any great ceremony is indeed like a dramatic performance. It has well-defined roles and acts because it must be performed over and again, in similar ways, by different players.

There are two broad categories of roles: those of the kinsmen of the dead person and those of his fellows in the community. His kin are the bereaved who are being purified and restored to society; his kith—fellow villagers and other Kotas—help restore the bereaved and help speed the spirit on its way.

On the first morning of the Dry Funeral, a band of musicians gathers and plays a lament. With the opening notes of the funeral tune, it becomes clearly apparent, even to a stranger, which villagers have lost a relative during the past year. Bereaved women stop in their tracks. A rush of sorrow suffuses them; they sit down where they are, cover their heads with their shoulder cloths, and wail and sob through much of that day and the next. Men of a bereaved household have much to do in preparation for the ceremony and do not drop everything to mourn aloud as do the bereaved women. But even they stop from time to time to weep.

Most grief-stricken of all are the widows and widowers. They must observe the most stringent mourning taboos and undergo the most extensive purificatory ritual. Much of the ritual of the funerals revolves about them. The siblings and children of a dead person have important, but less extensive, roles to play in the ceremony. Interestingly, the parents of a dead person have no formal part in the funeral. They may be personally as grief-stricken as bereaved parents can be in any society, but the cultural plan of the ritual does not make special provision for them. They may not even go through the formal gestures and symbols of mourning.

Leading roles in the category of participants who are not bereaved kinsmen are taken by priests. They lead in the ritual, except for certain especially sensitive acts such as setting flame to the funeral pyre. Then a specially chosen boy leads. A boy must lead because he is pure; his youth has preserved him from those defiling experiences which tarnish any man, even a priest. Other ceremonial roles are taken, respectively, by secular officers, fellow villagers, visiting Kota villagers, and by neighboring people who are not Kotas.

The ceremony falls into four main acts: First there is a week during which the year's dead are memorialized one by one. During that week strict mourning taboos are observed by bereaved kinsmen; other villagers dance every night, partly as a distraction from the mourners, partly to show both the viability and the concern of society.

The next act takes place on the day of the second cremation. A procession winds out of the village; in it are men carrying funeral goods to be placed on the pyre. The bit of skull bone is taken out and carried to the cremation ground. There the bone, the goods, and the personal ornaments of the widow or widower are placed on the pyre and it is set alight. The bereaved and some of the participants spend the night at the cremation ground.

The third phase of the ceremony begins when the morning star is seen by those who have spent the night at the funeral place. The mood changes abruptly. There is dancing and feasting; widows and widowers perform rituals in several stages which bring them progressively closer to normal social life. At nightfall the pot is smashed, all run back to the place of life, the village. That night the widows and widowers have sexual relations, preferably with a sibling of the dead spouse, thus symbolizing yet another step back to normal relations.

Finally there are two days of singing and dancing. The village houses are ritually purified. Then the visitors leave and villagers take up the ordinary round of life again.

By these roles and these prescriptions for action, Kota culture provides a way of answering the question which Kota society and every society must answer—what to do about death? The body is properly removed. The bereaved are successfully brought through their shock and sorrow back to normal status and relations. The villagers duly commemorate the death and turn back to everyday pursuits with a sense of having done the right and proper things about the social loss.

These are the manifest purposes accomplished by the ceremony, the purposes which villagers recognize and can explain. But the Dry Funeral celebration has other functions as well which are not so apparent to the participants, which are more implicit than explicit.

One such function is the reaffirmation of the social order. The role taken by each participant has to do with one or another of the groupings which make up Kota and Nilgiri society. These groupings range from the family, through the kinship circle, to the village, the Kota people, the Nilgiri peoples. There are economic and social obligations entailed in each of the groupings. These reciprocal obligations are remembered, re-enacted, and thus reinforced in the course of the ceremony.

The cohesion of the family is then clearly demonstrated. All in a bereaved household work hard to provide the necessary goods for the pyre and food for the feast. All in the deceased's family stay together in the house during the first week of the Dry Funeral, dressed in old and tattered clothes, hair unkempt, voices low, sadness heavy over all the household.

Kin relationship beyond the family is also reaffirmed during the ceremony. Relatives come to console the bereaved family and contribute to the funeral expenses. Every Kota who considers himself related to the dead person makes a point of attending the Dry Funeral and bowing to the relic of the deceased before it is recremated.

Other social groupings are represented in the ceremony: clan membership is acknowledged and confirmed; village affiliation—both of the dead and of the living—is shown. At certain points, a representative from each of the Kota villages plays a formal part in the ritual, thus reminding the assembly of the unity of the Kotas. There is also a place in the ceremony for associates of the bereaved families who are not Kotas; representatives of the neighboring peoples attend and, in their proper way, participate. A Kota is thus reminded, in the context of the funeral ceremony, of the parts and personnel of his social order. He can see, demonstrated in action, how its various parts serve him and must be served by him.

Participation in the ceremony has yet another effect on the participants. It gives them a renewed sense of belonging to a social whole, to the entire community of Kotas. The villagers and visitors go in procession, led by music, to clear the cremation ground, build the pyre, prepare the feast, and do other work in preparation for the ceremony. These group activities and the dancing which follows not only bring general enjoyment but enhance feelings of social unison.

There is no inclination to enlarge the intensity or scope of the mourners' grief. The bereaved are given a formal opportunity for complete self-immersion in grief, but there is also an effort to curtail their sorrow, to distract them by pleasing figures of the dance. Funeral dancing is not approved in scriptural Hinduism, and as the Kotas have become more influenced by the practices of high-caste Hindu villagers, they have become more uncertain about the propriety of dancing at a funeral.

The ceremony is being changed in this and in other directions, but it is still an occasion when many Kotas work together and together accomplish a religiously proper and personally enjoyable goal, the successful staging of the ceremony. This joint accomplishment bolsters Kota cohesion and sometimes helps smooth over factional rifts.

A third social consequence of enacting the cermony is that the order of precedence within Kota society is formally repeated and in that manner officially reinforced. Just as a participant gets from the ceremony a sense of the social whole and of the various groupings within the whole, so does he also derive a sense of the proper order in social life. For example, there is a strict order of precedence in the funeral procession, at the feast, and in all phases of the rite. Briefly put, the order is this: all men come before all women; officials and elders before all other men; officials before elders; religious officials before secular officials. Within any category, seniors in age come before their juniors.

This same order of rank applies in all life situations, as in the serving of an ordinary meal. But at great occasions like the second funeral, the whole assembly of Kotas formally, publicly, and impressively rehearses the proper precedence among the constituent parts of society.

Another social consequence which flows from performing the Dry Funeral is the completion of the proper order of a person's career. Every social transition is marked by some appropriate ritual. Hence the final step should also be celebrated appropriately by a person's kin and fellows. "A proper progress through life means a funeral." This comment by Raymond Firth on the people of the Polynesian island of Tikopia applies to the Kotas as well. "The death of every person must be followed by a reaffirmation of the social character of human existence."[2]

The Dry Funeral performance also has personal, psychological meanings for individual men and women. A Kota woman whose husband has died, reacts in ways which are the common, human manifestations of grief. She appears shocked and disoriented by her loss; she can think of nothing but her grief, she is bewildered, she withdraws. Her keening is culturally stereotyped, and much of her specific behavior as a mourning widow is prescribed by the cultural requirements for the role of new widow but in seeing her, we understand that there is also personal sorrow and genuine disorientation in her behavior.

For this widow, as well as for other bereaved persons, the performance of the Dry Funeral effectively assuages grief and provides personal reorientation. After the first outburst of grieving at the Green Funeral, there is a period of months of relative quietude. The second funeral provides an occasion for summoning up a person's latent grief, for expressing it, and then for terminating it. In the eleven days of the ceremony there is ample opportunity for venting one's sorrow. Perhaps for that reason the grief is more easily and finally dispersed after the rite. The several phases of the ceremony bring the bereaved back to normal status in gradual and socially approved stages.[3]

As in any major ceremony, incidental consequences ensue. Young men find occasion then to look over girls from various villages. A mature man who has prospered may take the occasion to demonstrate his achievements by providing lavish funeral goods, perhaps for a distant relative. One man, whose main personal victories came from his wide knowledge of ritual, found special satisfaction in playing a director's role in guiding the complex rites of the Dry Funeral. Such personal purposes, no less than the larger societal needs, are served by the celebration of the Dry Funeral.

2

Comparable purposes, both personal and social, are accomplished by the performance of death ceremonies in other societies. But there are great variations in the manner of bringing about such integrative results. As we examine the range of variation we find that among some peoples, funeral ceremonies are great public events; in other societies they are conducted swiftly, quietly, almost furtively. The whole of a social order may be represented at the funeral, or only a small section of it.

Two American Indian tribes of the Southwest, the Cocopa and the Hopi, respectively exemplify extremes of emphasis and of de-emphasis, in the observance of funeral rites. Among the Cocopa, death ceremonies are the major events of tribal life; among the Hopi, they are brief and hurried affairs.

The Cocopa, who lived mainly along what is now the Arizona-Sonora border, practiced some agriculture, but depended largely on hunting and gathering. Theirs was a relatively simple culture; they possessed few goods, they conducted few ceremonies.[4] The whole tribe, in the late nineteenth century, consisted of some twelve hundred people, scattered in small settlements. People from several settlements might come together for a harvest fiesta, but many more would gather for the occasion of a mourning ceremony. The death ceremonies were the principal religious and social events of the tribe.

Soon after a death, the mourning members of the family became transported into an ecstacy of violent grief behavior. They cried, wailed, and screamed from the time of the death, without much interruption, for twenty-four hours or more until the body was cremated. The cremation ritual was directed mainly at inducing the spirit of the dead person to go on to the afterworld. To help persuade the spirit to depart, clothes, food, and equipment were destroyed so that the spirit could have these things in the hereafter.

Some time after the cremation, and with purposes analogous to those of the Kota second funeral, a Cocopa family would give a mourning ceremony to commemorate its dead. Then a large part of the tribe would gather, there would be speeches and lamentations for the dead. At all other times, the names of the dead could not be mentioned; at this mourning ceremony dead relatives were recalled publicly, summoned to mingle with the assembled tribesmen, and impersonated by men and women dressed in ceremonial costumes to resemble specific deceased persons. Presents were given to visitors, and valuable goods, including a ceremonial house and the ceremonial costumes, were burned for the benefit of the spirits. Kelly gives his impression that ". . . this action symbolized a desire to be free of the dead, and that the ceremony served, in part, to bring lurking spirits into the open, and, in dramatic fashion, to rid the earth of them by banning them again in the physical form of the costumes worn by the impersonators."⁵

The cremation ritual dealt mainly with the disposal of the body and with helping the bereaved over the initial shock. At the subsequent mourning ceremony, the focus was more on religious and social integration than on the personal adjustment of the bereaved. Yet this very strengthening of social integration doomed the Cocopa to a relatively sparse level of subsistence. Because funeral rites were the main expression of Cocopa tribal enterprise and because the destruction and lavish consumption of wealth were integral parts of the funeral complex, the Cocopa "were forever barred from the accumulation of capital goods, the development of complex tools and equipment, and the building of elaborate houses, temples or monuments. They were, in effect, held to a hand-to-mouth existence which was more efficiently pursued by independent families and small political units."⁶

The old tradition of death practices continued in force when Kelly worked among the Cocopa between 1940 and 1947. At that time, not one of the tribe had acquired and kept more wealth than a bare minimum of household goods and a secondhand automobile. No Cocopa had dared to inherit anything, money or property, from a dead relative. The one change in this, perhaps indicative of changes to come, was that in a few families a dead relative's automobile was not burned but was traded in for another model.

3

At the other end of the state of Arizona and at a vastly different level of culture, live the Hopi. They are one of the Pueblo tribes—agriculturists who follow a highly ritualized, complex way of life. In recent years, automobiles and other appurtenances of Western material culture have become familiar sights in the eleven Hopi villages. Yet the traditional ways of religion, of ceremonialism, of social organization are still followed by many Hopi. Funeral rites continue to be held in the old tradition, and that tradition is one which minimizes the whole event of death and funerals.

The Hopi do not like the idea of death and they are afraid of the newly dead. Their funeral rites are small, private affairs, quickly over and best forgotten. Those who are bereaved may well feel the pain of loss as deeply as do mourners in any society, but they give themselves over to no overt transport of grief of the kind expected of mourners among the Cocopa, Kotas, and in many another society.   The Hopi cherish the middle way: they seek to avoid excess of any kind; their most desirable universe is one in which all is measured, deliberate, and under control.   Weeping may be unavoidable, but it is not encouraged, for any cause.   If one must weep— Hopi parents have told their children—it is best to weep alone, outside the village, where no one can see.[7]

As soon as a death occurs in a family, the women of the household do lament; they cry a bit and speak of their loss.   But there is no formal wailing nor is there a public gathering.   The body is quickly prepared for burial and put into its grave as soon as possible. A woman relative washes the head; prayer feathers and a cotton mask are put on the corpse; it is wrapped and carried off straightway by the men of the household.

As with the Kotas and many other peoples of the world, contact with death brings pollution.   Before persons who are thus polluted can resume normal relations with men and with the gods, they must divest themselves of the taint.   Hence, on their return from the burying ground, the members of the household purify themselves ritually.   The next morning a male relative of the deceased puts meal and prayer sticks on the new grave, prays for rain—a central good of Hopi life—and asks the spirit not to return to the village. To ensure the departure of the deceased, the relative symbolically closes the trail back to the village by drawing charcoal lines across it.   When he comes back to the bereaved household, all wash their hair and purify themselves in piñon smoke.   "They should then try to forget the deceased and continue with life as usual."[8]

The spirit is believed to rise from the grave on the fourth morning and to follow the path to the land of the dead, somewhere in the general area of the Grand Canyon.   It then becomes one of the great assembly of supernaturals.   With these the Hopi are greatly concerned.   The supernatural spirits are not Hopi; they are a different class of being and Hopi culture provides rules and means for dealing with them.   The spirits are depersonalized entities; they do not have the characteristics of deceased friends and relatives. The Hopi go to great lengths to make sure that the dichotomy of quick and dead is sharp and clear.   Many rites having to do with spirits conclude with a ritual device which breaks off contact between mortals and spirits.[9]

The Hopi are one people who express no desire whatsoever to recall the memory of their deceased, whether for good or ill.   Some years ago a visitor to one of the Hopi villages took a picture of a young woman. On a later visit to the village, he learned that the young woman had died, so he presented the enlarged photograph which he had with him to her mother. The next day the mother begged him to take the picture back, saying that it reminded her too vividly of her bereavement. The anthropologist's footnote to this account adds that "no Pueblo Indian of the older generation wants a picture of a deceased relative."[10] Among the Hopi and other Pueblo peoples, "Fear of the dead and the will to forget them as individuals are extreme, but the dead have to remove from the living, not the living from the dead."[11] That is, the mourners do not have to destroy all mementos and property of the deceased; that would be quite contrary to Hopi precepts of balance, moderation, and thrift. Property is inherited and distributed in prescribed ways among various classes of heirs.

The emphasis in the funeral ceremony is quite different from other motifs in Hopi practice. Most life-cycle and calendrical rites are conducted with very elaborate ceremony, in contrast to the quick and meager ritual of the funeral occasion. Hopi society is an elaborate structure of interlocking organizations. In most ceremonies, members of different socio-religious organizations take part or attend at some stage. But the funeral ceremony is restricted mainly to the immediate household; there is little provision to show the multiple roles which the deceased may have occupied in the social network. The sovereign desire is to dismiss the body and the event. The urge is to dispatch the spirit to another realm where it will not challenge the Hopi ideals of good, harmonious, happy existence in *this* world and where, as a being of another and well-known kind, it can be methodically controlled by the ritual apparatus of Hopi culture.

4

Quite a different outlook on death and on life is shown in the funeral rites of the Roman Catholic people of Barra, the southernmost island group in Scotland's Outer Hebrides. Burial rites there, as F. G. Vallee describes them,[12] take place in five stages. Only the close relatives are involved in the first; the total community is included in the last stage. When the final funeral bell tolls, every islander participates, in some degree, in the observances of the occasion.

The first act of the sequence begins when it becomes clear that a person is approaching his end. The close relatives rally around to help. It is important to make sure that a priest will be present at the proper time to bestow the last rites—these rites are a most essential element in the "happy death" which the Barra Catholic asks for in his prayers.

Death is not a tabooed subject for conversation. A failing person may well discuss with his friends and relatives the likelihood of his being alive, say, next autumn. Nor is there in this culture any great dread of the departed spirit. "In no case that I knew of was it assumed that the soul of a particular individual went to hell after death, no matter how evil his life in terms of the community *mores*."[13]

When death occurs, the next stage of the ceremony is set in train. The news is spread throughout the community of some two thousand people. No group recreation takes place until after the burial; those in the neighborhood abstain from their regular work.

The chief mourner—the man most closely related to the deceased—goes to the public house to buy whiskey and beer for those who will assemble and to arrange for coffin and shroud. This is the first public act in the ritual sequence; the chief mourner receives condolences from the men at the bar.

As the news spreads, those who have had close social ties with the deceased gather to pay their respects. Cousins, in-laws, and close friends come. They bring supplementary food and refreshments; some of them stay through the night, which is the night of the wake. The "watchers" during the night are mostly men. They talk through the night about seamanship, fishing, sheep, and similar subjects of male interest. Drinking whiskey and beer is part of the ritual idiom but there is no immoderation in drinking. A few women, mainly those of the household, are present and busy themselves about the kitchen. The men take turns through the night in keeping vigil beside the body. Several times during the night the whole company goes into the death room and all pray.

From Vallee's account of these formalities, it seems reasonable to infer that the wake serves both psychological and social purposes. The assembled kinsmen and friends are solicitous and helpful, giving psychic support to the bereaved. In their presence the mourners can give necessary vent to their grief but are constrained from intense and incapacitating brooding about their loss. The participants at the wake, by their presence, also assure the mourners (and themselves as well) that the bonds of kinship and friendship continue, that the death has not irreparably ruptured the web of social life.

In the afternoon on the day after the wake, the coffin is carried in procession to the chapel. In the funeral procession are the deceased's relatives, friends, and neighbors. Every man is given a turn at helping to bear the coffin, no matter how short the distance it is carried.

The final stage of the ceremony begins with a Requiem Mass on the following morning. Then the coffin is carried, again in procession, to the cemetery. This is a larger procession than on the previous day; people from a wide area attend. At the grave the priest conducts the burial service. After the interment, mourners disperse to kneel and pray at graves of other deceased relatives. Members of the bereaved household return home and are visited by their kinsmen.

The name of the dead person is recalled at High Mass each Sunday for a year in every Catholic congregation on the island. In the dead person's home church his name is formally mentioned in this way for two years after his death.

The people of Barra seem to have a smooth and easy set of patterns for dealing with the event of death. There appears, at least overtly, to be no great fear of the dead, no anxiety about speeding on the departed spirit, and no avoidance of the topic or of the memory of the deceased. Most men and women participate in some ten to fifteen funerals in their neighborhood every year; death ceremonies for them are normal events. Vallee notes how the sacred and secular elements are blended in the funeral. The occasion is a religious one complete with priest, prayers, and holy services. "Yet in the midst of these forms and acts of sanctity, mourners chat easily of ships and sheep, are concerned with ensuring that there is no shortage of liquor and food. Frequent attendance at these rites does more than breed familiarity with death; it intensifies the awareness of belonging to a community."[14]

The ritual sequence is complex; only the bare outline has been sketched here. It is a clearly known, frequently repeated sequence; hence hundreds can smoothly and spontaneously participate in a funeral. Even the few Protestants on the island know precisely when to take part and when to withdraw from the rites.

Funerals on Barra differ from those of our previous examples in that they are regulated and led by priests of the Roman Catholic

Church—an institution which extends far beyond the given community in space, time, and authority. Catholic ritual prescribes certain funeral rites and Catholic dogma provides certain beliefs about death. But there is also a great deal in any Catholic funeral which is not laid down in the canons of the Church. In Barra, for example, the wake, the whiskey, and the procession are important elements of the ceremony, but are not prescribed by the Church.

Among other peoples who are Roman Catholic in religion, a funeral ceremony includes the same prescribed rites, but it may also include many different elements of social participation, cultural practice, and emotional emphasis. The Church does decree certain requirements for funerals and will not countenance practices which run counter to its theological precepts. But the limits of these requirements are quite broad; within them there is notable variation between, say, a Catholic funeral on Barra and one in Bavaria or in the Philippines. Hence, while funeral rites on Barra appear to be smoothly attuned to social and personal needs, among another people of the same religion the funeral may not allay personal tensions or promote social concord in the same manner as on Barra.

5

Sometimes the very form of the funeral reflects personal ambivalences which arise from conflicting social and cultural conditions. Thus the Chiricahua and Mescalero Apache Indians of the American Southwest show two kinds of formal response to bereavement. Both are broadly similar to those previously mentioned for another southwestern tribe, the Cocopa. On the one side there is vigorous and public expression of grief by the relatives of a deceased; on the other side there is rigorous effort to banish all trace of the death and all memory of the deceased. There is a period when it is proper for mourners to give vent to their grief, and then they do so in quite violent fashion. At other times, the name and memory of a dead person must be expunged from recall and remembrance.

In his analysis of Apache death customs, M. E. Opler notes that "there is the tendency to publicly signify grief and attest to the loss, and an elaborately socialized machinery for banishing that grief and the objects and words which might awake it."[15]

These apparently contradictory practices, Opler suggests, are one manifestation of the ambivalence an Apache feels toward his relatives. Throughout his life an Apache is taught to assist and support his relatives, to avenge their wrongs at any cost. He in turn depends on them and under the economic and social conditions of aboriginal Apache life could not survive without them. But he was also taught to be independent and self-reliant, and this quality too was necessary for successful living in his natural and social environment.

The two demands, for group solidarity and for individual independence, often created conflict within the Apache individual. He generally acceded to the demands of his family group, but there was left in him a residue of resentment and hostility toward them. This hostility was shown in various ways. One was the belief that every Apache who received supernatural power was obliged to pay for this power with the life of a close relative, perhaps one of his children. Since "practically every Apache realized a supernatural experience," a person commonly feared those of his close relatives who were known to have particularly powerful supernatural helpers.[16]

Hence the two kinds of bereavement reaction, Opler suggests, reflect the personal ambivalence which an Apache felt about his relatives—including his parents, his siblings, and his wife's parents and siblings. The permitted florid mourning behavior expressed the emotional loss of a loved person on whom one was greatly dependent. The strong cultural directives to obliterate all trace of a deceased may be "the result of repressed and unconscious resentment and dislike of relatives which have their roots in the actual circumstances and events of Apache life."[17]

The cultural fiat to mourn and then to dismiss the memory of a dead relative evidently made it easier for an Apache to dismiss the fear he had of the relative when he was alive and of his ghost after he was dead. Such overt fear of one's close kin is not commonly manifested among the various peoples of the world.

More usual in human societies is another sort of ambivalence about death and funeral rites. Bronislaw Malinowski depicted the feelings of bereaved survivors in these words: "The emotions are extremely complex and even contradictory; the dominant elements, love of the dead and loathing of the corpse, passionate attachment to the personality still lingering about the body and a shuddering fear of the gruesome thing that has been left over, these two elements seem to mingle and play into each other."[18] In the Melanesian funeral rites which he had observed, Malinowski commented, there was shown a desire to maintain the tie with the deceased and the parallel tendency to break the bond. By performing the prescribed religious acts, men can resolve this conflict, counteract "the centrifugal forces of fear, dismay, demoralization," and can reintegrate themselves as a group and reestablish their morale.[19]

6

Yet traditional rites are not always sufficient for the occasion and its stress. An illuminating analysis of a funeral in a small town in Java shows how, in that case, the use of the customary funeral ceremony brought on social discord rather than integration and brought more trouble than solace to the bereaved.[20] The principal difficulty lay in the fact that the traditional rites, which were suited to the needs of the occasion in an agricultural, village, folk milieu, are not as appropriate to the needs of the villagers who are transplanted to town life, where economic and political orientations differ from those of the village.

The episode occurred in 1954 when a ten-year-old boy, who was living with his uncle and aunt in one of the crowded neighborhoods of a town in east-central Java, suddenly died. The uncle dispatched a telegram to the boy's parents and then sent for a Modin, a Moslem religious official, to conduct the funeral in the customary, traditional manner.

In form, the traditional Javanese funeral is a combination of Islamic precept and indigenous practice, of scriptural dogma and local belief. As in the Roman Catholic rites on Barra, the requirements of the universalistic, scriptural religion are met in the idiom of native tradition. In Javanese village tradition, the funeral ceremony is one variety of a generic ceremony, called slametan, which is given at crucial points, not only of the life cycle, but of the agricultural and ceremonial cycle as well.

The slametan is mainly a communal feast, performed under religious auspices, for a group of neighbors. "The demands of the labor—intensive rice and dry-crop agricultural process require the perpetuation of specific modes of technical cooperation and enforce a sense of community in the otherwise rather self-contained families—a sense of community which the slametan clearly reinforces."[21] The traditional funeral slametan is directed by an Islamic official, the Modin, who supervises the preparation of the body for burial, leads in the chanting of Arabic prayers, and reads a graveside speech to the deceased, reminding him of his duties as a believing Moslem.

This ritual form is carried through quickly and in a mood reminiscent of that described for Hopi funerals. The mourners are supposed to be relatively calm and undemonstrative. "Tears are not approved of and certainly not encouraged; the effort is to get the job done, not to linger over the pleasures of grief . . . the whole momentum of the Javanese ritual system is supposed to carry one through grief without severe emotional disturbance."²² Such was the expectation of the dead boy's uncle when he began funeral preparations and sent for the Modin.

But when the Modin came, the uncle's expectation was not realized and, to the great chagrin of the boy's family and their friends, the Modin refused to lead the funeral rites. This untoward, discomfiting, and exceptional refusal came about for these reasons.

There was in 1954 a great cultural-political split in this town, and elsewhere in Java. Those on one side were Islamic purists who wanted to emphasize the scriptural sanctions and diminish the indigenous practices. Those of the other side wanted to stress the indigenous practices and mute the Islamic elements. Allegiance to one or another side was expressed through political affiliation. In this town, the Islamic patriots belonged to the country's largest Moslem party, *Masjumi*, which supported an "Islamic State" for Indonesia rather than a secular republic. Those townsmen who advocated the indigenous tradition belonged to another political party, *Permai*, which was smaller nationally but locally strong. Its platform was a fusion of Marxist politics, anti-Islamic ideas, and nativist religion.

Worried about controlling the conflict between the two parties, the local administrative officer had called together the religious officials, the Modins, most of whom were *Masjumi* leaders. He instructed them not to participate in funeral rites for supporters of the *Permai* party.

Hence, on the morning of July 17, 1954, when a Modin arrived at the house where the boy had died, he saw a *Permai* poster displayed there and refused to perform the ceremony. He rubbed in his refusal by saying piously that since the *Permai* people belonged to another religion, he did not know the correct burial rituals for it. All he knew was Islam.

Though the *Permai* people are anti-Islam, they still had no other funeral rite than that traditionally performed and led by a Modin. The dead boy's uncle had never thought that his political allegiance would present such a distressing problem. The funeral preparations were halted, the people of the bereaved household were distraught, and the uncle exploded in rage—rather uncharacteristic behavior for a Javanese. Friends of the family gathered, but no one knew what to do.

When the dead boy's father and mother arrived, the aunt—who had earlier given vent to loud, unrestrained wailing—now rushed to her sister and the two women "dissolved into wild hysterics." These unusual and shocking outbursts made the assembled people all the more nervous and uneasy.

At last, through the good offices of a go-between, the dead boy's father requested an Islamic funeral, implying that he was not of the *Permai* party. The Modin then carried through the usual burial rites. But three days later, at the first commemorative feast, the usual slametan procedure—which includes an Islamic chant for the dead—was not followed. Instead there was a political speech and philosophical discussion, together with a strange and atypical talk by the dead boy's father expressing his feelings and his confusion.

His confusion arose because the traditional ceremony had become unsuited to his social circumstances. The ceremony functioned well when the group to be consolidated was a set of village neighbors who shared many close ties—economic, religious, personal, social. But in the town neighborhood, such village bonds are not as relevant; the important bonds are based on ideology, class, occupation, and politics rather than on local proximity. Hence the traditional funeral ceremony, when held now in an urban setting, "increasingly served to remind people that the neighborhood bonds they are strengthening through a dramatic enactment are no longer the bonds which emphatically hold them together."[23] The boy's funeral provides an example of the incongruity between the old ceremonial form and the new social conditions. It is likely that this incongruity will not long exist. Ceremonial forms can be changed. In future years these funeral rites may be altered and may then accord better with the broad purposes of personal and social integration for which men, in Java as elsewhere, commonly perform the last rites.

7

"A funeral rite," Raymond Firth observes, "is a social rite *par excellence*. Its ostensible object is the dead person, but it benefits not the dead, but the living."[24] This comment occurs in the course of an analysis of an incident involving a clash of interests in a chief's family in Tikopia. A grandson of the old chief has been lost at sea. The boy's father wants to prepare a suitably elaborate funeral ceremony; his brothers—the other sons of the chief—want to postpone the funeral lest it detract from a festival for the clan gods which the family should soon give in properly lavish style. There is a flare-up of temper; there is mollification by neutral people; finally the funeral is given precedence and familial solidarity is, at least overtly, re-established.

For the very reason that funerals so often are occasions when social solidarity ought to be displayed in a society, they can also present situations where the lack of solidarity is dramatically highlighted. In the Kota Dry Funeral, there is a juncture when all Kotas who are present at the ceremony come forward, one by one, to give a parting bow of respect to the relic of each deceased.

Around this gesture of social unity, violent quarrels often rage.[25] When kinsmen of a deceased Kota are fervent supporters of one of the two opposing factions in Kota society, they may try to prevent a person of the other faction from making this gesture of respect and solidarity. This is tantamount to declaring that those of the other faction are not Kotas at all—a declaration which neither side will quietly accept. Thus a ritual action which symbolized concord has frequently triggered a good deal of discord. Yet among the Kotas, as in other societies, neutral people try to bring about a compromise; the ceremony is somehow completed with as much show of social unity as can be managed—especially for funerals of the great men of the tribe.

Such show of unity is graphically depicted, on the grand scene of European history, by photographs of some memorable funeral corteges. If we turn to the picture of the glittering array of monarchs in the procession behind the coffin of Edward VII or the picture of the more somberly clad pallbearers carrying the coffin of Josef Stalin, we can appreciate that differences may be sunk, if only temporarily, on the occasion of a funeral.

In earlier European history, the State funeral was an important symbol of the continuity of monarchical power. In medieval France, for example, the death of a king might be followed by great disorder, because his successor was not sovereign until his coronation. By the sixteenth century, however, a new king in France exercised full powers from the moment of his predecessor's death. The royal funeral became not only a symbol of proper succession but also one of the agencies for the smooth transfer of power.[26]

Funeral monuments like the Pyramids and the Taj Mahal attest
to the political aspects which have long been entailed in state funerals.
Codes of testamentary law reflect the economic aspects of death
rites. The rites, the codes, the monuments—whether for a great
personage or for an ordinary person—have often expressed religious
ideas of immortality as well as those societal concepts which we
have here discussed.[27]

In some societies, the belief in immortality is considered to be
most important for the consolation of the bereaved; in other societies,
as among the Kotas, the concept of the afterworld is not of any
great interest. At funerals, social forces may be effectively rallied
to solace the mourners or there may be special social conditions
which hamper their readjustment.

In modern American society, E. H. Volkart suggests, such great
attachment to the particular members of one's family is built up
that readjustment becomes very difficult after their death. "Thus
whereas we stress the sense of loss and recognize the need for replacement, basically the culture creates conditions in which the deceased
is irreplaceable because he cannot ever really be duplicated. . . . In
this way the bereaved person has no automatic cultural solution
to the problem of replacement."[28]

American culture has, in certain respects, and for some Americans,
become deritualized. Persons bereaved by a death sometimes find
that they have no clear prescription as to what to do next. In
such cases, each has to work out a solution for himself. After
the typical period of shock and disorganization, these mourners can
receive little help toward personal reorganization. When individual
solutions to such recurrent and poignant problems are repeatedly
made, they may tend to coalesce and to become institutionalized.
Hence it may be that the people who have reacted strongly against
the older rituals—because they were rituals—may institute some
new version of the old ritual forms.

Death ceremonies, like other cultural forms, are changed in time
by those who use them as a result of changes in their social, cultural,
and psychological environments. Yet the fundamental psychological
and social purposes which are accomplished by funeral rites remain
quite similar. These purposes, illustrated in the Kota example, can
be met in many different ways. One way is the extravagant mourning ceremony of the Cocopa; another is the sparse, hurried ceremony
of the Hopi. The death rites may be taken in the community's
normal stride, as in Barra, or may touch on especially conflicting

feelings among the survivors, as with the Apache. A funeral may rouse social conflict, as in the example from Java, but funeral rites are generally intended to be a means of strengthening group solidarity.

Rituals for death can have many uses for life. And the study of these rites can illuminate much about a culture and a society. Thus the Kotas' certainty about the effectiveness of their Dry Funeral provides a clue to their general certainty about dealings with the supernatural. The violent quarrels which have taken place at Kota funerals direct our attention to certain values which they hold most dear. Once we have suitable analyses, from a number of peoples, of the ways in which death ceremonies (and other biologically based universals) fit into, reflect, and reinforce cultural themes, it will be possible to go on to some really interesting problems. For example, the Hopi funeral rites and those in the Javanese town are very dissimilar in specific detail but seem quite alike in mood. Is the similarity only a superficially apparent one, is it an epiphenomenon of little consequence, or does it give evidence of structural similarity of some kind between two societies widely different in the content of their cultures? In this and in other ways, the melancholy subjects of funerals may provide one good entryway to the analysis of cultures and to the understanding of peoples.

References

1. D. G. Mandelbaum, "Form, Variation, and Meaning of a Ceremony," in R. F. Spencer (Ed.), *Method and Perspective in Anthropology* (Minneapolis: University of Minnesota Press, 1954), pp. 60–102.
2. R. Firth, *Elements of Social Organization* (London: Henry E. Walter, Ltd., 1951), p. 64.
3. *Ibid.*, p. 63.
4. W. H. Kelly, "Cocopa Attitudes and Practices with Respect to Death and Mourning," *Southwestern Journal of Anthropology*, 5 (1949), 151–164.
5. *Ibid.*, p. 161.
6. *Ibid.*
7. R. B. Brandt, *Hopi Ethics*, (Chicago: University of Chicago Press, 1954), p. 221.
8. F. Eggan, *Social Organization of the Western Pueblos*, (Chicago, University of Chicago Press, 1950), pp. 57–58.
9. E. A. Kennard, "Hopi Reactions to Death," *American Anthropologist*, 29 (1937), 491–492.
10. M. Titiev, "Old Oraibi," *Papers of the Peabody Museum*, (Cambridge: Harvard University, 1944), Vol. 22, No. 1, p. 21.
11. E. C. Parsons, *Pueblo Indian Religion* (2 vols.), (Chicago: University of Chicago Press, 1939), p. 1150.

12. F. G. Vallee, "Burial and Mourning Customs in a Hebridian Community," *Journal of the Royal Anthropological Institute*, 85 (1955), 119–130.
13. *Ibid.*, p. 121.
14. *Ibid.*, p. 128.
15. M. E. Opler, "An Interpretation of Ambivalence of Two American Indian Tribes," *Journal of Social Psychology*, 7 (1936), 92.
16. *Ibid.*, p. 100.
17. *Ibid.*, p. 107.
18. B. Malinowski, *Magic, Science, and Religion and Other Essays* (Glencoe, Ill.: Free Press, 1948), p. 30.
19. *Ibid.*, pp. 32–35.
20. C. Geertz, "Ritual and Social Change: Javanese Example," *American Anthropologist*, 59 (1957), 32–54.
21. *Ibid.*, p. 36.
22. *Ibid.*, p. 40.
23. *Ibid.*, p. 52.
24. R. Firth, *op. cit.*
25. D. G. Mandelbaum, "The World and the World View of the Kota," in M. Marriott (Ed.), *Village India* (Chicago: University of Chicago Press, 1955), pp. 226–229.
26. R. E. Giesey, "The Royal Funeral Ceremony in Renaissance France," unpublished doctoral dissertation, University of California, Berkeley, 1954.
27. B. S. Puckle, *Funeral Customs*, (London, 1926); M. F. Ashley-Montagu, *Immortality* (New York: Grove Press, 1955); E. Bendann, *Death Customs: An Analytical Study of Burial Rites*, (New York: Knopf, 1930); J. G. Frazer, *The Belief in Immortality and the Worship of the Dead* (3 vols.) (London: Macmillan, 1913–1922).
28. E. H. Volkart (in collaboration with S. T. Michael), "Bereavement and Mental Health," in A. H. Leighton, J. A. Clausen, and R. N. Wilson (Eds.), *Explorations in Social Psychiatry*, (New York: Basic Books, 1957), pp. 299–300.

W. Lloyd Warner

The City of the Dead

The Cemetery

Yankee City cemeteries are collective representations which reflect and express many of the community's basic beliefs and values about what kind of society it is, what the persons of men are, and where

Reprinted from *The Living and Dead* (New Haven: Yale University Press, 1959), 9, by permission of the author and publisher.

each fits into the secular world of the living and the spiritual society of the dead.[1] Whenever the living think about the deaths of others they necessarily express some of their own concern about their own extinction. The cemetery provides them with enduring, visible symbols which help them to contemplate man's fate and their own separate destinies. The cemetery and its gravestones are the hard, enduring signs which anchor each man's projections of his intermost fantasies and private fears about the certainty of his own death—and the uncertainty of his ultimate future—on an external symbolic object made safe by tradition and the sanctions of religion.

The social boundaries of the sacred dead and the secular world of the profane living are set apart and joined *materially* in Yankee City by clearly defined physical limits marked by ordinary walls, fences, and hedges. The living and the dead are *spiritually* joined and divided by ceremonies for the dead—among them funerals which occur daily, Memorial Day rites, and the dedication and consecration of burial ground—which separate the sacred and profane realms by use of these symbolic methods. All are founded on, and give expression to, the feelings and beliefs of the people of Yankee City. Rituals of consecration have transformed a small part of the common soil of the town into a sacred place and dedicated this land of the dead to God, to the sacred souls of the departed, and to the souls of the living whose bodies are destined for such an end. The rituals which establish graveyards tacitly imply formal rules and precepts which define the relations of the profane and sacred worlds of the living and the dead. The funeral—a formal rite of separation of the recently dead from the living—is, broadly speaking, an unending ritual, for although funerals are separate rites, they occur with such continuing frequency that they maintain a constant stream of ritual connection between the dead and the living. Once a year the cult of the dead in the Memorial Day rites for the whole community strengthens and reexpresses what the chain of separate funerals accomplishes throughout the year.

The funeral symbolically removes the *time*-bound individual from control by the forward direction of human time. He no longer moves from the past towards the future, for now (in the minds of the living, he is in the unmoving, sanctified stillness of an ever-present eternity. At death the ageing process, conceptually a form of human time existing in the nature of things, loses its control of the individual. The march of events no longer has meaning for what he has become. His timeless ("eternal") soul is in a

sacred realm where human and social time lose most of their meanings; his dead, ephemeral body becomes part of a process where
human time has little significance. The time of the living as the
society conceives it cannot be understood without knowledge of
"dead" time. In many ways the two are contrary to each other.
As opposites, dead and live time express the duality of existence,
the sacred and the profane, the "controlled" and the "uncontrollable." The ephemeral and the eternal, activity and inertness, are
all part of the meaning of the duality of live and dead time.
The popularity of the play and motion picture "Death takes a Holiday," was built largely on the symbolic point that human time
no longer had control over human destiny; events were timeless
because the *time of death* was no longer in opposition to the *time
of life*. Rather the "holiday" of death meant that the sacred time
of eternity had been substituted for the secular time of man. Holidays and holy days are moments in the calendar where ordinary
time is flouted. The author of the play, however, also made another
point when he used the term "holiday" (rather than "holy day");
he allowed his audience to gratify their longing to translate into
the sacred, eternal time of the dead the pleasant, sensuous world
of the living.

The cemetery, separate and distinct from the living, yet forever
a material part of Yankee City's cultural equipment, bridges these
two times, ending the one and beginning the other. As man changes
physically, the "conveyor belt" of social time redefines his changing
place in the community and moves him onward until finally, at
death, it ceremonially dumps him into a new set of meanings where
human time no longer defines his existence. The cemetery's several
material symbols play their part in relating the time of eternity
to human time. Man's fate, as Yankee City conceives it, can be
found in these signs. Let us examine them.

The cemeteries in Yankee City are divided into lots of varying
sizes which are ordinarily the property of particular families, occasionally of associations. The burial plots are referred to by the
surnames of the families who own them. The individual graves,
with their individual stone markers, are arranged within the limits
of the lots—more often than not according to the status of the
dead individuals within the family and the dictates of mortuary style
prevailing at the time of their deaths.

The emotions and thoughts of the living about their dead always
express the antithetical elements that enter into the placement of

the dead. Human time continually makes its demands for controlling eternity; maintenance of the identity of the dead is partly dependent on placing them in living time and space. Human space concepts continue to be used to locate the dead. Location of the dead in time and space helps to maintain their reality to those who wish to continue their relations with them. The cemetery contributes its material signs to help maintain this system of meanings and feelings.

The cemetery as a collective representation is both a city and a garden of the dead. The two symbols fuse and merge in the collective thinking of the people of Yankee City. The most modern cemetery in the community, well over a hundred years in age, accents its natural surroundings and emphasizes the symbols of nature, but only as they are fashioned and expressed within the limits and control of men and society in the design of a formal garden. It is a miniature, symbolic replica of the gardenlike dwelling area of a better-class suburb, or an elaboration of the formal gardens of aristocratic families. It is a symbolic city built in the form of a garden of the dead.

"Garden" and "city" are both feminine images in our culture, the former a dependent symbol of the more ancient Mother Earth. The garden is also a symbol of both life and death. As a *place* it symbolizes life, vitality, growth, and the fertility of the earth. As a symbol of the *processes* occurring there it expresses feelings about man's involvement in the eternal cycle of life and death, its shrubs and flowers come and go and are born again, its life dies, decays, and enriches the soil where new plants and shrubs are reborn and flower again. Summer and winter, life and death, eternally repeat themselves in the processes of the garden—an artifact formed by, and subject to, the will of man.

Elm Highland, the most modern cemetery of Yankee City, was consecrated in the first half of the last century as a "rural burial place" where landscape gardening united "the beautiful in nature with sculptural art, thereby creating a garden cemetery." The citizens composed two original hymns for its consecration. Both explicitly use maternal and female symbols to refer to the cemetery and the return of the living to a maternal and female resting place. The one from which the following quote was taken also recognizes the cemetery as a "City of Our Dead" and refers to the common fate of the living and the dead and their mutual hope for immortality through their relations with the supernatural power of Christ.

We have appoint, by solemn rite,
On this sequestered, peaceful site,
With flowery grass and shadowy tree,
The City of Our Dead to be.

Though this now sacred turf must break
Our dearest forms of life to take;
On Nature's calm, maternal breast
'Tis meet her weary children rest.

May He, who, pitying, "touched the bier,"
Console each future mourner here;
And all the dead at last arise
With joy to meet Him in the skies!

The author of the hymn explicitly speaks of the return of the "weary children" to the "maternal breast" of Nature where they find eternal "rest." The more obvious female symbolism involved with the insertion of the body into the open grave which then encloses it in the "body of Mother Earth" is not acceptable at the conscious level to members of our culture. Unconsciously, the open grave and the uterus are compatible; they also fit the social assumptions of our rites of passage. The rite and facts of birth separate the new individual from the womb of the mother and, following the events between the rites and facts of death, complete the life cycle by returning the human body to the maternal body of Nature. The Christian rites of baptism and those surrounding death symbolically recognize the meanings assigned to these facts. In the Catholic Church, for example, the liturgy of Holy Saturday explicitly views baptism as both a birth and a death rite while bringing to the manifest level of understanding the vaginal significance of the "immersion" in the water of the font. On the other hand, Extreme Unction and Christian funerals nonlogically—but with great effectiveness—symbolically state the meanings of death as both an ending and a beginning, as a rite of death and a rite of birth.

The author of the sacred poem, in speaking of the "weary children" finding "rest," puts the fixed eternal world of sacred time in opposition to the weariness of those *moving* through human time. The return of the "children" to the breast of the mother, back to the beginning of time for them where the beginning and the ending are one, touches and may evoke powerful yet unsatisfied human feelings and use them positively to reduce anxiety about death. Whether the "peaceful" equilibrium, and quiet of prenatal existence influence the postnatal meaning of experience is debatable, but the strong desire to maintain close an unchanging relations with the mother and the infantile need to possess her are well documented human longings. These feelings, morally stated in the sacred symbols of consecration, nonmorally felt in the unconscious longings of men, are bound to the female symbol of Nature, the beginning and ending of human time. The cemetery as an object dedicated to God and man and consecrated to "our dead to be," its graves, and the cemetery as a city and garden, are all culturally controlled female symbols. One must suspect that their significance not only derives from the logical and nonlogical meanings of culture but lies deeply rooted in the life of the human animal.

The fundamental *sacred* problem of the graveyard is to provide suitable symbols to refer to and express man's hope of immortality through the sacred belief and ritual of Christianity, and to reduce his anxiety and fear about death as marking the obliteration of his personality—the end of life for himself and for those he loves. The assurance of life hereafter for the dead already in the cemetery and for those being buried is an assurance of life hereafter for the living. Maintaining the dead as members of society maintains the continuing life of the living. The living's assurance of life everlasting is dependent on their keeping the dead alive. Should the dead really die, in the belief of those who put them to rest, then they, too, must die. The cemetery is an enduring physical emblem, a substantial and visible symbol of this agreement among men that they will not let each other die. For a very few, it is a sacred or sometimes an open admission that the power of tradition and convention is greater than the strength of their own rational convictions.

The fundamental *secular* problem the graveyard solves is to rid the living of the decaying corpse, thus freeing them from the nauseous smells of corruption and from the horror of seeing the natural decomposition of a human body, thereby helping to maintain the satisfying images of themselves as persistent and immortal beings. Another social function of the graveyard is to provide a firm and fixed social place, ritually consecrated for this purpose, where the disturbed sentiments of human beings about their loved dead can settle and find peace and certainty. Death destroys the equilibrium of the family and other intimate groups in which the deceased participated during his life. When it comes, the interaction and exchange of intimate gestures and symbols, resulting in each individual's personality internalizing part of the person of the other with whom he intimately interacts, ceases. This process no longer provides a mirror, however opaque and distorted, in which the individual may feel he sees his own reflection and thus realize himself as a social being. The belief in immortality, strengthened and reinforced by the funeral rite, helps correct some of the feeling in the survivor of loss of self. For the survivor to continue to see and feel himself still living in, and related to the dead life of the other it is necessary for him to reconstruct his image of the other; but in doing this he must also rethink who he himself is, at least insofar as he relates himself to the dead person. This constitutes an essential part of the social-psychological processes of the living during the transition of death.

The cemetery provides the living with a sacred realm they have created by means of their social control of divine power, a function of sacred symbolism, in which they can deposit the impure and unclean corpse in a grave that belongs to it not so much as a corpse but as a sacred person, in a grave which also belongs to them, the living. The grave with its markings is a place where the living can symbolically maintain and express their intimate relations with the dead. There is a kinship of kind, too; today's dead are yesterday's living, and today's living are tomorrow's dead. Each is identified with the other's fate. No one escapes.

The grave is marked so that the living can approach it as something that belongs to a separate personality; it is not merely a symbol that refers generally and abstractly to all the dead. The cemetery is a symbolic meeting place for the dead and the living, for the realms of the sacred and profane, for the natural and for the supernatural. It is a social emblem, whole and entire, yet composed of many autonomous and separate individual symbols which give visible expression to our social relations to the supernatural and to the pure realm of the spirit. It is a meeting place which faces out to death and the sacred absolute and back to the secular realities of the finite and the living. In it the time of man and the time of God are united. It is a "final resting place" where the disturbed and bruised sentiments of the living members of the society mark the natural death and ultimate disposition of an individual organism and its detachment from the species, thus fixing a place in time where the living can relate themselves in human, understandable, emotional terms to the spiritualized personality now in the timeless realm of the supernatural other world. The members of the societies of the living and the dead meet here as "God's children" and are accordingly one people. The cemetery as a collective representation repeats and expresses the social structure of the living as a symbolic replica; a city of the dead, it is a symbolic replica of the living community. The spiritual part of the city of the Christian dead, often thought of as part of the City of God, is sometimes equated with the Invisible Body of Christ. For many Christians, each is an integral part of a greater mystery . . . .

Transition Technicians—the Funeral and Other Rites of Transition and the Power and Prestige of the Professions

It is clear that the symbolic significance of the cemetery as a material artifact reflecting the community life of Yankee City and the private worlds of its members cannot be fully comprehended by an examination limited to the grave itself. The symbolic rites which relate the living to the dead are integral parts of the whole life situation.

The movement of a man through his lifetime, from a fixed placental placement within his mother's womb to his death and the ultimate fixed point of his tombstone and final containment in his grave as a dead organism, is punctuated by a number of critical moments of transition which all societies ritualize and publicly mark with suitable observances to impress the significance of the individual and the group on living members of the community. These are the important times of birth, puberty, marriage, and death. The usual progress of all such rites of transition, as Van Gennep has demonstrated, are characterized by three phases: separation, margin, and aggregation. The first period of separation consists of symbolic behavior signifying the detachment of the individual from an earlier fixed point in the social structure; during the intermediate period of margin the status of the individual is ambiguous—it is not fixed for him or his society—he moves in a world where he is no longer what he was nor has attained what he is to be; in the last phase, of aggregation, the passage is made complete. The individual is again in a fixed status and reintegrated into his society. He is in a new status—new for him, but a traditional one for the society, a status which the society defines as the end and goal of a particular transition rite. The society recognizes and consecrates the successful achievement of the passage of the individual.[2]

At the same time his change of status and the reordering of

his relations with other members of the society are recognized and sanctioned. The transition phases of separation, margin, and aggregation always involve others who are in direct relation with the individual during this time. They, too, are in positions of uneasiness and confusion which are expressed in their feelings and actions. The different societies have developed traditional symbols which express the varying feelings of other members of the society, usually the family of the person concerned, and direct their actions to an attainment of the ultimate goal of each transition.

The informal and nonofficial behavior which is always a part of all transition rites is often a channel of expression for paradoxical emotions and sentiments which are not altogether inappropriate. The "tears of joy" at a wedding, symbolically a time of joy, may express feelings of loss, deprivation, and even hostility felt by members of the two families; the informal gatherings of friends and relatives after the funeral for bread and drink among peoples where wakes are not sanctioned, when laughter and tears are intermingled, often allow feelings to be expressed publicly and relations established which the official funeral has not permitted. In our society the unofficial behavior of fathers during the period of birth and confinement of the expectant mother, often a source of amusement and a target for the satirist, is an informal expression of the social sentiments formalized by the *couvade* in "primitive" societies. These sentiments of anxiety about themselves in the crisis are not provided for in our symbolic usage at the birth transition.

The symbols of our *rites de passage* of birth, death, and the others occurring between them always operate at four levels of behavior and consequently involve sentiments, emotions, and values which are of the deepest significance to the whole social system and powerfully affect the participating individuals. The levels of behavior are: species activity, technological and social action, and the action system which relates men to the supernatural.

Throughout the life span and in all rites, the social personality of the living—the product of the individual's interaction with other members of the society and the sum of the social positions he has occupied while living in the social structure—influences, and is influenced directly and indirectly by, the rest of the society. This means that the effects of the social personality of each individual are felt by other members of the group and retained as part of their memories. Consequently, when a member of a community dies, his social personality is not immediately extinguished. His physical lifetime is ended, but social existence continues. It exists so long as memory of it is felt by the living members of the group.

As the chart indicates, death does not destroy the social personality, for in the memory of others it continues to exist, and only disappears when all trace of it is obliterated from the memory of the living and it no longer exerts an influence upon them. Thus the social personality starts in the sacred realm, passes through a secular existence, and returns to the sacred world of the dead. Birthdays and anniversaries of marriage are symbolic recognitions of the original events. They usually function within the realm of the family, contribute to its solidarity by allowing its members to reassert their own values and beliefs about themselves, and allow the social value of the person and the occasion to be reasserted in symbolic form by the group. The flowers given to a mother

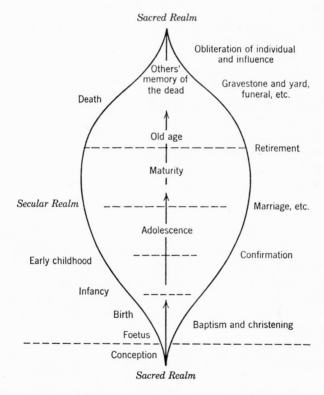

The expansion and contraction of the social personality (during the passage of the individual through life).

on her birthday or to a wife on a wedding anniversary, or placed on a parent's grave, revive and restate by yearly ritual the changing yet continuing meaning of an individual's life to him and his society.

Our complex western European society, during the long periods of its increasing differentiation, has developed a number of occupational statuses closely related to the several rites of passage which mark and define the passage of social time from birth to death. They are largely the older and more honored professions, which possess extraordinary positions of privilege, power, and prestige. Very early in the development of this culture they assumed functions in the rites and crises of transition that once were the duties and obligations of the families involved. Since the families of the changing individual are primarily concerned with his crises of change, it would be expected that their members might conduct the several rites. Although at such times family members are very active, professional men are called in to take charge: doctors, lawyers, ministers, priests, and, to a lesser extent, teachers assume leading roles in one or more of the several crises. They are the transition technicians standing by as the time conveyor belt transports and transforms those who compose its traffic. They manipulate the highly valued symbols and play their part in defining and establishing what is happening to the lifetime of each individual and what this means within the social time of the group.

The activities between death and burial are filled with tension, grief, and disorder in the social world which immediately surrounds the deceased. During mortal illnesses, fear mingled with hope in the thoughts of the dying person, his family, and the friends who surround him, has created strong anxiety and tension in the relations of all those intimately involved. For some, the sacrament of Extreme Unction provides a rite of transition which effectively separates and removes the soul of the living from the ordinary secular world, transports it, and places it in a position where it can be integrated into the spiritual world. Only a minority of Protestants now summon the spiritual aid of the minister to help them through the period of the death crisis. The feelings of fear and guilt which fill the emotions and thinking of family and friends often prevent them from calling in the minister, since his extraordinary visit might be interpreted as a sign that the techniques of science are no longer effective—that the minister as a representative of the sacred world is assuming the dominant place until then occupied by the doctor. His appearance could signify the certainty of approaching death.

There are significant differences between the relative status of priests and ministers in the community. The priest is of significance to the less as well as the extremely devout Catholics in all rites of transition. The fundamental human crises have been ritualized by the Catholic Church to the point where all the principal ones are raised to the ritual importance of sacraments. Five of the seven sacraments are directly related to times of crisis and transition in human life. The other two are also used in transition rites. Baptism for birth; confirmation for the child's passage from early immaturity to the beginnings of maturity—from the exclusive dominance of the family to a more responsible and larger participation in the society; the sacrament of marriage for sexual cohabitation and the passage of the individual from the family of his birth to his family of reproduction; and Extreme Unction for death: all are associated with transitions and life crises. For one devoted to a celibate existence, ordination is essentially a substitute for the marriage rite; it transforms the secular man of the world, living in the larger profane realm of the flesh, into a member of an adult spiritual order—a member of the sacred realm of the Church. Only the sacraments of the Eucharist and penance are not directly symbolic expressions of critical transition periods in which there is a marked change of the individual's status in the structure of the community.

The symbolic role and ecclesiastic authority of the priest in all these rituals are very great. The part he plays and the symbols he manipulates are of the very greatest supernatural significance, for they invest the transitional crises and the *rite de passage* occasioned by each of them with the absolute power of the Divine presence. Through the priest, the eternal Divine elements become part of, and are directly related to, a secular, mundane, transitory moment in one individual's life. The symbolic role and activity of the priest, backed by the authority of the Church and confirmed by the faith of the communicant, raise him to a position of highest professional rank.

The position of the priest in the Irish community as well as in the French Canadian group in Yankee City is very high. Since they belong to ethnic groups which rank below the old Americans and since their religion is considered inferior to that of the Protestants, they do not enjoy a status in the larger community commensurate with that held in the several Catholic communities of French Canada or southern Ireland.

Protestant ministers occupy a variable position in professional status and in class levels. They rank in social class from upper-lower to upper class, most of them being upper-middle. Despite the fact that the status of Protestantism is high (particularly certain indigenous forms of New England Protestantism) and the ministers largely of old American background and New England heritage, they cannot be sure of the secure place held by the priest within his own immediate community. Compared with priests, doctors, and lawyers, their position is weak. The role of the minister since the Reformation has been increasingly secularized. Many of the sacred symbols largely centered in *rites de passage* celebrating events of importance in the lives of the people have been destroyed, and those that remain are often weak and not of great importance. When the great system of sacred symbols was broken or destroyed by the forces that produced Protestantism and the absolute power largely removed from those which remained, much of the authority inherent to the cloth disappeared. God's vicars need his signs to make manifest what it is that they and He are. Words are important symbols, but the mysteries of the Word need other symbolic usages to manifest the full power of God.

Most of the symbols visible and perceptible to the senses have been removed by the hostility of Protestant reform. Vivid and sensuous ceremonies that capture the inner world of the individual, colorful images that elicit and contain the fantasies of his private life, have been abandoned and condemned. The Protestant minister, weakly armed with an anemic liturgical apparatus and devitalized spiritual imagery, has had his spiritual power reduced; the reinforcement of visual drama often needed to make his words significant to his congregation has been taken from him. He is often reduced to the use of verbal symbols, now impoverished by the debilitating effect of two centuries of science. Their potency with a Protestant audience, now highly secularized, is dependent not only on supernatural sanction but on their scientific and rational validity. He is in the awkward position of having to make sense with the symbols he uses, not only to the sacred but to the most secular part of the profane world. In the various times of transition the minister is often humiliated by having to compete with undertakers for the central role in burying the dead, with justices of the peace for the marriage rite, and with a varied assortment of speakers representing all parts of society at high school and college graduation exercises.

Although the liturgical life of the Protestant church has not disappeared but is still alive and in many ways vital, even in the Evangelical churches it does not possess the symbolic strength nor the validity of faith that it has among the Catholic faithful. Although verbal symbols are significant and necessary parts of any great liturgy, they are not by themselves as effective as those which depend on visual symbols as well as those appealing to the other senses.

For most Protestants, funeral orations and sermons by the minister are still believed necessary and important. An analysis of a number of them indicates that the primary function of the eulogy is to translate the profane person in the feelings of those who mourn from secular living into the sacred world of the dead and of Deity.

The funeral oration must reassure the living that immortality is a fact, that the personality of the dead has not ceased to exist, and that spiritual life has no ending, since death is only the transition from life in the present to eternal life in a spiritual world. The establishment of these spiritual truths in the minds and emotions of the audience prepares them for the next important step: the transformation of the total person, once a living combination of good and bad and of spiritual and profane elements, into a spiritual person who is a certain, or at least very likely, candidate for immortality. Thus his lifetime, bound by ideas of transition, is transposed into the eternal time of death. Essentially, from the point of view of what is being done to the dead person, the whole is an initiation rite and compares very closely with the initiation rites which many pass through in life.

Since at most funerals the whole group of mourners is composed of individuals who have considerable knowledge of the habits and activities of the deceased, each individual if questioned could often mention traits of the deceased which as evidence might cause an entirely just—not to say harsh—judge to refuse the candidate admittance to a happier life. The task of the minister is a delicate one. He must touch lightly on the earthly traits of the dead and then move gracefully over to his positive virtues and his spiritual qualities. Since he possesses an immortal soul given him by God, and since those most lacking in spiritual grace and moral competence are never categorically evil, these small and often insignificant positive traits of the personality are easily substituted in the words of a skillful speaker for the whole person, and the transfiguration takes place. The symbolic functions of the eulogy are to transform what are memories of the secular living into ideas of the sacred

dead, and to re-form recollection of the personality sufficiently to
make it possible for everyone to believe that entrance into heaven
or any of its contemporary vague substitutes is not blocked or
impossible.

The symbolic activities of the audience are minor but sufficient
to allow them some participation, at least to the point of permitting
them to affirm informally what the speaker asserts. The accompani-
ment of the casket in a funeral procession to the cemetery and
the brief ceremonies there allow the living to demonstrate their
love and respect to the end.

The doctor plays one of the more sympathetic roles of modern
science. He is able to personify its optimism and insistence that
all problems must be solved, for the public believes that science
has its own miracles which can effectively pull back dying men
from the edge of the grave. As long as the doctor continues to
function as the central figure during a serious illness, everyone
concerned can continue to believe that the sick person has his chance
to live.

The role of the physician at the death of a patient who is a
beloved member of a family is very complex and often difficult.
Ordinarily he functions as a friend and an expertly trained professional who, with life and death in his hands, solves all problems
and keeps human beings alive; but at death this role must be relinquished. His own conception of his role and his professional
oath demand that under the most pessimistic circumstances, where
death seems certain, he try to keep the patient alive and "hope
for the best." His dominant position in the death crisis makes it
difficult for him to shift openly from the role of the protector of
life to one who prepares the family for approaching death by predicting its likelihood. Yet in many instances this is what he must
somehow do. The tremendous pressure placed on him by those
who transform their hope for the recovery of their loved ones into
a firm belief that a hopelessly ill person will not die often makes
it impossible to prepare the family for the imminence of dissolution.
The doctor, to function in the combined role of scientist, friend,
and citizen, must be a symbol of life rather than of death.

Despite the doctor's being the scientist and the "man in white"
who brings new miracles to the sick to make them well and who,
as the family physician, is friend and confessor, with intimate and
privileged knowledge about family members and the relations among
them, his role is not entirely positive. Although the formal symbols

which surround him are positive and life-giving, the informal ones are negative. There is often a feeling of ambivalence, hostility, and distrust mixed with the faith, trust, pride, and genuine affection among members of a family for the profession. In Yankee City the grim jokes about the undertakers being beneficiaries of the doctors' mistakes, the stories about various instruments being left in the body after the operation or excessive charges and pink pills and bottles of highly colored liquids being no more than chalk and colored water, as well as the sexual jokes about the doctor shifting from his professional, bedside manner to an all too human masculine one, all testify to this feeling of ambivalence about doctors.

The gossip about various doctors which appeared in our interviews again testified to themes of fear and hostility about them—tempered, it must be remembered, by willing submission to their "fatherly authority" and by genuine trust in their skill and love and respect for them as persons. The ambivalence towards doctors is usually divided symbolically into two types of concept, one being "my doctor" in whom I take pride and the other, the "sawbones" who is suspected of varying infractions of the moral code, professional incompetence, and exclusive interest in his fees, as well as malpractice. Doctors in the intermediate position between these two types, when known by the informant, are likely to be well thought of or treated with indifference.

When a patient dies, a doctor must be sure that the family and other members of the community do not saddle him with responsibility for the death. In one sense, the physician is in a strong position because he is the professional expert who alone can make final judgment of the causes of the event. Professional ethics and mutual protection demand that his colleagues speak approvingly, keep quiet, or defend him, should gossip and rumor attack him. The surgeon, because of his central role in a dramatic situation, is particularly subject to threats of unpleasant criticism.

The doctor can announce the cause of death, sign the death certificate, and usually depend on the community and its officials to accept his pronouncement. But, given the various types of personality among those who grieve and feel guilty about their covert or open hostility to the deceased, the doctor must play his role carefully and well to make sure he will not be blamed and possibly have his reputation and career destroyed. His professional reputation must be reinforced by moral authority. Should there be doubts about his private moral life there may also arise questions as to

his professional competence.   Since doctors receive little or no training in problems of human relations, it is clear that each learns
informally and by trial and error how to handle this difficult problem; sometimes by the quiet, sardonic advice of other doctors.   Moreover, the society itself helps to protect the doctor, for, after all,
its members believe—and must believe—that the profession is necessary to heal the sick and prevent death.   Individual faith and trust
are needed by all who use doctors to reduce their anxiety and con-
quer fear.   It is not strange that most members of the community
have a personal interest in protecting their faith in their own doctors
by helping to protect the community's faith in the medical profession.

The doctor, particularly the surgeon, must take care of his own
internal psychological problems.   He must learn how to convince
himself most of the time that he has done everything to save the
patient or he may find it impossible to cope with the moral pressure
of a succession of unpleasant outcomes.   Self-confidence is often
attained by allowing the role he plays for his patients to convince
him that he is what they believe him to be.   Since any doctor
must always play a positive public role for his clients and act out
beliefs and sentiments he may not feel, but which he knows are
expected by his patients and their families, whose fear and anxiety
demand constant reassurance from his deportment, he often learns
to allow his experiences with his patients to convince him that
he is what they think he is.   His conception of himself in time
largely corresponds with the role in which the public sees him.
If he cannot achieve this he pays an intolerable and sometimes
tragic price internally for his efforts to manage his own self-
evaluations . . . .

The role of the undertaker has developed very rapidly in the
last few generations and is likely to continue to increase the social
area it controls.   Whereas it was once customary for the family
with the help of friends to "lay out the dead" and prepare the
corpse for burial as well as to "sit up" with it to show respect
and indicate that duty, honor, and love were being bestowed upon
the dead person's memory, the undertaker is now called immediately
after death to take charge.   At death the second phase of the general
period of crisis begins; the first being the period of the last illness
and the second the time between death and burial.   The mortician
has developed his place by satisfying a need for which those in
distress were willing to pay.   Basically he is a private enterpriser
who will do the ritually unclean and physically distasteful work

of disposing of the dead in a manner satisfying to the living, at a price which they can pay . . . .

As a skilled artisan he uses the expertness of the embalmer, thereby drawing upon some medical knowledge. He must also be proficient in the art of the beauty shop and the cosmetician to perform the last toilette of the corpse. This, of course, includes washing, powdering, painting, the use of paraffin, and other devices of the beauty shop. He must see to it that the corpse is properly clothed and that it conforms to the expectations of its audience, particularly the bereaved family. In this he functions to save responsible members of the family and their friends from performing the menial and unpleasant tasks necessary to prepare a body for burial. He does the physical work of taking the ritually unclean, usually diseased, corpse with its unpleasant appearance and transforming it from a lifeless object to the sculptured image of a living human being who is resting in sleep. The contemporary image of the corpse is that of a human being temporarily resting with his eyes closed, or perhaps someone who has but recently gone to sleep and will soon waken.

The corpse, although a dead human being, is supposed to "look well." Those who pass by in procession to look upon the deceased want a glorified, or at least peaceful, image of the live person they knew and loved. The undertaker closes the staring eyes, the gaping mouth, strengthens the sagging muscles, and with the aid of cosmetics and the help of soft silks and satins in the coffin's interior provides the central character of the tragic ritual with the proper appearance. Some of the favorite expressions of those who pass by "to pay their last tribute" are: "He looked very well—" "He looked just like he did when he was well—" or "You would think he was taking a nap or was resting his eyes for a minute." The people of Yankee City do not use formal death masks to look at what they want to see in death. But the skill of the undertaker provides an informal one which says that the dead who wear it look like life, that they are only asleep and will soon awaken. The art of the undertaker, despite its extreme secularity and its traffic with the impure things of this world, provides a symbolic product which fits very neatly into the needs of the symbolic life of Yankee City.

In performing these ritually unclean tasks the undertaker reduces the horror the living feel when in contact with the cold and "unnatural" remains of a loved person, particularly during the uncertain

in-between stage of the funeral rites of passage, when anxieties
are greatest. The undertaker helps to remove the pollution and
corruption of death at less emotional cost to the living. In the
language concerned with rites of transition, he allows the living
to pass through the phases of separation and margin with less pain
than if he were not present.

The staging and arrangements for the funeral ritual are largely
in the undertaker's hands. He must place the coffin and arrange
the flowers so that their dramatic effect is most easily brought out.
He must be unobtrusively responsible for making certain that during the moments of intense emotion and sorrow no awkward situations arise. He must be sure that family, near kindred, and friends
are properly placed in the audience, that pallbearers are chosen
who are symbolically correct and physically capable. He must be
certain that all arrangements have been made with the proper
officials at the cemetery and with the police escort for the funeral
procession. Above all, he must be the competent stage manager
and impresario who conducts the ritual of the tragic drama, beginning with the mortuary chapel, church, or home, that continues
and coheres as a tragic procession across the crowded streets of
the city to the open grave in the cemetery. In one sense he is
the producer who fashions the whole enterprise so that other per-
formers, including the minister, the eulogist, the organist, the
vocalist, family, and mourners, can act becomingly and get the
approval and praise for the funeral's success and receive the sensuous
satisfaction that the funeral's symbolism evokes. At the same time
all this must be performed in such a way that the uncontrolled
grief and random behavior of the living when they face the dead
will not destroy the form of the ritual.

Despite the fact that the undertaker performs a necessary, useful
service and provides necessary goods for an inevitable event, that
the skills and services he brings to bear are of a high order, and
that he is usually well paid and very often successful as an entre-
preneur, there is considerable evidence that neither he nor his cus-
tomers are content with his present symbols and status within the
occupational and social hierarchy of Yankee City. There is an increasing tendency on the part of the undertaker to borrow the ritual
and sacred symbols of the minister and other professional men to
provide an outward cover for what he is and does.

His place of business is not a factory or an office but a "chapel"
or a "home." Its furniture and arrangement often suggest the altar

and auditorium of a church. He frequently dresses in ritual clothes reserved for roles of extreme formality, high etiquette, and prestige. His advertisements, while cautious and careful not to use symbols indicating a particular sect (unless specialized for that purpose), tend to borrow from the language of religion. The brochures and other attendant literature used to advertise the functions of the enterprise skillfully draw on the traditional symbols of the church.

Although the social processes continue to turn the role of the undertaker from that of businessman into professional mortician, there is a considerable hostility to it. It cannot be forgotten that he handles the unclean aspects of death while the minister controls the clean and spiritual phases of it. The undertaker makes a business profit, whereas the minister is given a professional fee. The deep hostilities and fears men have for death, unless very carefully controlled and phrased, can turn the undertaker into a scapegoat, the ritual uncleanliness of his task being identified with his role and person. The thousands of undertaker jokes that appear on the radio and in other mass media as well as in informal gossip, which relate him to the more despised and feared features of death, are ample testimony to this fact. To hold this hostility in check it is necessary for him to surround his functions with sacred symbols and to profess a very high code of ethics. These uplifting efforts are often successfully attacked. For example, in Yankee City an undertaker was the principal sponsor of a nondenominational Easter service on one of the historic hills of the community. Although popular, the service met with considerable ambivalent "kidding" and comment about his skill in advertising his business and putting himself right with everyone so that he would get their trade. This despite the fact that he was known as a conscientious Christian. Undertakers have become the modern target of many of the same jokes as were once directed at gravediggers.

Unless the place of the church and its supernatural symbols increases in importance, it seems likely that the professional role of the undertaker and his use of sacred symbols will continue to grow. His present prominence demands that his business enterprise receive the protection of professional ethics as well as the social form of sacred symbols. It is even possible that in the more remote future the church may incorporate the mortician into its system of functionaries or perhaps take over his functions as part of its own duties; in some sects the custom of referring members to an undertaker of the membership, presumably holding harmonious and trustworthy religious views, already approaches this. Death being at the very center of the sacred life of any society, the functionary who plays a prominent role in its rites is likely to become heavily ritualized and develop a sacred role.

The Life Span of a Cemetery and the Continuing Life of a Community

As long as the cemetery is being filled with a fresh stream of the recently dead it stays symbolically a live and vital emblem, telling the living of the meaning of life and death. But when the family, the kindred, and other members of the community gradually discontinue burying their loved ones there, the cemetery, in a manner of speaking, dies its own death as a meaningful symbol of life and death, for it ceases to exist as a living sacred emblem and, through time, becomes an historical monument. As a symbolic object it, too, is subject to the meaning of time. Its spirituality then resides in a different context, for it becomes an object of historical value in stable communities rather than a sacred collective representation effectively relating the dead to the living.

The active cemetery, funerals, and mourning symbols ritually look to the sacred life of the future while marking the secular end of the lifetime of the individual, while the "dead" cemeteries look backward to the life of the past. Their gravestones are not so much symbols of a man's death as the fact that he and the others once lived and constituted in their aggregate a way of life and a society. If a cemetery holds no future for *our own* deaths to mark our passage from the living to the dead—if we cannot project the life of our time into it—then its dead belong to the *life* of the past. The gravestones become artifacts that refer to the past; the cemetery becomes a symbol speaking of the people of the past to those of the present and stands for the regard of the present for its own past. But man's hope for immortality, his hope for the future, cannot be evoked by such historical symbols. They must be projected into cemeteries and into other symbols which represent man's beliefs and feelings about himself.

There are eleven cemeteries in Yankee City. Each has been filled with the city's dead for part or all of the period from the 1600's until the present. Only six were decorated on Memorial Day. The others were neither repaired nor decorated and were no longer being used as burial grounds. The graves were filled with the ancient dead. Their living descendants did not recognize them for a number of reasons: the family had moved west or gone elsewhere; the intermediate kindred connecting them with the living were buried in more recently established cemeteries, which did not extend to the earlier generations, but received the homage of the living; the dead had no living representatives, or the living representatives had no interest in, or knowledge of, their ancestors. The last two reasons are really one, for connections with the dead are always present but the knowledge or interest to trace these relations may not be.

. . . In a stable community such as Yankee City there is little chance that they face an ultimate loss of all value and that their land will be captured for business enterprise. Such seems to be the fate of many cemeteries in rapidly changing and growing communities where the social structure and population are unstable, this instability in the social system being reflected in the people's disregard of the cemetery as a collective representation to express either their sentiments for the dead or their feelings about the past. In an unstable community, where the changing social structure is reflected in disregard of the cemetery as a collective representation and it no longer has sacred value, the sentiments attached by social groupings such as the family and association disappear. The community loses its values for itself as a totality. Without traditions and a feeling for social continuity, the living lose their feelings for the social character of the graveyard.

When cemeteries no longer receive fresh burials which continue to tie the emotions of the living to the recently dead and thereby connect the living in a chain of generations to an early ancestry, the graveyards must lose their sacred quality and become objects of historical ritual. The lifetime of individuals and the living meanings of cemeteries are curiously interdependent, for both are dependent on an ascription of sacred meaning bestowed upon them by those who live. The symbols of death say what life is and those of life define what death must be. The meanings of man's fate are forever what he makes them.

References

1. Emile Durkheim, *The Elementary Forms of the Religious Life*, trans. J. W. Swain (New York: Macmillan, 1915).
2. Arnold van Gennep, *Les Rites de Passage* (Paris: Émile Nourry, 1909).

Octavio Paz

The Day of the Dead

The solitary Mexican loves fiestas and public gatherings. Any occasion for getting together will serve as a pretext to stop the flow
of time and commemorate men and events with festivals and ceremonies. We are a ritual people, and this characteristic enriches
both our imaginations and our sensibilities, which are equally sharp
and alert. The art of the fiesta has been debased almost everywhere
else, but not in Mexico. There are few places in the world where
it is possible to take part in a spectacle like our great religious
fiestas with their violent primary colors, their bizarre costumes and
dances, their fireworks and ceremonies, and their inexhaustible
welter of surprises: the fruit, candy, toys, and other objects sold
on these days in the plazas and open-air markets.

Our calendar is crowded with fiestas. There are certain days
when the whole country, from the more remote villages to the largest
cities, prays, shouts, feasts, gets drunk and kills, in honor of the
Virgin of Guadalupe or Benito Juárez. Each year on the 15th of
September, at eleven o'clock at night, we celebrate the fiesta of
the *Grito*[1] in all the plazas of the Republic, and the excited crowds
actually shout for a whole hour . . . the better, perhaps, to remain
silent for the rest of the year. During the days before and after
the 12th of December,[2] time comes to a full stop, and instead of
pushing us toward a deceptive tomorrow that is always beyond
our reach, offers us a complete and perfect today of dancing and
revelry, or communion with the most ancient and secret Mexico.
Time is no longer succession, and becomes what it originally was
and is: the present, in which past and future are reconciled.

But the fiestas which the Church and State provide for the country
as a whole are not enough. The life of every city and village
is ruled by a patron saint whose blessing is celebrated with devout
regularity. Neighborhoods and trades also have their annual fiestas,
their ceremonies and fairs. And each one of us—atheist, Catholic,
or merely indifferent—has his own saint's day, which he observes
every year. It is impossible to calculate how many fiestas we have
and how much time and money we spend on them. I remember

Reprinted from *The Labyrinth of Solitude: Life and Thought in Mexico*, translated by Lysander Kemp (New York: Grove Press, Inc., 1961), by permission of
the author and publisher.

asking the mayor of a village near Mitla, several years ago, "What is the income of the village government?" "About 3,000 pesos a year. We are very poor. But the Governor and the Federal Government always help us to meet our expenses." "And how are the 3,000 pesos spent?" "Mostly on fiestas, senor. We are a small village, but we have two patron saints."

This reply is not surprising. Our poverty can be measured by the frequency and luxuriousness of our holidays. Wealthy countries have very few: there is neither the time nor the desire for them, and they are not necessary. The people have other things to do, and when they amuse themselves they do so in small groups. The modern masses are agglomerations of solitary individuals. On great occasions in Paris or New York, when the populace gathers in the squares or stadiums, the absence of people, in the sense of *a* people, is remarkable: there are couples and small groups, but they never form a living community in which the individual is at once dissolved and redeemed. But how could a poor Mexican live without the two or three annual fiestas that make up for his poverty and misery? Fiestas are our only luxury. They replace, and are perhaps better than, the theater and vacations, Anglo-Saxon weekends and cocktail parties, the bourgeois reception, the Mediterranean café.

In all of these ceremonies—national or local, trade or family—the Mexican opens out. They all give him a chance to reveal himself and to converse with God, country, friends or relations. During these days the silent Mexican whistles, shouts, sings, shoots off fireworks, discharges his pistol into the air. He discharges his soul. And his shout, like the rockets we love so much, ascends to the heavens, explodes into green, red, blue and white lights, and falls dizzily to earth with a trail of golden sparks. This is the night when friends who have not exchanged more than the prescribed courtesies for months get drunk together, trade confidences, weep over the same troubles, discover that they are brothers, and sometimes, to prove it, kill each other. The night is full of songs and loud cries. The lover wakes up his sweetheart with an orchestra. There are jokes and conversations from balcony to balcony, sidewalk to sidewalk. Nobody talks quietly. Hats fly in the air. Laughter and curses ring like silver pesos. Guitars are brought out. Now and then, it is true, the happiness ends badly, in quarrels, insults, pistol shots, stabbings. But these too are part of the fiesta, for the Mexican does not seek amusement: he seeks to escape from himself, to leap over the wall of solitude that confines him during the rest of the year. All are possessed by violence and frenzy. Their souls explode like the colors and voices and emotions. Do they forget themselves and show their true faces? Nobody knows. The important thing is to go out, open a way, get drunk on noise, people, colors. Mexico is celebrating a fiesta. And this fiesta, shot through with lightning and delirium, is the brilliant reverse to our silence and apathy, our reticence and gloom.

According to the interpretation of French sociologists, the fiesta is an excess, an expense. By means of this squandering the community protects itself against the envy of the gods or of men. Sacrifices and offerings placate or buy off the gods and the patron saints. Wasting money and expending energy affirms the community's wealth in both. This luxury is a proof of health, a show of abundance and power. Or a magic trap. For squandering is an effort to attract abundance by contagion. Money calls to money. When life is thrown away it increases; the orgy, which is sexual expenditure, is also a ceremony of regeneration; waste gives strength. New Year celebrations, in every culture, signify something beyond the mere observance of a date on the calendar. The day is a pause; time is stopped, is actually annihilated. The rites that celebrate its death are intended to provoke its rebirth, because they mark not only the end of an old year but also the beginning of a new. Everything attracts its opposite. The fiesta's function, then, is more utilitarian than we think: waste attracts or promotes wealth, and is an invesment like any other, except that the returns on it cannot be measured or counted. What is sought is potency, life, health. In this sense the fiesta, like the gift and the offering, is one of the most ancient of economic forms.

This interpretation has always seemed to me to be incomplete. The fiesta is by nature sacred, literally or figuratively, and above all it is the advent of the unusual. It is governed by its own special rules, that set it apart from other days, and it has a logic, an ethic and even an economy that are often in conflict with everyday norms. It all occurs in an enchanted world: time is transformed to a mythical past or a total present; space, the scene of the fiesta, is turned into a gaily decorated world of its own; and the persons taking part cast off all human or social rank and become, for the moment, living images. And everything takes place as if it were not so, as if it were a dream. But whatever happens, our actions have a greater lightness, a different gravity. They take on other meanings and with them we contract new obligations. We throw down our burdens of time and reason.

In certain fiestas the very notion of order disappears. Chaos comes back and license rules. Anything is permitted: the customary hierarchies vanish, along with all social, sex, caste, and trade distinctions. Men disguise themselves as women, gentlemen as slaves, the poor as the rich. The army, the clergy and the law are ridiculed. Obligatory sacrilege, ritual profanation is committed. Love becomes promiscuity. Sometimes the fiesta becomes a Black Mass. Regulations, habits, and customs are violated. Respectable people put away the dignified expressions and conservative clothes that isolate them, dress up in gaudy colors, hide behind a mask, and escape from themselves.

Therefore the fiesta is not only an excess, a ritual squandering of the goods painfully accumulated during the rest of the year; it is also a revolt, a sudden immersion in the formless, in pure being. By means of the fiesta society frees itself from the norms it has established. It ridicules its gods, its principles, and its laws: it denies its own self.

The fiesta is a revolution in the most literal sense of the word. In the confusion that it generates, society is dissolved, is drowned, insofar as it is an organism ruled according to certain laws and principles. But it drowns in itself, in its own original chaos or liberty. Everything is untied: good and evil, day and night, the sacred and the profane. Everything merges, loses shape and individuality, and returns to the primordial mass. The fiesta is a cosmic experiment, an experiment in disorder, reuniting contradictory elements and principles in order to bring about a renascence of life. Ritual death promotes a rebirth; vomiting increases the appetite; the orgy, sterile in itself, renews the fertility of the mother or of the earth. The fiesta is a return to a remote and undifferentiated state, prenatal or presocial. It is a return that is also a beginning, in accordance with the dialectic that is inherent in social processes.

The group emerges purified and strengthened from this plunge into chaos. It has immersed itself in its own origins, in the womb from which it came. To express it in another way, the fiesta denies society as an organic system of differentiated forms and principles, but affirms it as a source of creative energy. It is a true "re-creation," the opposite of the "recreation" characterizing modern vacations, which do not entail any rites or ceremonies whatever and are as individualistic and sterile as the world that invented them.

Society communes with itself during the fiesta. Its members return to original chaos and freedom. Social structures break down and new relationships, unexpected rules, capricious hierarchies are created. In the general disorder everybody forgets himself and enters into otherwise forbidden situations and places. The bounds between audience and actors, officials and servants, are erased. Everybody takes part in the fiesta, everybody is caught up in its whirlwind. Whatever its mood, its character, its meaning, the fiesta is participation, and this trait distinguishes it from all other ceremonies and social phenomena. Lay or religious, orgy or saturnalia, the fiesta is a social act based on the full participation of all its celebrants.

Thanks to the fiesta the Mexican opens out, participates, communes with his fellows and with the values that give meaning to his religious or political existence. And it is significant that a country as sorrowful as ours should have so many and such joyous fiestas. Their frequency, their brilliance and excitement, the enthusiasm with which we take part, all suggest that without them we would explode. They free us, if only momentarily, from the thwarted impulses, the inflammable desires that we carry within us. But the Mexican fiesta is not merely a return to an original state of formless and normless liberty: the Mexican is not seeking to return, but to escape from himself, to exceed himself. Our fiestas are explosions. Life and death, joy and sorrow, music and mere noise are united, not to recreate or recognize themselves, but to swallow each other up. There is nothing so joyous as a Mexican fiesta, but there is also nothing so sorrowful. Fiesta night is also a night of mourning.

If we hide within ourselves in our daily lives, we discharge ourselves in the whirlwind of the fiesta. It is more than an opening out: we rend ourselves open. Everything—music, love, friendship—ends in tumult and violence. The frenzy of our festivals shows the extent to which our solitude closes us off from communication with the world. We are familiar with delirium, with songs and shouts, with the monologue . . . but not with the dialogue. Our fiestas, like our confidences, our loves, our attempts to reorder our society, are violent breaks with the old or the established. Each time we try to express ourselves we have to break with ourselves. And the fiesta is only one example, perhaps the most typical, of this violent break. It is not difficult to name others, equally revealing: our games, which are always going to extremes, often mortal; our profligate spending, the reverse of our timid investments and business enterprises; our confessions. The somber Mexican, closed up in himself, suddenly explodes, tears open his breast and reveals himself, though not without a certain complacency, and not without choosing a stopping-place in the shameful or terrible mazes of his intimacy. We are not frank, but our sincerity can reach extremes that horrify a European. The explosive, dramatic, sometimes even suicidal manner in which we strip ourselves, surrender ourselves, is evidence that something inhibits and suffocates us. Something impedes us from being. And since we cannot or dare not confront our own selves, we resort to the fiesta. It fires us into the void; it is a drunken rapture that burns itself out, a pistol shot in the air, a skyrocket.

Death is a mirror which reflects the vain gesticulations of the living. The whole motley confusion of acts, omissions, regrets, and hopes which is the life each one of us finds in death, not meaning or explanation, but an end. Death defines life; a death depicts a life in immutable forms; we do not change except to disappear. Our deaths illuminate our lives. If our deaths lack meaning, our lives also lacked it. Therefore we are apt to say, when somebody has died a violent death, "He got what he was looking for." Each of us dies the death he is looking for, the death he has made for himself. A Christian death or a dog's death are ways of dying that reflect ways of living. If death betrays us and we die badly, everyone laments the fact, because we should die as we have lived. Death, like life, is not transferable. If we do not die as we lived, it is because the life we lived was not really ours; it did not belong to us, just as the bad death that kills us does not belong to us. Tell me how you die and I will tell you who you are.

The opposition between life and death was not so absolute to the ancient Mexicans as it is to us. Life extended into death, and vice versa. Death was not the natural end of life but one phase of an infinite cycle. Life, death, and resurrection were stages of a cosmic process which repeated itself continuously. Life had no higher function than to flow into death, its opposite and complement; and death, in turn, was not an end in itself: man fed the insatiable hunger of life with his death. Sacrifices had a double purpose: on the one hand man participated in the creative process, and the same time paying back to the gods the debt contracted by his species; on the other hand he nourished cosmic life and also social life, which was nurtured by the former.

Perhaps the most characteristic aspect of this conception is the impersonal nature of the sacrifice. Since their lives did not belong to them, their deaths lacked any personal meaning. The dead—including warriors killed in battle and women dying in childbirth, companions of Huitzilopochtli the sun god—disappeared at the end of a certain period, to return to the undifferentiated country of the shadows, to be melted into the air, the earth, the fire, the animating substance of the universe. Our indigenous ancestors did not believe that their deaths belonged to them, just as they never thought that their lives were really theirs in the Christian sense. Everything was examined to determine, from birth, the life and death of each man; his social class, the year, the place, the day, the hour. The Aztec was as little responsible for his actions as for his death.

Space and time were bound together and formed an inseparable whole. There was a particular "time" for each place, each of the cardinal points, and the center in which they were immobilized. And this complex of space-time possessed its own virtues and powers, which profoundly influenced and determined human life. To be born on a certain day was to pertain to a place, a time, a color, and a destiny. All was traced out in advance. Where we dissociate space and time, mere stage sets for the actions of our lives, there were as many "space-times" for the Aztecs as there were combinations in the priestly calendar, each one endowed with a particular qualitative significance, superior to human will.

Religion and destiny ruled their lives, as mortality and freedom rule ours. We live under the sign of liberty, and everything—even Greek fatality and the grace of the theologians—is election and struggle, but for the Aztecs the problem reduced itself to investigating the never-clear will of the gods. Only the gods were free, and only they had the power to choose—and therefore, in a profound sense, to sin. The Aztec religion is full of great sinful gods— Quetzalcóatl in the major example—who grow weak and abandon their believers, in the same way that Christians sometimes deny God. The conquest of Mexico would be inexplicable without the treachery of the gods, who denied their own people.

The advent of Catholicism radically modified this situation. Sacrifice and the idea of salvation, formerly collective, became personal. Freedom was humanized, embodied in man. To the ancient Aztecs the essential thing was to assure the continuity of creation; sacrifice did not bring about salvation in another world, but cosmic health; the universe, and not the individual, was given life by the blood and death of human beings. For Christians it is the individual who counts. The world—history, society—is condemned beforehand. The death of Christ saved each man in particular. Each one of us is Man, and represents the hopes and possibilities of the species. Redemption is a personal task.

Both attitudes, opposed as they may seem, have a common note: life, collective or individual, looks forward to a death that in its way is a new life. Life only justifies and transcends itself when it is realized in death, and death is also a transcendence, in that it is a new life. To Christians death is a transition, a somersault between two lives, the temporal and the otherworldly; to the Aztecs it was the profoundest way of participating in the continuous regeneration of the creative forces, which were always in danger of being extinguished if they were not provided with blood, the sacred food. In both systems life and death lack autonomy, are the two sides of a single reality. They are references to invisible realities.

Modern death does not have any significance that transcends it or that refers to other values. It is rarely anything more than the inevitable conclusion of a natural process. In a world of facts, death is merely one more fact. But since it is such a disagreeable fact, contrary to all our concepts and to the very meaning of our lives, the philosophy of progress ("Progress toward what, and from what?" Schiller asked) pretends to make it disappear, like a magician palming a coin. Everything in the modern world functions as if death did not exist. Nobody takes it into account, it is suppressed everywhere: in political pronouncements, commercial advertising, public morality, and popular customs; in the promise of cut-rate health and happiness offered to all of us by hospitals, drugstores, and playing fields. But death enters into everything we undertake, and it is no longer a transition but a great gaping mouth that nothing can satisfy. The century of health, hygiene and contraceptives, miracle drugs and synthetic foods, is also the century of the concentration camp and the police state, Hiroshima and the murder story. Nobody thinks about death, about his own death, as Rilke asked us to do, because nobody lives a personal life. Collective slaughter is the fruit of a collectivized way of life.

Death also lacks meaning for the modern Mexican. It is no longer a transition, an access to another life more alive than our own. But although we do not view death as a transcendence, we have not eliminated it from our daily lives. The word death is not pronounced in New York, in Paris, in London, because it burns the lips. The Mexican, in contrast, is familiar with death, jokes about it, caresses it, sleeps with it, celebrates it; it is one of his favorite toys and his most steadfast love. True, there is perhaps as much fear in his attitude as in that of others, but at least death is not hidden away: he looks at it face to face, with impatience, disdain or irony. "If they are going to kill me tomorrow, let them kill me right away."[3]

The Mexican's indifference towards death is fostered by his indifference towards life. He views not only death but also life as nontranscendent. Our songs, proverbs, fiestas and popular beliefs show very clearly that the reason death cannot frighten us is that "life has cured us of fear." It is natural, even desirable, to die, and the sooner the better. We kill because life—our own or another's—is of no value. Life and death are inseparable, and when the former lacks meaning, the latter becomes equally meaningless. Mexican death is the mirror of Mexican life. And the Mexican shuts himself away and ignores both of them.

Our contempt for death is not at odds with the cult we have made of it. Death is present in our fiestas, our games, our loves, and our thoughts. To die and to kill are ideas that rarely leave us. We are seduced by death. The fascination it exerts over us is the result, perhaps, of our hermitlike solitude, and of the fury with which we break out of it. The pressure of our vitality, which can only express itself in forms that betray it, explains the deadly nature, aggressive or suicidal, of our explosions. When we explode we touch against the highest point of that tension, we graze the very zenith of life. And there, at the height of our frenzy, suddenly we feel dizzy: it is then that death attracts us.

Another factor is that death revenges us against life, strips it of all its vanities and pretensions and converts it into what it really is: a few neat bones and a dreadful grimace. In a closed world where everything is death, only death has value. But our affirmation is negative. Sugar-candy skulls, and tissue-paper skulls, and skeletons strung with fireworks . . . our popular images always poke fun at life, affirming the nothingness and insignificance of human existence. We decorate our houses with death's-heads, we eat bread in the shape of bones on the Day of the Dead, we love the songs and stories in which death laughs and cracks jokes, but all this boastful familiarity does not rid us of the question we all ask: What is death? We have not thought up a new answer. And each time we ask, we shrug our shoulders: Why should I care about death if I have never cared about life?

Does the Mexican open out in the presence of death? He praises it, celebrates it, cultivates it, embraces it, but he never surrenders himself to it. Everything is remote and strange to him, and nothing more so than death. He does not surrender himself to it because surrender entails a sacrifice. And a sacrifice, in turn, demands that someone must give and someone receive. That is, someone must open out and face a reality that transcends him. In a closed, nontranscendent world, death neither gives nor receives: it consumes itself and is self-gratifying. Therefore our relations with death are intimate—more intimate, perhaps, than those of any other people—but empty of meaning and devoid of erotic emotion. Death in Mexico is sterile, not fecund like that of the Aztecs and the Christians.

Nothing is more opposed to this attitude than that of the Europeans and North Americans. Their laws, customs, and public and private ethics all tend to preserve human life. This protection does not prevent the number of ingenious and refined murders, of perfect crimes and crime-waves, from increasing. The professional criminals who plot their murders with a precision impossible to a Mexican, the delight they take in describing their experiences and methods, the fascination with which the press and public follow their confessions, and the recognized inefficiency of the systems of prevention, show that the respect for life of which Western civilization is so proud is either incomplete or hypocritical.

The cult of life, if it is truly profound and total, is also the cult of death, because the two are inseparable. A civilization that denies death ends by denying life. The perfection of modern crime is not merely a consequence of modern technical progress and the vogue of the murder story: it derives from the contempt for life which is inevitably implicit in any attempt to hide death away and pretend it does not exist. It might be added that modern technical skills and the popularity of crime stories are, like concentration camps and collective extermination, the results of an optimistic and unilateral conception of existence. It is useless to exclude death from our images, our words, our ideas, because death will obliterate all of us, beginning with those who ignore it or pretend to ignore it.

When the Mexican kills—for revenge, pleasure, or caprice—he kills a person, a human being. Modern criminals and statesmen do not kill: they abolish. They experiment with beings who have lost their human qualities. Prisoners in the concentration camps are first degraded, changed into mere objects; then they are exterminated en masse. The typical criminal in the large cities—beyond the specific motives for his crimes—realizes on a small scale what the modern leader realizes on a grand scale. He too experiments, in his own way: he poisons, destroys corpses with acids, dismembers them, converts them into objects. The ancient relationship between victim and murderer, which is the only thing that humanizes murder, that makes it even thinkable, has disappeared. As in the novels of Sade, there is no longer anything except torturers and objects, instruments of pleasure and destruction. And the nonexistence of the victim makes the infinite solitude of the murderer even more intolerable. Murder is still a relationship in Mexico, and in this sense it has the same liberating significance as the fiesta or the confession. Hence its drama, its poetry and—why not say it?—its grandeur. Through murder we achieve a momentary transcendence.

At the beginning of his eight Duino Elegy, Rilke says that the "creature," in his condition of animal innocence, "beholds the open" . . . unlike ourselves, who never look forward, towards the absolute. Fear makes us turn our backs on death, and by refusing to contemplate it we shut ourselves off from life, which is a totality that includes it. The "open" is where contraries are reconciled, where light and shadow are fused. This conception restores death's original meaning: death and life are opposites that complement each other. Both are halves of a sphere that we, subjects of time and space, can only glimpse. In the prenatal world, life and death are merged; in ours, opposed; in the world beyond, reunited again, not in the animal innocence that precedes sin and the knowledge of sin, but as in innocence regained. Man can transcend the temporal opposition separating them (and residing not in them but in his own consciousness) and perceive them as a superior whole. This recognition can take place only through detachment: he must renounce his temporal life and his nostalgia for limbo, for the animal world. He must open himself out to death if he wishes to open himself out to life. Then he will be "like the angels."

Thus there are two attitudes towards death: one, pointing forward, that conceives of it as creation; the other, pointing backward, that expresses itself as a fascination with nothingness or as a nostalgia for limbo. No Mexican or Spanish-American poet, with the possible exception of César Vallejo, approaches the first of these two concepts. The absence of a mystic—and only a mystic is capable of offering insights like those of Rilke—indicates the extent to which modern Mexican culture is insensible to religion. But two Mexican poets, José Gorostiza and Xavier Villaurrutia represent the second of these two attitudes. For Gorostiza life is a "death without end," a perpetual falling into nothingness; for Villaurrutia it is no more than a "nostalgia for death."

The phrase that Villaurrutia chose for his book, *Nostalgia de la Muerte*, is not merely a lucky hit. The author has used it in order to tell us the ultimate meaning of his poetry. Death as nostalgia, rather than as the fruition or end of life, is death as origin. The ancient, original source is a bone, not a womb. This statement runs the risk of seeming either an empty paradox or an old commonplace: "For thou art dust, and unto dust shalt thou return." I believe that the poet hopes to find in death (which is, in effect, our origin) a revelation that his temporal life has denied him: the true meaning of life. When we die,

The second hand
will race around its dial,
all will be contained in an instant . . .
and perhaps it will be possible
to live, even after death.[4]

A return to original death would be a return to the life before life, the life before death: to limbo, to the maternal source.

Muerte sin Fin, the poem by José Gorostiza, is perhaps the best evidence we have in Latin America of a truly modern consciousness, one that is turned in upon itself, imprisoned in its own blinding clarity. The poet, in a sort of lucid fury, wants to rip the mask off existence in order to see it as it is. The dialogue between man and the world, which is as old as poetry and love, is transformed into a dialogue between the water and the glass that contains it, between the thought and the form into which it is poured and which it eventually corrodes. The poet warns us from his prison of appearances—trees and thoughts, stones and emotions, days and nights and twilights are all simply metaphors, mere colored ribbons—that the breath which informs matter, shaping it and giving it form, is the same breath that corrodes and withers and defeats it. It is a drama without personae, since all are merely reflections, the various disguises of a suicide who talks to himself in a language of mirrors and echoes, and the mind also is nothing more than a reflection of death, of death in love with itself. Everything is immersed in its own clarity and brilliance, everything is directed toward this transparent death: life is only a metaphor, an invention with which death—death too!—wants to deceive itself. The poem is a variation on the old theme of Narcissus, although there is no allusion to it in the text. And it is not only the consciousness that contemplates itself in its empty, transparent water (both mirror and eye at the same time, as in the Valéry poem): nothingness, which imitates form and life, which feigns corruption and death, strips itself naked and turns in upon itself, loves itself, falls into itself; a tireless death without end.

If we open out during fiestas, then, or when we are drunk or exchanging confidences, we do it so violently that we wound ourselves. And we shrug our shoulders at death, as at life, confronting it in silence or with a contemptuous smile. The fiesta, the crime of passion and the gratuitous crime reveal that the equilibrium of which we are so proud is only a mask, always in danger of being ripped off by a sudden explosion of our intimacy.

All of these attitudes indicate that the Mexican senses the presence of a stigma both on himself and on the flesh of his country. It is diffused but nonetheless living, original, and ineradicable. Our gestures and expressions all attempt to hide this wound, which is always open, always ready to catch fire and burn under the rays of a stranger's glance.

Now, every separation causes a wound. Without stopping to investigate how and when the separation is brought about, I want to point out that any break (with ourselves or those around us, with the past or the present) creates a feeling of solitude. In extreme cases—separation from one's parents, matrix, or native land, the death of the gods or a painful self-consciousness—solitude is identified with orphanhood. And both of them generally manifest themselves as a sense of sin. The penalties and guilty feelings inflicted by a state of separation can be considered, thanks to the ideas of expiation and redemption, as necessary sacrifices, as pledges or promises of a future communion that puts an end to the long exile. The guilt can vanish, the wound heal over, the separation resolve itself in communion. Solitude thus assumes a purgative, purifying character. The solitary or isolated individual transcends his solitude, accepting it as a proof or promise of communion.

The Mexican does not transcend his solitude. On the contrary, he locks himself up in it. We live in our solitude like Philoctetes on his island, fearing rather than hoping to return to the world. We cannot bear the presence of our companions. We hide within ourselves—except when we rend ourselves open in our frenzy—and the solitude in which we suffer has no reference either to a redeemer or a creator. We oscillate between intimacy and withdrawal, between a shout and a silence, between a fiesta and a wake, without ever truly surrendering ourselves. Our indifference hides life behind a death mask; our wild shout rips off this mask and shoots into the sky, where it swells, explodes, and falls back in silence and defeat. Either way, the Mexican shuts himself off from the world; from life and from death.

References

1. Padre Hidalgo's call-to-arms against Spain, 1810.
2. Fiesta of the Virgin of Guadalupe.
3. From the popular folk song *La Adelita*.
4. Quoted from Xavier Villaurrutia's poem *Décima Muerte*.

BIBLIOGRAPHY

Abely, X., and M. Leconte, "Attempt to Interpret Manic Reactions After Sorrow," *American Journal of Medical Psychology*, 96 (1938), 232–240.

Abrahamsson, Hans, *The Origin of Death: Studies in African Mythology*, unpublished thesis, Upsala College, 1951.

Adlerstein, A. M., *The Relationship Between Religious Belief and Death Affect*, unpublished doctoral dissertation, Princeton University, 1958.

Aginsky, B. W., "The Socio-psychological Significance of Death Among the Pomo Indians," *American Imago*, 1 (1940), 1–11.

Aldrich, C. K., "The Dying Patient's Grief," *Journal of the American Medical Association*, 184 (1963), 329–331.

Alexander, I. E., and A. M. Adlerstein, "Affective Responses to the Concept of Death in a Population of Children and Early Adolescents," *Journal of Genetic Psychology*, 93 (1958), 167–177.

—— and ——, "Death and Religion," in H. Feifel (Ed.), *The Meaning of Death* (New York: McGraw-Hill, 1959), pp. 271–283.

——, and ——, "Studies in the Psychology of Death," in Henry P. David and J. C. Brengelmann (Eds.), *Perspectives in Personality Research* (New York: Springer Publishing Co., 1960), pp. 65–92.

——, R. S. Colley, and A. M. Adlerstein, "Is Death a Matter of Indifference?" *Journal of Psychology*, 43 (1957), 277–283.

Altman, Leon L., "'West' as a Symbol of Death," *Psychiatric Quarterly*, 28 (1959), 236–241.

397

Anderson, Charles, "Aspects of Pathological Grief and Mourning," *International Journal of Psychoanalysis*, 30 (1949), 48–55.

Angrist, A. A., "A Pathologist's Experience with Attitudes Toward Death," *Rhode Island Medical Journal*, 43 (1960), 693–697.

Anthony, Sylvia, "A Study of the Development of the Concept of Death," (M.A. thesis abstract), *British Journal of Educational Psychology*, 9 (1939), 276–277.

——, *The Child's Discovery of Death* (New York: Harcourt, Brace and Co., 1940).

Archibald, Herbert C., D. Bell, C. Miller, and R. D. Tuddenham, "Bereavement in Childhood and Adult Psychiatric Disturbances," *Psychosomatic Medicine*, 24 (1962), 343–351.

Aronson, Gerald J., "Treatment of the Dying Person," in H. Feifel (Ed.), *The Meaning of Death* (New York: McGraw-Hill, 1959), pp. 251–258.

Autton, N., "A Study of Bereavement, 2 . . . . To Comfort All That Mourn," *Nursing Times*, 58 (1962), 1551–1552.

Bacon, Francis, "Of Death," *Bacon's Essays* (Ed. by S. H. Reynolds) (Oxford: Clarendon Press, 1890), pp. 12–18.

Baker, J. M., and K. C. Sorensen, "A Patient's Concern with Death," *American Journal of Nursing*, 63 (1963), 90–92.

Baler, Lenin A., and Peggy J. Golde, "Conjugal Bereavement: A Strategic Area of Research in Preventive Psychiatry," *Working Papers in Community Mental Health* (Harvard School of Public Health), 2 (Spring), 1964.

Banks, Sam A., "Dialogue on Death: Freudian and Christian Views," *Pastoral Psychology*, 14 (1963), 41–49.

Banta, Thomas J., "The Kennedy Assassination: Early Thoughts and Emotions," paper presented to meeting of the Midwest Psychological Association, St. Louis, 1964.

Barber, Theodore X., "Death by Suggestion," *Psychosomatic Medicine*, 23 (1961), 153–155.

Barnacle, Clarke H., "Grief Reactions and Their Treatment," *Diseases of the Nervous System*, 10 (1949), 173–176.

Barry, Herbert, "Orphanhood as a Factor in Psychoses," *Journal of Abnormal and Social Psychology*, 30 (1936), 431–438.

——, "A Study of Bereavement: An Approach to Problems in Mental Disease," *American Journal of Orthopsychiatry*, 9 (1939), 355–359.

——, "Significance of Maternal Bereavement Before the Age Eight in Psychiatric Patients," *Archives of Neurological Psychiatry*, 62 (1949), 630–637.

——, and W. A. Bousfield, "Incidence of Orphanhood Among Fifteen Hundred Psychotic Patients," *Journal of Genetic Psychology*, 50 (1937), 198–202.

——, and Erich Lindemann, "Critical Ages for Maternal Bereavement in Psychoneurosis," *Psychosomatic Medicine*, 22 (1960), 166–181.

Bataille, Georges, *Death and Sensuality: A Study of Eroticism and the Taboo* (New York: Walker, 1962).

Beatty, D., "Shall We Talk About Death?" *Pastoral Psychology*, 6 (1955), 11–14.

Becker, Howard, "The Sorrow of Bereavement," *Journal of Abnormal and Social Psychology*, 27 (1933), 391–410.

——, and David K. Bruner, "Attitudes Toward Death and the Dead and Some Possible Causes of Ghost Fear," *Mental Hygiene*, 15 (1931), 828–837.

Beigler, Jerome S, "Anxiety as an Aid in the Prognostication of Impending Death," *Archives of Neurological Psychiatry*, 77 (1957), 171–177.

Bendann, Effie, *Death Customs: An Analytical Study of Burial Rites* (New York: Knopf, 1930).

Bender, Lauretta, *Aggression, Hostility and Anxiety in Children* (Springfield, Ill.: C. C Thomas, 1953), pp. 40–65.

Beres, David, and Samuel J. Obers, "The Effects of Extreme Deprivation in Infancy on Psychic Structures in Adolescence," *The Psychoanalytic Study of the Child*, 5 (1950), 212–235.

Bergler, Edmund, "Psychopathology and Duration of Mourning in Neurotics," *Journal of Clinical Psychopathology*, 3 (1948), 478–482.

Bluestone, H. and C. C. McGahee, "Reaction to Extreme Stress: Impending Death by Execution," *American Journal of Psychiatry*, 119 (1962), 393–396.

Blum, G. S., and S. Rosenzweig, "The Incidence of Sibling and Parental Deaths in the Anamnesis of Female Schizophrenics," *Journal of General Psychology*, 31 (1944), 3–13.

Borkenau, Franz, "The Concept of Death," *The Twentieth Century*, 157 (1955), 313–329.

Bowlby, John, "Grief and Mourning in Infancy and Early Childhood," *The Psychoanalytic Study of the Child*, 15 (1960), 9–52.

——, "Separation Anxiety," *International Journal of Psychoanalysis*, 41 (1960), 89–113.

——, "Childhood Mourning and Its Implications for Psychiatry," *American Journal of Psychiatry*, 118 (1961), 481–498.

——, "Processes of Mourning," *International Journal of Psychoanalysis*, 42 (1961), 317–340.

——, "Loss, Detachment and Defense," in *The Psychopathology of Loss*, in press.

——, "Pathological Mourning and Childhood Mourning," *Journal of the American Psychoanalytic Association*, 11 (1963), 500–541.

Bowman, LeRoy, *The American Funeral* (Washington: Public Affairs Press, 1959).

Bozeman, Mary F., Charles E. Orbach, and Arthur M. Sutherland, "Psychological Impact of Cancer and Its Treatment: III. The Adaptation of Mothers to the Threatened Loss of Their Children Through Leukemia: Part I.," *Cancer*, 8 (1955), 1–19.

Brewster, Henry H., "Grief: A Disrupted Human Relationship," *Human Organization*, 9 (1950), 19–22.

——, "Separation Reaction in Psychosomatic Disease and Neurosis," *Psychosomatic Medicine*, 14 (1952), 154–160.

Brill, A. A., "Thoughts on Life and Death or Vidonian All Souls' Eve," *Psychiatric Quarterly*, 21 (1947), 199–211.

Brodsky, B., "Liebestod Fantasies in a Patient Faced with a Fatal Illness," *International Journal of Psychoanalysis*, 40 (1959), 13–16.

——, "The Self-Representation, Anality and the Fear of Dying," *Journal of the American Psychoanalytic Association*, 7 (1959), 95–108.

Bromberg, Walter, and Paul Schilder, "Death and Dying," *Psychoanalytic Review*, 20 (1933), 133–185.

——, and ——, "The Attitudes of Psychoneurotics Toward Death," *Psychoanalytic Review*, 23 (1936), 1–25.

Brown, Felix, "Depression and Childhood Bereavement," *Journal of Mental Science*, 107 (1961), 754–777.

Brown, Norman O., *Life Against Death* (Middletown, Conn.: Wesleyan University Press, 1959).

Bulger, Roger, "The Dying Patient and His Doctor," *Harvard Medical Alumni Bulletin*, 34 (1960), 23.

——, "Doctors and Dying" (editorial), *Archives of Internal Medicine*, 112 (1963), 327–332.

Burton, Arthur, "Death as a Countertransference," *Psychoanalysis and the Psychoanalytic Review*, 49 (1962), 3–20.

Cain, Albert C., and Barbara S. Cain, "On Replacing a Child" (Digest of paper presented at meeting of American Orthopsychiatric Association, Los Angeles, 1962), *American Journal of Orthopsychiatry*, 32 (1962), 297–298.

——, Irene Fast, and Mary Erickson, "Children's Disturbed Reactions to the Death of a Sibling," *American Journal of Orthopsychiatry*, 34 (1964), 741–752.

Cannon, Walter B., " 'Voodoo' Death," *American Anthropologist*, 44 (1942), 169–181.

Cappon, D., "The Dying," *Psychiatric Quarterly*, 33 (1959), 466–489.

——, "Attitudes of and Towards the Dying," *Canadian Medical Association Journal*, 87 (1962), 693–700.

Caprio, F. S., "A Psycho-social Study of Primitive Conceptions of Death," *Journal of Criminal Psychopathology*, 5 (1943), 303–317.

——, "Ethnological Attitudes Toward Death: A Psychoanalytic Evaluation," *Journal of Clinical and Experimental Psychopathology*, 7 (1946), 737–752.

——, "A Study of Some Psychological Reactions During Prepubescence to the Idea of Death," *Psychiatric Quarterly*, 24 (1950), 495–505.

Carmichael, B., "The Death Wish in Daily Life," *Psychoanalytic Review*, 30 (1943), 59–66.

Carnell, E. J., "Fear of Death," *Christian Century*, 80 (1963), 136–137.

Carpenter, Edmund S., "Eternal Life and Self-definition Among the Aivilik Eskimos," *American Journal of Psychiatry*, 110 (1954), 840–843.

Carr, J. L., 'The Coroner and the Common Law. III. Death and its Medical Imputations," *California Medicine*, 93 (1960), 32–34.

Carstairs, G. M., "Attitudes to Death and Suicide in an Indian Cultural Setting." *International Journal of Social Psychiatry*, 1 (1955), 33–41.

Chadwick, Mary, "Notes Upon the Fear of Death," *International Journal of Psychoanalysis*, 10 (1929), 321–334.

Chodoff, P., "A Psychiatric Approach to the Dying Patient," *Cancer*, 10 (1960), 29–32.

Choron, Jacques, *Death and Western Thought* (New York: Collier-Macmillan, 1963).

Christ, A. E., "Attitudes Toward Death Among a Group of Acute Geriatric Psychiatric Patients," *Journal of Gerontology*, 16 (1961), 56–59.

Christenson, L., "The Physician's Role in Terminal Illness and Death," *Minnesota Medicine*, 46 (1963), 881–883.

Cleveland, F. P., " 'Masquerades': Homicide, Suicide, Accident or Natural Death," *Journal of Indiana Medical Association*, 53 (1960), 2181–2184.

———, "The Dance of Death," *Journal of the American Medical Association*, 176 (1961), 142–143.

Cobb, Beatrix, "Psychological Impact of Long Illness and Death of a Child on the Family Circle," *Journal of Pediatrics*, 49 (1956), 746–751.

Cochrane, A. L., "Elie Metschnikoff and his Theory of an 'Instinct de la Mort'," *International Journal of Psychoanalysis*, 15 (1934), 265–270.

Cohen, M., and L. M. Lipton, "Spontaneous Remission of Schizophrenic Psychoses Following Maternal Death," *Psychiatric Quarterly*, 24 (1950), 716–725.

Colliers Encyclopedia, "Death Customs and Rites" (New York: Collier and Son, Corp., 1958), Vol. 6, pp. 310–317.

Corey, Lawrence G., "An Analogue of Resistance to Death Awareness," *Journal of Gerontology*, 16 (1961), 59–60.

Cousinet, R., "L'Idee de la Mort chez les Enfants," *Journal of Normal and Pathological Psychology*, 36 (1939), 65–75.

Creegan, R. F., "A Symbolic Action During Bereavement," *Journal of Abnormal and Social Psychology*, 37 (1942), 403–405.

Curphey, Theodore J., "The Role of the Forensic Pathologist in the Multidisciplinary Approach to Death," paper presented to meeting of the American Psychological Association, Los Angeles, 1964.

Custer, H. R., "Nursing Care of the Dying," *Hospital Programs*, 42 (1961), 68.

DeJarast, S. G., "Mourning in Relation to Learning" (in Spanish), *Revista de Psicoanalisis*, 15 (1958), 31–35.

Deutsch, Felix, "Euthanasia: A Clinical Study," *Psychoanalytic Quarterly*, 5 (1936), 347–368.

Deutsch, Helene, "A Two-year-old Boy's First Love Comes to Grief," in L. Jessner and E. Pavenstedt (Eds.), *Dynamics of Psychopathology in Childhood* (New York: Grune and Stratton, 1959).

———, "Absence of Grief," *Psychoanalytic Quarterly*, 6 (1937), 12–22.

Devereux, George, "Primitive Psychiatry, Funeral Suicide and the Mohave Social Structure," *Bulletin of the History of Medicine*, 11 (1942), 522–542.

———, "Social Structure and the Economy of Affective Bonds," *Psychoanalytic Review*, 29 (1942), 303–314.

DeVos, George, and Hiroshi Wagatsuma, "Psycho-cultural Significance of Concern Over Death and Illness Among Rural Japanese," *International Journal of Social Psychiatry*, 5 (1959), 5–19.

Diggory, James C., "Death and Self-Esteem," paper presented to meeting of the American Psychological Association, St. Louis, 1962.

———, and Doreen Z. Rothman, "Values Destroyed by Death," *Journal of Abnormal and Social Psychology*, 63 (1961), 205–210.

Earle, A. M., and B. V. Earle, "Early Maternal Deprivation and Later Psychiatric Illness," *American Journal of Orthopsychiatry*, 31 (1961), 181–186.

Eissler, Kurt R., *The Psychiatrist and the Dying Patient* (New York: International University Press, 1955).

Eliot, Thomas D., "The Adjustive Behavior of Bereaved Families: A New Field for Research," *Social Forces*, 8 (1930), 543–549.

———, "Bereavement as a Problem for Family Research and Technique," *The Family*, 11 (1930), 114–115.

——, "The Bereaved Family," *Annals of the American Academy of Political and Social Sciences*, 160 (1932), 184–190.

——, "A Step Toward the Social Psychology of Bereavement," *Journal of Abnormal and Social Psychology*, 27 (1933), 380–390.

——, "Bereavement as a Field of Social Research," *Bulletin of the Society for Social Research*, 17 (1938), 4.

——, ". . . Of the Shadow of Death, " *Annals of the American Academy of Political and Social Sciences*, 229 (1943), 87–99.

——, "War Bereavements and Their Recovery," *Marriage and Family Living*, 8 (1946), 1–6.

——, "Attitudes Toward Euthanasia," *Research Studies of the State College of Washington*, 15 (1947), 131–134.

——, "Bereavement: Inevitable but Not Insurmountable," in H. Becker and R. Hill (Eds.), *Family, Marriage and Parenthood* (Boston: Heath, 1955), pp. 641–668.

Encyclopedia Americana, "Death" (New York: American Corporation, 1959), Vol. 8, pp. 539–544.

Encyclopaedia Britannica, "Dead," "Death," "Death Rates" (Chicago: William Benton, 1961), Vol. 7, pp. 96–98; 108–114.

Encyclopedia of the Social Sciences, "Death Customs" (New York: Macmillan, 1931), Vol. 5, pp. 21–27.

Engel, G., "Is Grief a Disease?" *Psychosomatic Medicine*, 23 (1961), 18–22.

Evelson, E., and R. Grinberg, "The Child's Concept of Death," (in Spanish), *Revista de Psicoanálisis*, 19 (1962), 344–350.

Fairbairn, W. R. D., "The Effect of the King's Death Upon Patients Under Analysis," *International Journal of Psychoanalysis*, 17 (1936), 278–284.

Fairbanks, Rollin J., "Ministering to the Dying," *Journal of Pastoral Care*, 2 (1948), 6–14.

Fast, Irene, and Albert C. Cain, "Disturbances in Parent-Child Relationships Following Bereavement," unpublished paper, University of Michigan, 1963.

——, and ——, "Fears of Death in Bereaved Children and Adults," (digest of paper presented to the American Orthopsychiatric Association, Chicago, 1964), *American Journal of Orthopsychiatry*, 34 (1964), 278–279.

Federn, Paul, "The Reality of the Death Instinct," *Psychoanalytic Review*, 19 (1932), 129–150.

Feifel, Herman, "Attitudes of Mentally Ill Patients Toward Death," *Journal of Nervous and Mental Disease*, 122 (1955), 375–380.

——, "Older Persons Look at Death," *Geriatrics*, 11 (1956), 127–130.

——, (Ed.), *The Meaning of Death* (New York: McGraw-Hill, 1959).

——, "Attitudes Toward Death in Some Normal and Mentally Ill Populations," in H. Feifel (Ed.), *The Meaning of Death* (New York: McGraw-Hill, 1959), pp. 114–130.

——, "Death-Relevant Variable in Psychology," in R. May (Ed.), *Existential Psychology* (New York: Random House, 1961), pp. 61–74.

——, "Scientific Research in Taboo Areas—Death," *American Behavioral Scientist*, 5 (1962), 28–30.

——, "Death," in A. Deutsch (Ed.), *The Encyclopedia of Mental Health* (New York: Franklin Watts, 1963), Vol. 2, pp. 427–450.

——, "Death," in Norman L. Farberow (Ed.), *Taboo Topics* (New York: Atherton Press, 1963), pp. 8–21.

——, "The Problem of Death," paper presented to meeting of the American Psychological Association, Los Angeles, 1964.

Fenichel, Otto, "A Critique of the Death Instinct," (1935), in *The Collected Papers of Otto Fenichel* (New York: W. W. Norton and Co., 1953), Vol. I, pp. 363–372.

Fleming, Joan, and Sol Altschul, "Activation of Mourning and Growth by Psychoanalysis," *Bulletin of the Philadelphia Association of Psychoanalysts,* 9 (1959), 37–38.

——, and ——, V. Zielinski, and M. Forman, "The Influence of Parent Loss in Childhood on Personality Development and Ego Structure," paper read at meeting of the American Psychoanalytic Association, San Francisco, 1958.

Flügel, J. C., "Death Instinct, Homeostasis and Allied Concepts," *International Journal of Psychoanalysis* (Supplement), 34 (1953), 43–74.

Fodor, N., "Jung's Sermons to the Dead," *Psychoanalytic Review*, 51 (1964), 74–78.

Folck, Marilyn Melcher, and Phyllis J. Nie, "Nursing Students Learn to Face Death," *Nursing Outlook*, 7 (1959), 510–513.

Forest, Jack D., "The Major Emphasis of the Funeral," *Pastoral Psychology*, 14 (1963), 19–24.

Foster, L. E., Erich Lindemann, and Rollin J. Fairbanks, "Grief," *Pastoral Psychology*, 1 (1950), 28–30.

Foxe, A. N., "Critique of Freud's Concept of a Death Instinct," *Psychoanalytic Review*, 30 (1943), 417–427.

Frankl, Viktor E., *From Death Camp to Existentialism: A Psychiatrist's Path to a New Therapy* (Boston: Beacon Press, 1959).

——, "Psychiatry and Man's Quest for Meaning," *Journal of Religion and Health*, 1 (1962), 93–103.

Frazer, James G., *The Fear of the Dead in Primitive Religion* (London: Macmillan, 1933) (3 volumes).

Freud, Anna, "Discussion of 'Grief and Mourning in Infancy and Early Childhood' by Bowlby," *The Psychoanalytic Study of the Child*, 15 (1960), 53–94.

——, *War and Children* (New York: International University Press, 1942).

Freud, Sigmund, "Dreams of the Death of Persons of Whom the Dreamer is Fond," (1900), *Standard Edition* (London: Hogarth, 1953), Vol. 4, pp. 248–271.

——, "The Theme of the Three Caskets," (1913), *Collected Papers* (New York: Basic Books, 1959), Vol. 4. pp. 244–256.

——, "Thoughts for the Times on War and Death," (1915), *Collected Papers* (New York: Basic Books, 1959), Vol. 4, pp. 288–317.

——, "Mourning and Melancholia," (1917), *Collected Papers* (New York: Basic Books, 1959), Vol. 4, pp. 152–170.

——, "The Uncanny," (1919), *Collected Papers*, (New York: Basic Books, 1959), Vol. 4, pp. 368–407.

——, "Beyond the Pleasure Principle," (1920), *Standard Edition* (London: Hogarth, 1955), Vol. 18, pp. 7–64.

——, "Inhibitions, Symptoms and Anxiety," (1926), *Standard Edition* (London: Hogarth, 1959), Vol. 20, pp. 87–174.

———, "Dostoevsky and Parricide," (1928), *Collected Papers*, (New York: Basic Books, 1959), Vol. 5, pp. 222–242.

Friedlander, Kate, "On the 'Longing to Die'," *International Journal of Psychoanalysis*, 21 (1940), 416–426.

Friedman, D. B., "Death Anxiety and the Primal Scene," *Psychoanalytic Review*, 48 (1961), 108–119.

Friedman, Stanford B., P. Chodoff, J. W. Mason, and D. A. Hamburg, "Behavioral Observations of Parents Anticipating the Death of a Child," *Pediatrics*, 32 (1963), 610–625.

Friedman, S. M., "An Empirical Study of the Castration and Oedipus Complexes," *Genetic Psychology Monographs*, 46 (1952), 61–130.

Fritz, Mary Apolline, "A Study of Widowhood," *Sociology and Social Research*, 14 (1930), 553–559.

Fulcomer, David M., "The Adjustive Behavior of Some Recently Bereaved Spouses," unpublished doctoral dissertation, Northwestern University, 1942.

Fulton, Robert, "Attitudes Toward Death: A Discussion," *Journal of Gerontology*, 16 (1961), 63–65.

———, "The Clergyman and The Funeral Director: A Study in Role Conflict," *Social Forces*, 39 (1961), 317–323.

———, *The Sacred and the Secular: Attitudes of the American Public Toward Death* (Milwaukee: Bulfin, 1963), 23 pp.

———, "Death and the Self," *Journal of Religion and Health*, 3 (1964), 359–368.

———, and William A. Faunce, "The Sociology of Death: A Neglected Area of Research," *Social Forces*, 36 (1958), 205–209.

———, and Gilbert Geis, "Death and Social Values," *Indian Journal of Social Research*, 3 (1962), 7–14.

———, and ———, "Ritual and Role Conflict: The Rabbi and the Funeral Director," Los Angeles: California State College, 1964. Mimeographed, 16 pp.

———, and Phyllis Langton, "Attitudes Toward Death: An Emerging Mental Health Problem," *Nursing Forum*, 3 (1964), 104–112.

Galdston, Iago, "Eros and Thanatos: A Critique and Elaboration of Freud's Death Wish," *American Journal of Psychoanalysis*, 15 (1955), 123–134.

Gavey, C., *The Management of the "Hopeless" Case* (London: H. K. Lewis, 1952).

Gealy, Fred D., "The Biblical Understanding of Death," *Pastoral Psychology*, 14 (1963), 33–40.

Gibson, P. C., "The Dying Patient," *Practitioner*, 186 (1961), 85–91.

Giesey, R. E., "The Royal Funeral Ceremony in Renaissance France," unpublished doctoral dissertation, University of California at Berkeley, 1954.

Glaser, Barney G., and Anselm L. Strauss, "Expecting Patients to Die: Temporal Aspects of Status Passage," San Francisco, University of California Medical Center, 1963. Mimeographed, 22 pp.

———, and ———, "The Social Loss of Dying Patients," San Francisco, University of California Medical Center, 1963. Mimeographed, 12 pp.

Glidden, Thomas, "The American Funeral," *Pastoral Psychology*, 14 (1963), 9–18.

Gluckman, Max, "Mortuary Customs and the Belief in Survival After Death Among the South-eastern Bantu," *Bantu Studies* (Johannesburg: University of the Witwaterstrand Press), Vol. 11, pp. 117–136.

Goody, Jack, "Death and Social Control Among the Lo Dagaa," *Man*, 59 (1959 b), 134–138.

——, *Death, Property and the Ancestors. A Study of the Mortuary Customs of the Lo Dagaa of West Africa* (Palo Alto: Stanford University Press, 1962).

Gorer, Geoffrey, "The Pornography of Death," in W. Phillips and P. Rahv (Eds.), *Modern Writing* (New York: Berkeley, 1956), pp. 56–62.

Gottlieb, Carla, "Modern Art and Death," in H. Feifel (Ed.), *The Meaning of Death* (New York: McGraw-Hill, 1959), pp. 157–188.

Gough, E. K., "Cults of the Dead Among the Nayars," *Journal of American Folklore*, 71 (1958), 446–478.

Graham, J. B., "Acceptance of Death—Beginning of Life," *North Carolina Medical Journal*, 24 (1963), 317–319.

Green, W. A., "Role of a Vicarious Object in the Adaptation of Object Loss: I. Use of a Vicarious Object," *Psychosomatic Medicine*, 20 (1958), 344–350.

Greenberg, N. H., John G. Loesch, and Martin Lakin, "Life Situations Associated with the Onset of Pregnancy: I The Role of Separation in a Group of Unmarried Women," *Psychosomatic Medicine*, 21 (1959), 296–311.

Greenberger, E. S., "Fantasies of Women Confronting Death: A Study of Critically Ill Patients," unpublished doctoral dissertation, Radcliffe College, 1961.

Greenson, Ralph R., "Sleep, Dreams and Death," transcript of radio broadcast on station K.P.F.K., Los Angeles, November 16, 1961. Mimeographed, 12 pp.

Greer, Ina May, "Grief Must Be Faced," *Christian Century*, 62 (1945), 269–271.

Gregory, Ian, "Studies of Parental Deprivation in Psychiatric Patients," *American Journal of Psychiatry*, 115 (1958), 432–442.

Grotjahn, Martin, "About the Representation of Death in the Art of Antiquity and in the Unconscious of Modern Man," in George B. Wilber and Warner Muensterberger (Eds.), *Psychoanalysis and Culture* (New York: International University Press, 1951), pp. 410–424.

——, "Ego Identity and the Fear of Death and Dying," *Hillside Hospital Journal*, 9 (1960), 147–155.

Habenstein, R. W., and W. M. Lamers, *The History of American Funeral Directing* (Milwaukee: Bulfin, 1955).

——, and ——, *Funeral Customs the World Over* (Milwaukee: Bulfin, 1961).

Hackett, Thomas P., and Avery D. Weisman, "The Treatment of the Dying," *Current Psychiatric Therapy*, 2 (1962), 121–126.

Hall, G. S., "A Study of Fears," *American Journal of Psychology*, 8 (1897), 147–249.

——, "Thanatophobia and Immortality," *American Journal of Psychology*, 26 (1915), 550–613.

Hamovitch, Maurice B., "Parental Reactions to the Death of a Child," City of Hope Medical Center, Duarte, California, 1962. Mimeographed, 27 pp.

——, "Research Interviewing in Terminal Illness," *Social Work*, 8 (1963), 4–9.

Harmer, Ruth M., *The High Cost of Dying* (New York: Crowell-Collier, 1963).

Harnik, J., "One Component of the Fear of Death in Early Infancy," *International Journal of Psychoanalysis*, 11 (1930), 485–491.

Hartland, E. Sidney, "Death and the Disposal of the Dead," in James Hastings (Ed.), *Encyclopaedia of Religion and Ethics* (New York: C. Scribner's Sons, 1912), Vol. 4, pp. 411–444.

Havighurst, Robert, "The Career of the Funeral Director," unpublished doctoral dissertation, University of Chicago, 1954.

Heckel, R. V., "The Day the President was Assassinated: Patient's Reaction in One Mental Hospital," *Mental Hospitals*, 15 (1964), 48.

Heinicke, C. M., "Some Effects of Separating Two-year-old Children from Their Parents: A Comparative Study," *Human Relations*, 9 (1956), 105–176.

Hertz, Robert, "A Contribution to the Study of the Collective Representation of Death," in *Death and the Right Hand* (translated from the French by Rodney and Claudia Needham) (Glencoe, Ill.: Free Press, 1960), pp. 29–86.

Hickerson, Harold, "The Feast of the Dead Among the Seventeenth Century Algonkians of the Upper Great Lakes," *American Anthropologist*, 62 (1960), 81–107.

Hilgard, Josephine R., "Anniversary Reactions in Parents Precipitated by Children," *Psychiatry*, 16 (1953), 73–80.

——, and M. F. Newman, "Anniversaries in Mental Illness," *Psychiatry*, 22 (1959), 113–121.

——, and ——, "Early Parental Deprivation in Schizophrenia and Alcoholism," *American Journal of Orthopsychiatry*, 33 (1963), 409–420.

——, and ——, "Parental Loss by Death in Childhood as an Etiological Factor Among Schizophrenic and Alcoholic Patients Compared with a Non-patient Community Sample," *Journal of Nervous and Mental Disease*, 137 (1963), 14–28.

——, ——, and F. Fisk, "Strength of Adult Ego Following Childhood Bereavement," *American Journal of Orthopsychiatry*, 30 (1960), 788–798.

Hinton, J. M., "The Physical and Mental Distress of the Dying," *Quarterly Journal of Medicine*, 32 (1963), 1–21.

——, "Problems in the Care of the Dying," *Journal of Chronic Diseases*, 17 (1961), 201–205.

Hocking, W. E., *The Meaning of Immortality in Human Experience* (New York: Harpers, 1957).

Hoffman, Francis H., and Morris W. Brody, "The Symptom: Fear of Death," *Psychoanalytic Review*, 44 (1957), 433–438.

Hoffman, Frederick J., "Mortality and Modern Literature," in H. Feifel (Ed.), *The Meaning of Death* (New York: McGraw-Hill, 1959), pp. 133–156.

Howard, J. D., "Fear of Death," *Journal of the Indiana Medical Association*, 54 (1961), 1773–1779.

Hutschnecker, Arnold A., "Personality Factors in Dying Patients," in H. Feifel (Ed.), *The Meaning of Death* (New York: McGraw-Hill, 1959), pp. 237–250.

Ingles, T., "Death on a Ward," *Nursing Outlook*, 12 (1964), 28.

Irion, Paul E., *The Funeral and the Mourners* (New York: Abingdon, 1954).

——, "The Funeral and the Integrity of the Church," *Pastoral Psychology*, 14 (1963), 25–32.

Jackson, Edgar N., "Grief and Religion," in H. Feifel (Ed.), *The Meaning of Death* (New York: McGraw-Hill, 1959), pp. 218–233.

——, "Grief and Guilt," *The Pastoral Counselor*, 1 (1963), 34–38.

——, *For the Living* (New York: Channel Press, 1963).

——, *You and Your Grief* (New York: Channel Press, 1963).

Jakobovits, I., "The Dying and Their Treatment in Jewish Law," *Hebrew Medical Journal*, 2 (1961), 242–251.

Jeffers, Frances C., C. R. Nichols, and C. Eisdorfer, "Attitudes of Older Persons Toward Death: A Preliminary Study," *Journal of Gerontology*, 16 (1961), 53–56.

Jelliffe, S. E., "The Death Instinct in Somatic and Psychopathology," *Psychoanalytic Review*, 20 (1933), 121–131.

Johannsen, Dorothea E., "Reactions to the Death of President Roosevelt," *Journal of Abnormal and Social Psychology*, 41 (1946), 218–222.

Jones, E., "On 'Dying Together'," in *Essays in Applied Psychoanalysis* (London: Hogarth, 1951), pp. 9–15.

Jones, K. S., "Death and Doctors," *Medical Journal of Australia*, 49 (1962), 329–334.

Jones, T. T., "Dignity in Death. The Application and Withholding of Interventive Measures," *Journal of the Louisiana Medical Society*, 13 (1961), 180–183.

Jones, William Tudor, *Metaphysics of Life and Death* (New York: George H. Doran Co., 1924).

Joseph, F., "Transference and Countertransference in the Case of a Dying Patient," *Psychoanalysis*, 49 (1962), 21–34.

Jung, Carl G., "The Soul and Death," in H. Feifel (Ed.), *The Meaning of Death* (New York: McGraw-Hill, 1959), pp. 3–15.

Kalish, Richard, A., "An Approach to the Study of Death Attitudes," *American Behavioral Scientist*, 6 (1963), 68–70.

——, "Dealing With the Grieving Family," *R.N.* 26 (1963), 81–84.

——, "Some Variables in Death Attitudes," *Journal of Social Psychology*, 59 (1963), 137–145.

Kalsey, Virginia, "As Life Ebbs," *American Journal of Nursing*, 48 (1948), 170–173.

Kanders, O., "Der Todesgedanke in der Nervose und in der Psychose," *Der Nervenartz*, 6 (1934), 288.

Kasper, August M., "The Doctor and Death," in H. Feifel (Ed.), *The Meaning of Death* (New York: McGraw-Hill, 1959), pp. 259–270.

Kastenbaum, Robert, "Time and Death in Adolescence," in H. Feifel (Ed.), *The Meaning of Death* (New York: McGraw-Hill, 1959), pp. 99–113.

——, and Charles E. Goldsmith, "The Funeral Director and the Meaning of Death," *American Funeral Director*, 86 (1963), April: pp. 35–37; May: pp. 47–48; June: pp. 45–46.

Kaufmann, Walter, "Existentialism and Death," in H. Feifel (Ed.), *The Meaning of Death* (New York: McGraw-Hill, 1959), pp. 39–63.

Keeler, W. R., "Children's Reaction to the Death of A Parent," in P. H. Hoch and J. Zubin (Eds.), *Depression* (New York: Grune and Stratton, 1954), pp. 109–120.

Kelly, William H., "Cocopa Attitudes and Practices with Respect to Death and Mourning," *Southwestern Journal of Anthropology*, 5 (1949), 151–164.

Kennard, E. A., "Hopi Reactions to Death," *American Anthropologist*, 29 (1937), 491–494.

Kephart, William M., "Status After Death," *American Sociological Review*, 15 (1950), 635–643.

Kevorkian, J., "The Eye of Death," *Clinical Symposia*, 13 (1961), 51–62.
Keyes, E. L., "The Fear of Death," *Harper's Magazine*, 99 (1909), 208–212.
Kidorf, Irwin W., "Jewish Tradition and the Freudian Theory of Mourning," *Journal of Religion and Health*, 2 (1963), 248–252.
Klein, Melanie, "Mourning and its Relation to Manic-depressive States," (1940), in *Contributions to Psychoanalysis* (London: Hogarth, 1948), pp. 311–338.
———, "A Contribution to the Theory of Anxiety and Guilt," *International Journal of Psychoanalysis*, 29 (1948), 114–123.
Klopfer, W. G., "Attitudes Toward Death in the Aged," unpublished master's thesis, City College, New York, 1947.
Knudson, Alfred G., and Joseph M. Natterson, "Participation of Parents in the Hospital Care of Fatally Ill Children," *Pediatrics*, 26 (1960), 482–490.
Kostrubala, T., "Therapy of the Terminally Ill Patient," *Illinois Medical Journal*, 124 (1963), 545–547.
Kotovsky, D., "Die Psychologie der Todesfurcht," *Monatsberichte*, 1 (1936), 21–40.
Koupernik, C., "A Drama of Our Times: Euthanasia," *Concours Medical*, 84 (1962), 4687–4688.
Krupp, George R., and Bernard Kligfeld, "The Bereavement Reaction: A Cross-cultural Evaluation," *Journal of Religion and Health*, 1 (1962), 222–246.
Leclaire, Serge, "La Mort dans la Vie de l'Obsédé," *Psychoanalyse*, 2 (1956), 111–144.
Lee, Reuel P., *Burial Customs, Ancient and Modern* (Minneapolis: The Arya Co., 1929).
Lehrman, Samuel R., "Reactions to Untimely Death," *Psychiatric Quarterly*, 30 (1956), 564–578.
Leshan L., and E. Leshan, "Psychotherapy and the Patient with a Limited Life Span," *Psychiatry*, 24 (1961), 318–323.
———, and R. E. Worthington, "Some Psychological Correlates of Neoplastic Disease: A Preliminary Report," *Journal of Clinical and Experimental Psychopathology and the Quarterly Review of Psychiatric Neurology*, 16 (1955), 281–288.
Letourneau, C. V., "A Soliloquy on Death," *Hospital Management*, 96 (1963), 58–60.
Lifton, Robert Jay, "Psychological Effects of the Atomic Bomb in Hiroshima: the Theme of Death," *Daedalus*, 92 (1963), 462–497.
Lindemann, Erich, "Symptomatology and Management of Acute Grief," *American Journal of Psychiatry*, 101 (1944), 141–148.
———, "Modifications in the Course of Ulcerative Colitis in Relationship to Changes in Life Situations and Reaction Patterns," in H. G. Wolff (Ed.), *Life Stress and Bodily Disease* (Baltimore: Williams and Wilkins Co., 1950), pp. 706–723.
———, and Ina May Greer, "A Study of Grief. Emotional Responses to Suicide," *Pastoral Psychology*, 4 (1953), 9–13.
———, "Psychological Aspects of Mourning," *The Director*, 31 (1961), 14–17.
Lipson, Channing T., "Denial and Mourning," *International Journal of Psychoanalysis*, 44 (1963), 104–107.
Loesser, Lewis H., and Thea Bry, "The Role of Death Fears in the Etiology of Phobic Anxiety as Reversal in Group Psychotherapy," *International Journal of Group Psychotherapy*, 10 (1960), 287–297.

Lourie, R. S., "The Pediatrician and the Handling of Terminal Illness," *Pediatrics*, 32 (1963), 477–479.

McClelland, D. C., "The Harlequin Complex," in R. W. White (Ed.), *The Study of Lives* (New York: Atherton Press, 1963), pp. 94–119.

McCully, R. S., "Fantasy Productions of Children With a Progressively Crippling and Fatal Illness," *Journal of Genetic Psychology*, 102 (1963), 203–216.

McDonald, Arthur, "Death Psychology of Historical Personages," *American Journal of Psychology*, 33 (1921), 552–556.

Madow, L., and S. E. Hardy, "Incidence and Analysis of the Broken Family in the Background of Neurosis," *American Journal of Orthopsychiatry*, 17 (1947), 521–528.

Maeterlinck, Maurice, *Our Eternity (Extension of Essay on Death)* (London: Methuen and Co., Ltd., 1913).

Mahler, Margaret S., "Helping Children to Accept Death," *Child Study*, 27 (1950), 98–99, 119–120.

Malinowski, Bronislaw, "Death and the Reintegration of the Group," in *Magic, Science and Religion* (New York: Doubleday, 1954), pp. 47–53.

Mandelbaum, David G., "Social Uses of Funeral Rites," in H. Feifel (Ed.), *The Meaning of Death* (New York: McGraw-Hill, 1959), pp. 189–217.

Marcuse, Herbert, "The Ideology of Death," in H. Feifel (Ed.), *The Meaning of Death* (New York: McGraw-Hill, 1959), pp. 64–76.

Marris, P. *Widows and Their Families* (London: Routledge and Kegan Paul, 1958).

Martí-Ibáñez, Felix, "The Pale Sweetheart," (editorial), *M.D. of Canada*, September (1964), 7–9.

Maurer, Adah, "Maturation of Attitudes Toward Death," paper presented at meeting of the American Psychological Association, Los Angeles, 1964.

Means, Marie Hackl, "Fears of One Thousand College Women," *Journal of Abnormal and Social Psychology*, 31 (1936), 291–311.

Meiss, M., "The Oedipal Problem of a Fatherless Child," *The Psychoanalytic Study of the Child*, 7 (1952), 216–229.

Meissner, W. W., "Affective Response to Psychoanalytic Death Symbols," *Journal of Abnormal and Social Psychology*, 56 (1958), 295–299.

Melcher, Achim, "Der Tod als Thema der Neueren Medizinischen Literatur," *Jahrbuch für Psychologie und Psychotherapie*, 3 (1955), 371–382.

Melikian, L. H., "The Use of Selected T.A.T. Cards Among Arab University Students: A Cross-Cultural Study," *Journal of Social Psychology*, 62 (1964), 3–19.

Meninger, E., "Death from Psychic Causes," *Bulletin of the Menninger Clinic*, 12 (1948), 31–36.

Menninger, Karl, *Man Against Himself* (New York: Harcourt, Brace and Co., 1938).

——, "Dr. Karl's Reading Notes," *Menninger Library Journal*, 1 (1956), 15.

Meyerson, Abraham, "Prolonged Cases of Grief Reactions Treated by Electric Shock," *New England Journal of Medicine*, 230 (1944), 255–256.

Middaugh, Bruce L., "The Ministry of Bereavement," *Pastoral Psychology*, 1 (1950).

Middleton, W. C., "Some Reactions Toward Death Among College Students," *Journal of Abnormal and Social Psychology*, 31 (1936), 165–173.

Mira y Lōpez, E., "Psychopathology of Anger and Fear Reactions in Wartime," *American Clinician*, 5 (1943), 98 ff.

Mitchell, Nellie D., "The Significance of the Loss of the Father Through Death," (digest of paper read at meeting of the American Orthopsychiatric Association, Chicago, 1964), *American Journal of Orthopsychiatry*, 34 (1964), 279–280.

Mitford, Jessica, *The American Way of Death* (New York: Simon and Schuster, 1963).

Mitra, D. N., "Mourning Customs and Modern Life in Bengal," *American Journal of Sociology*, 52 (1947), 309–311.

Moellenhoff, F., "Ideas of Children About Death," *Bulletin of the Menninger Clinic*, 3 (1939), 148–156.

Monsour, Karem J., "Asthma and the Fear of Death," *Psychoanalytic Quarterly*, 29 (1960), 56–71.

Moreno, J. L., "The Social Atom and Death," *Sociometry*, 10 (1947), 80–84.

Moriarty, D. M., "Early Loss and the Fear of Mothering," *Psychoanalysis and the Psychoanalytic Review*, 49 (1962), 63–69.

Morin, Edgar, *L'Homme et la Mort dans L'Histoire* (Paris: Corrêa, 1951).

Moritz, Alan R., and Norman Zamcheck, "Sudden and Unexpected Death of Young Soldiers," *Archives of Pathology*, 42 (1946), 459–494.

Morrissey, James R., "A Note on Interviews with Children Facing Imminent Death," *Social Casework*, 44 (1963), 343–345.

Muensterberger, Warner, "Vom Ursprung des Todes," *Psyche*, 17 (1963), 169–184.

Murgoci, A., "Customs Connected with Death and Burial Among the Roumanians," *Folk-Lore*, 30 (1919), 89–102.

Murphy, Gardner, "Discussion," in H. Feifel, (Ed.), *The Meaning of Death* (New York: McGraw-Hill, 1959), pp. 317–340.

Nagy, Maria H., "The Child's Theories Concerning Death," *Journal of Genetic Psychology*, 73 (1948), 3–27.

Natterson, J. M., and A. G. Knudson, "Observations Concerning Fear of Death in Fatally Ill Children and Their Mothers," *Psychosomatic Medicine*, 22 (1960), 456–466.

Nemtzow, Jesse, and Stanley R. Lesser, "Reactions of Children and Parents to the Death of President Kennedy" (digest of paper read at meeting of the American Orthopsychiatric Association, Chicago, 1964), *American Journal of Orthopsychiatry*, 34 (1964), 280–281.

Noon, John A., "A Preliminary Examination of the Death Concepts of the Ibo," *American Anthropologist*, 44 (1942), 638–654.

Norton, J., "Treatment of a Dying Patient," *The Psychoanalytic Study of the Child*, 18 (1963), 541–560.

O'Connor, Sister May Catharine, *The Art of Dying Well—The Development of Ars Moriendi* (New York: Columbia University Press, 1942).

Oltman, J. E., J. McGarry, and S. Friedman, "Parental Deprivation and the 'Broken Home' in Dementia Praecox and Other Mental Disorders," *American Journal of Psychiatry*, 108 (1952), 685–693.

Opler, Morris E., "The Lipan Apache Death Complex and Its Extensions," *Southwestern Journal of Anthropology*, 1 (1945), 122–141.

——, "Reactions to Death Among the Mescalero Apache," *Southwestern Journal of Anthropology*, 2 (1946), 454–467.

——, and William E. Bittle, "The Death Practices and Eschatology of the Kiowa Apache," *Southwestern Journal of Anthropology*, 17 (1961), 383–394.

Orbach, Charles E., "The Multiple Meanings of the Loss of a Child," *American Journal of Psychotherapy*, 13 (1959), 906–915.

——, Arthur M. Sutherland, and Mary F. Bozeman, "Psychological Impact of Cancer and Its Treatment: III. The Adaptation of Mothers to the Threatened Loss of Their Children Through Leukemia: Part II.," *Cancer*, 8 (1955), 20–33.

Orlansky, Harold, "Reactions to the Death of President Roosevelt," *Journal of Social Psychology*, 26 (1947), 235–266.

Osborne, Ernest, *When You Lose a Loved One*, Public Affairs Pamphlet #269, 1958.

Osipov, N., "Starch ze Smrti (Fear of Death)," *Rev. Neurol. Psychiat. Praha*, 32 (1935), 17–25.

Ostow, Mortimer, "The Death Instinct—a Contribution to the Study of Instincts," *International Journal of Psychoanalysis*, 39 (1958), 5–16.

Parkes, C. M., "Recent Bereavement as a Cause of Mental Illness," *British Journal of Psychiatry*, 110 (1964), 198–204.

Parsons, Talcott, "Death in American Society—A Brief Working Paper," *The American Behavioral Scientist*, 6 (1963), 61–65.

Paton, Lewis Bayles, *Spiritism and the Cult of the Dead in Antiquity* (New York: Macmillan, 1921).

Paz, Octavio, "The Day of the Dead," in *Labyrinth of Solitude: Life and Thought in Mexico* (translated by Lysander Kemp) (New York: Grove Press, 1961), pp. 47–64.

Peck, M., "Notes on Identification in a Case of Depression Reactive to the Death of a Love Object," *Psychoanalytic Quarterly*, 8 (1939), 1–17.

Peniston, D. H., "The Importance of Death Education in Family Life," *Family Life Coordinator*, 11 (1962), 15–18.

Perske, Robert, "Death and Ministry: Episode and Response," *Pastoral Psychology*, 15 (1964), 25–35.

Pollock, G. H., "Mourning and Adaptation," *International Journal of Psychoanalysis*, 42 (1961), 341–361.

——, "Childhood Parent and Sibling Loss in Adult Patients," *Archives of Genetic Psychiatry*, 7 (1962), 295–306.

Pretty, L. C., "Ministering to the Bereaved and Dying," *Nebraska State Medical Journal*, 44 (1959), 243–249.

Puckle, Bertram S., *Funeral Customs* (London: T. W. Laurie, Ltd., 1926).

Quint, Jeanne, and Anselm L. Strauss, "Nursing Students, Assignments and Dying Patients," *Nursing Outlook*, 12 (1964), 24–27.

——, "Mastectomy—Symbol of Cure or Warning Sign?" *American Academy of General Practice*, 29 (1964), 119–124.

Radó, Sándor, "The Problem of Melancholia," *International Journal of Psychoanalysis*, 9 (1928), 420–438.

Rezek, J. R., "Dying and Death," *Journal of Forensic Science*, 8 (1963), 200–208.

Rhudick, P. J., and A. S. Dibner, "Age, Personality and Health Correlates of Death Concerns in Normal Aged Individuals," *Journal of Gerontology*, 16 (1961), 44–49.

Richmond, J. B., and H. A. Waisman, "Psychologic Aspects of Management of Children with Malignant Disease," *American Medical Association Journal of the Diseases of Children*, 89 (1955), 42–47.

Richter, C. P., "On the Phenomenon of Sudden Death in Animals and Man," *Psychosomatic Medicine*, 19 (1957), 191–198.

——, "The Phenomenon of Unexplained Sudden Death in Animals and Man," in H. Feifel (Ed.), *The Meaning of Death* (New York: McGraw-Hill, 1959), pp. 302–313.

Ristus, Ruth, "The Loneliness of Death," *The American Journal of Nursing*, 58 (1958), 1283–1284.

Roberts, W. W., "The Death Instinct in Morbid Anxiety," *Journal of the Royal Army Medical Corps*, 81 (1943), 61–73.

Rochlin, G., "Loss and Restitution," *The Psychoanalytic Study of the Child*, 8 (1953), 288–309.

——, "The Loss Complex," *Journal of the American Psychoanalytic Association*, 7 (1959), 299–316.

Rogers, William F., "Needs of the Bereaved," *Pastoral Psychology*, 1 (1950), 17–21.

Rosenthal, Hattie, "Psychotherapy for the Dying," *American Journal of Psychotherapy*, 11 (1957), 626–633.

——, "The Fear of Death as an Indispensable Factor in Psychotherapy," *American Journal of Psychotherapy*, 17 (1963), 619–630.

Rosenzweig, Saul, "Sibling Death as a Psychological Experience with Reference to Schizophrenia," *Psychoanalytic Review*, 30 (1943), 177–186.

——, and D. Bray, "Sibling Deaths in Anamnesis of Schizophrenic Patients," *Archives of Neurological Psychiatry*, 49 (1943), 71–92.

Rosner, Albert, "Mourning Before the Fact," *Journal of the American Psychoanalytic Association*, 10 (1962), 564–570.

Ruff, Frank, "Have We the Right to Prolong Dying?" *Medical Economics*, 37 (1960), 39–44.

Rush, Alfred Clement, *Death and Burial in Christian Antiquity* (Washington, D.C.: The Catholic University of America Press, 1941).

Russell, Bertrand, "Your Child and the Fear of Death," *The Forum*, 81 (1929), 174–178.

Sachs, Hans, "Beauty, Life and Death," *American Imago*, 1 (1940), 81–133.

Sandler, David, "The Study of Bereavement," in K. D. Kroupa and D. Sandler (Eds.), *Community Mental Health: Theory, Practice and Research*. Unpublished manuscript, Harvard University, 1962.

Sarnoff, Irving, and Seth M. Corwin, "Castration Anxiety and the Fear of Death," *Journal of Personality*, 27 (1959), 374–385.

Saul, L. J., "Reactions of a Man to Natural Death," *Psychoanalytic Quarterly*, 28 (1959), 383–386.

Schaffer, H. R., and W. M. Callender, "Psychological Effects of Hospitalization in Infancy," *Pediatrics*, 24 (1959), 528–539.

Scharl, Adele E., "Regression and Restitution in Object-loss: Clinical Observations," *The Psychoanalytic Study of the Child*, 16 (1961), 471–480.

Scher, Jordan, "On Death: The Final Construction," paper presented at meeting of the American Psychological Association, Los Angeles, 1964.

Schilder, Paul, "The Attitude of Murderers Toward Death," *Journal of Abnormal and Social Psychology*, 31 (1936), 348–363.

——, and D. Wechsler, "The Attitudes of Children Toward Death," *Pedagogical Seminary and the Journal of Genetic Psychology,* 45 (1934), 406–451.

Schmale, A. H., "Relationship of Separation and Depression to Disease," *Psychosomatic Medicine,* 20 (1958), 259–277.

Schneck, J. M., "Unconscious Relationship Between Hypnosis and Death," *Psychoanalytic Review,* 38 (1951), 271–275.

Schur, Max, "Discussion of Dr. John Bowlby's Paper ('Grief and Mourning in Infancy and Early Childhood')," *The Psychoanalytic Study of the Child,* 15 (1960), 63–84.

Scott, C. A., "Old Age and Death," *American Journal of Psychology,* 8 (1896), 67–122.

Searles, H. F., "Schizophrenia and the Inevitability of Death," *Psychiatric Quarterly,* 35 (1961), 631–665.

Segal, Hanna, "Fear of Death: Notes on the Analysis of an Old Man," *International Journal of Psychoanalysis,* 39 (1958), 178–181.

Seigman, Aron W., "Background and Personality Factors Associated With Feelings and Attitudes About Death," paper presented at meeting of The Society for the Scientific Study of Religion, Cambridge, Massachusetts, 1961.

Shaler, Nathaniel Southgate, *The Individual: A Study of Life and Death* (New York: D. Appleton and Co., 1901).

Shambaugh, B., "A Study of Loss Reactions in a Seven-year-old," *The Psychoanalytic Study of the Child,* 16 (1961), 510–552.

Sheatsley, Paul, "Impact of the Assassination of President Kennedy," paper presented at meeting of the American Psychological Association, Los Angeles, 1964.

Sherrill, Lewis J., and Helen H. Sherrill, "Interpreting Death to Children," *International Journal of Religious Education,* 28 (1951), 4–6.

Shneidman, Edwin S., "Orientations Toward Death: A Vital Aspect of the Study of Lives," in R. W. White (Ed.), *The Study of Lives* (New York: Atherton Press, 1963), pp. 201–227.

——, "Suicide, Sleep and Death," *Journal of Consulting Psychology,* 28 (1964), 95–106.

——, "Some Reflections on Interrelationships Among Suicide, Sleep, and Death," paper presented at meeting of the American Psychological Association, Los Angeles, 1964.

Shontz, Franklin C., and Stephen L. Fink, "A Psychobiological Analysis of Discomfort, Pain and Death," *Journal of General Psychology,* 60 (1959), 275–287.

Shoor, Mervyn, and Mary H. Speed, "Delinquency as a Manifestation of the Mourning Process," *The Psychiatric Quarterly,* 37 (1963), 540–558.

Shrut, Samuel D., "Attitudes Toward Old Age and Death," *Mental Hygiene,* 42 (1958), 259–266.

Sigal, Roberta, "Child and Adult Reactions to the Assassination of President Kennedy," paper presented at meeting of the American Psychological Association, Los Angeles, 1964.

Simmel, E., "Self-preservation and the Death Instinct," *Psychoanalytic Quarterly,* 13 (1944), 160–185.

Slater, Philip E., "Prolegomena to a Psychoanalytic Theory of Aging and Death," in R. Kastenbaum (Ed.), *New Thoughts on Old Age* (New York: Springer, 1964), Chapter 2.

Solnit, A. J., and M. Green, "Psychological Considerations in the Management of Deaths on Pediatric Hospital Services: I. The Doctor and the Child's Family," *Pediatrics,* 24 (1959), 106–112.

Stacey, C. L., and K. Marken, "The Attitudes of College Students and Penitentiary Inmates Toward Death and A Future Life," *Psychiatric Quarterly, (Supplement),* 26 (1952), 27–32.

——, and Marie L. Reichen, "Attitudes Toward Death and Future Life Among Normal and Subnormal Adolescent Girls," *Exceptional Children,* 20 (1954), 259–262.

Staff, Clement, "Death is no Outsider," *Psychoanalysis,* 2 (1953), 56–70.

Steinzor, Bernard, "Death and the Construction of Reality," in John G. Peatman and Eugene L. Hartley (Eds.), *Festschrift for Gardner Murphy* (New York: Harper, 1960), pp. 358–375.

Sterba, Richard, "On Halloween," *American Imago,* 5 (1948), 213–224.

Stern, Karl, Gwendolyn M. Williams, and Miguel Prados, "Grief Reactions in Later Life," *American Journal of Psychiatry,* 108 (1951), 289–294.

Stevens, A. C., "Facing Death," *Nursing Times,* 58 (1962), 777–778.

Strauss, Anselm L., Barney Glaser, and Jeanne C. Quint, "The Non-accountability of Terminal Care," *Hospitals,* 38 (1964), 73–87.

Swenson, Wendell M., "Attitudes Toward Death Among the Aged," *Minnesota Medicine,* 42 (1959), 399–402.

——, "Attitudes Toward Death in an Aged Population," *Journal of Gerontology,* 16 (1961), 49–52.

Teahan, John E., and S. Golin, "Reactions to the President's Assassination as a Function of Sex Ideology, Perceived Parental Attitudes and Symbolic Significance," paper presented to meeting of the Midwest Psychological Association, St. Louis, 1964.

Teicher, J. D., " 'Combat Fatigue' or Death Anxiety Neurosis," *Journal of Nervous and Mental Disease,* 117 (1953), 234–243.

Thompson, Edward John, *Suttee: A Historical and Philosophical Enquiry into the Hindu Rite of Widow Burning* (London: G. Allen and Unwin, 1928).

Tillich, Paul, "The Eternal Now," in H. Feifel (Ed.), *The Meaning of Death* (New York: McGraw-Hill, 1959), pp. 30–38.

Ulanov, Barry, *Death—A Book of Preparation and Consolation* (New York: Sheed and Ward, 1959).

Van Gennep, Arnold, *The Rites of Passage* (London: Routledge and Kegan Paul, 1960).

Volkart, Edmund H., and Stanley T. Michael, "Bereavement and Mental Health," in A. H. Leighton, J. A. Clausen, and R. N. Wilson (Eds.), *Explorations in Social Psychology* (New York: Basic Books, 1957), pp. 281–307.

Voneder, Sophie, *Wie die Menschen Durch die Dunkle Pforte Schreiten* (Vienna: Europäischer Verlag, no date).

Von Lerchenthal, Erich, "Death From Psychic Causes," *Bulletin of the Menninger Clinic,* 12 (1948), 31–36.

Vulliamy, Colwyn Edward, *Immortal Man—A Study of Funeral Customs and of Beliefs in Regard to the Nature and Fate of the Soul* (London: Methuen and Co., 1926).

Wahl, Charles W., "The Fear of Death," *Bulletin of the Menninger Clinic,* 22 (1958), 214–223.

——, "The Physician's Management of the Dying Patient," *Current Psychiatric Therapy*, 2 (1962), 127–136.

——, R. Leslie, and N. Kennedy, *Helping the Dying Patient and His Family* (New York: National Association of Social Workers, 1960).

Walkenstein, Eileen, "The Death Experience in Insulin Coma Treatment," *American Journal of Psychiatry*, 112 (1956), 985–990.

Walters, Mary Jane, "Psychic Death: Report of a Possible Case," *Archives of Neurological Psychiatry*, 52 (1944), 84–85.

Warner, W. Lloyd, "The City of the Dead," in *The Living and the Dead* (New Haven: Yale University Press, 1959), pp. 280–320.

Waugh, Evelyn, "Death in Hollywood," *Life Magazine*, 23 (1947), 73–84.

Weisman, Avery D., and Thomas P. Hackett, "Predilection to Death," *Psychosomatic Medicine*, 23 (1961), 232–256.

——, and ——, "The Dying Patient," *Forest Hospital Publications* (Des Plaines, Ill.), 1 (1962), 16–21.

Whetmore, Robert, "The Role of Grief in Psychoanalysis," *International Journal of Psychoanalysis*, 44 (1963), 97–103.

Williams, Glanville L., *The Sanctity of Life and the Criminal Law* (New York: Knopf, 1957).

Williams, H., "On a Teaching Hospital's Responsibility to Counsel Parents Concerning Their Child's Death," *Medical Journal of Australia*, 2 (1963), 643–645.

Wittgenstein, G., "Fear of Dying and of Death as a Requirement of the Maturation Process in Man," *Hippokrates*, 31 (1960), 765–769.

Wolf, Anna W. M., *Helping Your Child to Understand Death* (New York: Child Study Association of America, 1958).

Wolff, Kurt H., "A Partial Analysis of Student Reaction to President Roosevelt's Death," *Journal of Social Psychology*, 26 (1947), 35–53.

Worchester, Alfred, *The Care of the Aged, the Dying and the Dead.* (Springfield, Ill.: C. C. Thomas, 1950).

Wrightman, Lawrence S., and F. C. Noble, "Reactions to the President's Assassination and Changes in Philosophies of Human Nature," paper presented to meeting of the Midwest Psychological Association, St. Louis, 1964.

Yamazaki, S, "The Physical Attitudes of Youths Toward Death," *Japanese Journal of Psychology*, 15 (1940), 469–475.

Yarrow, H. C., "A Further Contribution to the Study of the Mortuary Customs of the North American Indians," *First Annual Report, Bureau of American Ethnology*, 1 (1879–1880), 87–203.

Yarrow, Leon, "Maternal Deprivation: Toward an Empirical and Conceptual Re-evaluation," *Psychological Bulletin*, 58 (1961), 459–490.

Young, William H., "Death of a Patient During Psychotherapy," *Psychiatry*, 23 (1960), 103–108.

Zilboorg, Gregory, "Fear of Death," *Psychoanalytic Quarterly*, 12 (1943), 465–475.